ASSURED SELF, RESTIVE SELF

ASSURED SELF, RESTIVE SELF

Encounters with Crisis

Edited by

Prasanta Chakravarty

B L O O M S B U R Y
NEW DELHI • LONDON • OXFORD • NEW YORK • SYDNEY

BLOOMSBURY INDIA
Bloomsbury Publishing India Pvt. Ltd
Second Floor, LSC Building No. 4, DDA Complex, Pocket C – 6 & 7,
Vasant Kunj, New Delhi, 110070

First published in India 2023
This edition published 2023

Bloomsbury Academic India
An imprint of Bloomsbury Publishing Plc

ISBN: HB: 978-93-54359-91-0; eBook: 978-93-54359-81-1
2 4 6 8 10 9 7 5 3 1

Typeset in Manipal Technologies Limited
Printed and bound in India by Replika Press Pvt. Ltd.

CONTENTS

LIST OF FIGURES

INTRODUCTION: ASSURED SELF, RESTIVE SELF

Prasanta Chakravarty

> A crisis of illness, bereavement, separation, natural disaster, could be the opportunity to make contact with deeper levels of the terrors of the soul, to loose and to bind, to bind and to loose. A soul, which is not bound, is as mad as one with cemented boundaries. To grow in love-ability is to accept the boundaries of oneself and others, while remaining vulnerable, woundable, around the bounds. Acknowledgement of conditionality is the only unconditionality of human love.
>
> — Gillian Rose, *Love's Work*

> It is the personality of man, conscious of its inexhaustible abundance; it has the paradox in it that it is more than itself; it is more than as it is seen, as it is known, as it is used.
>
> —Rabindranath Tagore, *Personality*

> Let me be someone else as well, play someone else: a pioneer, a deserter, a soccer referee or at least a linesman.
>
> —Peter Handke, *Quiet Places*

> The soul is prosthetic: an artifice annexed to the person. And so, I will describe what the uncertain experience of interiority could be in representation, rather than in consciousness.
>
> —Lisa Robertson, *Nilling*

In a short kernel of a work titled *Inwardness*, the evolved harvest of a long association with the question of selfhood, the philosopher Jonardon Ganeri rejects the reclusive quest for self-contemplation or self-illumination (2021). He feels that the route to renunciation, traversed first by finding the *true Self*, is a foredoomed enterprise. Is it even possible to discover the neutral point of perfect repose by saving or holding up the 'centre' or the 'inmost sanctum' of our selves even as we go on about the varied and various encounters in and with the world? Can there be an absolute schism between the Self and the world so that each can be dealt with on its own terms? Memory is deceptive. Self-awareness keeps receding. Contrary to certain beliefs, the Self can hardly be illuminated on its own, without some kind of original concealment that can perhaps only be peeled off by and by. Even the act of peeling off various layers of selfhood may not lead to any authentic core but to further concealment and mystery.

It is more likely that selves may be revealed through networks of mediation: through interfaces with our doubles, in dream and in waking, for we are many-faced, masked and often confused. A certain reflective saturation about the indeterminate and open-ended nature of truth can also take place by means of a dialogue, sometimes with acute disagreement, between the Self and the Other. The Self can emerge only in and within temporality; call it history if you will. What then constitutes a system of interiority even as the world rushes in to ruffle and light us up at once? In his many works, Ganeri talks about a method that can redirect our attention from fixity of thought and from regarding only the centre of our own selves as the only site through which the world may pass. He calls this method *protreptic* (Ganeri 2007).[1] Encountering truth and truth's contingencies, which we shall call *crisis* in this book, is not a matter of winning debates, if we are to follow this method. Through mediation, one might rather become receptive to systems of interiority. The wise one

> is as open to the truth as the sand dune is to the desert wind. He lets the truth blow through him, to affect not only his beliefs but also his hopes, his ideals, the stories he tells about himself, the concerns he has for himself and others. (Ganeri 2007)

In such circumstances, selves can only be multiple, heteronymous in nature and networked to each other with no fixed centre from which to view the world. This dispersal of the Self means that there are multiple 'I's—what Ganeri calls 'more 'I's than I myself' (2021). To acknowledge multiple 'I's is to invest in diverse perspectives of the Self and its mediation with the world. To accept the notion of diverse perspectives is not to undermine reality or to authenticate frame neutrality. It is also not a concession to pragmatism. Such an acknowledgement is simply to redirect our attention to the plural and multifarious nature of the cosmos, especially when battered by forms of fate and crises that may beset the Self that is constantly in mediation with the world. The heteronymous selves would often contradict each other in the manner that Walt Whitman proclaimed famously: 'Do I contradict myself? Very well then, I contradict myself (I am large, I contain multitudes)' (1855/2004). The day-dreamer and flaneur Fernando Pessoa would, of course, disperse his selves into the world of imagination in and through heteronyms. The question that this volume asks is whether such heteronomy and the expansion of selfhood help in encountering a crisis when it strikes.[2]

The other option to get a better handle of the Self's relation to the world is to 'decreate' the Self, effected through a rigorous process of minimising its scope and by withholding judgement on the world, though each Self must encounter the world all the time and is always steeped in it. The worldling of the being is a given. Decreation, a term coined by Simone Weil, pertains to clearing oneself of the certainty that is the unified Self and focusing instead attentively on our surroundings and interlocutors (Weil [1966] 2009). Decreation is to partake in a process of waiting, a way of reordering the body and the mind—to live without bringing any act of one's will to the encounters. Minimising or stripping away the Self is the very antipode of multiplying the Self, but engagement with the world goes on unabated. Decreation is rather another way of decentring or off-centring the Self, an emptying of the soul. To be attentive to our interlocutors means to bracket off the Self and immerse in the design and the kaleidoscopic brilliance of existence. The crucial question that this volume asks, once again, is: In what manner does the decreated Self help us encounter the *crises*—relational, political, historical, cosmological and in art practice —that must hit the many mediations of the Self with the world?

Ganeri and others like him who tell us about the expanded and/or the subtracted Self offer us sagacity. By not seeking any assured or fixed Self, such views give us another kind of assurance: that by multiplying or decreating the Self, we are able to not only get a better handle on the very conundrum that the Self is but also make our encounters with the world open-ended and blithe. Such moves implicitly tell us that minimising or multiplying the Self are ways to keep us away from the individual will and the ills of self-interest. These ways also tell us that by winning over selfhood, it is possible to reconnect with the mystery of the infinite universe. Such an insight is wonderful indeed, save that it has to be bookended with a couple of caveats. To begin with, we are fallible creatures made of bones and blood, and as such, ideas of preconceived wisdom almost always elude us. Prior cultivation of sagacity is of little use when the Self clashes or selves clash with powerful conjunctures—ruptures in temporal flow. Second, contingency and crises as forces do not always care about our being assured. The whole phenomenon of crises is there to destabilise all prudence and perspicacity. It arrives with a raw and untrumpeted power of its own. This volume wishes to put the thesis about the subtracted and/or the expanded Self to greater tests.

Contingent and unsettled times foment precisely such a mood and ambience: that of unsettlement, strangeness and even menace. Such times also produce specific equations among selves within a given culture, often masked, partial and callous while negotiating with each other. Such times also produce difficult questions within the Self itself. Contradictions of selfhood make it difficult for the Self to hold on to its precarious equilibrium. Seams begin to burst. Hopes of assurance may not lead to tranquillity of the soul but may well end up fostering behavioural and therapeutic inertia among several sections of the society.

Restiveness, on the other hand, could turn desultory, rather than creative, in unsettlement. Keeping these circumstances in mind, the literary critic, linguist and activist G.N. Devy tries to address the voice of the threatened Self by delving deep into the foremost point of a crisis among negotiating and expressive selves: the question of silence, which he finds more disturbing than overt violence. The greatest challenge to our times is the unnegotiability of selfhood with and through language itself: 'When dialogue becomes impossible and an undesirable silence dominates, relations become impossible and thought acquires the colour of violence' (Devy 2019). A whole culture turns silent in distrust, agony and contempt in which selfhoods operate though unspeakability. Devy homes in on three possible reasons for this cultural aphasia—political domination leading to lowering of self-esteem, alienation originating out of acute technology-driven narcissism and neurological-evolutionary changes whereby the very idea of being human becomes a question. But, can we hold on to a prior and sacrosanct idea of the human?

The poet and essayist Anne Carson is engrossed and perturbed by the same subject—that of muteness as a condition. In an essay titled *Stillness*, Carson considers the idea of 'silence between two thoughts' that mediating selves sometimes face (2021). Hesitation, impasse and impossibility of decision-making in difficult encounters are often responsible for making selves undecidable and, hence, still. Carson takes the help of her favourite poet, Emily Dickinson, to make the point about such distress when one 'cannot see to see'. The moment precipitates a kind of artistic crisis: that of generating artistic inspiration—'the time when insight fails and motive goes blank and you cannot "see to see"' (Carson 2021). Such a predicament implies a stillness of the pause, which makes it both 'fixed and fluid, servile and adventurous'. Carson's larger theme is that of the state of suspended animation, and that state is not always benign. To live in suspended animation is to enter the state of coma, one that lies beyond all sanctuaries. The state of stillness is also when time is emptied out in people's lives, from within selves: like in detention camps or among stateless people. Carson refers to Giorgio Agamben's formulations about stranded and placeless people here (2021). To encounter such a form of crisis is to turn mute. The pivotal question is whether such muteness reserves within itself the seedbeds of the initiative that forms of crises offer to each troubled but evolving selfhood. Is Carson's muteness a form of turning quiet and melancholic, as Devy has diagnosed? Or is it one way to set free the troubled and grated selves?

Contours of Crisis

To address a crisis is to address latency. The intimations of accelerated time *is* a crisis—when everyday immediacy and certain historical conjunctures are aligned together. It is supposedly the obverse of stability or continuity. Crisis is an omen as well as an opportunity to exceed and outvie the ills of the omen for the selfhoods entangled in it. Is such an entanglement analytical or rhetorical/emotional?

The Oxford English Dictionary (OED) defines the sociopolitical nature of a crisis as 'a vitally important or decisive stage in the progress of anything; also, a state of affairs in which a decisive change for better or worse is imminent; now applied especially to times of difficulty, insecurity, and suspense in politics or commerce' (*Oxford English Dictionary* 1971).

Crisis gives us a sense that there is no blueprint to confront its tentacles and that actors caught in its web must grope and search for a way out. This sense goes back to the origin of the word *crisis*: *kpisis* (kpinein: to sift, to decide), that is, discrimination or decision.[3] The actors must take decisions that are as considered as they are intuitive and immediate. Decisions cannot be deferred since the crisis cannot be extended. Yet, such decisions cannot be cavalier or immediate, for the nature of the initiatives or their lack make or mar future prospects for those selves who must confront or are entangled in the crisis. Hence, OED puts stress on the phrase 'better or worse'. Crisis is the condition of the present that may innovatively read the past but most certainly must consider the future in so far as the demand for initiatives goes. A crisis splices open time.

There is also an exaggerated sense of drama in crises, which may not always dovetail with the conjectures of historical grand narratives. If a crisis is placed at the level of the relationalities or the turmoil within selves, its nature turns micro. Selves seem to be under the 'spell' of a crisis, as it were. Much of the volume is about the nature of such microcrises—as observed through the lens of phenomenology, psychology, theology, fiction or behaviourism. However, a crisis simultaneously has a sense of enormity, as one notices sudden changes in nature, historical turns and cultural battles. Calibration of, and engagement with, crisis is a matter of scaling.

Personal crisis is not the subject of this book. It is not about delving into individual lives, though the book has much to do with ordinary lives caught in the web of conjunctures. The crisis within the selves, as the opposite, marks the shifts in the relationship that selves and communities may have as they come face to face with hastening interruptions of and within temporality. The interruptions themselves could be artificial or more geo-cosmic in nature. However, the sense of an immediate conjunction is palpable in a crisis so that the question of rectification does not arise. Decision-making capacities of the individual actors, though, often prove to be crucial in deciding the turns and twists of the crisis itself. There is also a larger and inner tectonic shift within selfhood, relationalities and the inner dynamics of communities in such times—all these have little to do with the various ups and downs that human beings must experience in their personal lives at any given point of time. Individual lives get 'caught in the crossfire' as it has happened all through the journeys of human actors working in time.

Typically, a crisis could take three possible turns. It can arise out of or give a sense of fatalism to actors—burgeoning from and succumbing to the dicta of forces to which selves are pliable and plastic. The very idea of selfhood may turn deeply precarious in the face of such a material sense of calamity. The second kind of interest in a crisis emanates from agitation and apprehension. Selves with such an orientation would be restive. Alarm and fluster are often reactions to crisis situations, but to be disconcerted could very well be weaved into the crisis itself. The alarmist Self would almost hope and wish for limit-experiences to precipitate. Such restive selves often summon crises, a pattern already imprinted in their souls. This is the gothic sense of crisis: encounters of selfhood in the obliviousness of the abyss. The third kind of selfhoods are selves thrown and bewildered in and by a crisis. They are baffled and mystified, and the question of decision-making does not arise when such eccentric selves encounter a crisis. Such selves are forever stunned by the pulverising force of the crisis, though such bafflement may sometimes lead to a larger sense of bewilderment with creation itself.

There is a fourth possibility. The beings who are most galvanised by a crisis will not wish to designate such moments in time with the term *crisis* at all. These are the radicals who see each moment of calamity as an opportunity for purge and redemption—to be brought about in the name of justice and change. Each crisis is a possibility to such selves. Crisis is the other name for wreaking cleansing terror. Decisions must be taken to prolong the happy conjunctions of crises. This insurrectionary nature of a crisis is to supersede it wholesale through the unleashing of an enormous hopeful force. In a kindred spirit, Antonio Negri says, 'The immeasurable does not derive so much from the relationship that is disproportionate with the time of crisis as much as it does from the absolute organization that the consciousness of the crisis impresses on the project so as to supersede the crisis' (1991).

There is a more pragmatic way of dealing with a crisis: managing it. Such a manner of looking into a crisis is a staple in diplomatic circles, international relations and disciplines that deal with managing risk.[4] The idea of containment, so crucial to managing the onslaught of a crisis, depends on human agency, which is not the subject of the book. Crisis management is also entirely dependent on the imminence of the present and its transience (in Freedan's words, 'an asteroid hurtling toward the earth' [2017]), which is a foreshortening of the predicament. Anticipation of decisions in a crisis is in no way purely interventionist if placed within the larger historico-philosophical canvas. Instead, a crisis is most densely observed if placed between an oppressive sense of necessity and resolution, between paralysis and accelerated response. The imminent decisive change is always a potential, and it may continue to remain so rather than quickly leading to any realisation or resolution based on prompt action.

History and Crisis

In a moving homage to the genius of Johann Peter Hebel, W.G. Sebald narrates how Hebel, who had the rarest of abilities to lift the veil that separates us from the world beyond, was nevertheless deeply troubled by the calamitous events that occurred between 1789 and 1810 in Europe, and the limitless reach of violence so that 'one can never know, first thing in the morning, what will happen by nightfall' (Sebald 2014). Hebel marks the precipitation of history in its very hastening. He never supported the status quo but was horrified by the toll that the telescoping of time and the 'ever-accelerating maelstrom of destruction' takes on human bodies and minds and on relationships in such times. The nature of a whole culture alters, which turns covetous, gets obsessed with fame and order and loses all sense of patience and understanding (Sebald 2014). All higher principles of rational thought are overturned. The transience of all glory is especially marked in Hebel's revelatory prose. Sebald ends the section with these words:

> The view from the Milky Way down to the bleak and blackened ruins of the earth spinning in space could not appear more strange, and yet the childhood we spent on it, and which echoes through the words of the *Hausfreund*, seems scarcely more distant than the day before last. (Sebald 2014)

There is a sense of déjà vu, most certainly, to Sebald's pronouncement, in many parts of the world at this point of time.

That a crisis is a liminal historical moment and a hiatus, indeed, a pressure on time itself, is marked by Sumit Sarkar in his well-known essay on the 19th-century ascetic Ramakrishna's critique of the notion of *chakri* or clerical jobs (1992). It was a time when a series of opposites began to attract each other. People tried to bridge diverse 'worlds' or 'levels' of frontiers that were 'difficult' in themselves and yet 'had to be crossed' (Sarkar 1992). In this case, the crisis is made manifest by a change to the new colonial lifestyle of the imposed drudgery of routinised education and the travails of time-bound clerical jobs/ chakri in mercantile and government offices: 'Chakri thus became a "chronotype" of alienated time and space' (Sarkar 1992). Rural labour was being replaced by urban work processes and a bourgeois idea of time and discipline. Ramakrishna provides a kind of sanctified escape from such a drudgery: 'the solace and comfort of an inner space, distanced from an every-day world dominated increasingly by money and alien power' (Sarkar 1992). Sarkar captures the uncertain world of the urban poor and their cultural milieu in colonial Bengal through the idea of *Kaliyuga* as a time of rupture. He ends his essay on a pessimistic note though—that such a comforting escape from crisis may have a limited appeal and does not get rid of the structural nature of the crisis altogether. In the claustrophobic world of clericality, eventually, there is little hope. Placing Sarkar's concerns in the current scenario, one may be tempted to ask: How do human beings fare as they operate within the cybernetic-capitalist forms? What is the nature of comfort for the drudgery of the ones who program endless algorithms or plan trolling and pickup mechanisms in our times? Do greed and boredom breed reptilian selves?

Sebald and Sarkar proffer specific ideas of crisis: while the first reflects on acceleration and frenzy, the second considers the spiritual void and alienation owing to the structural shifts that the modern idea of service helps stimulate. Half a century ago, in a seminal essay, Randolph Starn wondered whether historians ought to treat a crisis in a discrete fashion, or consider it under the heading of 'general crisis' in the context of a Europe-wide debate on the 17th century being a key period of interruption and innovation (Starn 1971). Starn iterated the medical and martial origins of the word but also emphasised the rhetorical roots of Greek drama to which Thucydides returned every time he used the term historically. So, the original bodywork of crisis 'functioned to stage events with the tragic irony that [Thucydides] shared with Aeschylus and Sophocles.... As much as key moments in a process of change, crisis situations became moments of truth where the significance of men and events were brought to light' (Starn 1971). Here is how history and the literary, truths about the real and fiction, science and rhetoric, come together. The decisive moment of a crisis is also a recasting that must be imagined without any causal logic whatsoever.

Starn also suggests that instead of taking the term for granted, historians must clearly understand the nature of the decisive turning points, the antecedents and the consequences of crises. A crisis pattern would be 'open-ended, unpredictable, dynamic' (Starn 1971). Crises could be read as transition moments between one phase to another, whether time is imagined in cycles or horizontally. The term *crisis* especially has a modern ring to it: ranging from concerns of commerce to such speculative and modern ones like *crisis of conscience*. To those who wish to conserve social mores, order and values—a crisis is a malady, a symptom of the incapacity of humans to transcend history. Weakness of authority allows a crisis to creep in, and therefore, order must be restored. In extreme forms, any transition would seem like a crisis to such minds. On the other hand, the radicals discover in a crisis a partner concept to rupture. Citizen Thomas Paine thought that crises

> produce as much good as hurt … they produce as much good as hurt. Their duration is always short; the mind soon grows through them, and acquires a firmer habit than before. But their peculiar advantage is, that they are the touchstones of sincerity and hypocrisy.… They sift out the hidden thoughts of men, and to the world. (Paine 1776/2018)

Dislocation marks the turning point to positive change in time. To the accelerationist, crisis must be invented from time to time to achieve the goals of justice. To the radical, a crisis clears the ground for action to take place. All spiritual growth takes place in leaps and bounds, and such expediency is the very motor of history.

In the widest historical sense, to study a crisis is to get drawn into certain patterns of human, natural and social acts, which may not always have a causal link to each other and yet are able to portray or predict certain trends. Such trends direct us towards human fallibilities, surreptitious skirmishes and betrayals as well as make us conscious of the power of unknown and unfathomable circumstances. What does taking an initiative mean in the face of such pulverising superventions? How do selves battle within and negotiate with time's ravishing overtures?

To Jakob Burckhardt, moments of crisis decisively test and shape vital institutions and national character itself (1943). Crisis is revelatory: it brings forth the vitality and exigent discontinuities of history. Crisis transforms history into an arena where contending forces fight dark and underground battles that cannot always be detected through the lens of cause and effect or overt factual evidences. One must acknowledge that much of the sense of crisis in modern imagination is also economic in nature. A crisis threatens the future. It is a matter of reading contradictions of history among the Marxists. However, every crisis may not be another step towards any steady progress. It is a domain where a tug of war of divergent interest groups takes place—sometimes in the open, but often in the dark on a subterranean plane. A crisis often destabilises the standard narratives of linear time. The Annales historians and others became extremely attentive to the long-term and short-term fluctuations of economic progress and downturns.

Starn concludes his essay with two caveats, which are worth iterating (1971). For one, a crisis is twice removed from the evidences to which historians must apply it. It is not 'out there' to be gathered in. Second: historians of crisis often tend to see pathology where there are none. If we are preoccupied with sickness, we may end up neglecting the patient. Crisis is a working framework—a premise and a tool for scaffolding.

Unlike Starn, Reinhart Koselleck fundamentally posits the question of historical displacement in terms of a movement from criticism to crisis, which happened sometime in 18th-century Europe (1988). The rational, moral and natural claim of critique is entrenched in doubt about prejudice and the spiritual order of tradition. History was placed against myth. The more the idea of critique of established values took root, the more it gained universality by creating the polar binaries of unreason and reason. Criticism gradually became its own foe—mendacious to its own cause. Most of all, it lacked 'self-insight'. Truth, duty, virtue and right, all became politicised through the idea of critique, effected through dualism. Critique levelled everything and everyone. The disciplinary name that the Illuminati, the moral citizen, placed once religion was supplanted was: philosophy of history. The philosophy of history was an admixture of 'Rousseauesque concept of nature, moralizing Christianity and the generally accepted notions of progress' (Koselleck 1988). The moral inner space of the Illuminati was divided though: Did they wish to abolish the State too along with community values or did they place their faith in immediate revolutionary goals and acts in order to abolish all established norms? Choosing the latter option would disturb the moderation that reasonable critique claimed for itself. The political planning of the Self was indirect. The shift from critique to crisis happens at this stage: when moral law of reason and conscience failed to provide justifications for the wholesale abolishing of all normative frameworks. Nation and nature could not hold together the impeding disquiet among a large number of people.

Civil war was ignited. For Koselleck, the 'explosive revolutionary force inherent in moral dualism legitimated the civil war' (1988). Crisis meant the political crisis of the State as a whole—'the collapse of all property relations, convulsion and unpredictable unrest'. Soon, crisis turned into a moral tribunal. Despotism and freedom became braided. It was impossible to distinguish one from the other. Further, much of the crisis was concealed and furtive, which itself intensified it further. Here, Koselleck makes a simple but powerful statement that also guides much of this volume: 'The crisis was a crisis only because its political nature was essentially covered up.' How does this cover-up happen? Did the selves involved in the crisis evade, participate in or suppress the process of covering up? At what cost was there such a cover-up on intimate and interacting spaces?

Janet Roitman makes an incisive 'critique' of Koselleck's framework of crisis (2014). Indeed, the mounting of Koselleck's thesis hinges on the idea that a crisis is essentially historical temporality over which a certain consciousness acts. History takes the form of 'world-immanent' justice, brought about by the reactions of the various selves that alter within the capsule of the crisis. Crisis, conceived in such a manner, becomes the disclosure of epistemological limits: 'Crisis-claims evoke a moral demand for a difference between the past and the future. And crisis-claims evoke the possibility for new forms of historical subjectivity, transpiring through determinations of the limits of reason and knowledge' (Roitman 2014). Actors begin to question what went wrong. According to Roitman, by placing critique as preceding crisis, Koselleck turns the latter into a 'transcendental placeholder in the occupation of an immanent world' (2014). As a placeholder for contingency, crisis allows us to think the 'otherwise'. In the same context, she quotes William Rasch:

> If . . . moral codes (commandments), Holy Scripture, papal and royal edicts, and the voice of prophets and visionaries no longer deliver direct evidence of the transcendent realm, but rather become historicized and seen as socially constructed artifacts, the task of reclaiming authority must be negotiated within the domain of an immanence that has been loosed from its transcendent anchorage. The world is as it is, but it could be otherwise. (Rasch 1995)

The immanent has to then turn back onto itself in order to think the 'otherwise'. The task itself becomes a quasi-transcendental quest.

Crisis, as addressed by Koselleck then, is a 'blind spot in narrative construction' (Roitman 2014). A crisis is real to the extent that it hopes to delve into the necessary fiction involved in the real. The crevasse resides between the empirical and the unstated. Hence, Roitman's query: Given that the chasm is forever a deferral and a radical gap, how can we ever know what crisis is? She posits the problem quite pointedly:

> What is at issue is our alienation from history and the potential for revelation of true value and the true significance of events—of redemption, emancipation, deliverance. I ask: how can we claim to represent that chasm? What is the basis of a claim to know the locus of our alienation from underlying value, from material value, from real value, from truth value? (Roitman 2014)

These are questions that must be addressed. Crisis cannot turn into a sociology of error. The judgements we come with cannot be post-hoc and convenient, once the placeholder is already in place. Further, it serves no one any good if crisis is protracted to become a general rubric to describe all things persistently pathological around us. Most importantly, any study of crises must resist the easy journey from prognosis to prophecy or vice versa. In other words, the 'epochal consciousness' that marks the shift in temporality must be open-ended rather than predetermined to be a successful detective and solve time's riddles.

The shift in temporality is read in terms of economic construct and failure by some historians. Julian Borchardt, for instance, feels that a 'crisis constitutes a grave disturbance of the equilibrium between production and consumption' (1932).[5] A crisis disturbs the economic ideal. Commodities remain unsaleable whereas they are needed by a large number of people. The division of labour disrupts self-production and eventually leads to overproduction. To the Marxist historian, crisis is another name for the lack of independence of the producer, who turns into a wage labourer. However, he welcomes such crises for 'by means of ... [the crisis] alone the constantly increasing requirements of the consumers can be satisfied' (Borchardt 1932). In the final section of his essay on the subject, he refers to Friedrich Engels's work *Principles of Communism* to remind us that as vaster quantities would be produced, the problem from capitalism will be to find more and more consumers. The system shall break under its own weight, for 'it is to be feared that the economic structure of modern society will not be able to withstand for long the immense perturbations in which it is continually exposed' (Borchardt 1932). The crisis can only be solved by means of an increase in consumption. Is this an accelerationist argument or a marking of the contradictions that lie within the structure of capitalism?

Eric Hobsbawm places the concerns of Borchardt historically and within a larger canvas—under the rubric of the 'general crisis' of the

17th century—the last phase of transition from the feudal to a capitalist economy in Europe (1954). Hobsbawm marks epidemics, a spurt in population, price rise, decline of trade and commerce, uneven expansion of Europe, social revolt in western and eastern Europe and the rise of absolutist territorial states and concomitant war as certain effects arising out an underlying crisis. These were all obstacles in the way of capitalist expansion. Hobsbawm seeks the causes for such crises. The problem, he feels, is that the transition required for the metamorphosis to happen from the feudal system to a capitalist mode of production was uneven and not at all smooth. The conditions for capitalism to flourish—like a large and free labour force, surplus for productive investment and an expanding market for goods—were always not available. Indeed, capitalism was parasitic on the feudal world. However, the spectre of the feudal spirit (a combination of 'natural economy' and tribalism) could not be overcome easily for a smooth transition towards/to industrial revolution. The rural society created its own limits, and the feudal businessman could not turn fully capitalist. The crisis or the glut intensified. Hobsbawm follows this primary thesis by further reading the contradictions of expansion in home and colonial markets. Besides, there were a huge rise in labour costs. He sums up his conclusions succinctly: 'Economic expansion took place within a social framework which it was not yet strong enough to burst, and in ways adapted to it rather than to the world of modern capitalism' (Hobsbawm 1954). Unlike Borchardt, Hobsbawm does not offer a solution or a retrospective corrective measure though.[6]

There is now a debate on the left side of the political spectrum whether the current situation of arbitrary violence and proliferation of personal dependencies in the world can be designated as new-age techno-feudalism, or whether the mode of production still remains an advanced and expansive form of capitalism. The debates are around ideas of innovation, digital dispossession, cognitive/fictitious capitalism, predation and surveillance (Morozov 2022).

The question of a pointed historical argument has now taken a more global dimension, although with local and regional variations. In *Age of Anger*, Pankaj Mishra, for instance, draws a line through various conjectures in the long 20th century to our time—as a meandering culture shaped out of misfits and moral scandalmongers and certain political and artistic demagogues taking advantage of a sense of mass discontent and cynicism from time to time (2017). In the bargain, a kind of *negative solidarity* is formed and perpetrated, and unadulterated *ressentiment* reigns. Mishra calls this condition 'universal crisis'. It is a strange global civil war—protracted and stuttering. The crisis of our times is not necessarily horror but bafflement arising out of the sense 'that anything can happen anywhere to anybody at any time' (Mishra 2017). The idea of crisis for our times, therefore, is more a kind of structure of feeling, a matter of disposition and the dissonances arising out of sharp opinions about large and small matters leading to devastating effects over large swathes of humanity. The end of rational argument means launching sneers at the other without providing any alternative. Mike Davis has called the present crisis of the global village 'pathological presentism' (2022): 'making all calculations on the basis of short-term bottom-lines in order to allow the super-rich to consume all the good things of the earth within their lifetimes'. To read such a structure of feeling historically and dispassionately is a daunting task.

Myths and Life-Worlds

To place crisis within the markers of known social temporality is important, and yet it may have passed through a more ancient trajectory. The recent readings of crisis notwithstanding, like the thesis proffered by Burckhardt, Hobsbawm or Koselleck, the idea of crisis, calamity and possible recovery (never guaranteed) began when cosmic forces and heavenly interventions started toying with the lives and fortunes of corporeal beings. Hence, Thucydides goes back to the tragedians, who could mediate between the divine and the temporal orders. In his inimitable style, Jan Patočka tells us the primal story:

> It can happen that the gods at times feel neglected or irritated by men, it can happen that at times they forget themselves to such an extent that it occurs to them to eradicate humanity altogether. Therein lies the origin of the interpretation of a certain event that could well have been a geological calamity and the preservation of humanity afterwards. Such destruction is an example of the work of the gods. (Patočka 1996)

Creation must be annihilated at certain junctures: call it crisis or calamity. The originary myths of civilisations, therefore, often begin after an interruption—gods turn angry and produce deluge and earthquakes. However, the same gods of wisdom also know that corporeal life must not be destroyed and that new order must be renewed from time to time. The chosen ones arrive in a 'premonitory dream' so that the saving ship is built for them to embark upon (Patočka 1996).

The ordinance of the gods and the menace that it brings forth to the world is instantly vivid to all corporeal bodies. The humans immediately realise their vulnerability and dependability. They understand that human labour or pragmatism cannot secure their lives. In this context, Patočka says that 'history differs from prehistoric humanity by the *shaking of accepted meaning*' (1996). The original mystery that shakes the accepted meanings of human journey is, therefore, another way of defining crisis. Crisis, in this sense, is the accumulated release of tremendous force. The force of such conflicts can be felt until they are neutralised and entropy restored. Individuals are mere tools in such times. To Patočka, such finitude is also a *front*:

> The Front is not simply a line of fire, the interface of people attacking each other, but that it is also in some way the 'crest of the wave' that bears the world of humans toward its new destiny . . . it seems that there one finds oneself at the extreme limit of what has happened and what is to be done. (1996)

Whoever lives through the Front becomes a different being. The forces do not distinguish. The forces destroy and organise a juncture. The vehemence of crisis comes from a total mobilisation of pent-up energy that must be exhausted. Crisis is never resolved or silenced.

Edmund Husserl places such a notion of crisis squarely within the context of the rise of the sciences in his unfinished work of 1936, *The Crisis of European Sciences and Transcendent Phenomenology*. He called his framework 'teleological-historical reflections' (Husserl 1970). The work is as much a response to his time (seeking the *essence* of history) as it is systematic. Crisis, for Husserl, constitutes 'the fate of human spirit, undecided and hanging in balance'.[7] Husserl stood stoutly against the anti-rational and anti-intellectual tendencies of his time. He realised that taking recourse to instrumental reason (excessive specialisation) also meant a desperate dive into wishy-washy varieties of irrationalism. His grand plan was to write the fifth section of his work entirely on the theme of the responsibility of humanity for itself. In this context, he wishes to reinstate life-world.

Husserl makes an early distinction by referring to Aristotle, who defines participatory citizenship both in terms of *archê*, which means authority/dominion', and *krisis*, which means taking part in political decision-making (Husserl 1970). Citizens make choices in times of crisis—which is, at once, the burden that conflicts generate and the shouldering of them. The shouldering of a crisis does not lie in any bureaucratic or managerial solution. There is a unity in the situation itself. That must be appreciated foremost. The citizen must be involved and attentive to the problem at hand. The citizen must be concerned about the good of the polis and, hence, is invested in the crisis. Thomas Dodd reminds us that the modern distinction between critique/reflection and crisis that Koselleck makes (and which Roitman questions) is missing in Aristotle (2004). According to Dodd, critique 'does not represent being in, or being concerned with, and above all not *charged with* a "crisis"'. There is no distinction between one *who chooses* and one who has to *make a choice*.

Husserl actually follows the crisis of reason and the rise of scepticism. With the objectivist science and extreme forms of doubt, the viability of the modern European Self and the Self's attachment to any coherent sense of the world and the cosmos was in question. The connection of doubt (Europe as a rational culture) with the lived world has severed, and that is the real crisis: 'Merely fact-minded sciences make merely fact-minded people' (Husserl 1970) In this context, Husserl wishes to radically reformulate the culture and self-understanding of science. Husserl's project is to reinstate the ideal of reason, which the scientific culture has muddied, in its earlier glory. Dodd calls Husserl's method 'spiritual therapeutics' in which critique is not merely objective judgement but calm and intellectual insight into the possibilities to deal with a situation of crisis (2004). Decisions are not blind assertions but descriptions that try to grapple with the situation at hand. If critique still sounds judgemental, Dodd has suggested the Aristotelian solution to a situation of crisis, that is to say that the concerned citizens must come to 'grips' with the crisis. The decision would follow. Of course, Aristotle's claims are public-spirited, and so are the selves involved in such negotiations.

To Husserl, therefore, a crisis is not a complete breakdown of reason but a partial existence with life in reason through objectification and festishisation of its original possibilities (1970). It is the life-crisis of humanity as such. To him, at that conjuncture in time, the crisis was that humans had become rational beings without realising what they had jettisoned in espousing total scientificity in running life. This sense had gradually percolated in lives—and the percolation itself is a crisis. To Husserl, there is nothing exceptional about crisis. It is a condition. Such an idea of crisis takes shape when comprehension and certainty are mired in their opposites. Rationality becomes unintelligible to itself, which is the crisis. Dodd gives us the holistic scenario of Husserl's concerns:

> 'Crisis' could then be used as a term that would cover *both* the situation of conflict, of doubt and uncertainty over the question of the meaning of true being for those who speak on behalf of its realization, *and* the understanding that guides the one who is in the midst of just such a conflict. (2004)

Science does remain a majestic movement of world discovery (arising out of the original question: What is there?), but the meaning of it must be reached through transcendental philosophy. So, Husserl says: 'A superior survey of the world must be launched, unfettered by myth and the whole tradition: universal knowledge, absolutely free from prejudice, of the world and man, ultimately recognizing in the world its inherent reason and teleology and its highest principle' (1970).

What does surveying mean in the face of the large crisis? Is not the very idea that reason is valid across time and space itself in crisis? Self-directed feelings and rhetoric have supplanted criticality in every sphere of life.

By trying to understand the inner driving force of the teleology of the crisis, the philosopher seeks to reintegrate the goal of science to the life-world—this was Husserl's wager. Husserl was surely addressing the inner being in crisis, for he says,

> If man loses this faith, it means nothing less than the loss of faith 'in himself', in his own true being. This true being is not something he always already has, with the self-evidence of the 'I am', but something he only has and can have in the form of the struggle for his truth, the struggle to make himself true. (Husserl 1970)

He was invested in the contemplative consideration of an existential kind rather than in any Cartesian-style 'introspection'. With such a consideration in mind, addressing a crisis means trying to realise the ideal of a certain lawfulness in the being's life-world. However, instead of taking the route that Ganeri does, Husserl holds on to the certainty of selfhood operating within a certain 'givenness'.

Since Husserl questions positivism and empiricism, truth is realised in neither an objective nor a subjective manner. Objects are given, and subjects perceive through such givenness. The meaning content of the world is independent of 'my' subjective concerns for the world; it exists as such (the word outlasts 'me'), and yet selves must keep on negotiating with the incidental givenness of the world and pass through ruptures and crises. Therefore, 'if subjectivity constitutes the world, it constitutes a totality in which it must recognize itself as only the smallest part' (Kidder 1987). Objective science aspires to correct this constitution of the Self within its life-world by means of 'abandoning the whimsy of imagination, correcting the illusions of the senses, and ridding culture of the inconclusiveness and error of unmethodical thought' (Kidder 1987). It aspires to purify the distortions of the subjective world into order. In this context, selves must grapple with the crisis as an interruption within the concatenation of moments in the life-world and in the manners of givenenness. Husserl creates a transcendental subject though, which 'as an entity in the world ... must prescind from aspects such as spatial extension, natural behaviors, personality' (Kidder 1987). To consider the imaginative and free variations within the life-world may free the Self from the sense of crisis. The transcendental subject is a kind of philosophic solitude that is ensconced within the inter-subjective community of the humans:

> I am not an ego, who still has his you, his we, his total community of cosubjects in natural validity. All of mankind, and the whole distinction and ordering of personal pronouns has become a phenomenon within my *epoche*; and so has the privilege of I-the-man among other men. (Husserl 1970)

Selves, therefore, may *participate* in crisis but never gesture towards any easy cure. The questioning spirit of science must be backed, yet it must be sought to appreciate the givenness of the cosmos. Therefore, a counterintuitive measure is sought: *to come to grips with crisis, its inner dynamics must be heightened and not dispelled.* Crisis must be pushed to its culmination. Besides, to address crisis is to actually consider the 'surrounding world' (*Umwelt*). Hence, Dodd defines the Husserlian sense of crisis as 'a kind of spiritual rebirth, or re-creation of a future out of an exhausted belief' (2004).

The juncture where the ontological and the historical may meet is navigated by a space that has been called *minimal* by Rodolphe Gasche: the zone of the relational (1999). Relations are not ontologically deficient 'things', Gasche emphasises. Relations are rather elemental and a substance at its minutest. Relations reveal themselves as 'transobjective'. Gasche actually goes further into the limit-problems as philosophy's building blocks from which relations are derived and the selves begin to encounter relations. At the juncture of relations, the possibility of 'being-towards-something' manifests itself in all its bareness—marking not only the in-betweenness of selves but also a tendency to be inclined towards the thinking of the being as such. However, radical non-relation hovers too at this very juncture. Therefore, at the minimal level, the potential crisis of the selves is most delicately poised. Gasche's formulation takes us away from the way 'relations' are traditionally conceived, say, as objective determinations of things or as propositional functions of statements.

Gasche considers relations in a non-formalist and non-empirical manner: 'Encounter, arrival, address, contact, touch, belonging, distance, accord, agreement, determination, measuring, translation, and communication are some such forms of relation' (Gasche 1999). In concrete terms, the modes of such minimal relations would constitute in the practice of the caesura, rhythm and the zigzag. In relations, there is a demand—a demand of each Self to the Other, which breaks down in crisis. The demand is a comportment. Gasche describes these modes of comportment as the tying of knots upon knots that stretch and hold them into some cluster of traits (1999). But these knots start to accumulate often by chance or luck, for the demand of the other is pure fortuity. The same minimalism is, therefore, also responsible for the crisis to take root—the result of a similar event of fortuity.

Spacing and distance among different selves in relation are needed to avert crisis and chaos. Spacing revaluates values and affirms the necessity of contradiction to inscribe the traits. We project relations, traits of the Self, onto the Other. Relations circulate as names.

Relations mediate selves, history and mythological patterns. Therefore, in the Indian context, selfhood has been fundamentally seen as 'the condition of being a locus of various psychological states, that is, being the kind of thing which possesses and synthesizes such states such that they are co-located' (Dasti and Bryant 2014). The idea of co-location immediately refracts all sense of any stable identity. Even the very idea of common experience is more often than not rejected as superficial and false. Either there is a deeper and contemplative Self that can take on all the tribulations of the world, or as the major Buddhist schools have deduced, there is no enduring Self at all, just bundles of properties or psychophysical aggregates (the five *skandhas*) that keep shifting and evolving with relationship to transient events:

> Madhyamaka Buddhists conversely argue that moral responsibility is not to be found in an enduring self, but in the network of relationships, states, and interconnections that constitute our rich identities. Only by navigating these connections will we understand the fact that human agency and the responsibilities that go along with it are multivalent and narrative-dependent aspects of conventional reality.[8] (Dasti and Bryant 2014)

The idea of a person is a conceptual imputation. So, the *Anatta-lakkhana Sutta*: *The 'Discourse on the Characteristic of Not-Self'* attests to the impermanence of the aggregates: 'This is not mine, this I am not, this is not my Self.' The same is then said of feeling, perception, the constructing activities and consciousness. Seeing in this way, the learned noble disciple turns away from the (*nibbindati*) material form and also from feeling, perception, constructing activities and consciousness. Turning away, he becomes dispassionate; through dispassion, [his mind] is freed (Edelglass and Garfield 2009). In Milindapañha or 'Milinda's Questions', the venerable Nagasena famously tells King Milinda that

> just as a 'chariot' is not any chariot component or the totality of components, or something separate from the components, but a conventional term applied by common usage to the rightly assembled collection of components, so when there is the functioning collection of five aggregates the term 'a being' or 'a person' is applied. (Edelglass and Garfield 2009)

There is only a conglomerate of ongoing interacting processes in the everyday when mental and physical faculties meet and disperse. There is no Self or person-essence as such.

In other Indic traditions, the process of interaction is highlighted. The empirical ego has no place in the interactive space. Components of the Self are rather related to dynamic processes of living. The point about the knot is first located within the Self in the question of *aham* and *asmat* (first-person I persona), as explained by Arindam Chakrabarti, say, through the writings of Gadadhara and Madhusudana Saraswati (2019). Between consciousness and the felt body lies a confused entity: 'In intimate friendship, in moral reasoning and in aesthetic communion, the subjective but inter-substitutible "I" offers the possibility of becoming a "you" to another self' (Chakrabarti 2019). Each 'relishes' the other. From a monist of view, Ramachandra Gandhi emphasises the Self's infinite congress and assimilation with its Other in every form:

> The apparent otherness of fellow human beings, non-human living beings, non-human matter and nature and environing nothingness melts down in the fire of moksha, revealing self's infinite variety of self-images in an ecstatic dance of ethically and ecologically sensitive interdependence and existential autonomy. (1994)

Relational Crisis and Selfhood

The obverse of voicelessness is verbosity—relentless burgeoning of expressions, images and opinions that are thrown at others in their full literalism. What does it mean to turn silent under pressure or to exchange banalities—for determining the nature of human relationships, behavioural alterations in group dynamics and for the terms that decide community norms? Sometimes, garrulousness happens when a large number of people seem to be desperately hankering for care and counsel from within a self-perpetuating climate of hatred and jealousy, striving for a particular kind of recognition of personhood that is identical with itself. The subtleties of relationality can be said to have come under some form of crisis, ironically with the advent of the so-called 'relational turn' in culture speak. Simone Drichel's introduction to an edited work called *Relationality*, for instance, places the arguments along two coordinates (2020). First, there is a critique of what was known as the 'critical mind', now described in terms of the 'solitary, autonomous individual' (Drichel 2020). The charge is that the post-1960s generation has produced lonely and disconnected individuals, a category she christens as 'existential cowboys' (Drichel 2020). This is a straightforward critique of the Enlightenment legacy—of punctilious thinking and passionate, risky undertaking where individuals would take charge of their lives and accept the consequences of living life critically.

The foundational nature of the crisis, which is inflected culturally at this point, has to do with the traumatised psyche, beleaguered, forever anxious and depressed. Drichel traverses the path from the biomedical to the psycho-social to make her point. She asserts that the issue is

> no longer simply an individual's problem (and an individual's responsibility) but rather a problem of the 'connective tissue' between individuals: we are becoming anxious and depressed at unprecedented levels not (or not only) because we lack certain neurotransmitters but because we have become creatures of disconnection. (Drichel 2020)

Such a state apparently has to directly do with a decreased level of anxiety and trust and an increase in indifference and violence. Notably, Drichel does not address the larger concerns of Devy—which functions at the evolutionary level of humanity itself.

Similarly, in a recent work titled *The Crisis of Connection*, Niobe Way talks about an emerging field: the 'Science of human connection' (Way et al. 2018). The resurgent emphasis on connection, she claims, has been possible with insights from neuroscience, developmental psychology and sociology, evolutionary anthropology, health sciences and primatology. There is a remarkable anxiety to nurture a Self that refuses to be actually vulnerable and wants to latch on to its identity within the framework of a certain behavioural consciousness. The more you try to connect, the more therapeutic the Self turns.

What is the nature and basis of relation/s in such interventions? There are a few noticeable traits. The overall frameworks are projected with an aspiration and a concern to latch on to and fortify secure living. The frameworks that undergird such relationalities are often health and well-being. Giorgio Agamben has called this the medicalisation of our lives: the medical as the new religion (2020). These are models of self-interest with no deepening of selfhood within the relational, largely scaffolded on a pre-emptive sense of precariousness in individuals with little real interest in the fragility, the evolution and the becoming of relations. The very dispossession of the Self is misconstrued. Besides, there is little striving of the Self itself.

Second, positive relations are often imagined or put in terms of communion or kinship that itself is skin-deep, rather than based on any critical solidarity or deep passion or searching ways to live deeply or with fulfilment. The bonds that hold society together are invariably family, school, workplace and religious organisations. However, the manner in which such institutions are imagined is often thin and behavioural in their interactive scope and ambit.

Third, in a corollary, the philosophic basis of relations is always dualistic and, therefore, concerned with identity rather than plurality, difference or fragmentation. The internal dynamics and contradictions of 'I' are also rejected or ignored. At its best, the 'I' is fixed within a certain economy. Consequently, the vocabulary is about constantly projecting and presenting personhood rather than the Self. Again, Agamben has most succinctly diagnosed the 'malady' of dualism in medical terms:

> Medicine articulates these ideas in a Gnostic or Manichean sense; that is to say, through an exacerbated dualistic opposition. There is a malign god or principle—namely, the disease, whose specific agents are, say, bacteria and viruses—and a beneficent god or principle—which is not health, but recovery, whose cultic agents are doctors and therapy. (Agamben 2020)

Cultic devotees must celebrate the liturgy of the righteous trauma. The locus is personhood. That relationship is bandied about as a badge of loyalty for tribal associations.

These half-baked, limiting and utterly conservative contemporary takes on personal ordeals currently being broadcasted in new-age bourgeois circles must bring us back to Gasche and the radical minimal. Gasche never tries to fix the being but rather talks about the nethermost Self (1999). There is no concern for transparency or sincerity in his formulations for there is no self-knowledge possible in such repetition. Nietzsche's response to the relation with oneself, Gasche reminds us, was its untimeliness. He goes back to Parmenides (1999). Non-contemporaneity is non-identity: 'a self that is not present to itself, and that, by relating to itself in a temporality distinct from that of the present now and its modalities, forever differs from itself' (Gasche, 1999). The obverse of the verticality of the Self is the becoming of the Self—the Dionysian and the Heraclitian impulses of eternal joy reigns, which includes the joy of destroying.

Relations happen in between the non-identical being and its becoming—the third space, which is an interval and an estrangement.

The Self is neutral and impartial to the flow of life. Gasche has a beautiful name for the interval: *dithyramb*. Such a relation is not the Hegelian reciprocity that leads to reflexive determination in two interactive consciousnesses. From the world of appearances, which is chained up in the calculative and the social-symbolic, the distancing actually marks a depth and a tendency. It helps fulfil a commitment between selfhoods touching each other. The return of appearances (intentions or references) is the real crisis—which is the return of the 'wooded ridge' of language.

This foregrounding of appearances in transactions is the reason Walter Benjamin gives so much importance to literal/verbatim translations. Relations are translations. Relations are yearnings to be translated into a new vocabulary. Translatability actually breaks the crisis of wallowing in identity. It disregards content and challenges the original's structure of reference by way of distancing it from itself and thereby creating a space for relation to blossom. Translation breaks the intentions of the language by destroying its unity. Translations entangle the possibilities within each language. Benjamin and Gasche, therefore, think that afterlife (translation) and not the natural life of two languages form an innermost relation. The selves are spontaneous and receptive to each other. Selves are anticipative and intimating. What is foreign to oneself is owned. Crisis is the opposite: fostered by mythical entanglements. Difference needs to be set free, for relations are but a fleeting touch, a kinship of souls. Hence, Benjamin's eloquent voice declares:

> Just as a tangent touches a circle lightly [fluchtigl and at but one point-establishing, with this touch rather than with the point, the law according to which it is to continue on its straight path to infinity-a translation touches the original lightly and only at the infinitely small point of sense, thereupon pursuing its own course according to the laws of fidelity in the freedom of linguistic flux. (Benjamin [1923] 1968)

Relations are not something to be fixed—an 'issue' *present-at-hand*. They are not gathered together for letting something to be seen from itself as itself. That would mean going back to self-identity. Relations are rather the rarest of *attunements*; they arrive within our thrown condition. Relations also demand attention. Relations are a comportment that opens up the space of minimal cohering and minimal agreeing. They are a constellation of bare mood.

Incoherence and distancing are essential to form relations and, therefore, important to avert the crisis of narcissism that keeps foregrounding anxiety and depression. A relation is a *presenting comportment*. Relations can only happen among and within improper and acutely differing notions of determinations and identities—of tone and style and of levels of argumentation and feelings. Relationality breaks unity and all harmony for it is a process and act of continuous weaving among selves. The floundering of this minimal coherence is the crisis. Relations are what accords, in a finely tuned manner, only after passing through radical opacity. They must foster the web of manifold voices. Relations are but a withdrawing and disclosure of certain counter-traits in conversation; it is a process of preparation for an eventual translatability of each interactive Self.

The pathways that relationalities go through are zigzag and meandering. They cannot be unidimensional. The open comportment takes root gradually as the traits criss-cross and swing. It is a constant vibration of selves in oscillation. The ropeway swings too, like the one trying to connect jagged edges in a glacial blizzard. Relations take root only via decentring, being 'out of joint'. Gasche notes the necessity of dis-accord in advancing the proximity of the selves: there are proxies, concealment and indeterminations (1999). The counter-traits of dis-accord stall crisis by foregrounding difference rather than by blocking the pathway. These dissimulations are all anticipatory to atonements. Letting be is also concealment. Appearances obfuscate, and withdrawal and retreat take the selves to openness. Every dis-accord must eventually be wrenched from concealment, but 'letting be' must still remain an everlasting mystery for the selves in conversation. 'Letting be' is resolutely an open bearing.

When the Self withdraws, there is an effect of two veilings: the hiddenness that follows relationality and the primordial hiddenness. However, the veiled trait is folded unequally over itself. There is forgetfulness and reconcealment. Thus, everything that lingers awhile stands unfinished. Relations must stand on the minimal, on radical undecidability. Gasche calls this 'invisible of all invisibles' (1999). Is the effacing of relationality a crisis?

Instead, if the will and wish to foreground the 'I' (the transcendental ego) becomes the condition for establishing relationality, the terms of the relation are already decided in advance.[9] Relations become tied to each other, which are no relations—for example, as it happens in a contract. In a contract, relations turn into co-relations or synchronous relations. The transcendental ego retains its primacy in such situations. For a minimal relationality to take root, the reverse should happen: the relation itself must be of primary significance. Robert Bernasconi has, therefore, rightly suggested:

> Is it possible that relationality does not link two or more preexisting individuals, but that in relationality the relation is in some sense prior to the relata? This would mean that the relata are to be approached in terms of the relation and not vice versa. There is no I, only a relation. (Drichel 2020)

Perhaps in the tradition of Martin Buber and Levinas, it is pivotal to realise that separation is a precondition of the relationship to the Other. All relations must be asymmetrical. The Self does not have to be renounced nor the politics of relationality ignored. The Self need not be seen purely as a hostage to the Other. It is not a matter of being substituted by the Other. The Self may turn lucid instead. To turn lucid is to acknowledge the strangeness of humans vis-à-vis one another. Is the minimal obligation to the Other, placed against pure self-preservation, perhaps one way to address the crisis of relationalities?[10] The obligation is not only to pardon and compassion but to arguments and radical disagreements too. However, the responsibility is 'mine' in preserving and taking forward the minimalism—there is always a pre-history of 'me'. All proximity is a surplus that beckons us beyond the objective. Relations are at once immersions, and yet, relations are without relations. It is crucial to realise the involuntariness of all relationalities even in their most jagged of predicaments. All relations are fluid in this fundamental sense. Commitments are never a therapy. Perhaps, having such a sense of commitment in mind, Christopher Lasch sagaciously pronounced almost half a century ago:

> The best hope of emotional maturity, then, appears to lie in a recognition of our need for and dependence on people who nevertheless remain separate from ourselves and refuse to submit to our whims. It lies in a recognition of others not as projections of our own desires but as independent beings with desires of their own. More broadly, it lies in acceptance of our limits.[11] (Lasch [1979] 2018)

While the effacement of the subject arising out of exhaustion does not address relational crisis (the subject that no one could own, for instance), most certainly, the torment comes from the Other, which once again makes separation a crucial aspect of attachment. Hence, in his essay *No Identity*, Levinas quotes from the Song of Songs (Song of Solomon, 5:6): 'I opened to my beloved, but my beloved had withdrawn himself and was gone; my soul failed when he spake; I sought him but I could not find him; I called him, but he gave me no answer; he had disappeared' (1970). *The beloved takes me out of my self.* The beloved shatters my complacency. Hence, the Punjabi poet and seer Shiv Kumar

Batalvi writes: 'Let us sing of separation/Separation is king/ A body that does not know separation/ Is but a corpse' (Batalvi, n.d.).

If this prior celebration of the Other smacks of unconditionality that does not consider contingencies or the ups and downs in a relationship, it is imperative to realise that the likes of Levinas and Batalvi are deeply distrustful of behavioural and sentimentalised forms of 'connections' and trauma alike. Indeed, within the notion of minimal relationship also must lie vexed ambivalence. There is no redoubled home for relations to arrive at as a destination. In her remarkable works on relationality, Gillian Rose, therefore, is troubled by the literature of alternative healing, which she says is 'poor psychology, worse theology and no notion of justice at all' (Rose 1995). Such new-age therapies re-insinuate

> the most remorseless protestantism. It burdens the individual soul with an inner predestination: you have eternal life only if you dissolve the difficulty of living, of love, of self and other, of the other in the self, if you are translucid, without inner or outer boundaries. If you lead a normally unhappy life, you are predestined to eternal damnation, you will not live.... It denies that there is no love without power; that we are at the mercy of others and that we have others in our mercy. Existence is robbed of its weight, its gravity, when it is deprived of its agon. (Rose 1995)

Lovers hardly know what they hope and fear, for that is what makes the condition of being in love throbbing and ethereal at once. Love, for Rose, therefore, is a 'supernatural conviction of unexpressed mutual desire and a mortal unsureness concerning declaration and consummation' (1995). Edges are a part of all relations; and relations are always a mix of reserve and exposure. The sureness of the Self, for Rose, is the readiness to be unsure.

Clair Colebrook, in her recent writings, also notes the debilitating effects of moralism on relationality and becoming (2021). She is concerned about the impoverishment in conceiving and framing relations, since complexities arising out of relations are shunned by citing humanistic concerns in these times. There is no prehension of the Self's own becoming nor are the encounters among forces that might foster new vistas of relations welcome. The primary problem for Colebrook is the emergence of a 'global and simultaneous relationality: I imagine every other as somewhat like myself; therefore I am' (Colebrook quoted in Drichel 2020). The virtual collectivity of humans and the concomitant humanism foisted upon living beings is creating a self-recognition that wants to save and sustain itself. Rose's apprehensions have come true most harrowingly at this time. The narcissistic form of relationality is puritanically righteous in saving the personhood and, through that, the world. The species awareness has turned geological in the Anthropocene and its management becomes imperative. Such a realisation is necessary for ensuring human flourishing and its *proper* reproduction. How can one imagine the open-endedness and the creative forces of relationality that shun rigidities? Is there an underground art of existence, after all, where selves can come out of the game of recognition and maintenance? Can we imagine centripetality in relations rather than their proliferation?

Identity is territory—its jealous safeguarding. Errantry is detour: this is the crux of Edouard Glissant's thought about nations that morph. Selves discover and rediscover themselves. Errantry is a resolute act of rejection of boundaries. It revels in abandonment. Errantry means a relation underlined by destructured poetics through which selves may find themselves. Errantry will not accept any monolingual end fiction. An errant Self is mad and distracted; he is consumed in a state of internal exile. He is not interested in any pleasurable compensation. The errant Self is immersed in the threatened beauty of the universe, in his surroundings. Opacity beckons him, beyond which there is pure idiocy. Errantry does not possess, nor does it wish to sum it up. Errantry travels zigzag with no general aim. Errantry embraces sudden epiphanies, which arrives through disarmed investments.

Errantry is rambling; it dishevels all narrative. The poetics of relations, like rambling, cannot be reported. It runs chaotically onwards. Nothing is absolute. Relations explode and meander and explode again—in between networks. Trajectories happen to be. There are no assimilations. Relations are, therefore, latent and opaque—its mystique is contact with all things conjectural. Therefore, relations offer and weave the totality of all possibilities; their infinite fluctuations. Relations secrete, like the chaotic history of nations and people. They stutter, break and rejoice again and move. Sediments accumulate, but the future is open to all relations. Its opacity propels the absolute transparency of inexhaustible expectations. Variations thus enter when selves, like cultures, come into contact with each other. Rambling is redundant disclosure, a rerouting of projections. Errant rambling echoes the ongoing and the fluid chaos of living; it moves in motion and music.[12]

Rambling into chaos is also endurance. Contradictory passions make and mar relations. Yet that is one surest way of addressing a crisis. As Anne Dufourmantelle has said, 'Far from "doing" something or preparing for it—for the Greeks, saying yes to fate meant the possibility of freedom from it: Letting fatality run its course is not the same as submitting to it' (2021). Endurance is entering headlong into chaos. The miraculous may come only after enduring chaos. Its residue arrives out of nowhere.

Self and Fiction/Fictional Self

The Self in fiction can be anything and everything. It is unconstrained and uncontainable. It breaks away from the frames of the social, even if it works with and alongside the latter. Fictional selves can turn meditative or contemplative if they so wish. They can double and redouble themselves in dreams and in fantasy. They may well reflect social relations in being buffeted by the machinations and ways of historical circumstances. They can also be completely rambunctious and irreverent, breaking free of finitude by means of being imagined and by mobilising imagination in and through their own actions. Above all looms fate and contingency. The fictional selves that the artist creates—in tragedy and in lyric, in romances and in operas, in sketches and in nocturnes—are all protean and free. They shimmer and scintillate. The fictive Self is an ever-elusive genie, evolving and antithetical, vile and noble at once, as Rousseau had imagined. Art highlights the chaos and contingency of life, playing up the intersections of fate and human decisions. Contradictions do not bother art. Crisis, therefore, strikes when such an enormous freedom overwhelms the guardians of good life and health, who are scared of the power of imagination. Moral agents fear the intensity that fantasy may have upon life itself. Moral agents have always sought to propitiate gods and evil forces, which all powerful art must foreground and play with.

Referring to Western civilisation, Jean Starobinski perceptively points out that the discovery of the Self coincides with the discovery of imagination, and that the two discoveries are the same (Starobinski 2003). He is referring to the romantic-modernist sensibility, of course, inaugurated by the likes of Rousseau and the Schlegels. In every creation, the author now distributes his substance: 'What is your substance, whereof are you made/ That millions of strange shadows on you tend? / Since every one hath, every one, one shade/And you but one, can every shadow lend' (Sonnet 153; Shakespeare [1609] 2010). Selves are but shadows dispersed in every *blessed shape* we have known in fiction, which is also life.

The more a certain kind of romantic strand sought to salvage the sincere inner selfhood, the more doubling and fashioning dispersed its bounded nature. Creators of art have fictively tried to mould and nurture the Self, but it slips away. It prefers to stand testimony to the history of contingent conflicts and temporal flux. Even in the best of *bildungsromans* or in the poetry of healing/dwelling (such as in Novalis, Wordsworth or Emerson), the fixity of the Self is put to question. Bringing the 'man to home' has proven to be an exasperating possibility. Instead, self-reflection becomes the predominant mode of imagining fictiveness, and with it comes suffering and what Irving Howe has called a 'despotic possessiveness' of consciousness (1991). One direction is egoism and developmental quest (like in Crusoe and his descendants). The other is alienation and angst where self-extension is thwarted (right from the creature's failed attempts to communion in *Frankenstein* to its numerous modernist progenies), while the third is the implosion and complete dispersal of the Self.

The democratisation of the egotistic persona makes a dramatic announcement in Walt Whitman's 'Song of Myself': 'These one and all tend inward toward me, and I tend outward to them/And such as it is to be of these more or less I am' (Whitman [1855] 2004). Here is the blithe and hopeful Self in the salad bowl—grandiose, pragmatic and yet, often lonely. The obverse happens when fantasy and reality collide—all forms of identity and knowable Self collapse, such as in certain works of Luigi Pirandello or Alain Robbe-Grillet. The possession of all selves within and distancing from each of those show how identity is knit. The creator and receiver of fiction do not discover a Self really but invent it rather through the delineation and actualisation of various roles, which are not consistent or symmetric to each other. In the classical and modern sensibilities, the working out of the roles are detached—in the former, in deference to proportion and unity, and in the latter, in trying to achieve objective clarity by internalising the notion of role-playing itself. Relations pass through *bundles of perception*. In romantic fiction, however, by contrast, a sense of 'being alone together' is overwhelming. Here, subjectivities arise and take shape in the encounters among those roles in the course of the narrative. Often, even the most intimate encounters are asymmetrical, for there is a constant tension between solitary inwardness and interpersonal exposure and between mutual feeling and an incommunicable core of the Self. Consequently, romantic poetry and fiction is suffused with estranging forms of intimacy (Yousef 2013).

In each case, one thing remains constant: that there is no direct congruence between the being's consciousness and its natural Self in fiction. The fictive Self is indeed an elaborate conceit where criss-crossing personae are exposed to untrammelled emotional chaos. So, also with thought, reflective selves travel towards thinking. Thinking can never be housed in any distinct arrogance.

The sense or the bafflement with the fictive Self and the harbinger to the query: 'What is our substance, wherefore we are made?'—is self-reflective in nature. Yet, the reflection is never about full knowledge of the Self. Rather, it is about its obverse, to take lightly the righteous idea about assertions of the first person, for all experiences are as real as they are elusive. Reason is as inadequate in fathoming the Self's journeys and vacillations as is desire. The elusiveness of desire is marked by the ironical turns of self-reflection in the romantic-modern sensibility. Yet, desire comes back time and again to undercut all objective distancing. Both self-indulgence and austerity measures must lead to a sense of exhaustion and void. The tension creates and unmakes the modern Self. Once the dead end is realised, the Self disperses, turns meditative and stoic or becomes ironic in its utterances. From here, it is a small step to the looping back to therapy and salvific quests in fiction.

On one hand, we are still trying to grapple with the hollowing out of words, the losing of language—the *shrouded soundlessness* of a culture. On the other hand, there is the relentless buzz of the crowd and the news cycle and the acceleration of associations, which is the *excited unease* of a culture. Both conditions deny the interpretative in-between space. Is it possible to renew the productive tension between whatever is assured/quiet and its obverse, the restive, the volatile and the creative? Is it not between our sense of dwelling and our sense of contingency that selves play?

The tension between the rival selves, though distressed, is still pregnant with prospects perhaps. The in-between space still reserves the potential to transcend hesitation, statelessness and the crisis of inspiration. A culture in coma may still be able to come out of it.[13] Perhaps, there is hope in Carson' *pause* and in Devy's too, who contrasts *caesura* with repressive silence? This is the 'Quiet Place' that Peter Handke has sought all his life: a place where the Self may turn 'ebullient, a place filled with invigorating, unfocussed energy', a space of awakened enthusiasm (Handke 2022).

The space of privacy in Western modernity has to do with at least one genre in literature where the Self comes closest to the first-person 'I': autobiographies/self-narratives. The romantic notions of life writing have much to do with crafting the first person in the way that Rousseau had envisaged. It eventually led to the modern appreciation of autobiographies as a chronologically consistent narrative of a self-conscious personality. Autobiographies written in such a manner resist the dissipation of personhood and hope to shore up authentic forms of inwardness instead by creating and documenting inner accounts of unique individuals. Psychological veracity determines modern life-representations. Besides, intimacy becomes a mode to express emotions—the reader becomes privy to the childhood, upbringing, love life and other anxieties of the confessional author. William Hazlitt's 1823 autobiography *Liber Amoris* is a good example. However, such an idea of writing life is not universal. For instance, Arabic, Japanese (*nikki*) and Tibetan (*ragnam*) autobiographies often raise mystical, philosophical possibilities and the hope of communicating literary pleasure to their readers. Some autobiographies are co-authored with later additions and redactions. Political memories also have little to do with the personal portrayal of the Self.[14] In the context of Indian first-person narratives, Udaya Kumar has shown how certain life-representations from Kerala are actually interventions in public life and public discussions. Such interventions are extremely concerned with historical change (2008). Truth telling in such autobiographies is about sharing and giving shape to historical memory. Kumar calls such networks 'perceptual economies' where objects and emotional states, new subjectivities and life practices are formed through correlations among eventual change.[15]

On the other hand, what D.H. Lawrence (1981) would call the 'old stable ego'—integral and self-consistent—would be battered constantly since the advent of modernity (which has had a ripple effect all around the world). Such an ego found a remarkable, if unfinished, dimension in the long 20th century though various cultural-political acts and artifices. In certain instances, dissipation and disintegration of selfhood in modernism as a phenomenon is intricately related to the ways of trying to re-engage with traces of the lost Self—in Ezra Pound's Mauberley (1957) and Henry James's Lambert Strether (*The Ambassadors,* 2011), for instance. Conversely, and more often, the modern and the modernist personae have immersed themselves in creative freedom itself, by relegating or multiplying the Self—as encountered in the narrative voice of Shakespeare's *Sonnets* or in Stephen Daedalus in Joyce's *Portrait of the Artist as a Young Man* (2023). In other times, modernist quests have led to the primitive heart of darkness. Still others took to a politics of grand style, outrage and martyrdom, as we encounter in the works and actions of Stefan George or Gabriele D'Annunzio.

However, that quest of the idiosyncratic Self got refracted and then dissipated—first in the self-defeating irony of detached simulacrum, followed by an extended reaction in search of the authentic: a revenge of the sentimental tribes formed out of cabals constituting the banal and behavioural 'I' persona. The consumptive and insecure tribes seek a series of 'teasing meantimes', instead of partaking in any beautiful detour through art's suggestivity or force. The teasing meantimes are rather virtual and make-believe distractions in culture, not investments in aesthetics. Consequently, all politics gets refracted from those who indulge in such faithless simulacra. However, the simulacrum, the virtual data design, is not fictional at all. It is auretic, and the aura is operatic, not naïve. The more moral certainties become the staple of everyday show business, the more the very perplexity of the condition of living have come to appear suspect to a large swathe of humanity, cutting across the ideological spectrum. All doubt turns into new-age belief, which is really a receptacle to unleash faithlessness and cruelty over selfhood itself. As Boris Groys succinctly puts it, 'virtual means having virtue' (2021). The real crisis is that without polyphony and without contradiction, selves in fiction can hardly be sustained. But we confront a culture where no mystique is allowed. Everything must be revealed in the age of uncovering and display.

Indeed, without earning the capacity to be perplexed by life's inexplicable opacity, there is no appreciation of the variegated texture of art's detour and its inflections. Confronted with the crisis of indeterminacy, art effaces its own figurations. It lurches, and as art lurches and stutters alongside living, it begins to shimmer. It embraces indeterminacy joyously. In this manner, selves in art lie bare and baffled—saturated with historicity and flux. Lisa Robertson has called such a state 'incandescent and erotic duration' (2012). The greatest crisis to art is the assault on such a sense of pulsating duration, which is also the zone of I's *groundlessness*, its *lingering* and eventual *desertion*. Art unbinds the subject in such groundlessness. All unbinding is the revelation of the Self's opacity; its secret—filtered through untimely colours and tropes, metaphors and inflections of every nature.

The moment art begins to seek security through self-conscious sanctimony, all fictional selves appear to be fraudulent. The problematique is placed instead in terms of hunting the truth. Buffeted by a sense of being lost, we begin to seek measure. Hence, there is the hope that art would reveal the hidden *gestell* and, along with that, the inner harmony of the universe: art turns into a receptacle for proportion and proportionate living. Such a revelatory hope fosters a spiritualised superiority of centrifugal mysticism. It could also foster the obverse: that art must reveal the truth about social fractures and the play of power and the quest for that ever-eluding justice for a large swathe of humanity. In sanctimony, sometimes, the two come dangerously close. Living is attested, though an economy of commensurate virtue in search of a purer and more honest experience. Angry malcontents take over to unleash honesty over a trembling culture. Neither wandering conviviality nor a flight of imagination and wonder is the quest. The swerve of the uncanny eludes the discourse of demand.

References

Agamben, Giorgio. 2020. 'The Medical Religion.' *Where Are We Now?: The Epidemic as Politics*. Trans. Valeria Dani. London: Urtext Ltd.

Baron, Hans. 1955. *The Crisis of the Early Italian Renaissance*. Princeton, N.J.: Princeton University Press.

Batalvi, Shiv Kumar. n.d. 'Shiv Kumar Batalvi.' Accessed 8 January 2023. https://apnaorg.com/poetry/suman/4.html

Benjamin, Walter. (1923) 1968. 'The Task of the Translator.' *Illuminations: Essays and Reflections.* RHUS. Page numbers from 1923 edition.

Borchardt, Julian. 1932. 'The Essence of Marx's Theory of Crises.' In *Karl Marx, Capital, The Communist Manifesto, and Other Writings*, edited by Max Eastman, 302–314. New York: The Modern Library.

Burckhardt, Jakob. 1943. *Reflections on History*. Translated by M.D.H. London: George Allen and Unwin Ltd.

Carson, Anne. 2021. 'Stillness.' *Critical Inquiry* 48 (1): 1–22.

Chakrabarti, Arindam. 2019. *Realisms Interlinked: Object, Subjects, and Other Subjects.* New Delhi, London, Oxford, New York, Sydney: Bloomsbury.

Colebrook, Claire. 2021. 'A Cut in Relationality: Art at the End of the World.' In *Relationality,* edited by Simone Drichel. London and New York: Routledge.

Collins, Stephen. 1982. *Selfless Persons.* Cambridge: Cambridge University Press.

Dasti, Matthew R., and Edwin F. Bryant. 2014. *Free Will, Agency, and Selfhood in Indian Philosophy.* Oxford and New York: Oxford University Press.

Davis, Mike. 2022. 'Thanatos Triumphant.' *New Left Review, Sidecar*. Accessed July 2022. https://newleftreview.org/sidecar/posts/thanatos-triumphant

Dessein, Bart, ed. 1999. 'The Notion of Self in Buddhism.' *Communication and Cognition* 32, no 1/2.

Devy, G.N. 2019. *The Question of Silence: A Parabiography.* Hyderabad: Orient BlackSwan.

Dodd, James. 2004. *Crisis and Reflection: An Essay on Husserl's Crisis of the European Sciences.* New York, Boston, Dordrecht, London. Moscow: Kluwer Academic Publishers.

Drichel, Simone. 2020. 'The Most Perfectly Autonomous Man: Relational Subjectivity and Crisis of Connection.' In *Relationaliy*, edited by Simone Drichel. New York and London: Routledge.

Dufourmantelle, Anne. 2021. *In Defense of Secrets.* Translated by Lindsay Turner. New York: Fordham University Press.

Edelglass, William, and Jay L. Garfield. 2009. *Buddhist Philosophy: Essential Readings.* Oxford and New York: Oxford University Press.

Erikson, Eric H. 1968. *Identity: Youth and Crisis.* New York and London: W.W. Norton.

Faruque, Muhammad U. 2021. *Sculpting the Self: Islam, Selfhood, and Human Flourishing.* Ann Arbor: University of Michigan Press.

Ferguson, Niall. 2021. *Doom: The Politics of Catastrophe.* New York: Penguin Press.

Flood, Gavin. 2004. *The Ascetic Self: Subjectivity, Memory and Tradition.* Cambridge: Cambridge University Press.

Freedan, Michael. 2017. 'Crisis? How Is that a Crisis?!' *Contributions to the History of Concepts* 12 (2): 12–28.

Gallagher, Shaun, ed. 2011. *The Oxford Handbook of the Self.* Oxford: Oxford University Press.

Ganeri, Jonardon. 2007. *The Concealed Art of the Soul: Theories of Self and Practices of Truth in Indian Ethics and Epistemology.* Oxford: Oxford University Press.

———. 2017. *Attention, Not Self.* Oxford: Oxford University Press.
———. 2021. *Inwardness: An Outsider's Guide.* New York: Columbia University Press.
Gandhi, Ramachandra. 1994. *Sita's Kitchen: A Testimony of Faith and Enquiry.* New Delhi: Wiley Eastern Limited.
Gasche, Rodolphe. 1999. *Of Minimal Things: Studies on the Notion of Relation.* Stanford: Stanford University Press.
Groys, Boris. 2021. 'Art on the Internet.' School of Visual Arts, 28 May 2021. YouTube video, 1:13:05. Accessed June 2022. https://www.youtube.com/watch?v=WmFiAN5AU4o&t=1281s
Gyatso, Janet B. 1989. 'Autobiography in Tibetan Religious Literature: Reflections on Its Modes of Self-Presentation.' *Tibetan Studies—Proceedings of the 5th Seminar of the International Association for Tibetan Studies.* Vol. 2. Narita: Naritasan Shinshoji. Language, History and Culture.
Hall, Donald. 2004. *Subjectivity.* London: Routledge.
Handke, Peter. *Quiet Places.* 2022. New York: Farrar, Strauss and Giroux.
Hardt, Michael. 2007. 'The Violence of Capital.' *New Left Review* 48 (November-December):153–160.
Harvey, Peter. 1995. *The Selfless Mind.* Richmond, UK: Curzon.
Hobsbawm, E.J. 1954. 'The General Crisis of the European Economy in the 17th Century.' *Past and Present* 5: 33–53.
Howe, Irving. 1991. 'The Self in Literature.' *Salmagundi,* Spring-Summer 1991, no. 90/91: 56–77.
Husserl, Edmund. 1970. *The Crisis of European Sciences and Transcendental Phenomenology.* Translated by David Carr. Evanston: Northwestern University Press.
James, Henry. 2011. *Novels 1903-1911: The Ambassadors / The Golden Bowl / The Outcry.* New York: Library of America.
Joyce, James. 2023. *A Portrait of the Artist as a Young Man.* London: Macmillan Popular Classics.
Kaukua, Jari. 2015. *Self-Awareness in Islamic Philosophy: Avicenna and Beyond.* Cambridge: Cambridge University Press.
Kenny, Anthony. 1988. *The Self.* Milwaukee, WI: Marquette University Press.
Kidder, Paul. 1987. 'Husserl's Paradox.' *Research in Phenomenology* 17: 227–242.
Koselleck, Reinhart. 1988. *Critique and Crisis: Enlightenment and Pathogenesis of Modern Society.* Cambridge, M.A.: MIT Press.
———. 2002. *The Practice of Conceptual History: Timing History, Spacing Concepts.* Stanford, C.A.: Stanford University Press.
Koselleck, Reinhart, and Michaela W. Richter. 2006. 'Crisis.' *Journal of the History of Ideas* 67 (2): 357–400.
Kumar. Udaya. 2008 'Autobiography as a Way of Writing History Personal Narratives from Kerala and the Inhabitation of Modernity.' In *History in the Vernacular,* edited by Raziuddin Aquil and Partha Chatterjee. Ranikhet: Permanent Black.
———. 2016. *Writing the First Person: Literature, History and Autobiography in Modern Kerala.* Ranikhet: Permanent Black.

Lasch, Christopher. (1979) 2018. *The Culture of Narcissism: American Life in an Age of Diminishing Expectations.* London and New York: W. W Norton and Company.

———. 1985. *The Minimal Self: Psychic Survival in Troubled Times.*

Lawrence, D.H. 1981. *The Letters of D. H. Lawrence.* Vol. II. Edited by George J. Zytaruk and James T. Boulton. Cambridge: Cambridge University Press.

Levinas, Emmanuel. 1970. 'No Identity' [In French]. *L'Ephémère* 13: 27–44. Reprinted in *Humanisme de l'autre homme.* 1972. Montpellier: Fata Morgana. 83–101.

Long, A.A. 2015. *Greek Models of Mind and Self.* Cambridge, MA: Harvard University Press.

Lowe, E.J. 1991. 'Substance and Selfhood.' *Philosophy* 66 (255): 81–99.

MacIntyre, Alasdair. 1978. *Against the Self-Images of the Age.* Notre Dame, IN: University of Notre Dame Press.

Marx, Karl. 1976. *Capital.* Translated by Ben Fowkes and David Fernbach. New York and London: Penguin.

Mead, George H. 1962. *Mind, Self, and Society.* Chicago, IL: University of Chicago Press.

Mishra, Pankaj. 2017. *Age of Anger: A History of the Present.* New Delhi: Juggernaut.

Morozov, Evgeny. 2022. 'Critique of Techno-Feudal Reason.' *New Left Review*, no. 133/134. Accessed 8 January 2023. https://newleftreview.org/issues/ii133/articles/evgeny-morozov-critique-of-techno-feudal-reason

Natanson, Maurice. 1974. *Edmund Husserl: Philosopher of Infinite Tasks.* Evanston, Illinois: Northwestern University Press.

Nedelsky, Jennifer. 2011. *Law's Relation: A Relational Theory of Self, Autonomy and Law.* New York: Oxford University Press.

Negri, Antonio. 1991. *The Savage Anomaly: The Power of Spinoza's Metaphysics and Politics.* Translated by Michael Hardt. Minneapolis and Oxford: University of Minnesota Press.

Oliver-Smith, Anthony, and Susanna M. Hoffman, eds. 2020. *The Angry Earth: Disaster in Anthropological Perspective.* London and New York: Routledge.

Oxford English Dictionary. 1971. Oxford: Oxford University Press.

Paine, Thomas. 2018. *Writings of Thomas Paine—Volume 1 (1774–1779): The American Crisis.* Delhi: Lector House, LLP.

Parfit, Derek. 1987. *Reasons and Persons.* Oxford: Clarendon Press.

Patočka, Jan. 1996. *Essays in the Philosophy of History.* Translated by Erazim Kohak. Chicago and La Salle, Illinois: Open Court.

Polanyi, Karl. 2001. *The Great Transformation: The Political and Economic Origins of Our Time.* Boston: Beacon Press.

Pound, Ezra. 1957. *Selected Poems of Ezra Pound.* Cambridge, MA: New Directions.

Raghuramaraju, A., ed. 2013. *Ramachandra Gandhi: The Man and His Philosophy.* New Delhi: Routledge.

Rasch, William. 1995. 'Immanent Systems, Transcendental Temptations, and the Limits of Ethics.' *Cultural Critique*, Spring 1995, No. 30: 193–221.

Remes, Pauliina, and Juha Sihvola, ed. 2008. *Ancient Philosophy of the Self.* Dordrecht and London: Springer.

Reynolds, Dwight F, ed. 2001. *Interpreting the Self: Autobiography in the Arabic Literary Tradition.* Berkeley, Los Angeles, London: University Of California Press.

Robertson, Lisa. 2012. *Nilling: Prose Essays.* Toronto: Book Thug.

Roitman, Janet. 2014. *Anti-Crisis.* Durham and London, Duke University Press.

Rose, Gillian. 1995. *Love's Work: A Reckoning with Life.* New York: Schocken Books.

Sanil, V. 2013. *Ramachandra Gandhi: The Man and His Philosophy.* Edited by A. Raghuramaraju. New Delhi: Routledge.

Sarkar, Sumit. 1992. '"Kaliyuga", "Chakri" and "Bhakti": Ramakrishna and His Times.' *Economic and Political Weekly* 27 (29): 1543–1559 and 1561–1566.

Sebald, Winfried Georg. 2014. *A Place in the Country.* London: Penguin.

Sen, Manidipa, ed. 2019. *Problem of the Self: Consciousness, Subjectivity and the Other.* Delhi: Aakar Books.

Shakespeare, William. (1609) 2010. *The Oxford Shakespeare: The Complete Sonnets and Poems.* Oxford, UK: Oxford University Press.

Shank, J.B. 2008. 'Crisis: A Useful Category of Post-Social Scientific Historical Analysis?' *The American Historical Review* 113 (4): 1090–1099.

Siderits, Mark. 2003. *Personal Identity and Buddhist Philosophy: Empty Persons.* Oxford: Ashgate.

Soichi Saeki. 'The Autobiography in Japan.' *The Journal of Japanese Studies* 11 (2): 357–368.

Sorabji, Richard. 2006. *Self: Ancient and Modern Insights about Individuality, Life, and Death.* Chicago, IL: University of Chicago Press.

Starn, Randolph. 1971. 'Historians and "Crisis".' *Past & Present*, No. 52: 3–22.

Starobinski, Jean. 2003. *Action and Reaction: The Life and Adventures of a Couple.* New York: Zone Books.

Sweijs, Tim, Artur Usanov, and Rik Rutten. 2016. 'Back to the Brink: Escalation and Interstate Crisis.' *Hague Centre for Strategic Studies.* The Hague. ISBN/EAN: 978-94-92102-33-1.

Tagore, Rabindranath. 1996. *The English Writings of Rabindranath Tagore.* Vol. 3. Edited by Sisir Kumar Das. New Delhi: Sahitya Academy.

Tangjia, Wang. 2014. 'A Philosophical Analysis of the Concept of Crisis.' *Frontiers of Philosophy in China* 9 (2): 254–267.

Taylor, Charles. 1989. *Sources of the Self: The Making of the Modern Identity.* Cambridge, MA: Harvard University Press.

Thiel, Udo. 2011. *The Early Modern Subject: Self-Consciousness and Personal Identity from Descartes to Hume.* Oxford: Oxford University Press.

Way, Niobe, Alisha Ali, Carol Gilligan, and Pedro Noguera. 2018. *The Crisis of Connection: Roots, Consequences, and Solutions.* New York: New York University Press.

Weil, Simone. (1966) 2009. *Waiting for God.* Translated by Emma Craufurd. New York: HarperCollins.

Weston, Michael. 2001. *Philosophy, Literature and Human Good.* London and New York: Routledge.

Whitman, Walt. (1855) 2004. *Complete Poems.* New York: Penguin Books.

Williams, Bernard. 1973. *Problems of the Self.* Cambridge: Cambridge University Press.
Yousef, Nancy. 2013. *Romantic Intimacy.* Stanford, California: Stanford University Press.
Zahavi, Dan. 2014. *Self and Other: Exploring Subjectivity, Empathy, and Shame.* Oxford: Oxford University Press.
Zweig, Paul. 1968. *The Heresy of Self-Love.* New York: Basic Books.

Notes

1 *Protrope* or *protreptikon* means turning pupils and interlocutors in a certain direction. This is a method of introductory persuasion, rather than giving direct counsel, advancing a hypothesis, indulging in 'midwifery' or getting into an act of diatribe or propaganda. Protreptic is *urging towards* a range of discourses rather than offering a single schema of demonstration and refutation. It is the obverse of rousing.

2 The idea of expanding or *sculpting* the Self is sometimes used in the sense of cultivating it or orienting it in certain directions, like charity, devotion, trust, patience or bravery. The mode becomes a 'way of life'. Muhammad U. Faruque has used such a concept of expansive, mindful and transformative Self in *Sculpting the Self* (2021). Such a project seems to be more about an ethico-spiritual quest of self-knowledge and self-growth, mediated via notions of flourishing, self-cultivation, self-transcendence and the transformation of the Self itself. It is more about detachment than decreation.

3 Related notions to crisis, such as 'tension' or 'strain', mostly work at a more micro-level. Sometimes, 'convulsion' is used in a more general sense to denote crisis. Contradiction, in socialist vocabulary, has an affinity to crisis. Conjuncture is another allied but more neutral term.

4 For instance, in an essay titled 'Back to the Brink' (2016), Tim Sweijs, Artur Usanov and Rik Rutten say:

> Crises, it is claimed, have therefore become the 'surrogate for war' and are instrumental in resolving 'without violence, or with only minimal violence' interstate disputes 'that are too severe to be settled by ordinary means and that in earlier times would have been settled by war.' In this rendering, crises are a necessary safety valve, especially in a world in which nuclear weapons have dramatically raised the costs of going to war.

5 On Marx and 'crisis theory', see Marx (1976, 2: Chapters. 7–9, 13–21, 3: chap. 30); Borchardt (1932, 302–314); and Hardt (2007). See also Hobsbawm (1954).

6 See Karl Polanyi (2001) to weigh the contemporary ways by which the relationship between the market and the political institutions are now being worked out, especially when fundamental democratic values are

taking a beating in large parts of the world. Does the question of economics still trump the political decisions, or do ideological and cultural issues now find a primary place in determining the nature of crisis in the West as well as in other parts of the world? Polanyi's context was the major societal shift that was taking place as a result of the Great Depression and the First World War.

7 See the 'Translator's Introduction' by David Carr to the English translation of Husserl's text.

8 See Collins (1982) and Siderits (2003). See also Dessein (1999) and Harvey (1995). In modern Western philosophy, the best delineation of reduced personhood can be found in Derek Parfit's contributions, which argue that though persons exist, 'we could give a complete description of reality without claiming that persons exist' (1987). Parfit's thesis negatively claims that a person is not a separately existing entity, distinct from his or her brain, body and experiences. Its positive claim is that 'a person's existence just consists in the existence of a brain and body, and the occurrence of a series of interrelated physical and mental events'.

9 Paul Zweig engagingly traces the intuitive history of self-regarding motivations in *The Heresy of Self-Love.* Zweig focuses on 'the West's millennia-long fascination with Narcissus: deploring his inhuman solitude, admiring him as a figure of fulfilment and transcendence' (1968). Surprisingly, Narcissus proves to be a figure of serene resistance, of meditative renitence, opposing everything current, common, collective, a mirror, so to speak, of the 'ambivalent war-fare—call it a dialectic—between subversive individuals and the large, moralised embrace of society.

10 In *Self and Other: Exploring Subjectivity, Empathy, and Shame,* Dan Zahavi tries to connect the experiential Self with the normative Self to bridge relationality (2014). He argues for the co-constitution of Self and Other and for a self-relation constitutive of selfhood by being socialised into a publicly shared space of normativity—such as empathy and shame. Zahavi transcends identity but keeps the tension between norms and experience alive. For an expanded liberal exploration of relations that does not relinquish the autonomy of personhood, see also Nedelsky (2011).

11 See also MacIntyre (1978). MacIntyre extends the argument of self-regarding sensibility to certain contemporary ideologies and practices that have made relationality moribund. He particularly finds the self-images of Christianity, Marxism and psychoanalysis to be illusive.

12 In an incisive essay titled *Rambling Wisdom*, V. Sanil refers to Ramachandra Gandhi's very mode of enunciation as 'inspired garbling' (2013). He says,

> In addressing you I do not refer to you. I do not identify you with a description. In addressing I do not seek your attention. Instead I mean you. I identify you non-referentially, non-descriptively and as Ramu would insist in his later works, non-dualistically. What does it mean to mean you? To mean you means to bring you into self-awareness. To be self-aware is not to become aware

> of something as opposed to something else. It is to be aware of oneself as coincided with the circumambient emptiness—the not thingness.

13 One recalls the final sections of Rabindranath Tagore's *Crisis in Civilization,* where he writes:

> As I look around I see the crumbling ruins of a proud civilization strewn like a vast heap of futility. And yet I shall not commit the grievous sin of losing faith in Man. I would rather look forward to the opening of a new chapter in his history after the cataclysm is over and the atmosphere rendered clean with the spirit of service and sacrifice. (1996)

14 See Reynolds (2001), Gyatso (1989, 465–478) and Soichi (1985, 357–368).
15 See Udaya Kumar (2008, 2016).

I

LINEAGES OF THE SELF

1

THE FORMATION AND TRANSFORMATION OF THE SELF IN ANCIENT GREEK POLITICAL DISCOURSE

Vijay Tankha

This chapter aims to provide a broad survey of ideas relating to the Self and its identification with different aspects of thought and consciousness in some representative writings of the Greeks. I aim to connect different conceptions of the Self to the political and social matrix that gave it its form and function. Starting with epic and heroic ideas of selfhood and consciousness as found in Homer's poetry, I trace doctrines that emerge from the 6th century BCE and form the basis for the more developed accounts of soul and Self (here used interchangeably) that we encounter later in the works of Plato and Aristotle. I show, through the analogies and metaphors in some representative works, how conceptions of the Self reflected the social and political (rather than merely the religious and ethical) matrix of the times. The Self or soul as the seat of consciousness, as the knowing subject, represented the interests and outlook of an elite class who, distinguishing themselves from lower social orders, created not only a moral and political vocabulary but also a metaphysical one in which the soul is given a prominent role.

Further, in the better-known writings of the philosophers, the idea of the soul and its relation to knowledge underwent a transformation that was elaborated through a complex and still influential psychology, even as it supported a conservative ideology. Such an outlook was consolidated, if not masked, by the creation of a sociopolitical ethic coordinated with an epistemology. It was filled out by an appealing metaphysics that advanced traditional ideas and sentiments. In the detailed eschatology that we find in some accounts of the afterlife in Plato's works, room was made for the knowing subject or Self that conferred near-divine status on it. The identification of the soul with both consciousness and agency provided thinkers of this period with an ethics that was at odds with the more egalitarian aspects of popular politics.

The Greek contribution to Western thought is considered overwhelming. Indeed, in some ways, Western thinking, if not a footnote to Greek philosophy, may be seen as a series of appendices, whose utility, even when questioned, will use categories that have already been conceptualised: logic, physics and ethics. Kant distinguished these three domains as constituting the body of philosophy, and they also form the body of early Greek philosophy.

What is touted as the Greek miracle and as a cause for wonder has no identifiable or agreed-upon origins. Like life itself, its trigger remains mysterious. Whether it was climate, geography or the special insight of extraordinary men, it engendered uniquely both science and philosophy. These are announced as the products of reason, Greece's unquestioned contribution to humanity. The implication is that all other civilisations lacked this concept. In a sense, there is no equivalent concept in the other surviving civilisational texts of antiquity, Chinese or Indic. Neither tradition has a man-defining term like *logos*. Clearly, this is not a deficiency as both traditions have had great longevity. However, neither has bequeathed as enduring a concept to the world as the idea of the rational man. Rationality is the flower of Greek philosophy. Those who dismiss Western logo-centricism do so in its shadow. The mark of reason is, minimally, one might suppose, the use of arguments rather than declamation, assertions or wise adages. Arguments, if you look very closely, are discernible in the speculations of the earliest natural philosophers, Aristotle's *phusiologoi* (those who talk about nature). With rapid strides, arguments (*logoi*) took over all forms of thought, whether in poetry or prose, metaphors and analogies, even where they did not give way completely, accompanied scarcely suppressed syllogisms. However, the use of arguments is not the same as reason, though often confused with it. Reason as a faculty that characterises humans is as much a construct as the soul, with which it becomes mysteriously identified, eventually leading to Aristotle's definition of man as 'the rational animal'.[1]

However, Aristotle had another definition also used to define man: *zoon politikon* or 'man is by nature a political animal' because he lives in a community (the polis), determined by and determining it. Perhaps, the political animal took on the garb of the rational animal to make himself more equal than others.[2]

In the several centuries that separated Aristotle from his literary forbears, the epic poets, there was a discernible development in the idea of the Self and, with it, the understanding of man, who was not always rational but very much political for the political animal was primarily male.

Let us also leave the gods aside, though we know, as did some Greeks, that the gods are only little men writ large (Xenophanes, Heraclitus), and restrict our survey to what the poets said of men. Before philosophical prose developed, we have only the testimony of the poets, epic, lyric and tragic: these forms mark the chronology of archaic, early and classical Greece. In their work, the nature of the Self, its agency and its relation to the community (its politics) were conceived.

We find in the developed outlook of the Self, in Plato's *Republic*, the tripartition of the soul into reason, spirit and appetite, coordinated (not very happily) with a final contrast between the divine intellect and the mortal body. This contrast is affirmed so certainly that it appears not so much a construct as a discovery (echoed in other ancient systems of thought). The Self is routinely divided into what endures and what perishes, a division that still dominates popular conceptions of what it is to be. Yet this apparent self-evidence conceals a progressive construction of a political, rather than merely a psychological, order.

It is important therefore to try to see how the Platonic idea of the Self was a transformation and assimilation of different pre-Platonic ideas, located in the social matrix that gave them birth. While this is difficult to discern where textual evidence is sparse, it is most clearly seen as part of Plato's political programme, where ethics, epistemology and ontology are marshalled together to provide the scaffolding of an aristocratic anti-democratic politics. While Plato's dismissal of democracy is not news, how he develops and constitutes the Self as part of a political strategy has not been fully explored. This chapter is a step in that direction.

The Psyche

In Plato's *Republic*, as is well known, the three parts of the Self are coordinated with three virtues (*arête*) or excellences, which uniquely characterise each part: wisdom or knowledge the rational part, courage the spirited part and prudence or moderation the appetitive part. These together are further coordinated with three classes of citizens: rulers, soldiers and everybody else (the *demos*). The rational rulers stand in opposition to the pleasure- and money-loving populace. Between them, the class of guards may serve one or the other. While the final product is Plato's, harmonised in the analogy of city and soul, its ingredients have been collected, tested and mixed over time.

In his short work on the soul (*de Anima* in its Latin title), Aristotle traces two different ideas that came together to form a developed conception of the soul: movement and consciousness.[3] Reading this back into early Greek ideas, we can revisit Aristotle's claims: the *psyche* in the Homeric poems, while it is mentioned, has, as is well known, little active role to play in a man's life (a role taken up by other forces/organs differently designated), except to leave the body at death.

The difference between an ensouled and a lifeless body (the Self, *autos*) that is left for 'dogs and kites to feed upon' is the absence of the psyche in the latter, connecting it to movement, while retaining the idea of life breath, since a corpse (*nekros*) has neither motion nor breath. So psyche in epic poetry is sometimes understood as 'life breath'. The pre-Socratic thinker Thales credits the soul with motion, while breath, life and the cosmos are together aligned as early as Anaximenes. The soul then had neither agency nor responsibility in early epics, and its post-mortem existence was insubstantial as it lacked both memory and consciousness.[4]

In his journey to the underworld, Odysseus encounters the *psuchai* of the warriors killed in Troy ('shades' rather than 'souls'), who need to drink blood to be able to converse with the living hero. The idea of the relation of blood to life and consciousness persisted, especially among physicians (Boylan 2015). Yet, even in this insubstantial condition, the fact that Ajax still nurtures his anger against Odysseus or that Patrocles's soul appears to Achilles, bearing the memory of what it had suffered and enjoyed while living, might lead us to suppose that some elements of the personality survive into the afterlife. However, we must remember that these are poetic accounts, not an analytic treatise on the nature of the soul. That the shades of the dead need blood to speak to the living, the idea of their insubstantiality and lack of human vigour is stressed. What is important is not the soul but the fact of death and the heroic attitude to it.

Courage

In the heroic imagination, while death is the lot of every man, it distinguishes mortals from the gods (immortals). For men, only fame, won by great deeds, endures. Thus, Hektor, realising that Athena has tricked him and he is about to die, says, 'At least let me not perish without a struggle, ingloriously, but after having done something great, for future generations to learn of' (Fitzgerald 1974). In an oft-quoted passage, Sarpedon says to Glaukos,

> If ... we two were going to be unageing and immortal for ever, /neither would I myself fight in the front ranks /nor would I send you into the battle where men win glory. /But as it is, since the spirits of death stand over us /numberless, which it is not possible for a mortal

> to flee, /let us go—either we will give glory to boast of to someone else, or someone will give it to us.[5]

In Homer, while the psyche's main function is to leave the body, it does reappear as a shadow or *eidolon* of the individual as when the shade of his mother tells Odysseus the nature of the soul:

> This is the appointed way with mortals when one dies. For the sinews no longer hold the flesh and the bones together, but the strong might of blazing fire destroys these, as soon as life [thumos] leaves the white bones, and the spirit [psyche], like a dream, flits away.[6]

The shade lacks strength (*menos*), the very real aspect of the heroic Self, a word that appears with much greater frequency in epics than *psyche*. The dead are without power. The bloodless *psyche* is lifeless, which accounts for its inability to either know or influence earthly affairs. It lacks cognitive ability, though that is not what is missed. By contrast, Plato, censuring the poetic representation of the warrior's world, cites Homer on the insubstantial nature of post-mortem existence. He quotes two passages where the soul's lack of understanding (*phrenes/nous*) is emphasised.[7] Such passages, according to Plato, are to be censored as they are unsuitable for a fighting spirit. The lack or rarity of thought as a feature of the soul marks the contrast between the epic and the Platonic views of the nature of the soul and its post-mortem condition. In the heroic world view, death was not something to fear. Its post-mortem shadowy condition made it unappealing, not the loss of cognitive capacities (Lake 2000, 258–270).

The chief virtue of the hero, which constitutes his nature, is not knowledge but courage. Located in his thumos, it is the driving force, which gives both sexual and physical strength and enables a man to fight.[8] Plato later incorporates courage into the structure of the psyche, which he calls *thumoeides* (the form of the thumos), characteristic of those who, endowed by nature and trained accordingly, must guard the city/soul against foes both external and internal to it. The internal foes are the individual's desires and appetites, more dangerous than the external ones (the populace at large). Both Plato and Isocrates downgraded the value of courage in relation to the other virtues.

If death is the common lot, then it is unexceptional and cannot mark the better from the worse. The nobles, or *agathoi*, must share some feature other than merely living and dying, which is the general lot of mortals. In the heroic imagination, the warrior ethic valorised the lack of fear of death and hence, as we find, the identification of excellence (virtue) with courage or manliness.[9]

Prudence (Sophrosune)

If the Homeric ideal is one of martial prowess and courage in the face of death, its polar opposite is prudence or careful calculation, one of the many senses of the word *sophrosune*: an excellence or virtue better suited to communitarian goals.[10] For the agonistic heroic culture, the civic virtue of sophrosune is akin to cowardice. At best, a minor virtue in the epics (only four occurrences in Homer), it becomes increasingly important in the context of the city states.[11]

It is the second virtue that Plato conjoined to form a composite civic soul, better suited to ordinary persons than heroic exceptions. Its increasing importance in the politics of the city state marked the end of the archaic age as new communitarian values come to the fore. The citizens are characterised as sophron.[12]

Sophrosune is the wisdom that is not deceived by immediate gratification but 'looks to the end', an oft-repeated characteristic of true wisdom being farsighted. Sophrosune is implied as well by words that have to do with the loss or clouding of intellect and actions stemming from imprudent behaviour. Aristotle later characterised it as practical wisdom, emphasising its non-cognitive aspects, primarily with regard to bodily pleasures. The term applied increasingly to behaviour, it seems, rather than to thinking.[13] While its meaning shifts and develops, its unchanging sense when applied to women gives us a clue to its core meaning. Thus, the qualities expected of women (beauty, domestic skill and chastity) 'comprise feminine arête/excellence throughout antiquity' (North 1966, 21).[14] As a paradigm of feminine virtue, it came to characterise effeminate men.

The courage of the warrior defines him just as much as the prudence of the citizen. Each of these marks a different social role that the individual plays in the theatre of war on the one hand and within the order of the city on the other.

To be sophron is also to be modest and to know one's place as it were in the scheme of things. From the viewpoint of the elites, it is a virtue that the mass of citizens must aspire to. In early Greek poetry, much of which is political, sophrosune is as much a norm for the citizens as a whole as it is a trait of the elites that qualifies them to rule. Their intelligence and their ability for forethought and good planning confers status on them. By contrast, the masses (demos) are foolish and, even when they acquire wealth, may still be distinguished from those of noble birth.[15]

The aristocratic ideal is elaborated in the poetry of Theognis. It is not wealth as such that is important but the wealth that has been acquired justly. To acquire wealth justly, it is necessary to be steady in disposition, temperate and self-controlled (sophron; Cobb-Steven 1985, 171).[16] This set of concepts served a political purpose, conferring on some a capacity that distinguished them from those who sought to break into their ranks but lacked the mark of the (truly) well-born. 'In archaic poetry … Sophrosune is … related to conduct that avoids injustice to others … specifically with the orderly civic conduct that avoids internal conflicts … and so a political virtue' (Rademaker 2000, 82).

The complementary negative pole of moderation by the good (*agathoi*) is the immoderation and foolishness of those who are spent by wealth and cause discord (*stasis*) in the city through their actions. They harm both themselves and the polis, joining factions to disrupt civic life. They are stupefied by drink and are like rustics.[17] Such immoderate behaviour as a characteristic of the 'lower' classes may even be an imposed norm. By contrast, the elites are expected to show self-control or sophrosune on such occasions where the sense of restraint is emphasised. In *The Republic*, Plato castigates Homer for letting his heroes reveal their grief in lamentations, saying that it is not seemly for heroes to show such emotions.[18] Sophrosune, read back into the elite status of the warrior, is contrasted with the emotional outflow associated with peasants and other manual workers whose temperament is 'slavish'.

Plato normally associates sophrosune with the control of pleasure and the appetites.[19] In *The Republic*, it is primarily a virtue of the lowest class, those motivated by the desire for wealth/pleasure who, for their own good, agree to be controlled by their superiors. Sophrosune, though at first an aristocratic virtue, becomes the defining trait of the demos in the sense of 'knowing one's place', echoing the Delphic motto: 'Know thyself.'

Knowledge

In pre-democratic Greece (democracy came to Athens after the tyranny of Hippias in 490 BCE), the elites as a whole comprised the ruling class. They distinguished themselves from their inferiors by claiming an excellence or virtue that made them natural rulers: this was their superior skill, based on knowledge coupled with forethought. They could refer to themselves as the agathoi, the good, and look down upon the general agricultural workers as rustics (*agroitikos*). Terms for mind, intellect and the importance of thinking abound in the Theognidean corpus (an aristocratic anthology attributed to Theognis that spans two centuries). Thinking distinguishes the good (both well-born and virtuous) from their inferiors. Their excellence is knowledge.

The most common metaphors for good rulers in epic and early poetry are those of the shepherd and his flock and the pilot of a ship: the former capturing the relationship between the ruler and his people, the latter between the ruler and his city.[20] Both these metaphors are yoked together by Plato in the *Statesman*, a post-Republic dialogue. The idea that there should be only one ruler or one pilot is understandably an aristocratic one, made explicit in the *Iliad*: 'Let not all of the Achaeans try to be kings, multiple rule (*polykoiranie*)… one king (*basileus*) to whom Zeus gave judgements wherewith to formulate plans.'[21] The good king is like a shepherd who looks after the welfare of the people. The bucolic metaphor is both benign and sinister (questioned by Thrasymachus in *The Republic*).[22] The helmsman metaphor emphasises the knowledge and skill of the ruler and was commonplace in the literature of the times.

Knowledge is like a rudder, and the knowledgeable ruler is like a helmsman who guides both the ship of the Self and the city. Plato echoes and further trims this metaphor, contrasting the knowledgeable ruler with the ignorant masses whom clever politicians lead by the nose for their gain. Only the helmsman can save the city and the people.

> Just as the captain of a ship keeps watch for what is at any moment for the good of the vessel and the sailors … making his science his law, and thus preserves his fellow voyagers, so may not a right government be established in the same way by men who could rule by this principle?[23]

Soul and Body

Cults

Apart from the cults of the heroes enshrined in their tombs (*sema*), there were other cults that transformed the heroic understanding of death as the limit of life: Bacchic, Orphic and Pythagorean cults introduced new conceptions of the Self and its relation to the cosmos as a whole. There is, however, little direct evidence available about their doctrines and practices. The Elusian mystery cult does not mention immortality of the soul or transmigration, suggesting that these ideas only took hold with the Pythagoreans. The Orphics, with their formulaic 'the body is a tomb' (*soma sema*), reversed the aristocratic idea of the tomb as the memorial of the hero, turning life into a form of death (and, by implication, dying into life).[24]

The Orphics separated the body and the soul, making the former an encumbrance and a source of evil that must be escaped by a process of purification, bringing to the fore the idea of the soul as a moral agent and its destiny as independent of the body. Orphic doctrines must have offered a more egalitarian outlook to ordinary people, unmarked by social status. Orphic and Pythagorean ideas are difficult to date as their texts, where they exist, are late. However, their influence can be discerned in early philosophers like Heraclitus and Parmenides, the former in Ionia close to where Pythagoras began his career (Samos) and the latter where he ended it (southern Italy).

The transformation in the concept of the psyche that took place in these circles is noteworthy. The doctrine of transmigration presupposes that in the living being, man as an animal, there is an individual, constant something, an ego that preserves its identity by force of its essence, independent of the body that passes away. Thus, a new general concept of a living being is created, *empsychon*: 'a psyche within'. This psyche is obviously not the powerless, unconscious image of recollection in a gloomy Hades. Now it is unaffected by death (*athanatos*), which distinguished gods from men in Homer (Burkert 1985, 300).

Heraclitus and Parmenides

Heraclitus, who flourished around 500 BCE, adopted many Pythagorean ideas. He was one of the first to give importance to the soul as both a moral and a cognitive agent distinct from the physical world. 'You could not find the limits of the soul, though you travelled every way, so deep is its logos.'[25] This notion of the depth or profundity of the soul involves a dimension that is foreign to a physical organ or its function. Logos is given a new range of meanings: the logos or understanding of the psyche is so profound that there are no limits to it. The idea of limit has Pythagorean overtones as 'limit' and 'unlimited'(*peras/aperas*) stood at the head of the table of contraries, a formal Pythagorean classification of all things. For Heraclitus, the psyche lies outside all categories. It is not merely a unique object but the knowing subject that desires and suffers, though Heraclitus makes no clear mention of its post-mortem condition. Further, understanding and knowledge of things are, though rare, attributed to it.[26]

The contrast between human and divine knowledge is a regular motif in Greek literature, but while human knowledge was accepted as limited, many thinkers aimed at understanding what was not given directly in experience by paying close attention to what was—thus the use of analogies that underpin pre-Socratic thought. Heraclitus was no exception, but he did not dismiss outright the use of the senses. While there is a general bias against perception as a means to knowledge, we don't find that sharp contrast in Heraclitus.

His contemporary Parmenides, rejected sense experience, seeking direct knowledge of divinity/reality through the mind. Parmenides offered irrefutable and abstract arguments in favour of his conception of an abstract unchanging reality that can only be known but never sensed.[27] Access to truth (knowledge) is given in Parmenides through a divine revelation, not via the accumulation of sense experience. In Plato, the mind moves entirely within the mind and has no recourse to (confusing) sense perceptions.[28]

Socrates: Virtue and Knowledge

Whether it was the historical Socrates or a singular Platonic voice, the political and ethical ideas of Socrates marked a real change from speculative natural philosophy. There were many others like him, dubbed 'sophists' by Plato, who were part of a cultural revolution, a product of the democracy that placed Athens at the centre of an intellectual renaissance.

Arête/virtue is knowledge, said Socrates, paradoxically. Socrates is thought to have introduced ethics into the political life of the city. Two claims typically associated with him are that 'one must care for oneself' and that 'the unexamined life is not worth living'.[29] Both statements are conceptually linked and point to a common feature of a new philosophical praxis. To say that the unexamined life is not worth living is to claim the importance of philosophical examination in one's own life. Socrates tells us what he thinks this minimally involves: paying attention to what is important for one's soul and not paying attention to what is adventitious or unimportant.[30] The question that must dominate our concerns is: How should one live? What is the best kind of life? These are questions that philosophy alone can answer. In an important sense, the practice of philosophy is the answer to how to live best.[31] Philosophical examination must aim at revealing the real nature of the Self as a condition, we might suppose, of caring for it. We can only take care of the Self if we know what it is essentially.

For Socrates, care of the Self requires paying attention to virtue or arête: 'and I tell you that virtue is not derived from wealth, but that virtue is itself the source of wealth and all other goods, both for the individual and for the state'.[32]

The term translated as virtue, *arête*, is also translated as 'excellence'. While the term *arête*, like excellence, has a variety of uses and could characterise, as the English term does, both horses and knives, we can distinguish between moral and non-moral uses of the term. Socrates was primarily interested in the former.[33] It is not possible (or desirable) to unpack the claim that the only human excellence is knowledge: it is enough to note that if the care of the Self is connected intimately to knowledge, the Self or soul must not merely be capable of knowing but must be one whose essential nature is to know. Care of the Self, as a Socratic slogan, gives a new interpretation to the Delphic maxim 'Know thyself', making knowledge an excellence.[34]

Further, though Socrates was concerned most of all with 'care of the Self', he had no doctrine of post-mortem existence. In several of his early dialogues, Plato sought to unravel this paradox (or complicate it further). Knowledge or understanding is a chief function of the mind. The Homeric hero, while he exemplifies the virtue of courage, was not without intelligence. However, the intelligence was of a certain kind—closer to the argumentative skill that sophists would later boast they could teach, employing deception rather than truth (Detienne and Vernant 1991). Odysseus was its exemplar, in contrast to truth-telling Achilles.[35]

Plato

It is not necessary to summarise Plato's political philosophy while connecting it with his ethics and metaphysics, for he has already done so in several memorable images in the central books of *The Republic*. An analogy between the soul and the city structures the entire work. Outside both city and soul lie the realm of Forms, which are paradigms for both (though there is no Form of either). The soul is capable of knowledge of this realm, difficult though it is to achieve.

Plato's earlier theory of knowledge, often attributed to Socratic influence, if not an entirely Socratic understanding of what 'virtue is knowledge' means, takes knowledge as being constitutive of the Self and radically distinct from ignorance. Such knowledge, formally on par with other undisputed forms of specialised knowledge, has both a theoretical and practical component like them. Plato leaves undefined the precise nature of the knowledge that Socrates promotes: the early dialogues are seen as probes towards discovering what such knowledge entails.

The contrast between knowledge and ignorance had as its political correlate, as we have seen, the aristocratic idea foreshadowed in the lyric poets that only the knowledgeable are fit to rule while the majority of men (the demos) should be prudent and submit to be ruled by their betters. The masses were regularly castigated in the literature of the time as ignorant and undisciplined.[36]

Plato incorporates this aristocratic idea in his developed notion of the psyche: the appetites must be under the control of reason, which alone can determine what is good for the whole (body) just as the rulers can determine what is good for the whole of the body politic. The views of the many often lead to disastrous results and are not on par with those who know. This familiar aristocratic complaint was echoed in several Platonic dialogues, but Plato grounds it within an elaborate metaphysical frame.

One problematic consequence of the Socratic identification of intelligence with human excellence was its corollary: no man does wrong willingly (since if he knew what was good for him, he wouldn't do it; hence all wrongdoing is regarded as an intellectual failure, a mistake about one's own good). In the division of the soul that Plato advances in his middle dialogues, individuals are no longer absolved of their wrongdoing. However, its cause is placed in their appetites and desires, which are separated from the soul's intellectual and rational part. The three-part division of the soul in *The Republic* provides a model that is both psychological as well as political. The city is 'an individual writ large', the individual its analogue.[37] Social harmony is a form of psychic harmony. Both balance opposed forces (courage and prudence) under the control of the rational part.[38]

The soul is identified with the rational part, the most godlike aspect of human beings. The desires and appetites are tied to the body. The aim of man is freedom from all that is bodily. The soul is immortal and transmigrates. Immortality and transmigration are incorporated from Pythagorean ideas and developed at length, incorporating earlier ideas of the soul as the life principle, the source of motion and possessed of knowledge.[39]

The rational soul is a reflection of a rational cosmos. Plato uses the idea of the soul as the cause of motion to argue (fallaciously) that whatever moves (without an external force applied to it) must be ensouled. Being the origin of motion, it must be without an origin (or cause) and, consequently, without an end.[40] What is true for the soul holds true for the entire cosmos. The stars, for instance, move so precisely that they must be ensouled and so possess intelligence.[41]

That the order of the heavens must be reflected in the world order sums up Plato's political philosophy. The just soul reflects the cosmic order; injustice is the loss of rational control when it is overcome by the lower elements, whether in the soul or in the city.[42] That is why the cosmos is called cosmos (order), for reason (intelligence) informs its working and reveals itself to human reason. That such knowledge, the result of a long apprenticeship and extensive learning, which alone can grasp unchanging reality, is limited to the few is axiomatic and contrasts with the varied opinions of the many. The rulers who have knowledge will constitute the smallest part of the city: 'It is by virtue of its smallest class … and the wisdom that resides there, in the part that takes the lead and rules, that a city established on principles of nature would be wise as a whole.'[43]

The radical distinction between 'truth and opinion' ushered in by Parmenides enabled Plato to separate the many citizens (the *demos*) from the few (philosophers), who alone are naturally constituted to rule. In the psycho-politics of *The Republic*, *doxa*, translated as opinion, belief or conjecture, is equated, as these often are, with a state of mind.[44] The people at large are limited to opinion in their relationship with the world. In the words of Heraclitus, they are asleep, though believe in their own opinions when awake (Kahn 1979).[45]

Demos and Doxa

The opinions of the many are contrasted regularly (not merely by Plato) with the knowledge of the wise man (*sophos*). In the metaphor of the ship of state, the crew or people, stirred up (by a demagogue), take over the tiller and (without knowledge of navigation) attempt to sail the ship. The distinction between knowledge and opinion provided an epistemological frame in which the term *doxa* could be equated with falsehood or weakened as 'mere opinion'. However, doxa and its cognates also generally meant 'to think good', often translated as 'it seems good' or 'I think it good'. Notably, proclamations issued by the Boule (the council) on behalf of the democratic assembly would standardly begin with the locution 'It seems good/or is resolved (*edozen*) by the demos' (Rhodes and Osborne 2007, 41).[46] Plato, perhaps, alludes to this in the *Gorgias* when he writes that tyrants can 'deprive people of their property and expel them from their cities as it seems good (*dokei*) to them'.[47] Combining a democratic formula with the rule of a tyrant, he likens democracy to a kind of tyranny.

Knowledge and Perception

Parmenides had established that only the mind can grasp reality (to be known, reality had to be unchanging). Since the objects of the world were changing, they could not be known. Sense perception was confused and provided only contradictory impressions. The contrast between the mind and the senses was thus established. Later, some thinkers insisted that perception was the only evidential source of knowledge. Others thought the mind was either distracted by the senses and so should neglect them or, at best, use them as the basis for discerning what was real (even if the real was removed from experience). Many pre-Socratic thinkers worked with analogies: using everyday occurrences as models for (hidden) cosmic processes. Anaximander and Anaximenes come to mind, as do Heraclitus and Anaxagoras.[48] The Atomists, by contrast, held that reality is completely unlike what we experience but is the cause of everything that we do experience, the senses only giving us 'obscure' (that is, unclear) knowledge.[49]

The contrast of the mind with the senses, explicit in Plato's work, was patched on the distinction between the body and the soul, the latter equated with the mind, the only faculty that can apprehend truth. The soul in its rational aspect aligned with reality, both animated and conscious (Dodds 1973, 70).[50] That such reason was mostly a limited and masculine prerogative was spelt out later by Aristotle.[51]

If reason alone gives the truth and perception is reduced to many-sided opinion, we should expect that those who clung to perception or, more generally, to the truth of experience, would have questioned the primacy of truth and the claims of those who held it. Denying the truth and embracing a relativist epistemology, such thinkers emphasised the importance of inductive rather than deductive arguments, leading to probabilistic rather than certain (stochastic rather than apodeictic) conclusions.[52] The importance of likelihood or probability is one such feature of sophistic thinking criticised by Plato. We find that these thinkers did use such reasoning (in the general sense of making arguments), while denying, by implication, the need for a unique epistemological faculty necessary to apprehend the truth since they denied the possibility of such truth or, in some cases, the possibility of its apprehension.[53]

Protagoras and Antiphon

Although we might regard them as the intellectual successors of earlier poets with whom they share a claim to wisdom, the self-image of the Sophists was in keeping with a democratic outlook. Unlike the poet's claim of divine inspiration, the Sophist's skill, the art of persuasive speech, was a human contrivance.[54] It is said that the founders of the art of rhetoric, Korax and Tisias, devised it for the Sicilians who, having expelled their tyrants and established a democracy, needed to settle legal questions regarding the property of returning exiles. Both its democratic and juridical roots are revealed in this claim.[55]

While a pure empiricist epistemology is not explicitly argued for in early Greek writings (the Hippocratic treatises, especially *On Ancient Medicine,* are exceptions), there are arguments *against* treating perception as a basis for knowledge, a thesis ascribed by Plato to both Heraclitus and Protagoras, the former providing the ontological basis for the latter's relativist epistemology (according to Plato). Protagoras, an older contemporary of Socrates, makes more than one appearance in Plato's work. His claim to teach virtue is tied in knots by Socrates in Plato's eponymous dialogue and his famous dictum 'Man is the measure of all things' reduced to self-contradiction in the *Theaetetus*.[56]

'Protagoras, when he said that of all things the measure is man, meant that as things appear to me, then, so they actually are for me, and as they appear to you, so they actually are for you.'[57]

The *homo mensura* tenet, as it is called, puts Protagoras at the centre of a debate about the nature of knowledge and the Self. The dictum, the first line of a discourse titled *Truth* (or *Refutations*, the main text of which is lost), denied the independent and objective nature of truth by asserting the counter-claim 'all opinions are true', or as Plato infers (on his behalf), that 'no opinions are false'.[58]

Plato wrote over fifty years after Protagoras' *Truth*. Plato's accounts of his predecessors do not aim at historical verisimilitude but draw out what he thinks are their implications. This is the crux of his interpretative engagement, even as he is the earliest available source of their views. His numerous mentions of Protagoras alert us to the importance the latter holds for him.[59]

In the *Theaetetus*, Plato argues that Protagoras's claim leads to an untenable and self-contradictory relativism. Plato accepts the claim that all perceptions, as sensations, are true (for those who experience them), in the truistic sense that what is experienced is experienced. But Plato is unwilling to jettison a conception of truth independent of the beliefs and opinions of individuals.[60] He uses Protagoras's claim against itself: if no judgements are false, then the judgement 'the Protagorean thesis is false' is true, proving that 'no judgements are false' is false. The refutation is more subtle than this summary, but that argument does not concern us here.[61]

Protagoras, however, does not claim that mere experience is a criterion of truth, for he denies any such criterion, appealing instead, as later Pragmatists did, to utility. Some experiences (even at the level of sensations) are better because they are more beneficial than others. Protagoras does not deny the possibility of wisdom, basing it on experience (and natural talent), not on status or birth or wealth, the hallmarks of aristocratic self-regard. What Protagoras taught was the 'political art': 'One who comes to me will learn to order his own house in the best manner, and he will be able to speak and act most powerfully in the affairs of the state.'[62]

Protagoras claimed to teach *euboulia* (good judgement) with respect to both private and public matters.[63] Euboulia, or good counsel, links Protagoras to deliberations in both the courts and the assembly, where the aim was to arrive at the best possible outcome in the interest of both the individual and the polis. Euboulia contrasts with the *eunomia*, a term that captured the elitist vision of civic order in which distinct classes or categories fulfilled their respective functions, leading to harmony and balance between essentially opposed forces (a model coordinate with both natural philosophy and medicine).[64]

That such a skill could be taught to anyone presupposed a doctrine of natural equality, implicit in Protagoras's retelling of the myth of Prometheus. There, he claimed that without equitable distribution of moral virtues, human society could never have come about. The idea of equal distribution of divine gifts among the class of humans had anti-aristocratic overtones. Tradition had it that Protagoras was an ordinary labourer until he became a student of Democritus.[65] If excellence can be taught, then 'all human beings are able to display a certain degree of political virtue, which is what allows them to talk in the Assembly (and Protagoras to maintain that virtue is teachable)' (Zilioli 2007, 100–102).

Making doxa as respectable as knowledge in effect meant that there could be no wise men who ought to rule or whose decisions should determine the city's political affairs: The aristocratic complaint was: 'When questions concern affairs of the state, everyone is free to give advice ... rich and poor, high and low ... because they are under the impression that this kind of knowledge cannot be taught and so is not the preserve of any special skill.'[66]

For Protagoras, political excellence is a social achievement. Society itself teaches its young respect for the laws and a sense of fair play (justice). No individual or class of men (the aristocrats, for instance) can lay claim to knowledge because there are no independent grounds (outside the social milieu) that can provide criteria for distinguishing correct from false opinions. There are only beliefs (doxa), which are shared by society at large. Yet political wisdom is teachable, as Protagoras claimed. The political art was identified with the art of debate (rhetoric), which was deemed essential for effective participation in the democratic institutions of the time. Such an art would admit, if not welcome, the general claim that there are always (at least?) two sides to every question and that one who learnt it would be able 'to make the weaker argument stronger'. These claims, also attributed to Protagoras, were part and parcel of democratic practice.[67]

While each person is entitled to speak what he thinks, this need not mean that each person's opinion is as good as the other's or that every opinion has to be acted upon. Sophistic relativism and subjectivism provided the theoretical underpinning for direct democracy of the Athenian kind. While there are no ultimate truths that experts are privy to, their expertise is, from the democratic point of view, the ability to persuade others, replacing one belief with another and influencing behaviour, which happens all the time in democratic polities. People change their opinions. While the *homo mensura* tenet privileges subjective beliefs, it does not rule out inter-subjective ones.[68] Whenever a number of people agree, a common measure emerges, which is essentially how the Athenian democracy, for better or worse, functioned.[69]

The denial of objective knowledge is consistent with Protagoras's remark on the existence of the gods: 'Concerning the gods I cannot know either that they exist or that they do not exist.'[70] For Plato, the rational Self is immortal (in Aristotle, akin to the godlike) and can aspire to the company of the gods. If he was indeed a student of Democritus (a known atheist), Protagoras's agnosticism, for which the sources repeat, his books were burnt and he was exiled from Athens, may have been mitigated atheism and politically pragmatic. It also aligns with his empiricism: having no personal experience of them, he is unable to say whether they exist or not, and their presence (or absence) is irrelevant because they cannot be known.

The reasons he advances for this are also interesting. The quoted fragment continues, 'for there is much to prevent one's knowing: the obscurity of the subject and the shortness of man's life'.[71] We may infer from the phrase the 'shortness of man's life' that he had no doctrine of post-mortem existence. In any case, it is unlikely that Protagoras would have held the belief, coupled with atheism, that the soul survives death as this would be an unexampled combination in Greek thought.

Diogenes cites Plato when he says that for Protagoras, the soul (psyche) was nothing but sensation and that 'all things are true'.[72] Limiting the soul to sensation or sense experience is to limit it temporally, for sense perception, as we have seen, was consistently linked with the body (rather than the mind).

To say that the soul is sensation is to deny any separate status to reason over and above the functioning of the mind and the senses. The denial of truth is the denial of privileged access, which was, as we have seen, the hallmark of the aristocratic claim to rule. The democratic tendencies of Protagoras's ideas about the validity of opinions is in line with Athenian political practices where each person could vote and speak in the assembly. Free speech was Athen's hallmark, celebrated by its tragic poets and historians.[73]

If the soul is not immortal, instead of innate antenatal knowledge (the Platonic doctrine of anamnesis or recollection), the only route to knowledge is perception. While the sophists as a whole showed little interest in physical and physiological phenomena, they also showed little interest in theorising the nature of perception and its relationship to the mind. Yet we can see that perception was the keystone of their theory of knowledge and the unifying nature of the mind, not as independent of the body, but an integral part of what being human is. Their use of speech (another sense of logos) as a way of influencing action via emotions, again much castigated by Plato, shows their connection to the politics of the day. Gorgias is an example of one who extolls the power of persuasion, a key feature of democratic politics, where every man was equal to every other, a sentiment also expressed by the Sophist Antiphon.

> We (respect) and revere those who are of good parentage, but those who are not of good family we neither (respect) nor revere. In this behavior we have become like barbarians, one to another, when in fact by nature we all have the same nature in all particulars, barbarians and Greeks... For we all breathe out into the air by the mouth and the nose, and we all eat with our hands.[74]

Antiphon, in his fragments on knowledge, while acknowledging the role of the mind as the ruler of the body (thus admitting an aristocratic metaphor) holds that thought (gnome) rules the body but needs a starting point. The senses are the starting point. We all believe what we see with our eyes more than abstractions. However, when we speak, there is no permanent reality behind our words, nothing comparable to the results of seeing and knowing.[75]

Abstract knowledge privileges the (thinking) mind over the senses: the senses are downgraded in both Parmenides and Plato. The thinking aspect of the psyche is conceived as separate and separable from the more bodily aspects (desires and appetites), which are dependent upon the body for both expression and satisfaction. In the ordered soul, whether conceived as bipartite or tripartite, the rational should control the irrational. There will be degrees of such control. The purely rational soul is akin to the gods. Plato uses both ideas of the soul that Aristotle distinguishes, as animator and cause of motion and as the seat of consciousness. In *The Republic*, Plato combines the idea of the soul as that which gives life with the expression of its rational nature: not merely to live but to live well, that is, justly, where justice is the rational order of the cosmos reflected in the psychic order of the soul.

In conclusion, the Platonic conception of reason and rationality as the defining feature of man, whatever else it does, principally forms the basis of his aristocratic politics. Rationality was more than the ability to make or insist on making arguments. While thought and thinking in general were obviously commendable human capacities, the idea of a rational faculty that alone could access truth was as much a construct as the divine lineage claimed by noble families. Married to a notion of a permanent Self, it provided a conceptual weapon against democratic ideals of equality. We can see shades of shared ideas of deficiencies inherent in democratic regimes in metaphors for knowledgeable rulers as opposed to ignorant masses.

References

Adkins, A.W.H. 1960. *Merit and Responsibility*. Oxford: Clarendon Press.

Aristotle. 1985. *Nichomachean Ethics*. Translated by T.H. Irwin.

———. 2017. *De anima,* translated by C.D.C. Reeve. Indianapolis: Hackett.

———. 1991. *Complete Works*, edited by J. Barnes. 2 vols. Princeton: Princeton University Press.

Boylan, M. 2015. *The Origins of Ancient Greek Science Blood—A Philosophical Study.* London.

Burkert, W. 1985. *Greek Religion*. Blackwell.

Cobb-Steven, V. 1985. 'The Unsettled World of Theognis.' In *Theognis of Megara Poetry and the Polis*, edited by T.J. Figueira and G. Nagy. Baltimore.

Claus, B. 1977. *Towards the Soul.* New Haven.

Detienne, M., and J.P. Vernant. 1991. *Cunning Intelligence in Greek Culture and Society*. Chicago.

Diels, H., and W. Kranz. 1951–1952. *Die Fragmente der Vorsokratiker*, revised by W. Kranz. 6th ed. Berlin.

Diogenes Laertius. *Lives of the Philosophers*. 2 vols. Translated by R.D. Hicks. Cambridge: Harvard University Press.

Dodds, E.R. 1959. *Plato's Gorgias*. Oxford.

———. 1974. *The Ancient Concept of Progress*. Oxford.

Edmonds, J.M., trans. 1986. *Greek Elegy and Iambus*. Vol. 1. Cambridge: Harvard University Press.

Farrar, Cynthia. 1988. *The Origins of Democratic Thinking*. Cambridge.

Fitzgerald, Robert, trans. 1974. *Homer's Iliad*. New York.

Irwin, T. 1982. *Plato's Gorgias*. Oxford.

Kahn, Charles. 1979. *The Art and Thought of Heraclitus*. Cambridge.

Lake, G.P. 2000. *Plato's Homeric Dialogue* PhD disscussion (unpublished), Boston University.

Lattimore, R. 1965. *The Odyssey of Homer*. New York.

Maidment, K.J., trans. 1941. *Minor Attic Orators*. Vol. 1 (Antiphon). Cambridge: Harvard University Press.

Mansfeld, Jaap. 1981. 'Protagoras on Epistemological Obstacles and Persons.' In *The Sophists and Their Legacy*, edited by G.B. Kerferd. Weisbaden.

Moss, J. 2008. 'Appearances and Calculations: Plato's Division of the Soul.' *Oxford Studies in Ancient Philosophy* 34: 35–68.

North, Helen. 1966. *Sophrosune*. New York.

Plato. 1937. *The Republic*. 2 vols. Translated by Paul Shorey. Cambridge: Harvard University Press.

———. 1997. *Complete Works*, edited by J.M. Cooper and D.S. Hutchinson. Indianapolis: Hackett.

Rademaker, Adriaan. 2007. *Sophrosyne and the Rhetoric of Self Restraint*. Leiden.

Rhodes, P.J., and Robin Osborne, eds. 2007. *Greek Historical Inscriptions 404-323BC*. Oxford.

Van Hook, Larue, trans. 1945. *Isocrates*. 3 vols. Cambridge: Harvard University Press.

Vlastos, G., ed. 1956. *Plato's Protagoras*. New York.

———. 1971. *Plato, 1: Metaphysics and Epistemology*. NY: Doubleday Anchor.

———. 1981. *Platonic Studies*, 2nd ed. Princeton: Princeton University Press.

West, M.L. 1978. *Hesiod: Theogony. Edited with Prolegomena and Commentary*. Oxford.

Williams, B. 1981. 'Philosophy.' In *The Legacy of Greece*, edited by M.I. Finley. Oxford.

Woodruff, P. 2013. 'Eubolia as the Skill Protagoras Taught.' In *Protagoras of Abdera: The Man, His Measure*, edited by Johannes M.van Ophuijsen, Marlein van Raalte and Peter Stork, 179–193. Brill.

Zilioli, U. 2007. *Protagoras and the Challenge of Relativism*. Ashgate.

Notes

1 Aristotle, *Nicomachean Ethics* (henceforth EN) 1.13.

2 Aristotle, *EN* 1103a30, where he distinguishes the rational and irrational parts of the soul. Man is by nature a political animal (*Politics* 1253a).

3 Aristotle, *On the Soul* 403b 27–28.

4 Thales, Diels and Kranz (henceforth DK; 1951–1952), A2, whose source is Aristotle *On the Soul* (*De anima*) 405a19; Anaximenes, DK B2. The contrast between the ensouled and the unmoving corpse is vividly brought out in the oxymoron 'living corpse' by Sophocles (*Antigone* 1167).

5 *Iliad* 22.304–5, 2.322–28.

6 *Odyssey* 218–222, cited by Lake (2000, 262).

7 *Republic* 386d, quoting *Iliad* 23.103 and *Odyssey* 10.495. In the latter, only Tireisias has a mind (*nous*), while the rest flit about like shades.

8 Heraclitus (DK85) says, paradoxically, it is 'hard to fight with one's thumos', that is, 'it is hard to fight with that with which one fights' (Kahn 1979, 76–77).

9 A sense we find even in Plato (*Symposium* 208c–d): 'a deathless memory for valour (*arête*)' Alcestis, Achilles … asked … for themselves.

10 'This word is the translator's despair. Its original meaning is something like "having a healthy mind"'; it can mean any of the following: discretion, prudence, reasonableness, decency, good sense, moderation, temperance, self-control' (Vlastos 1956, viiin7).
11 I have relied here on North (1966) and Rademaker (2007).
12 As in Theognis (39–52) in Edmonds (1986); Adkins (1960, 246ff).
13 Aristotle, *EN* 1140b4.
14 See Aristotle (*Politics* 1335a) where it clearly means chaste as opposed to licentious behaviour.
15 'Among the best people there is minimum wantonness and injustice but a maximum of scrupulous care for what is good, whereas among the common people (*demos*), there is a maximum of ignorance, disorder, and wickedness' (*Ps-Xenophon* 1.5)
16 Theognis 39–52.
17 Theognis (475–96): drunkards lack sophrosune; 1138: sophrosune deified as divinities who have left the earth in these unrighteous times. The moderation of the citizen body despite debased leaders (v.41)
18 *Republic* 386–388.
19 *Gorgias* 491d; *Phaedo* 68c; *Philebus* 45d–e; *Laws* 710a.
20 *Stateman* 275b, 296e.
21 *Iliad* 204 ff.
22 *Republic* 343b.
23 Plato, *Politicus* 297e.
24 Heraclitus, enigmatic B 67.
25 DK B 45; Kahn (1979, 45).
26 Heraclitus ridicules human folly. Men are not awake (frs. 1; 73; 89) or like drunks (fr. 117) or children (frs. 70; 79; 121) or beasts (frs. 4; 9; 13; 29; 37; 83; 97).
27 Parmenides, DK B7.
28

> The clearest knowledge will surely be attained by one who approaches the true realities as far as possible by thought alone, not permitting sight or any other sense to intrude upon his thinking … one who gets rid, as far as possible of eyes and ears and, broadly speaking of the body altogether, knowing that when the body is the soul's partner it confuses the soul and prevents it from coming to possess truth and intelligence. (*Phaedo* 67e)

29 Plato, *Apology* 30a.
30 *Apology* 30a-b.
31 In a sense, this is also Plato's answer to the question about the best kind of life: the philosophic life, because it is a virtuous or moral life.
32 *Apology* 30b.
33 The connection between moral virtues and the soul is made explicit by Aristotle: 'Virtue is being in good condition as regards the soul' (*Politics* I. V. 8).

34 The relation of the soul with thought seems to have been associated with Socrates even by Aristophanes (*Clouds* 94, 414). See Claus (1977, 157). The school or institution that Socrates heads in the comedy is called a *phrontesterion* or 'a thinking place'. One translation names it the 'reflectory'.

35 *Iliad* 9. In the *Hippias Minor* (364c). Socrates sophistically inverts these claims.

36 Thus, in Herodotus, Megabyzus praises oligarchy and attacks the masses: 'Nothing is less intelligent and more arrogant than the "useless" mob' (Hdt. 3.81). In Attic tragedy, the *demos* is often feminised and depicted as disorderly and emotional. A possible example of this is the reaction of the Theban elders (citizens) to the signal that announces the fall of Troy in Aeschylus' *Agamemnon* (475–487).

37 *Republic* 369a.

38

> It belongs to the rational part (*logistikos*) to rule (*archein*) … being wise and exercising forethought on behalf of the whole soul … ruling principle and its two subjects [spirit and appetite], are at one in the belief that reason (*to logistikon*) ought to rule, and do not raise faction (*stasis*) against it. (*Republic* 441e, 442d)

39 Aristotle, *On the Soul* 407b.The proof for the immortality of the soul in the *Pheado* identifies it with the principle of life, essentially opposed to death. In the *Phaedrus*, the proof is based on eternal motion. In the *Meno*, the antenatal existence of the soul is proved on the basis of an untutored slave's ability to grasp truths independent of experience.

40 Similarly, the final proof in the *Phaedo* attempts to show that the soul is not just long-lived, which would be compatible with an attenuated doctrine of transmigration, but indestructible.

41 *Laws* 967a–e.

42 However, injustice is defined as a rebellion by the two lower parts against the rule of rationality (444b). The lower part related to the higher as a slave to its master: when the elements of the soul are 'displaced and confused', that constitutes injustice (*Republic* 444b).

43 *Republic* 428e.

44 The distinction between knowledge and opinion is first drawn by Plato in the *Gorgias* (454b), though the word there is *pistis* (conviction), which becomes a sub-category of *doxa* in *The Republic*. From the *Meno* onwards, *doxa* becomes the word he uses for opinion. See Dodds (1959, 206) on *Gorgias* 454b8.

45 DKB1,17.

46 The enactment formula of the Athenian assembly.

47 Gorgias 466d–e. Noted by Irwin (1982) ad loc.

48 'Thales the Milesian said it [the earth] remains floating like a log' (Thales DK A14). 'The stars do not move under the earth … but around it, just as a cap is moved around the head' (Anaximenes DKB3). The visible is a clue to the invisible (Anaxagoras DKB21a). Nature loves to hide (Heraclitus DKB123).

49 Democritus DKB11.

50 While limiting the emphasis on reason and rationality to Socrates, Dodds adds that reason also becomes the means to personal redemption. This is only to restate the strong version of the Socratic identification of virtue with knowledge, making knowledge both necessary and sufficient for virtue. The political correlate of this is that knowledge is both necessary and sufficient for ruling the city.

51 'The male is by nature (*phusis*) superior and the female inferior; the male is the ruler and the female is the subject. . . . The slave has not got deliberative reason at all and the female has got it, but without full authority' (*Politics* 1254b 13, 1260a 13).

52 Aristotle (*Rhetoric* 1402a) refers to the *techne* of Korax and the use of probabilistic arguments as used by Protagoras.

53 Gorgias DK B3 '*On The Non-Existent*'.

54 A summary of such ideas is to be found in Sophocles's 'Ode to man' (*Antigone* 322ff) where the knowledge and skill of man is emblematic of his indomitable nature and whose language separates him from the beasts he rules. This is not to claim that the ode is an absolute endorsement of human achievement within the context of the play.

55 Aristotle claims that rhetoric was invented by Korax and Tisias. He refers to a handbook of Korax of rhetorical principles (Aristotle, *Rhetoric*, II. 24. 11), and to his teacher Tisias (*Soph. Elench.* 183 b30).

56 Protagoras (480–420 BCE), belonged to the older generation of 5th-century thinkers, a contemporary of Herodotus, Aeschylus and Sophocles. He was professionally active in Athens in the 460s and 450s. In 443, he was asked (by the Athenians) to write a constitution for their colony at Thurii. We have no details of this constitution, but the fact that he was asked to, although non-Athenian, indicates his political and democratic leanings. His friendship with Pericles is subject of a well-known anecdote.

57 Plato, *Cratylus* 385e.

58 Plato, *Theaetetus* 166d-167d.

59 The dialogue *Protagoras* is named after him. He is cited in the *Meno*, *Hippias Major, Cratylus, Euthydemus, Phaedrus* and *Sophist*; His views are discussed in detail in the *Theaetetus*.

60 He ignores the real possibility that man, in Protagoras's dictum, may be understood generically.

61 Plato ascribes to Protagoras what might be called a naive relativism, demanding an ontology of extreme flux, so undermining his pragmatic defence. However, Protagoras is not committed to any particular ontology. The claim that human knowledge is partial is compatible with the claim that reality is both fixed and knowable (even if not known). Thinkers as distinct as Parmenides, Empedocles and the Atomists held some version of this thesis. What Protagoras rejected was privileged insight.

62 A claim put into his mouth in the dialogue named after him (*Protagoras* 319a).

63 On *Euboulia* or good judgement, see Woodruff (2013, 179–193).

64 Plato often assumes that correct judgement without knowledge is like a lucky guess or a gift of the gods. Techne is contrasted often with ignorance or having a knack (contrasting cooks with doctors in the *Gorgias*. 542 A 2–B 4). For Aristotle's distinction between euboulia and lucky guessing (*eustochia*), see *EN* 1142 b 2–4: 'Guessing is too fast to involve deliberation, and euboulia is a virtue of deliberation' (Woodruff 2013 pp. 187 nt. 10).
65 Diogenes Laertius, *Lives of the Eminent Philosophers* 9.8.53; 10.1.8.
66 Plato Protagoras 319d. Protagoras' response (320–328d) may be seen as the earliest defence of democracy.
67 DL 9.51 80DK A20 and Aristotle, *Rhetoric* 1402a23.
68 See Mansfeld (1981, 47).
69 On Protagoras as a thinker whose theories are fully organic to the Athenian democracy, see Farrar (1988, 77–98); see also Adkins (1973).
70 Protagoras B4.
71 80DK B4.
72 D.L. IX.51.
73 For example, Aeschylus, *Persians* 591–594, *Suppliants* 948, Euripides *Hippolytus* 421–423, *Suppliants* 438–441. At *Gorgias* 461e, Socrates makes an ironic reference to the claim that 'there is more freedom (in Athens) than anywhere else in Greece'.
74 Antiphon D.K B44.
75 Antiphon, DKB 70, 82;B 68; B 67.

2

AESTHETIC REPOSE (VIŚRĀNTI), THE SELF AND THE EMERGING FIGURE OF THE RASIKA IN EARLY MEDIEVAL INDIA

Parul Dave-Mukherji

The aesthetics of repose in modern art brings to mind paintings of languorous odalisques and reclining women by artists like Henri Matisse. In Indian aesthetics, there is a term for figures that strike such postures: the *ālasa kanyā*[1] or the indolent girls who often adorn the walls of medieval temples. Is the aesthetics of repose only about the poses and postures of the languid figures depicted in visual arts or does it concern the viewer, the spectator, the aesthete or the *rasika*? In other words, is the aesthetics of repose a matter of concern for the making of art or is it chiefly about the reception of art? Classical Sanskrit aesthetics waxes eloquent on the pleasure experienced by the connoisseur or the rasika.[2] Alas, there is not much on ālasa kanyā doubling up as a rasika or a woman connoisseur.[3] Aesthetic pleasure emerges as one of the key sites of the formation of selfhood in early medieval India.[4] This figure of the aesthete or rasika comes into prominence between the 9th and 10th century CE in Kashmir and, in the process, raises many questions about the right to experience aesthetic pleasure. Such an inquiry inadvertently lays open many vectors of social and political inequalities.

The figure of the rasika, a quintessentially male figure, has received much scholarly attention in recent times. He is largely assumed to be the refined figure of a *sahṛdaya* (literally, 'having the same heart') and part of the cultured elite who have the leisure and the cultural competence to experience aesthetic pleasure. Unlike the ālasa kanyās, who are too busy arching their bodies in various convoluted poses on temple doorways, the rasika or refined connoisseur has the wherewithal to enjoy an aesthetic experience or *rasa*. The rasika becomes a prime site to raise questions about a particular formation of the Self[5] in early medieval India. Given that the provenance of many aesthetic theories is Kashmir, we can assume a locale for the rise of this figure of the aesthete or rasika during the 9th and 10th century CE.

My main source for the figure of the rasika and its emergence in classical Sanskrit aesthetics is *Abhinavabhāratī*, Abhinavagupta's 10th-century commentary on Bharata's *Nāṭyaśāstra* (circa 1st century BCE). Scholarship on Sanskrit aesthetics underlines the salience of this commentary not only in the rise of the rasika but also in the manner in which Abhinavagupta supplies us with critical historiography of aesthetic theories that were prevalent three centuries before his time.[6]

Our focus will be on the 'aesthetic Self' that emerges from the writings of Abhinavagupta around the figure of the rasika and how he lays down some conditions for it to emerge: A rasika must have the ability to experience self-reflexivity or *vimarśa* and repose or *viśrānti*. When rasa involves a process of generalisation or commonisation of emotions or *sādhāraṇīkaraṇa*, the rasika overcomes the restricted Self of the here and now and arrives at an expanded Self.

The chapter will explore the contradictions in Abhinavagupta's aesthetic theory, which, on the one hand, undervalues the role of the actor [practitioner] to give greater visibility to the rasika and, at the same time, shows deep engagement with broadening the question of accessibility of drama to the wider public. Caught up in these contradictions is Abhinavagupta's rejection of *anukaraṇavāda* or the theory of [performative] mimesis[7] through which he makes his take on aesthetic theory clear.

In the process, I will be raising and addressing some of these questions: (i) Is this Self of the rasika/sahṛdaya thought of as pure consciousness, or does it bear any relationship with the performative body [of the actor]? (ii) How does Abhinavagupta reflect on Bharata's comparison of aesthetic pleasure with the delight of tasting food? (iii) Do Abhinavagupta's efforts to prioritise perception (*pratyakṣa*) over inference (*anumāna*) in the audience's reception of drama reflect his desire to imagine a larger public? (iv) How do the notions of repose (viśrānti) and self-reflexivity (vimarśa) participate in the making of an 'aesthetic Self'? (v) Finally, to what extent is the figure of a rasika gendered?

The Shift from the Actor (Naṭa) to the Aesthete (Rasika)

In the existing historiography of Indian aesthetics, Abhinavagupta has received a centrality, particularly for evolving a new aesthetic theory focusing on drama (*nāṭya*) around the 10th century CE. What is striking about his new take is how the figure of the rasika zooms into prominence. However, it was his predecessor Ānandavardhana, the author of *Dhvanyāloka* (c. 875), who inaugurated the theory of suggested meaning or *dhvani* in poetry. The figure of the sahṛdaya emerges as the recipient of poetry that relied heavily on suggestion (McCrea 2008, 117). In *Abhinavabhāratī* with its focus on *nāṭya*, Abhinavagupta intensified the emphasis on the audience, the spectator or the rasika. More importantly, this shift occurs at some cost to the figure of the actor (*naṭa*), whose salience as a performative agent gets suppressed by Abhinavagupta's theory to a large extent. This momentous shift of attention away from performance to reception is referred to by the experts of aesthetic theory as a 'paradigm transfer' (26). In poetics, too, the focus of the theorists moves from poetic composition to cognitive processes.[8] Can we connect the rise of the rasika in terms of what Lawrence McCrea calls the 'existence of a select group capable of appreciating it [poetry] fully' (115)?

However, the rasika has not always been the central figure in Indian aesthetics. Before Abhinavagupta, the theory of dramaturgy as proposed by Bharata laid much stress on the figure of the actor in the production of rasa. Right from the time of the *Nāṭyaśāstra*, Bharata made performance the centre of his theory of dramaturgy and envisioned his text as guiding the actors (Pollock 2016, 49).

Subsequently, other aestheticians commenting on the *Nāṭyaśāstra*, such as Bhaṭṭa Lollaṭa and Srī Śaṅkuka who preceded Abhinavagupta, continued to define the aesthetic experience that cohered around the actor. For Lollaṭa, rasa is first present in the character of the drama but gets projected by the spectators on the actor (naṭa) because of skilful acting. The actor is the main focal point. Śaṅkuka made a different pitch by asserting that emotions, as acted out by the actors, cannot be perceived directly by the audience but only inferred based on the virtuoso of acting. In that sense, even though the audience makes an oblique entry in Śaṅkuka's theory as those who infer emotions while watching drama, the actor remained the main agent whose skill is lauded in being able to convey emotions by *abhinaya* or acting.

Discrediting Śaṅkuka's imitation theory, Abhinavagupta, who draws his critique from the arguments of his teacher, Bhaṭṭa Tauta, claims that from the point of view of the audience, imitation is not visible.

'It, however, is falsified by the simple fact that the viewer actually perceives no distinction whatever between the character and the actor. In any case, the doctrine of imitation itself has already been refuted' (Pollock 2016, 211).

His systematic belittling of the actor runs parallel to his rejection of *anukaraṇa vāda*, which tended to place the actor on the centre stage, so to speak (Dave-Mukherji 2016, 71–92). His disparagement of the actor is also most visible in the way he reduces the role of the actor to being a mere *pātra* or a vessel and subordinates an actor to the poet or playwright whose text the actor has to follow. Through this metaphor of a *pātra* or vessel, Abhinavagupta empties the actor of any agency or ability to reflect.[9] It is almost as if such a 'subjectivisation' of the rasika happens at the cost of the practitioner.[10]

Evidently, in *Abhinavabhāratī*, the relationship between aesthetic experience and the performative bodies of the actors becomes extremely fraught. Does this privileging of the rasika speak of Abhinavagupta's elitism? Does he envisage a small constituency of connoisseurs who have specialist skills to appreciate and discern drama? The privileging of the connoisseurs might seem to be the case given his attention to artistic reception, which tends to displace attention from the performing bodies of the actors to the rasika. However, when we closely follow his question on the epistemology of drama—what are the main means of sense perception to experience drama?—we discern his pro-public stance. What is of particular concern to us is who populates the 'public sphere' for Abhinavagupta: for him, the public consists more of the rasikas, the critics and even the audience, rather than the practitioners of drama such as the actor.[11]

It is a matter of speculation whether this dramatic transition may be linked to some social or political crisis witnessed around the end of the first millennium in Kashmir. Crisis and aesthetics have rarely been studied in the historiography of premodern aesthetics in India. Sheldon Pollock has gone the furthest in this direction in his attempt to historicise concepts in Indian aesthetics and bring out the social (2006, 385). The one historic event that happened in Kashmir during Abhinavagupta's lifetime was foreign invasion (Wallis 2006, 231). Can this be read as a crisis that posed a challenge to the way the idea of selfhood had to be recalibrated? Were the existing patriarchal social structures in Kashmir shaken up by these turns of events? These are large questions that may be posed more as a heuristic rather than those yielding easy answers.

Abhinavaguptagupta's Take on Rasika and Food

In Indian aesthetics, comparing aesthetic delight to the pleasure of tasting a delicious cuisine is as old as Bharata, the author of the *Nāṭyaśāstra*. In modern scholarship on rasa aesthetics, much ink has been spilt on speculating about the centrality of the gustatory in Indian aesthetics (Schechner 1977, 333–334). Abhinavagupta's commentary on the *Nāṭyaśāstra* too reflects considerably on this culinary metaphor.

Rasa, explains Abhinavagupta, is a tasting of emotions, and its comparison with the act of eating brings out two salient features of aesthetic experience: temporality of drama and close coordination of the mind and the body. However, the food metaphor only goes this far. The state of tasting or *āsvādayatva*, used to describe an aesthetic experience, is now directed at the eyes than the tongue. For Abhinavagupta, aesthetic delight is primarily defined as a perceptual experience that involves seeing and hearing. Through the primacy of these two sense perceptions, *nāṭya* (drama) scores over kāvya (poem, play, poetics). Nāṭya is a state that the best kāvya can aspire for, as the best poems evoke images and turn the text into a visual experience. [12]

Let us explore the food metaphor more closely. The aesthetic pleasure of a rasika is time-bound for Abhinavagupta. He categorically states that rasa is strictly not an object but an event (*Nāṭyaśāstra* 2001, 90).[13] This proposition of the body in relation to food is very different compared to the German philosopher Immanuel Kant's dismissal of enjoyment gained from food (Kant 1931, 47).[14] If Kant's reference to food centres around the figure of a glutton who only satisfies his body while eating, Abhinavagupta and Bharata hold up a figure of a gourmet, a refined connoisseur of food for whom tasting involves a close conjunction of mind and the body (Pollock 2016, 42, 51).

Since drama unfolds in time as does the act of eating, temporality is a key vector of the theory of dramaturgy. This example of the act and the process of tasting (*āsvādana*) also implies that aesthetic pleasure or rasa experienced by the rasika is time-bound and does not outlive the duration of the drama. The stress on time ties in with the stress on visual epistemology: the rasa experience is understood as a perceptual (*dṛśya*) and auditory (*śrāvya*) experience but, as Abhinavagupta keeps reminding us, lasts only as long as the play lasts.

Abhinavagupta's Allegory of the Fiery Circle (Alāṭa Cakra) and His Imagination of the Public

One of the aims of Abhinavagupta's commentary on the *Nāṭyaśāstra* was to take a position on the existing debates on the nature of rasa. He had serious disagreements with his predecessors and their acceptance of anukaraṇa vāda. Abhinavagupta, as we noted, fiercely critiqued Śaṅkuka's theory on many grounds. The objection most relevant to our current discussion is that aesthetic experience can only be understood as immediate visual perception (*pratyakṣa*). What defines pleasure while watching a drama is its being a visual experience. Perception is the primary basis of aesthetic experience. Hence, he had a problem with Śaṅkuka's turn to inference, which, being a mediated experience involving perception and memory, lacked the directness of visual perception. Abhinavagupta disapproved of his opponent's turn to syllogism while explaining how we perceive emotions acted out on stage: just as there is no smoke without fire, there are no emotions without frowns, facial expressions and gestures. We infer emotions of love, joy and horror expressed by the actors through visible signs in form of gestures and facial expressions in the same manner in which we infer invisible fire from visible smoke.

To counter Śaṅkuka's use of the fire-smoke syllogism, Abhinavagupta turned to the allegory of a fiery circle or *alāṭa cakra*. It is a[n illusion of a] circle of fire produced by a torch in quick rotation: an event fully grounded in the immediate present and as happening right before one's own eyes (pratyakṣa). In his stress on the aesthetic experience of drama based on immediate knowledge, we discern his concern for the public: drama must be accessible to all. He makes his point by this visual example of the fiery circle (alāṭa cakra), which can not only easily be related to the everyday experience but is itself based on a performative act—the semblance of a fiery circle is created when a person holding it rotates it in a quick circular motion. This example was perfect to silence the supporters of the inference theory previously discussed. Alāṭa cakra is a *common* example drawn from everyday life based on an act that occurs before one's eyes (*sākṣātkāra*), while it is still being viewed. It forms part of a public (*laukika*) experience and is, hence, accessible to all, fulfilling the condition of commonality so central to Abhinavagupta's aesthetic theory.[15]

The same 'inclusive' logic underlies Abhinavagupta's distinction of two types of audience—the kāvya rasika/sahṛdaya (those who are well equipped to understand literature/poems/poetics) and the nāṭya spectator (those who enjoy watching drama), The former's heart is like 'a spotless mirror' and whose mind is 'no longer subjected to the anger, confusion, craving, and so on, typical of this phenomenal world' (Pollock 2016, 34). Such a rasika need not even see drama as he can experience rasa by the act of reading alone. Nāṭya as a genre envisaged by Bharata, Abhinavagupta reminds us, is meant for the second type of rasika who enjoys watching a drama. It is for such a viewer that Bharata, claims Abhinavagupta, had made provision for music and dances as strategies that will 'loosen the knot of the viewer's heart, hardened as it is by the anger, grief, and so on he bears inside' (209). In this sense, nāṭya can appeal to both the types of rasikas whereas kāvya is enjoyed only by the first type of rasika.

Hence, by upholding visual perception as the main epistemological means, Abhinavagupta gives higher stature to drama and subordinates it to kāvya.[16] Visual perception or the domain of the eyes is much more 'common' than that of kāvya; the latter resorts to *śabda* (words), which are a mediated form of knowledge much like the inference or *anumāna* that he had rejected. In this manner, Abhinavagupta foregrounds the specificity of drama and its difference from poetry, and indirectly underlines the importance of drama.

While there is no denying that the figure of the rasika proposed by Abhinavagupta assumes a male Self, his insistence on drama as epistemologically available to everyone runs counter to the usual assumption about the elitist status of a rasika. A better way to state this is that there is a deep ambivalence in Abhinavagupta's writings on the rasika. On the one hand, if he downplays the role of the actor to privilege the rasika, there is also a move to 'widen' reception by insisting on making performance epistemologically available to the general public. For this reason, Abhinavagupta rejected anumāna as mediated knowledge and its reliance on logic and poetics or *kāvyaśāstra* would tend to reduce the constituency of the rasikas to a small elite club.[17]

I will argue that while this broadening of the domain of aesthetic experience via pratyakṣa may be seen as inclusive, Abhinavagupta insists on sidelining the performers and their skill and artistic labour. The privileging of the viewer comes at a cost to a performer who is reduced by Abhinavagupta to be a vessel or a pātra that is incapable of any aesthetic delectation on his own and is made subordinate to the poet and playwright.[18]

That Abhinavagupta's 'public sphere' consists more of the rasikas than the actors shows his concern for an 'emotive community'. This community is carved out by laying stress on different kinds of commonality that act as threads binding different members of the public.[19]

While the status of the performer or the actor considerably declines in the aesthetic theory of Abhinavagupta, the rasika or the viewer/spectator of drama grows in stature. In the previous section, it was apparent that the rasika is not just an elitist reader of literature. Abhinavagupta includes him with the general audience who relish watching drama. With this view of a more inclusive viewership of drama, Abhinavagupta puts much stress on 'that which exists before our eyes' or pratyakṣa, and even grants higher status to drama over literature/poetics.[20] After all, the latter being text-based departs from perception as a means of knowledge and leans on indirect perception or *parokṣa*. Words/poems/text have to be heard or read before its meaning can be visualised.

Viśrānti and Vimarśa and Rasa as Self-tasting

For Abhinavagupta, if aesthetic experience in drama has to have this horizontal dimension of including the wider public, it also entails a vertical movement for reaching a higher Self. For the latter, he draws much of his inspiration from his teacher, Bhaṭṭa Nāyaka (c. 900), the author of the lost *Hṛdayadarpaṇa* (Mirror of the heart). This text was also known by another title connected with our concerns, *Sahṛdayadarpaṇa* (Mirror for the lover of literature). Bhaṭṭa Nāyaka was the first to discursively shift the focus from the actor to the rasika and thus bring about what Sheldon Pollock refers to as 'an aesthetic revolution' (2016, 144). According to Bhaṭṭa Nāyaka, the site of the production of rasa is neither the character nor the actor of drama but the mind of the viewer, reader or listener.

Bhaṭṭa Nāyaka, being a *Mimamsaka*,[21] drew his innovative ideas from the practice and interpretation of Vedic rituals: just as we apply to ourselves the ritual commands meant for others in a remote past and feel impelled to act and perform the ritual, in the same way, we appropriate the emotions felt by the characters in a given text and re-experience them as if they belong to us.[22] Through the connection he draws between rituals and literature, Bhaṭṭa Nāyaka offers a new argument about commonisation or sādhāraṇīkaraṇa, a concern that deeply moved Abhinavagupta. As we saw, commonisation was central to Abhinavagupta's agenda to horizontally expand the constituency of the public for drama, but following a cue from Bhaṭṭa Nāyaka, aesthetic relish could also be experienced along a vertical, transcendental axis. His teacher's *Hṛdayadarpaṇa* appears to have instructed Abhinavagupta about the role of the twin concepts of vimarśa and viśrānti in attaining the ultimate in aesthetic relish.

Vimarśa and Viśrānti

Bhaṭṭa Nāyaka, with his focus on the reception of aesthetic experience, underlines the power of literature to make the audience experience (*bhāvakatva*) and enjoy (*bhojakatva*) aesthetic experiences (rasa). The former is the power that makes the individual characters, settings and incidents in literary texts universal. Bhojakatva refers to the process of drawing enjoyment out of experiencing the universalised elements in drama or poetry. Both of these processes act as conditions for viśrānti and vimarśa. They prepare the rasika for the ultimate experience of rasa, which is none other than the tasting of the Self.

What also captures Abhinavagupta's imagination is the metaphor of the mirror as implicit in the *Hṛdayadarpaṇa*, which stresses the rasika's ability to reflect and experience aesthetic pleasure.[23] This ability to reflect is to be distinguished from the mindless and mechanical reflection of inert objects like crystals. Only the sahṛdaya or the rasika has the necessary subjectivity or vimarśa that equips him to enter commonisation (sādhāraṇīkaraṇa), a process of universalisation by which the emotions of the character in a text and/or as acted by the actor on the stage are experienced by the rasika as his own. Vimarśa is proposed as an ideal condition for the aesthetic experience; it leads to the tasting of the Self, paving the way for viśrānti.[24] When there is complete stillness and rest, full self-awareness is possible.

'In our view, what is being savored is simply one's own awareness, which is uniformly blissful' (Pollock 2016, 190).

Rasa as Higher than Religious Experience

Despite all the stress placed on self-awareness and self-reflectivity, Bhaṭṭa Nāyaka categorically asserts that an aesthetic experience is on a higher level than a religious experience. As the aesthetic experience is emotion-based, it can fall outside the ambit of even a yogi's experience whose understanding of the world is meant to be unmoved (*tatastha*) by emotions. 'Nothing can compare with aesthetic rasa,' says Bhaṭṭa Nāyaka, 'not even the rasa spiritual adepts bring forth' (Pollock 2016, 18–19).[25]

Viśrānti is a purely aesthetic category and is defined away from any religious sense. It takes place where the subject experiences the pleasure of consciousness through vimarśa and being untouched by the things of this world. This aesthetic experience of pure self-reflexivity and blissful repose is declared to be superior to even a religious experience.

To differentiate vimarśa as a self-reflexive reflection, Abhinavagupta brings in the example of crystals and their mindless capacity to reflect any objects that come within their range. However, vimarśa is about acute self-awareness and compares better to a coloured string that passes through the glass beads. These beads can reflect their surroundings, but the string retains its colour. As Pollock astutely points out, here, the string corresponds to the Self (2016, 388n136). The question remains, however, as to whose Self is implied by these visual examples of crystals, beads and coloured strings. Primarily, the rasika is implied, who, through the experience of commonisation or sādhāraṇīkaraṇa, attains a level where he can climb back to himself (self-reflexivity of vimarśa), experience repose (viśrānti)[26] and achieve a self-tasting that will bring about the ultimate aesthetic relish or *camatkāra*.

This self-tasting finds another visual exemplification when Abhinavagupta explains the process via a tree metaphor: He compares the seeds of rasa to [as planted by] the kavi/poet. They grow into the tree of kāvya. From the branches, the flowers bloom, which are like the actors and their acting (abhinaya), but the ultimate beneficiaries are the rasikas who enjoy [or are] the fruits of a drama (*Nāṭyaśāstra* 2001, 108). The rasikas brings back *carvaṇā* or (chewing, slow relishing) as ascribed to the experience of the rasika, a slow act of relishing with temporality built into it. After all, in drama, the rasa experience lasts as long as the performance continues.

The Gendering of Aesthetics

> tatra bhoktṛtve puruṣasya prādhānyam … prādhānadeva ca tasya bhogyenāparatantrīkaraṇamiti nāyikāntarayoge api na śṛṅgāra hānih. bhogyasya tu pāratantrayād evānyasamīlene śṛṅgārabhangamiti darśitam. (*Nāṭyaśāstra* 2001, 156)
>
> As for the erotic (*rati*), there is a male form and a female form, but when it comes to its enjoyment, men have a primacy; they are the enjoyers of pleasure (*bhoktā*) and women are the objects of enjoyment (*bhogyā*). (Translation mine)

The study of Indian aesthetics has rarely been seen through the lens of the politics of representation, especially that of gender. Pollock has gestured towards this through vernacular sociology of the aesthetic with respect to the *Nāṭyaśāstra* by Bharata. When he notes that the *Nāṭyaśāstra* 'institutes this social aesthetics, rigorously relating *rasa* and status', he largely implies class to gesture towards the inequality of social aesthetics (Pollock 2016, 27).

At one level, the rasa aesthetics centres around young highborn heterosexual couples such as the *nāyaka* and the *nayikā* (Pollock 2016, 26). They largely feature as legitimate agents of cause (*vibhāva*) and effects (*anubhava*) for bringing about, say, *śṛṅgāra* or erotic rasa. When it comes to the reception of an aesthetic experience, however, the rasikā or the woman aesthete remains an absent figure. Not everyone has equal aesthetic rights as the ability to 'feel' is not equally distributed, to draw from Jacques Ranciere's proposition for a politics of aesthetics (Groys 2008, 13–22).[27]

While it is easy to point out Bharata's gender bias in the *Nāṭyaśāstra*, Abhinavagupta's position on this issue is more ambivalent. Even in the general sense of the politics of representation, we noticed how fraught Abhinavagupta's position is regarding the status of the actor. The latter is demoted to being a passive container of emotions, which were originally articulated by the kavi or the poet. At the same time, Abhinavagupta ensures that, at least epistemologically, drama is accessible to the general public rather than only to the literary public (who read kāvya).

A similar inclusivity surfaces in Abhinavagupta's definition of the term *punsa*,[28] which literally means only 'man', but he stresses that in general parlance used by reliable people, *punsa* can mean 'human being' and thereby include 'man' and 'woman' (*Nāṭyaśāstra* 2001, 127).

This seemingly liberal understanding of the word 'man' as being gender-inclusive seems to run into conflict with the opening quotation of this section: men and women have unequal access to aesthetic relish. When it comes to the realm of acting, we come across the figures of the naṭa and its feminine pair, *naṭi*. Likewise, a nāyaka is coupled with a nayikā, and together, they bring about the śṛṅgāra rasa into existence. At this point, the social hierarchies, such as *uttama* (best), *madhyama* (middling) and *adhama* (inferior), intervene and map onto not only the nāyaka and nayikā but even the nine rasas. The rasas are divided into higher and lower rasas. The former are ranked higher as they pave the way for the human goals of life (*puruṣārtha*), and they are śṛṅgāra (the erotic), *raudra* (the wrathful), *vīra* (the heroic) and *śānta* (the peaceful). The latter include the lowbrow rasas such as *hāsya* (the comic),[29] *bhayānaka* (the fearful), *adbhuta* (the fantastic), *karuna* (the tragic) and *bibhatsa* (the macabre) (Pollock 2016, 327).

In this entire conceptual economy of rasa, the figure conspicuous by its total absence is that of a rasikā, a woman aesthete, or a *sahṛdayā*, a connoisseur. The absence of the rasikā is not just out of forgetfulness, but it structures the basic frame of rasa aesthetics. In the commentary on the śṛṅgāra rasa, Abhinavagupta exposes his political unconscious on gender, which resonates closely with the opening quote of this section.

After having declared men to be the bhoktā or those who have the right to enjoy rasa and women as the bhogyā or those who are to be enjoyed (*Nāṭyaśāstra* 2001, 155), Abhinavagupta proceeds to link the *sthayi bhāva* with the male subject and the thirty-three *vyabhicāri* or transitory bhāvas with the female bhogyā. He further comments on Bharata's definition of *śṛṅgāra* rasa that *puruṣa* here stands for the one who has the agency to experience (*samvedanātmakam*)[30], and, hence, is the subject of enjoyment or bhoktā (155). Hence, the bhoktā has the consciousness or agency to taste (āsvādana) and experience the sthāyi bhāva. The vyabhicāri or transitory bhāvas, on the other hand, are a form of bhogyā or an object to be enjoyed. Subjectivity is associated with the stability of male sthāyi or stable emotion whereas movement or transitory status of vyabhicāri bhavas demotes them to the status of a bhogyā. The latter condition of being in transition or movement disqualifies women from being the agent of aesthetic enjoyment as they cannot ever aspire to the state of viśrānti.[31]

The reader will now wonder about the gender dynamic underpinning the other related term, vimarśa, which formed the basis of the aesthetic thrill experienced by the rasika. Gender once again informs the way

Abhinavagupta describes *pratibhā* in another work of his called the *Tantrāloka* about the status of knowledge of an object already known (1938, 4.85). He brings up pratibhā in this context as a special form of insight in which the knower returns to the object of knowledge again and again and acquires fresh insight. Arindam Chakrabarti perceptively sees a connection between this kind of knowledge that deepened with more experience with the concept of vimarśa (literally 'reflection'; 2006, 291). Unsurprisingly, the figure of the bhogyā dominates Abhinavagupta's imagination and 'illustrates' this kind of deepened knowledge: 'when a lover pleases his beloved woman first by seeing her with his eyes, then embracing her for a long time, then by repeatedly ruminating on her with his mind. What shall we say about such repeated cognitions of the same subject?' (291).

Here, the figure of a woman is not just a paradigm of enjoyment in an aesthetic discourse but has moved up to being an exemplar of a grand philosophical idea. Yet she is trapped in the space of an allegory, an example, a metaphor and, inevitably, that of a bhogyā, not very dissimilar to the figure of the ālasa kanyā. What stops her from stepping down from the architectural bracket, from the commentary on the *Nāṭyaśāstra* or from the pages of philosophical discourse to sit along with the rasikas and enjoy a performance, a drama, a painting or poetry and feel the aesthetic frisson of rasa? It would imply an impossible transition from the status of a bhogyā to that of a *bhogī*—an aesthetic revolution of a more radical scale than the one accomplished by Bhaṭṭa Nāyaka.

Primary Texts

Nāṭyaśāstra of Srī Bharata Muni. 2001. Commentary by Abhinavaguptacarya and Manorama (Hindi Commentary). Part III. Chapters 12–18. Edited by Parasanatha Dvivedi. Varanasi: Sampurnanand Sanskrit Vidyalaya.

Naṭānkuśa: A Critique on Dramaturgy. 1994. Edited and Translated by K.G. Paulrose. New Delhi. Sangeet Naṭak Akademi.

References

Abhinavagupta. 1938. *Tantraloka*. Commentary by Jayaratha. Edited by Madhusudan Kaul Shastri. Bombay: Nirnaya Sagar Press.

Ali, Daud. 2004. *Courtly Culture and Political Life in Early Medieval India*. Cambridge: Cambridge University Press.

Bhaṭṭaraka, R.M. 2005. *Śilpa Prakāśa*. Edited by B. Baumer, R.P. Das and S. Das. Translated by A. Boner and S.R. Sharma. New Delhi: Indira Gandhi National Centre for the Arts, Motilal Banarsidass Publishers Pvt. Ltd.

Chakrabarti, Arindam. 2006. 'From Vimarsha to Vishrama: Your, I and the Tranquil Taste of Freedom.' *Evam: Forum for Indian Representations* 4: 1 & 2. Edited by Makarand Paranjape (editor) and Sunthar Visuvalingam (guest editor), 282–304. Special Issue titled 'Abhinavagupta: Reconsiderations.' New Delhi: Samvad India Foundation.

Dave-Mukherji, Parul. 2016. 'Who Is Afraid of Mimesis? Contesting the Common Sense of Indian Aesthetics through the Theory of "Mimesis" Anukaraṇa Vada.' In *The Bloomsbury Research Handbook of Indian Aesthetics and the Philosophy of Art*, edited by Arindam Chakrabarti, 71–92. London: Bloomsbury.

———. ed. 2001. *The Citrasūtra of the Viṣṇudharmottara Purāṇa*. Indira Gandhi National Centre for the Arts: New Delhi.

Groys, Boris. 2008. 'The Logic of Equal Aesthetic Rights.' In *Art Power*. Cambridge, MA: MIT.

Hogan, Patrick Colm. 1996. 'Toward a Cognitive Science of Poetics: Ānandavardhana, Abhinavagupta, and the Theory of Literature.' *Evam: Forum for Indian Representations* 4: 1 & 2. Edited by Makarand Paranjape (editor) and Sunthar Visuvalingam (guest editor), 305–319. Special Issue titled 'Abhinavagupta: Reconsiderations.' New Delhi: Samvad India Foundation.

———. 2006. 'Toward a Cognitive Science of Poetics: Ānandavardhana, Abhinavagupta, and the Theory of Literature.' *Evạm: Forum for Indian Representations* 4: 1 & 2. Edited by Makarand Paranjape (editor) and Sunthar Visuvalingam (guest editor), 305–320. Special Issue titled 'Abhinavagupta: Reconsiderations.' New Delhi: Samvad India Foundation.

Kant, Immanuel. 1931. *Critique of Judgement*. Translated by J.H. Bernard. London: Macmillan and Co. Ltd.

McCrea, Lawrence J. 2008. *The Teleology of Poetics in Medieval Kashmir*. Cambridge, Massachusetts and London: Harvard University Press.

Pollock, Sheldon. 2006. 'The Social Aesthetic and Sanskrit Literary Theory'. *Evam: Forum for Indian Representations* 4: 1 & 2. Edited by Makarand Paranjape (editor) and Sunthar Visuvalingam (guest editor), 382–413. Special Issue titled 'Abhinavagupta: Reconsiderations.' New Delhi: Samvad India Foundation.

———. 2016. *A Rasa Reader: Classical Indian Aesthetics*. New York: Columbia University Press.

Schechner, Richard. 1977. *Performance Theory*. Routledge: New York.

Wallis, Christopher D. 2006. 'The Descent of Power: Possession, Mysticism, and Metaphysics in the Shaiva Theology of Abhinavagupta,' *Evam: Forum for Indian Representations* 4: 1 & 2. Edited by Makarand Paranjape (editor) and Sunthar Visuvalingam (guest editor), 231–281. Special Issue titled 'Abhinavagupta: Reconsiderations.' New Delhi: Samvad India Foundation.

Notes

1 See references to ālasa kanyā in an Odia text by Bhaṭṭaraka (2005 395).

2 I follow Sheldon Pollock's translation of rasika as 'he who, or that which, has or tastes or experiences rasa' (2016, 14).

3 The textual tradition does not have the male counterpart of ālasa kanyā (indolent girl) like an ālasa *kumāra* (indolent young man) or ālasa *puruṣa* (indolent male), signalling how the asymmetries of the social world are registered by language.

4 Daud Ali points out that the rasika was both an aesthetic and moral category (2004, 193).

5 In a country like India where many kinds of inequalities prevail, 'Self' is a complicated concept. The Self under question is marked by time and space and a particular philosophical and, at times, religious persuasion. As Pollock, while drawing from Vishvanatha's definition of a rasika, says that he belongs to a class of 'certain special people' [who] have the capacity for relishing rasa, those who have a 'superabundance of sensitivity' (2016, 47).

6 The significance of Abhinavagupta's commentary on the *Nāṭyaśāstra* lies in its inclusion of a long-standing debate around aesthetic experience that started with Daṇḍin. He refers to different theories of poetics and dramaturgy as proposed by his predecessors that included Daṇḍin, Ānandavardhana, Bhaṭṭa Lollaṭa, Srī Śaṅkuka, Bhaṭṭa Tauta and Bhaṭṭa Nāyaka. *Abhinavabhāratī*'s historiography traces various views and positions on the nature of pleasure, a rare phenomenon in the aesthetic discourse, and offers us a glimpse into the Self under construction via the experience of aesthetic pleasure. It covers a period of a couple of centuries from around 8th to10th century CE in India.

7 See Dave-Mukherji (2016) for Abhinavagupta's critique of anukaraṇa vāda and his programmatic marginalisation of this discourse. Given the lack of any one-to-one correspondence between anukaraṇa vāda and a singular term in English along with the fact that anukaraṇa includes both mimesis and mimicry in classical dramaturgy, I have translated this Sanskrit term as the theory of performative mimesis.

8 It has been noted that this aesthetician from Kashmir 'turned his attention away from the linguistic and related abstractions which had preoccupied even Ānandavardhana focussing his attention on the human mind of the reader or a viewer of a literary work' (Colm 1996, 311).

9

> tena nāṭya eva rasā na loke ityarthah…kāvyanca nāṭyam eva. ata eva ca nate na rasah kutra tarhi…nate tarhi kim? āsvadanopayah. ata eva ca pātram iti ucyate. na hi patre madyasvadah. api tu tad upāyakah. tena pramukhapātre natopayoga ityalam. (*Nāṭyaśāstra* 2001, 99)
>
> Therefore, rasa is in Nāṭya, not in the world is the meaning. Kāvya is itself nāṭya. Then the question arises: if rasa is not in the actor, where is it to be located? Why is it [taken to be] in the actor? He [an actor] is only a means for tasting [rasa]. That is why he is called a vessel (pātra). The vessel can never taste the wine. It is only an instrument. It is enough to say that an actor is an instrument. (Translation mine)

10 If we expand practitioners to include the visual artists or a *citravid* (painter/artist/actor) for whom *anukrti* or imitation was also central as it involved

a performative activity of 'resemblance making' or what a *silpaśāstra* like the *Citrasūtra* of the *Viṣṇudharmottara Purāṇa* calls '*sādṛśya karaṇam*', Abhinavagupta's diatribe would include the visual artists. See Dave-Mukherji (2001, 202–203).

11 See Ali (2004, 190–191) for the importance of the rasika.

12 Incidentally, *Rupaka*, a term for the genre of drama as in *Daśarupaka*, is a visual metaphor.

13 Dvivedi edition p. 90.

14 Kant refers to a native American chief, an Iroquois Sachem who was visiting Paris, and it appalled Kant that what pleased this indigenous man in this city were cook-shops, not palaces.

15 'alātacakrādau sāksātkārāntareṇaiva balavatā tadhavadhāraṇād iti laukikas tāvad ayam kramah.'
In the case of [examples like] a fiery circle, etc., they are perceived on the basis of them happening right in front of one's eyes, and hence [such examples] are taken to be a common experience (*Nāṭyaśāstra* 2001, 66; translation mine).

16 In the section on various obstacles of rasa, lack of clarity of visual perception features as the fourth hindrance.

> Kimca pratityupāyānām abhāve katham pratitih?
> How can there be perception [of *rasa*] in the absence of the means of perception? (*Nāṭyaśāstra* 2001, 66; translation mine)

17 Generally, in Indian epistemology, there is a consensus agreement amongst most schools of philosophy that pratyakṣa or perception is the most valid means of knowledge. If we privilege mediate knowledge like anumāna in understanding aesthetic reception, claims Abhinavagupta, it will serve to alienate the general public for whom visual perception is more widely available than the logician's category of inference or anumāna or mediate knowledge.

18 In this regard, I would like to draw attention to a 16th-century text on performance, *Naṭānkusa*, that captures the debate between the actors or those who build their livelihood on *kriyā* or action of the artists, actors or that of the śāstrakāra, the ācāryas.

19 One such example of commonality discussed by Abhinavagupta is common mental traces (instinct) or *samskāra* (traces of previous birth) that are shared by all the spectators. It also explains why it is possible for everyone to enjoy even a negative rasa like *bhayānaka* rasa when it is being acted out on stage. At the level of generality or sādhāraṇīkaraṇa induced by an aesthetic experience, the Self rises above the constraints of the here and now and connects with past memories that have no causal connection with the present. Hence, fear is absent (*Nāṭyaśāstra* 2001, 61).

20 Abhinavagupta raises a serious objection to his teacher, Bhaṭṭa Tauta, who had undermined the role of perception in aesthetic experience. Abhinavagupta asserts:

> pratītyādi vyatiriktas ca samsāre ko bhoga iti na vidmah?
> We don't know of any enjoyment in this world that excludes perception etc. (*Nāṭyaśāstra* 2001, 55; translation mine)

'Perception' or 'what comes before one's eyes' is really about dṛśya and is epistemologically prior above other means of knowledge including that of hearing (srāvya).

Unfortunately, Bhaṭṭa Tauta's work *Kāvyakautuka* is lost, but parts of it are cited by Abhinavagupta in his commentary on the *Nāṭyaśāstra*.

21 Being a Mimamsaka, Bhaṭṭa Nāyaka followed a different model of interpreting language: language urges us to act and behave in the world we live in rather than being only a transmitter of knowledge.

22 Bhaṭṭa Nāyaka also proposed the two new concepts of bhāvakatva and bhojakatva. The former is the power which makes the individual characters, settings and incidents universal. Bhojakatva is the process of experiencing the universalised elements in drama or poetry leading to Rasa. Both of these processes act as conditions for viśrānti, which prepare the rasika for the ultimate experience of tasting the Self.

23 Reflection or *pratibimba* had a profound philosophical sense for a Saivite like Abhinavagupta and his *Pratibhijña* philosophy.

24 Here, Abhinavagupta consistently refers to the Sāṅkhya philosophy of Kapila, according to whom happiness can be understood as the predominance of the *sattva guṇa* over *rajas* or the action guṇa and the insensate *tamas* guṇa.

25 Sheldon Pollock translates viśrānti as absorption, where the subject experiences the pleasure of a consciousness untouched by the things of this world, superior even to the religious experience analogised to it (2016, 18–19).

26 Arindam Chakrabarti refers to viśrānti as 'a peaceful resting place in the heart' (2006, 290).

27 Abhinavagupta's use of the term *adhikāra*, while reflecting on the ideal reader of kāvya, is comparable with the idea of aesthetic right used by Groys following Ranciere. 'adhikārī catra vimalapratibhānasalihṛdayah': 'A person who is endowed with a spotless intuition and soft heart is the rightful reader' (*Nāṭyaśāstra* 2001, 59; translation mine).

28 'punsamiti manuṣyajāter narāṇām narīṇām ca.' [Generally speaking], the word *punsam* means 'of the category of human beings' [including] 'of women' and 'of men' (translation mine).

29 In his commentary on hāsya rasa, Abhinavagupta defines it as that which makes people laugh. Laughter is commonly seen in women owing to their [natural] lowly nature: 'hāsyati jana yasmāt tasmāt jñeyo raso hāsyah strīnīcaprakṛtāveṣa bhuyiṣṭham dṛsyate rasa' (*Nāṭyaśāstra* 2001, 164).

30 'puruṣa iti bhoktā samvedanātmakao abhipretah. bhoktaiva ca sthāyisamvidrupah. vyabhicāriṇistu bhogyasvabhāvāh' (*Nāṭyaśāstra* 2001, 155).

31 This male and female binary appears akin to the Sāṅkhya's division of the world into puruṣa and *prakṛti*.

II

SELF IN CRISIS

3

A DIFFICULT FREEDOM

Democracy, Disappointment and the Indefatigable

Aishwary Kumar

Being is becoming.

—Ambedkar, *The Buddha and His Dhamma*

But what is an architecture of becoming?

—Eisenman, *Written into the Void*

Architecture is a kind of eloquence of power in forms—now persuading, even flattering, now only commanding.

—Nietzsche, 'Skirmishes of an Untimely Man'

'I am not a part of the whole,' the moral and political philosopher Bhimrao Ambedkar (1891–1956), soon to become a new and fragile republic's most audacious constitutional theorist, declared in the Bombay Legislative Assembly in 1939. 'I am a part apart' (1978–2003, 10: 166).[1] Already, in his critique of Ambedkar's revolutionary manifesto *Annihilation of Caste* (1936) three years earlier, Mohandas Gandhi had sighed in nearly audible relief at the sort of political freedom that usually produced such exemplary declarations of independence from Ambedkar. 'Thank God,' Gandhi wrote of 'Ambedkar's 'indictment' of Hinduism in his newspaper *Harijan*, '[he] is singularly alone' (1999, 69, 206).[2] One would trust absolutely no anti-colonial wordsmith other than Gandhi to compress, in merely half a sentence of ironic brilliance, the majestic whole of Ambedkar's enduring, transcendent condition: his singular solitude.

It has since been said of this solitude more than once, more than ironically, and not without a trace of Brahminic malice that Ambedkar, at once the architect of India's constitutional founding and its anti-hero, died exactly as he had anticipated or perhaps even wanted, if not perversely deserved: in Nietzschean disappointment with the world of political morality; disenchanted with the system of laws that he (rightly) believed merely used the jargon of constitutionalism to legitimise the petty world of archaic, ritualised meanness; and betrayed by the moral and epistemological value he placed only ever on the power of his doubt. Repelled equally by the civilisational grandstanding of anti-colonial liberals and their ultranationalist counterparts, the philosophical sceptic in him was left without a homeland in a world full of nation states. A thinker racing defiantly against death to complete, in punishing illness, his masterwork *The Buddha and His Dhamma* (1956), it has been insinuated that Ambedkar finally saw the futility of his belief in modern legislative statecraft. As his trust in the power of constitutional norms to hold off against majoritarian assaults eroded, he turned to another belief, another religion, instead.

More than one nationalist has since had the temerity to suggest that this 'turn to religion' proved that Gandhi had been right all along about Ambedkar's inadequately theorised, metaphysical anger against Hinduism. Other myths have implied worse. Any turn to the language of religiosity in politics, it has been claimed, must itself always be, at its heart, secretly 'Gandhian', so that Ambedkar's final turn revealed him to be just that: an alienated soul who must return home—as he does—even if he exits it. The most obscurantist measure of all, both within nationalist institutions at home and the transnational outposts of this ideological apparatus overseas, has been the unrelenting and tacit drive to bury that which is singular in Ambedkar's critique of religious violence: the will to conversion and the monumental act of political faith through which this will was expressed in the final months of 1956, as Ambedkar exited Hinduism with half a million of his own, whose lives, in his searing words, had been reduced by the barbarity of caste 'from [their] millions to [mere] fractions' (1978–2003, 5: 229–246). It is a singularity whose inspiration Ambedkar drew from another classicism and its theory of government, another genealogy of Indian morals and, perhaps most obliquely, another conception of political forgiveness, one whose sources lay not in the epic traditions and their unforgiving heroes (favoured by reactionary and liberal nationalists in equal measure if for different ends) but instead in the one associated with the Mauryan imperium and the monarchical figure of Ashoka.

Significantly, Ashoka's turn to Buddhism nearly three centuries before Christ came not only at the height of the warrior's imperial dominance over the Gangetic north and beyond but also at the moment of his greatest, most bloody, and most desolate victory over the peninsular in Kalinga. In this moment of turn of sovereignty to Buddhism lies crystallised a political theory of conversion—the *conversion of violence to force*—that shines not in the grimness of Ashoka's desolate triumph but in the incandescence of his disappointment with war (and himself), not in his inconsolable disinterest in ruling but in the majesty of imperial justice. No atheological tradition other than Buddhism gives Ambedkar this revolutionary example of political disappointment and majestic judgement at one and the same time, one in which justice is sought not through a punitive exercise of power but through a force that is capable of yielding.[3] No religious tradition other than Buddhism gives him an epistemology of nothingness—a universality steeped in the primacy of non-self—and morals for the *transcendence* and reformation of power—yielding—at its sovereign source at one and the same time. Compressed in this atheological turn is the figure of a heroic exemplar who is not God but a fallible mortal, soaked in disappointment with his method, yet willing to forgive both himself and his vanquished others. Conversion enters Indian history through this turn, through this imperial *torsion*, one that is as classical as India's fabled non-violence, appearing on its horizon centuries before colonial Christianity maligns it and gives nationalism yet another reason to betray Ambedkar's exemplary inheritance.

This is an exemplarity rooted in forgiveness in which, for Ambedkar, the 'will to punish' is replaced by the will to conversion. This conversion occurs, however, not in the twilight of the idols—this is no fall into disenchanted, faithless nihilism—but at the high noon of Mauryan political sovereignty, one whose architecture of righteousness radiates its grace out from the centre of the imperial capital rather than from its monastic peripheries. In this exemplary genealogy of political faith, the architect converts to another religion not to relinquish power but to henceforth use it with justice. The architect turns to faith not to renounce the logic and gravity of force, or rule even, but to refuse the place of unforgiving vengeance in it.[4]

Yet the myth around Ambedkar's disappointment, with its morals willfully misread and its politics resentfully imputed, lives on. One disobedient doubt led to another reckless one until that day in December 1956 when Ambedkar finally departed, dying as restless a spirit as he had been born. In fact, the formidable nationalist C. Rajagopalachari, who had published exactly a decade earlier a tract of political calculus devoted entirely to denouncing Ambedkar's constitutional vision, titled *Ambedkar Refuted* (1946), uses in his 1956 obituary for Ambedkar the expression 'restless spirit' in as many words.[5] Perhaps, Rajagopalachari hoped that Ambedkar would find peace in death! To make it more ambiguous still, the obituary is not lacking in Rajagopalachari's grudging admiration of Ambedkar either, but that is the very point.

Figure 3.1. 'Rajaji's Tribute,' *Indian Express*, 7 December 1956

Regd. No. M. 2776 — Registered as a Newspaper in Ceylon

LARGEST CERTIFIED NET SALES AMONG ALL DAILY NEWSPAPERS IN INDIA.

MORNING

The Indian Express

PUBLISHED SIMULTANEOUSLY FROM MADRAS, BOMBAY & DELHI.

VOL. XXV. NO. 56. MADRAS: FRIDAY, DECEMBER 7, 1956. 10 PAGES: 1½ ANNAS.

24 HOURS

ANSWER'S

...TIONS BETWEEN 28th ...RUARY ... MAR. 14

...l Amnesty ...Offenders

(...pecial Correspondent)

NEW DELHI, Dec. 6.

...endation of the Election ...garding that the elections ... Feb. 28 and Mar. 14 has ... Government of India ... by the Election Commis... the dates will be issued at

...y has been decided upon with ...one election irregularities and ... during the first general elec... 1952) resulting in the disquali... ,000 persons throughout the

P.M.'s FLAG DAY APPEAL

Pakistan Preparing To 'Liberate' Kashmir

KARACHI, Dec. 6.

THE Pakistan Press today quoted "a Minister" of Pakistan-held Kashmir to say, "We have no faith left in the U.N. who have failed to do anything except discussing the (Kashmir) matter."

World Bank Selects Schemes For Aid

—T. T. K. URGES EARLY FLOW OF FUNDS

(From Our Special Representative)

NEW DELHI, Dec. 6.

THE Union Finance Minister, Mr. T. T. Krishnamachari, has impressed on the World Bank President, Mr. Eugene Black, that "it is essential for the flow of funds from the bank to commence at the earliest possible date" for such of the projects as have been selected by the bank for financial assistance.

The Letters

India's Case Strong

(Continued on Page 8 Column 8)

Ambedkar Dead: Houses Of Parliament Adjourn

A SYMBOL OF SOCIAL REVOLT, SAYS NEHRU

NEW DELHI, Dec. 6.

DR. B. R. AMBEDKAR, former Union Law Minister and one of the architects of India's Constitution, died here this morning.

(Continued on Page 8 Column 8)

THE 'MANU OF MODERN INDIA'

'A Restless Spirit Has Found Peace'

—RAJAJI'S TRIBUTE

MADRAS, Dec. 6.

...'S TUTORIAL INSTITUTE

...CES ITS BRANCH at TRICHY

Pre-University Students

NEELA PRODUCTIONS

MA...

It is not an absolute lack of admiration that drives nationalist mythology around Ambedkar's purported dejection with India's constitutional concord or with the anti-minority state it yielded. What drives nationalist mythology is a potent, prejudiced mixture of the majoritarian desire to appropriate Ambedkar, on the one hand, and on the other, its burning resentment against the indefatigable radicality of their founding architect's disappointment in them, one in which Ambedkar, by embracing Buddhism, leaves neither the moral sovereignty of majoritarian religiosity over public life intact nor the political purity of the national state, with its barely concealed theological undertones, unvanquished. Even Ashok Gopal's magisterial biography, aptly titled *A Part Apart* (2023), cannot help but conjure in its closing scenes the figure of the brooding architect, making it carry the grand finale of Ambedkar's constitutional act. The architect's inappropriable, mortal self might have long been buried in amnesia. But a silhouette of this figure is kept alive in nationalist consciousness and ultranationalist rhetoric alike, where it might be kept frozen in stasis until the catastrophic finale of the republic itself begins to unfold. Who is this architect? Or better still, what is an architect? And how to do democratic things with it again?

An Exemplary Disappointment

Indictments about Ambedkar's 'restless spirit' and his rhetorical 'overdoing' in 'a certain 'manner of language and utterance,' as Nehru (1956) put it in his own grudging obituary, which cut so close to his decisions and judgements—so close that nobody except Ambedkar himself might illuminate anything even vaguely resembling a truth about them—grow not only out of nationalism's wilful, curated amnesia about the figure it calls its architect; they also fester in its epistemological illiteracy about the structure of his moral doubt and his almost prophetic disappointment in India.

The most elementary truth is, humanity has never constructed anything durable without first doubting that it can be built at all. When the architect puts his first line—a line of force—on paper, he begins by drawing nothing more and nothing less than silhouettes of his doubt, fuelled by his passion for the possible. It is in the hands of the architect that human finitude first meets the insurmountable law of gravity, and the earthly desire for transcendence meets the force of natural law. To speak in the language of a radiant, transcendental faith as Ambedkar did for decades must, therefore, be taken, in equal part, to be a function of the architect's fundamental doubt, perhaps even a swerve away from his otherwise indefatigable faith—and Ambedkar's was invincible—in the human capacity to build durable forms in this life. The faith that Ambedkar brought militantly to life in 1956, weeks before his death, with half a million others born like him—outcastes who appeared for the first time as a people subject not to the caste contract but masters of their own judgement—was both a democratic overcoming and moral reaffirmation of this very doubt. In its architecture of disappointment, this faith was nothing like the old, dreary religiosity that his nationalist detractors had for so long championed.

Fanatics of extreme nationalism have always tarred conversion with their self-righteous brush, accusing Ambedkar of a calculus, as if their own decision to die with the religion they were born into has ever itself been free of calculations of privilege and generational gain. Why must a convert, a heretic, a radical atheist even, meet a burden of proof about his sacrificial clarity and truthfulness that those with nothing but moral inertia—indifference to their own plight and of others—are never asked to meet? How is the decision to stay on with what one is born with a more righteous decision than a rejection of that which does not let one live?

The moral point is, conversion is not a vow of monastic disinterest; it is an affirmation of life, of survival, of the power of judgement itself. It never claims to be a renunciation of interest. It only holds a sharp mirror to the brutal masquerade of ascetic disinterest behind which nationalism—and its majoritarian criterion of truth—perjures. Conversion seeks not a religion indigenous to this land or that; it is not lured by mysteries of this world or another. Nationalist attempts to frame its power in those terms miss the profoundly anti-authoritarian politics of human freedom at its core. At the heart of conversion instead lies a tenacious moral commitment to the gravity of truth and to a political world without majoritarian deception.[6] Conversion is a call to reclaim the earthly dignity of the outnumbered—the minor—in a world brutalised by hostile exclusions of the majority that surrounds, like a mob, even those it calls its own.

If conversion is a form of *pragmatism* at all, then—and by pragmatism, I mean a commitment to non-metaphysical, atheological truths that penetrate the studied wall of religious violence only to exit its economy of cruelty on its other side—it is because conversion's political expression is distinctly anti-authoritarian. The many forms and expressions of the jointure between 'pragmatism and *anti-authoritarianism*', as Richard Rorty (2021) cautions, disappoint too (and they do so more viciously than God). Given how obdurate the tentacles of majoritarian deception are, conversion cannot ever be a guarantee against disappointment. It can only ever be an indefatigable will to truth, one that perseveres and yet almost always finds itself bound ultimately towards disappointment in fellow human beings, if only with more forgiveness. If Ambedkar remains—despite his profound scepticism about the majoritarian will to stability—an architect of anything durable or immortal, it is of this bond between disappointment and truth, this fraught relation between forgiveness and democracy.

Whether or not he ever saw his own self in the classical figure of the architect, there are moments when it would seem that Ambedkar might himself call this immortal relation between disappointment and truth—the daunting battle for a justice without vengeance—the Constitution. In that sense, the architect is a singular witness to political disappointment and the many identities that swirl out of it. He is a bearer of judgement that cuts closest to the self and the self's reflexive knowledge of itself, its own identity only ever forged in response to those that surround it, sometimes with vengeance, often in resentment and, once in a while, in adoration. Nobody in the modern anti-colonial tradition with the exception of Frantz Fanon (2004, 97) is more aware of this fragile ambiguity of identity—of identities forged like 'empty shells' in the misanthropic crucible of nationalist zeal, its tribalism temporarily concealed by a forgetful euphoria—than Ambedkar. Yet nobody yields to this ambiguity with greater hope than Ambedkar, if only to be disappointed.

Yet the scaffolds of Ambedkar's own self, it has often been implied, could bear only one identity, or possessive individualism, at a time. Whether as an unbridled craftsman of constitutional law anchored in a modernist glorification of state power or as a disillusioned convert at war against Indic epistemologies of the 'self' and nationalist theologies of the 'soul', he could have only ever ended his life more alienated than he was born. Let us note, however, that neither the self nor the soul has ever been free from punitive liturgies of self-mastery and violent spectacles of modern self-determination. Both, Ambedkar had himself warned as if he were in a quiet dialogue with his enemies, would soon fuel the rhetoric of all stripes of fanatical nationalisms. Perhaps his affinity for classical Buddhist epistemologies of non-self (*anatta*) and, most fundamentally, emptiness (*sunnyata*) was anchored by this deep distrust of the majority and the 'risk' it brought to the democratic covenant in its misanthropic quest for limitless power, infinitude even (Kumar 2015). The appetite of the majority for self-concentration, the desire to make everything about itself and oneself, hid right under the skin of imperial and liberal visions of self-determination alike. But rather than quibbling with the prejudices that mark the verdict on the sources of Ambedkar's self, this chapter seeks to use them as beginnings for a moral psychology of democratic disappointment—and of its resentful other, which I will call the *majoritarian signature*—instead.

Can a constitutionalist's belief in popularly elected government as an instrument of the common good, despite the deceptions and perjuries that the government has always concealed, be a trusted antidote to the resentments of the very majority that authorises such a brutal signature (*signature* because we cannot, in Ambedkar's wake, think of the majority, in all its brutalism and passivity, without India's tacit, coercive caste contract)? Or is it a militantly melancholic faith in and embrace of disappointment—*unhope*, Du Bois (2015, 157) might say—instead that keeps the secretive heart of democracy beating against power?[7]

More oblique and less imperious than anger, disappointment lies somewhere between a value (that the reserved self silently nurses) and a miracle (that the dissolving self unavoidably yields to). Disappointment at once frees and drags the self into strife with itself, imbuing it with a truth-telling courage and an inconsolable force at one and the same time.[8] This force, under the grief of betrayal, yields itself—this force-bearing self—away so unconditionally, so fearlessly, fiercely even, that it can now see durable, immortal justice neither in ascetic delusions of self-mastery nor in the seething silences of masculine *ressentiment* (rarely two things) but in the freedom of others alone. Therein lies the irreducible difference between disappointment and resentment: both are effects of betrayal, and yet, only in disappointment does the self yield to the other; in resentment, on the other hand, the self inverts within and concentrates itself.

If you are disappointed, James Baldwin writes in his 1963 essay for the *New York Times* 'The Artist's Struggle for Integrity', 'you must understand that your pain is trivial, except insofar as you can connect it to other people's pain' (2010, 53). The disappointed self thinks not simply of and for the other; it yields its very place—the self's place—to the other. To be disappointed, in other words, is to have the courage not simply to *be* but instead the courage to *not* be. Baldwin, like Hannah Arendt, calls this yielding 'understanding'. Insofar as one's own self is given at all, insofar as its identity wields any truth in it, its givenness can be grasped only as the yield of the injurable, vulnerable other: the other who is no less desolate—and no less worthy of forgiveness—than oneself.

The exemplary power of disappointment for democracy—and its constant presence in it—lies in this capacity to forgive without forgetting, to begin again despite desolation, to yield and found at the same time. Ambedkar's disappointment in India was an antidote to the desolation he foresaw would be left behind by majoritarian resentments, not a denial of the republic's heroic idealism. The force of his disappointment—moral and epistemological—came precisely from the fact that he was, at the very seat of its constituent power, its unhopeful architect.

There is a long history and inheritance of revolutionary critique of political hope, a history in which prophetic solitude and inappropriable solidarity coalesce like a miracle at the moment of majestic despair. For without the solidarity, all pain is indeed trivial; its alternative, pace Arendt, is merely a powerless, wallowing 'pity'. This chapter engages with this aporia—the placeless passage between freedom and unhope—placing Ambedkar's theory of political judgement and his recalibration of the scaffolds, the very architecture, of the self at its centre. It is a self that, as Ambedkar posits with Marx, is always already a moving part in a cruel, unforgiving system of *relations of reproduction* of the self, albeit one that has a singularly Indian name: caste. In the process, the chapter examines why democracy, crippled by this reproducible (and reproductive) cruelty, must rethink the value of disappointment in politics. My beginning will be a figure in the history of political thought that has been braided on to Ambedkar's afterlife as if it were the entirety of his indefatigable arc—the figure of the architect—but one which he radically inverts for democracy, in his very disappointment with it.

The Gravity of Truth

Upon being asked about the aims of the October Revolution, Lenin had offered in November 1920 the unforgettable formula 'Communism is Soviet power plus electrification' (Lenin 1920). Hannah Arendt calls this revolutionary vision 'curious and long-forgotten', although she does lend it a decisive presence in postwar political theory (1963, 55). More recently, Jean-Luc Nancy has reclaimed the exact declaration, in Lenin's own words: 'Communism is Soviet power plus electrification' (2017, 357).

This revolutionary love of fabrication and planning, its rhetoric of grids and wires, on the one hand, and visions of almost annihilative surge, pulse and force, on the other, seems puzzling only because so much of modern political thought has been preoccupied with the destructive violence that accompanies modern revolutions at their inception that its most axiomatic principle, one that holds a revolution unto itself, is entirely lost. A 'revolution' is an acceptably theoretical term, it seems, to describe or cover up either the bloody fusillade launched over a colonial theatre or a genocidal orgy among neighbours ripped by civil war. Yet the true keeper of the modern revolutionary treasure is not the alleged arsonist but the scrupulous architect, not the polemist but the constitutionalist, not the technician of combat but the student of force, not the punishing priests of stasis but the forgiving partisans of crisis.

The revolution is a *politics of becoming given a new architecture*, one in which the architect is not so much a figure of stability as she is, right in the vortex of a crisis, the bearer of a promise: the promise that new lines of force will appear on the horizon, no matter how blurred the sky, and that they will endure, no matter how sprawling the ruins on earth. Architecture, Peter Eisenman writes of his craft, is the art of movement rather than of stasis (2007). The greatest revolutionaries—in politics as in architecture—are practitioners of dynamic, durable forms rather than of static, stable norms.[9] So only an architecture built out of annihilation, of 'blurring' and impurity, can be properly called an architecture of human freedom and of political becoming. The constitution that such an architecture of durability yields cannot also not be an 'exhumation,' an 'archaeology' of foundations. 'The task is one of gathering survivals of the past, placing them together and making them tell the story of their birth,' Ambedkar writes in his classic archeology of the caste sciences, *The Untouchables: Who Were They and Why They Became Untouchables* (1948). 'The task is analogous to that of the archaeologist who constructs a city from broken stones or the paleontologist who conceives an extinct animal from scattered bones and teeth or,' he declares finally, in a militant embrace of political theory as democratic imagination, 'of a painter who reads the lines of the horizon and the smallest vestiges on the slopes to make up a scene. In this sense, the book is a work of art even more than of history' (1978–2003, 7: 244).

To Ambedkar's unfinished work of art, which involves a politics not only of revolutionary memory but of democratic anti-amnesia, I shall return later in this chapter. Here, let us note the kinship he forges between founding and archaeology, or better still, between architecture and deconstruction. It is almost a universal element in political iconography that the revolutionary has always had one hand held out towards the future still to come. This is not because revolutionaries despise the shadow of the past lurking behind them but precisely because they are aware that this past leaves no shadow, that this past has been left unsaid, buried and broken, without a signature. The architect and the archaeologist share this passion for the hidden, grey signature that underwrites the mystical, cryptic and necessarily violent foundation of its authority. For Ambedkar, this passion was to always remain directed towards the dark matter of his country's communal, majoritarian signature, its scaffolds dug deep into the earth like the bones of an extinct species. There could be for him no constitutional architecture, then, without some anti-violent archaeology in it, and there could be no archaeology for him without some architecture of beginnings.

The architect of Greek laws, *rex*, as Arendt recalls, was always an outsider to the city, brought in to compose the civic statutes because he—like the architect of buildings who is concerned with nothing earthly other than the laws of gravity themselves—could disregard the murky complexities of social life and fabricate legal norms that would be almost indifferent to politics (2005, 182–183). If Arendt is right, then Ambedkar is an architect, arguably *the* architect of our time, only in the most paradoxical, Roman sense. This is not only because, unlike the Greek jurist, he sees the democratic constitution acquire its highest political form—its *freedom*—in the crucible of social life (which the Greek legislator strives to avoid) but also because of Ambedkar's acute judgement about constitutions and their constitutionality itself. In this judgement, being a partisan of moral durability is more fundamental to the task of constitutional—*transcendental*—founding than being simply a guarantor of comforting civilisational stability.

Here, then, is the enigma of Ambedkar, the architect: a figure at once marked by a transcendent exteriority, or an *untouchability*, he might say, and yet, a figure upon whom is inscribed the most granular knowledge of his country's vicious fallibilities; a figure who bears the weight of these failings very privately, often solitarily, until the very end, on his own body. It is the kind of solitude that attaches either to the grey, meticulous and patient craft of the architect or to the granular precision of the archaeologist. The later Foucault would say, almost in protest, 'genealogist!'[10] Whatever else he might be judged for, this radical ambiguity in Ambedkar—or revolutionary amphibiousness—is elemental. For Ambedkar's solitude ensues not only from the soaring flights of his democratic vision and constitutional hope (fitting of an architect) but in equal measure from the telluric—if you will, earth-grazing—gravity of political judgements (fitting of an archaeologist) about a civilisation's dark matter, its barbarism encrusted as the common law, its dead skin a haunting reminder of the routine, sanctioned decompositions of the human into a thing.

On the surface of it, the architect and the archaeologist rarely meet. They embody two seemingly incommensurable techniques. One draws the lines of a scaffold in the void, while the other digs up everything memory seeks to bury and avoid. One works often against gravity, the other always with it; sometimes they exchange places. They are strung apart at the extremities of that elliptical history and violent arc of human craftsmanship formed over millenia out of a locus of a million points. Each point holds within itself varying laws of and relation between hand and force, flesh and skill, bone and torque. These laws of force and techniques of the hand are themselves neither free of violence nor devoid of the will to punish, neither untainted by laws of inequality nor unsullied by the humanistic hubris that is jurisprudence.[11]

The first figural appearance of the architect in political thought appears not surprisingly, then, in the realm of jurisprudence as lawgiver: a figure who founds and fabricates, understands stability, and sees power not as license but as limit. The architect is an embodiment of good deeds, a reminder of the human capacity to found despite the cracks on the ground, an exemplar of what Arendt (1958) might call earthly immortality. He is a figure of groundless beginnings, a thinker of gravity who transcends all ground, precedent and lineage, and yet, precisely because he has touched the extreme limits of the possible, he is the closest witness to human finitude.[12]

The archaeologist, on the other hand, bears the memory of human finitude, of earthly mortality—sediments of a civilisation's felony—not as limit (or exception) but as a rule (or the law). Where the architect seeks stability, the archaeologist discerns a stasis. Where the architect is made responsible for beginnings, the archaeologist seeks origins. Where the architect finds materials for founding, the archaeologist discovers bones of species extinct as he rummages the ruins of cities destroyed no less by malice than they were by time. One of the great ironies of modern democratic politics is that its most fanatical enemies first attack ruins of cities long gone, laying even the oldest ruins to ruin anew, sometimes to simply try and find even older ruins underneath: violence against violence, an economy of violence, in other words. The archaeologist is the frontal figure in this assault on democratic truth by fanatics and economists of amnesia, the architect his transcendent other.[13] Both are figures of disappointment, inevitable bearers of a harsh truth, for neither one's passion for beginnings nor the other's love of memory eventually matter to a democracy gone rogue.

Perhaps that is why, in Ambedkar, the architect and the archaeologist perpetually appear—strung apart at their extremities—as equals.[14] To the extent that Ambedkar is now an unavoidable figure in global political thought, a theorist par excellence of disappointment done right, of disappointment done justice, one cannot even be imagined without the other. After all, the architect and the archaeologist do share a common bond with technique, a common quest for the machine, a common love of force. But this is not the force that makes, by unadulterated violence, a thing out of the living. The architect and the archaeologist are invested not so much in the *use of force* as they are artisans of an *imaginary of force*, or pace Benjamin, a *critique of force* (1996). It is at this point, where a revolutionary critique of force cuts into the economy of its use (and abuse) by the state for history, that Ambedkar fearlessly touches the nervous regime of nationalist amnesia and perjury. It is a point at which an architect's gravity-defying vision—his infinite passion for height, majesty and sovereignty even—bends and meets with the archaeologist's painful discovery of depth at the bottom of the earth, each layer revealing a disappointing inventory of lies, aggravating the solitude of the truthteller in its utter singularity.

Anger and Its Other

Here, in the architect's recalcitrant solitude and singular fullness, I argue, appears the faculty of political judgement. Political judgement seeks neither a world without crisis nor a subject fully in command of itself (judgement wouldn't be needed in such a flawless world). Quite to the contrary, judgement becomes fully itself—that is, most just, most passionate and most political—precisely in a world of inconsolable disappointment and catastrophic uncertainty, a world where the subject risks losing freedom itself. Only in the throes of disappointment does the self recover and return to itself in all its intensity and hopelessness. It makes itself the first and the last, perhaps the most unforgiving, subject of one's judgement. In disappointment, one judges oneself first (and last). When one judges oneself first, one also forgives the other. 'The alternative to forgiveness, but by no means its opposite,' Arendt writes, 'is punishment, and both have in common that they attempt to put an end to something that without interference could go on endlessly' (1958, 241).

This unforgiving, relentless castigation of the self might produce, every now and then, a certain anger. This anger is an effect, let us mark however, of *self-intensification*. It flows from a self-reflexive individualism, traversing a political path that is set distinctively apart from the nagging sense of self-injury or desolation. A truly political anger is always a function of self-reflexive judgement rather than of the desire to possess for oneself the right to always be proven right. Political judgement is this self-intensification given an emancipatory social form. Such judgement attaches not to rationality (or self-interest) but to the passion of the possible. It speaks in the tone not of impartiality—certainly not 'neutrality'—but of force. Its real centre is not the other but oneself, or better still, oneself as another first. 'I regard my feelings of hatred as a real force,' Ambedkar writes of this force that returns the self always to oneself in his 1943 essay 'Ranade, Gandhi and Jinnah.' 'They are only the reflex of the love I bear for the causes I believe in and I am in no way ashamed of it' (1978–2003, 1: 208).[15] I will call this sort of moral transparency in judging the self and the other—oneself as another—the foundations of *democratic anger*, one that is animated by moral epistemic and clarity rather than by the refusal to examine our suicidal resentments.

Resentment, on the other hand, grows in the isolationist, narcissist chamber of implosive *self-concentration.* Its primary impulse is the indictment of the other. While this punishing verdict against the other might be fuelled by a disdain towards liberal interest, and its demagoguery might be couched in claims of loss of the self and the hubris of disinterest, there is no self-reflexive judgement as such in it. Resentment is the moral psychological point where the self, stewing in its purportedly historic and endlessly unfolding injuries, matters even to itself only insofar as it seeks to appropriate the other into itself, into its circle of implosive—but for that reason, no less dogmatic—vehemence. Every other, especially those closest to oneself, is now merely a thing to be possessed, mastered, defaced.

If anger has democratic responsibility at its heart—'my response to racism is anger,' Audre Lorde (1984) writes in the searing first lines of her immortal essay 'The Uses of Anger'—then resentment has merely a seething desire for tyranny at its source, even if this desire is often couched in archaic myths of descent and purity, and even more perniciously, in snobbish rhetorics and postures of liberal dignity. In fact, the relation between the self's dignity, on the one hand, and the self-lacerating, fetishistic fuel of resentment, on the other, is both paradoxical and insoluble. For when pushed into an abyss beyond all restitution, it is often the most upright, the most ritualistic and the most monastic self that seeks solace in the defacement and violation of things. Rhetorics of dignity, especially normative ones whose sources are steeped in religious law and liturgy—in classical theatres of mastery and epics of sovereignty even—always risk lapsing or bursting into scenes of resentment.[16] The fetish for retributive violence is merely a step away from this delirious implosion, which launches a stream of indignant brutality against one's own and oneself.

Resentment is both the self-lacerating relinquishment of self-knowledge—*judgement*—and the toxic effacement of self-interest. Sometimes, it is fuelled by an ascetic phenomenology: a sacrificial relinquishment of the self itself, any trace of self-knowledge now in free fall into the abyss of an elusive purity that this self can seek only in predatory violence against its own. This paradoxical bond between monastic disinterest and suicidal vengeance, both of which require an almost sacrificial concentration of the self into itself—to the extremity that the very border between self-sacrifice and sacrificing the other has blurred—I submit, is the second source of the *postcolonial* self, its movement locked in stasis by the caste contract and its identity lodged in a resentful fetishism of the other.[17]

Yet resentment gnaws not merely at the scaffolds of individualism but at the foundations of civilisation itself. It is a seething infiltration of majoritarian cowardice into politics. It is always, in its opening gambit, a quiet, distant, almost snobbish act, for resentment has no style, no speech, and no language of its own. It might even have an ascetic disinterest in—and disdain for—political freedom itself.

In Nathuram Godse's disfigured self, for instance, this *unwilling freedom*—the resistance to even celebrate the country's independence unequivocally—turns into a *loathing of freedom.* Lacking in language or even speech proper (that is, a speech that might seek to address the minor, the outnumbered and the poor), resentment implodes and metastasises into a monastic and monstrous gesture at once, feeding a stream of slow, silent violence against the minority and the poor. Under conditions of tyranny, this steady, seething stream explodes in a sacrificial delirium, initially simmering and then insinuating itself into the moral fabric of social inequality, which it then painfully exploits to 'make inequality hurt' (Shklar 1984, 87).

It is this *insinuation of inequality into freedom*—an insinuation that is always religious and never non-violent—that Ambedkar warns of in November 1949 in his fabled speech to the Constituent Assembly. The perils of having founded a republic without finding a society is that its morally detached majority, mesmerised by nothing more powerfully than it is with rituals of dignity, an anti-political snobbery even, might not even recognise its loss of freedom when it slides into tyranny the next time. And this slide will happen silently, indifferently and perjuriously, with the desire for authoritarianism stretching, or quietly enabled, across divisions of political and existential commitments. Our age, we are frequently told, is 'the age of anger'. The problem is that such expressions do not illuminate much. If anything, they merely deflect us from the archaeological work of excavating the bonds of complicity between liberal grandstanding and fascist competencies. The 'communal majority', as Ambedkar calls it in the 1940s, is a figure in this genealogy of authoritarian desire and fascist competence, underwritten by the theologico-juridical sources of the modern self. There is not a trace of democratic anger or judgement in it, just a calm calculus that scaffolds the majoritarian will to punish.

There is a very difficult, patient, grey distinction to be maintained, then, between anger and resentment based on their motivations and effects. The anger of a Bhimrao Ambedkar or a Frantz Fanon is militantly different from the calm, ascetic rage of a Nathuram Godse. A revolutionary's anger is easy to denounce. One thinks here of more than one Brahmin theorist conceding he finds Ambedkar 'difficult to teach' because of his anger, which ironically is Ambedkar's very point:

his is a *difficult freedom* precisely because it is easy to hunt it down and tough to love.

Revolutionary anger is, by its very nature, a speech act with its own linguistic inventory, theatrical presence and rhetorical flourish. Its *signature* is its passionate anguish. Its lucid disappointment cuts through the majority's counter-revolutionary stasis like a sententious scalpel. Like an architect's fearless pencil cruising through the void, this anger seeks to begin again, even if only to be disappointed again. Yet in radical disappointment, 'not everything is lost. Responsibility cannot be lost, it can only be abdicated,' Baldwin writes of this indefatigable, anti-ascetic politics in the 1979 novel *Just above My Head*, his last (2000, 420). 'If one refuses abdication, one begins again' (Glaude Jr. 2020, 23). 'The dream was repudiated: so be it' (Baldwin 2000, 420).

Majesties of Judgement

Ambedkar understood that in a social universe in which majoritarian impulses festered in utter disregard of constitutional sanctions and in utter excess of their electoral mandate, disappointment could not be left to become the antithesis of democratic participation. Instead, disappointment must be embraced as the disobedient soul of political citizenship, a political friendship even (which he called *maitri*, often leaving it untranslated in his English writings), mounted on a refusal of dejection. Disappointment, for Ambedkar, is not the exhaustion of democratic promise. Instead, precisely because it is so perennial, it becomes a durable scaffold of the democracy still to come. This indefatigable attachment to one's own deep disappointment—but let us note, *a disappointment without desolation*—requires a faculty, a lesson and a craft, above all, of political judgement.

Without this judgement, disappointment turns into mere dejection, the involution of collective defeat into resentments of oneself for one's own self alone. How deeply must the Hindu fanatic despise himself, one can ask in Ambedkar's wake, to be able to hate even those that he and his ilk so resoundingly outnumber? Given this numerical and unforgiving dominance, 'how fatal,' Ambedkar asks in his theory of the 'communal deadlock,' must it be to dissent against this fanatical majority, let alone 'destroy' it? (1978–2003, 1: 377). For our purposes here, the question is more archaeological. How does one appropriate a figure who embraces that very thing, political disappointment, that his enemies accuse him of? This question has been posed in the history of political thought only for the architects of the laws, who, the Greeks believed, must always come from outside the city and must not belong. The architect, by the very nature of the craft, by the very dint of his recalcitrant work with force and forces, must be inappropriable.

In political judgement at its most rigorous, most truthful, most upright and most democratic above all, on the other hand, to modulate Paul Ricoeur's expression, one institutes the capacity to look at oneself as wholly another (2014). And because this self is now wholly given to the other (not as empathy or appropriation but as the irreducibility of identity), the freedom of the self now becomes, before everything else, the freedom of others. It is a sort of 'reflexive individualism' without which no revolution in norms, no fraternity of citizens, no politics of friendship and, above all, no equality of freedom is possible. Perhaps, the bearer of this individualism is always the exile, the outsider stranger to oneself, a soul that is a sum of its force field: in sum, the architect. The body of the architect out of whose hands the spirit of the laws is born remains forever marked by its inappropriable gravity, a transcendent exteriority. Unlike the curves of the artifice to which his hands give shape, the lines of the architect's force remain invisible, unseen, untouchable even.

Stranger to his own afterlife, Ambedkar was always hesitant to see himself as the architect of the world's longest written national constitution, disappointed as he remained with its majoritarian subterfuge. Yet it is precisely the moral reserve of the architect in him that mandates that an archaeology of this resolutely constitutional disappointment be undertaken, that its radical solitude be saved from nationalist condescension, and that disappointment itself, with its indefatigable intensity for justice, be reinscribed at the heart of a fraternally bound constitutional commitment. For in this disappointment of the architect, who, despite his moral anger, never crosses the rigorous limit and line of political and judicial constitutionality, lies not an inconsolable rage—one that consumes the modern majority—but instead, a profound theory of democratic judgement at whose empty centre is always, for Ambedkar, the outnumbered minor facing the full might of 'police power' and violence of the law (1978–2003, 5: 283).[18]

The unforgettable warning Ambedkar issues in the Constituent Assembly in November 1949 as he presents the 'Motion on the Draft Constitution' centres on the 'peril' of this extraconstitutional, asymmetrical, and unforgiving violence. 'How long shall we continue to live this life of contradictions?' he asks the Assembly (1978–2003, 13: 1216):

> How long shall we continue to deny equality in our social and economic life? If we continue to deny it for long, we will do so only by putting our political democracy in peril. We must remove this

> contradiction at the earliest possible moment or else those who suffer from inequality will blow up the structure of political democracy which is Assembly has to laboriously built up.

Left to fester, this slow entrenchment of inequality and vengeance might unleash a new age of violence against violence, a nihilistic 'grammar of anarchy' (1978–2003, 13: 1215). To compound the tragedy singular to caste society, this lawlessness would be no less Brahminic, no less marked by delusions of purity, and no less constituted by disdain for life and the living, even though its footsoldiers would barely be Brahmins by birth anymore. They would come from all castes, lured by the suicidal logic and the sacrificial apparatus—*dispositif*—that is Brahminism. The only antidote to this Brahminic nihilism is a 'recognition of the principle of fraternity…a sense of common brotherhood…[a desire to imbue] solidarity to social life'. Ambedkar closes, 'it is a difficult thing', this fraternally shared freedom of equals (1978–2003, 13: 1217).

Republics often risk losing their freedom, or worse, simply fail to keep it, if they delude themselves into believing—or lie about their belief—that their constitutions will save them from tyranny. Constitutions do not save republics; they only begin it (and that too with violence).[19] The durability of democratic politics, in Ambedkar's 'judgement', had nothing to do with its hubristic claim to stability. Caste, after all, has always seemed most stable to the technicians of nationalist discipline and accountants of public sacrifice. But the political forms it gives rise to have not yet yielded a durable freedom. Stilted as its foundations are on the soft clay of a republic's collective lying, the seemingly stable but vehement caste contract, with all its sanctions and coercions, might give in sooner than we might think to the ultra-majority's barely repressed tyrannical dream.

'It is perfectly possible to pervert the Constitution,' he reminds the assembly of his peers, 'without changing its form by merely changing the form of the administration' (Ambedkar 2002, 484–485). What prevents this perversion is not the artifice of the law but the cultivation of constitutional morals. This requires patient work, for constitutional morality is 'not a natural sentiment' and, prophetically, he adds, 'our people have yet to learn it' (484–485). The work here is the not the sentimental task of simply *willing*; it is the rigorous craft of *judging*. What Ambedkar calls 'constitutional morality' is perhaps the democratic counterpart, the only durable moral scaffold, of political judgement. Both are proper to the citizen, he cautions, but neither is natural to him. Both must be cultivated, but neither can be fabricated.[20]

Judgement, as word and concept, appears close to two dozen times in Ambedkar's interventions throughout the long deliberations of India's Constituent Assembly. Yet it must perhaps be a sign of the profound constitutional gravity that he assigns this word—which is to say, the primacy of the power of judgement in constitutional democracy—that he uses it just once in his most focused, philosophical meditation on constitutional morality itself, placing his own self—'In my judgement,' he affirms—at the centre of it. It is a singular use of a word so singular in its power and yet so elusive in its intricacy that, interrupted by death, even Arendt (1992) left her path through Kant's third *Critique* (2000) unfinished.

In Ambedkar's theory and critique of judgement, the concept comes alive precisely because of the hostility that surrounds his personhood. In him, judgement comes to be marked by a thinker's singular solitude in the midst of a frequently hostile assembly of peers that was India's Constituent Assembly. For all that, however, let us note that the word is used in a radically impolitic and profoundly untimely—which is not to say, ill-judged—manner. Where others bask in the reflected republican glory of a new founding, using the constitution to gloss over their deceptions and silences, the architect sees fissures of violence and cracks of perjury in the foundation. What seems most stable to the wilful eye of the nationalist is for the architect not the most durable. Nothing dissolves majoritarian hubris and its insatiable appetite for appropriating everything for itself more powerfully than this demythologised truth about our constitutional fragility, perfected by a truth-teller who found himself, as if by will, roundly outnumbered and singularly inappropriable.

Seven years later, this devastating sense of feeling 'outnumbered' reappears in *The Buddha and His Dhamma*, where an anti-war Siddharth, reduced to minority among the tribal war hawks willing to kill their neighbours over water, leaves the assembly in disappointment, only to later become the Buddha. Ambedkar's declaration of radical antinomy, which can be read as 'I am *not a part* of the whole. [But] I am [still] *a part* [of the whole, if only] *apart* [from the whole]', restages for its time the inimitably succinct definition of the homeless, derelict proletariat of *The Communist Manifesto* (1978–2003, 10: 166). There, as Étienne Balibar points out, Marx, in an equally brutal truth statement, calls the proletariat 'a class that is not a class of society' (2017, 148). The visceral antinomy here lies in the subject body of a class that, by its very name, is produced by a society within itself for itself. Yet this lonely class on the edges of nothingness, or at the end of time (*antjya*), never becomes a constituent of the society's self-representation, let alone its self-determination. This, perhaps, is also the tragic antinomy—the sovereign void—that lies at the heart of Ambedkar's revolutionary constitutionalism, fuelled in the 1940s by his verdict against any form of parliamentary democracy that chooses self-determination (and self-presentation) over the radical equality of its shared freedom.

The one comment most widely attributed to Ambedkar, 'Gandhiji, I have no homeland', must itself be understood in this militant context: not as Ambedkar's expression of the self's insufferable alienation from country, but instead, the self's revolutionary embrace of emptiness, its civic and disobedient recusal from participating in the logic of the caste contract now burnished, even more coercively, by the glories by India's anticolonial triumph. This recusal involves for Ambedkar, at the same time, tracing the silhouettes of a future subject that is as yet empty—fitting of *The Communist Manifesto*, where Marx says similarly of the proletariat hemmed in by predatory nationalism, 'The working men have no country. We cannot take from them what they have not got' (Marx, 2002, 41). If there is one event in the postcolonial world that might have seared the fact of this homelessness of the minority, the poor, and the outcaste upon nationalist consciousness, it was the one that appeared on its horizon in the immediate aftermath of the most radical judgement Ambedkar had ever made: making public his will to conversion. Instead, what followed was an epistemic stasis, a long winter for political faith that was now quarantined behind secularist etiquette, upon which grew a republic's founding, malignant hostility not only to conversion but to interrogations of its secularist snobbery—its punishing will to make inequality hurt—as such.[21]

The Majoritarian Signature

A civilisational resentment towards conversion drives the wilful nationalist misreading of Ambedkar's conception of the religious, and thus, of the mythology of his turn towards it. This is ironic, given the fact that the structure of political justice within which Ambedkar posits the conditions for the annihilation of caste, 'the religious' is not a figure of outright hostility, even if for him all hostilities ensue fundamentally from the communal appetite for sacrifice that religious traditions nourish in them. The religious temptation is the most archaic site of the law and right, which also makes it an ineluctable presence in any modern attempt to theorise equality and, most inextricably of all, for Ambedkar, political responsibility.

'The moment it degenerates into rules it ceases to be Religion, as it kills responsibility, which is the essence of a truly religious act,' goes that incandescent formula in a pivotal passage of *Annihilation of Caste*.

'I have, therefore, no hesitation in saying that such a religion must be destroyed and I say, there is nothing irreligious in working for the destruction of such a religion… to remove the misrepresentation that is caused by misnaming this Law as Religion' (1944, 87–88). To be responsible for the law requires an architect to demythologise the law's punitive will, in other words, the will that hides behind the religious and takes its name. Religion is simply the willful 'misrepresentation'—or misnamed double—of the law. Together, they constitute the theologico-juridical will to punish.

To speak of the religious as an architecture for a revolutionary's moral and political responsibility, as Ambedkar does here, however, is not to reduce revolution to theology. Quite to the contrary, it is to exit the inheritance of the passive, indifferent wretchedness that religiosity, in its sly civility, bestows upon the citizen. It is to reject the most originary theological demand that rituals of authority and obedience make on citizens: that they must abdicate all responsibility in the name of ascetic disinterest. It is to accept, above all, that any idiom and concept of responsibility as such must grapple first with the contagious presence of the theologico-juridical impasse before it overcomes the obdurate power of its stasis. If *Annihilation of Caste* is a treatise on that exemplary structure of political faith that alone might make possible the destruction of caste, it is so only because it is also a manifesto on the architecture of—*how not to abdicate*—political responsibility, how not to lose faith in equality and how not to sleepwalk into tyranny.

The inverse of this responsibility is abdication with an ascetic masquerade: the self-alienating precondition of India's 'armed neutrality', a war India wages with and against itself in its vicious passivity (1978–2003, 1: 64). It is a war that does not simply refuse to host strangers but also produces and reproduces strangers in its very midst. It is a strife, in other words, whose brutal logjam—or 'deadlock'—is at once reproducible and mutant, different in what it yields (and the desolation it leaves behind) every single time. Caste society is not stagnant or timeless in any simple sense, contrary to Orientalist and liberal claims about it then. Caste is the theft of time itself. What I have called the 'caste contract' is the punitive, theologico-juridical structure that enables this mutation—the ineluctable morphing of self-determination into the majoritarian will to total domination—and renders majoritarian habits of moral and political cruelty unpunishable. Of this unforgiving contract, caste is neither simply a juridical home nor just a theological origin nor, above all, only a sacrificial limit. Instead, precisely because it is all three, caste is an exemplary figure in the originary, even universal logic of violence as such.

In that sense, the paradox of what Ambedkar frames as the 'Indian political' (1941), right in the subtitle of *Thoughts on Pakistan*, composed on the eve of the subcontinent's independence from colonial rule, is also its most classical: obdurate in its logic and banal in its evil. An entire system of laws, rituals, office and duty—dharma—is built upon the contract whose very purpose is to make caste disappear in plain sight, rendering it unspoken and unsayable. It is a system policed and reinforced by a complex nexus of sacrificial obligations, disciplinary sanctions, and punitive limits (*maryada*), whose very use is to quarantine the human from the worldly, which is to say, sequester force from the collective pulse and impulse of the political itself.

One cannot comprehend the coercive, vehement stability of the caste contract unless one grasps, with Ambedkar, this dynamic—or vacillating—nexus between theology and government, between asceticism and disdain, one that reproduces itself through technologies of denial. That is, it lives on by denying that it exists at all, either as theology or as government. Dharma, one might still be told with a straight face by those who love to deface Ambedkar, is neither this nor that (*neti neti*). This is why caste can be wholly archaic in its juridical structure and wholly modern in its conceptual jargon for in its structure and its reproducibility—its *historicity*, if you will—it resembles both a machine and a mutant. Ancient as a technique of rule, it can mutate seamlessly into the art of modern government as its classical economy of sacrifice pivots around republican virtuosity and its debts—incurred by simply being born—are paid in deliriums of masculine duty. Caste does not exist, neither as racial apartheid nor, as Ambedkar puts it, as a settler colonial regime of 'barbed wire' (1978–2003, 1: 68). Caste is a 'notion', the *wholly other of segregation*, a bottomless relation of absolute wrong that leaves no footprints on the ground.

Perhaps, beneath its irrepressible rhythm as a democratic manifesto on freedom or as a radiant call to revolutionary intelligence, *Annihilation of Caste* is most fundamentally a treatise on the moral psychology of the modern majoritarian signature itself, a patient deconstruction of what Ambedkar insistently calls, including at a decisive moment in his discussion of stasis and war, the 'wrong'. Two threads are woven around his archaeology of the wrong. The first is that which he calls the 'wrong relationship', which takes the phenomenology of everyday 'indifference' and 'insult' and turns them into habits of moral cruelty with legal sanction—or judicial disdain—behind them (1978–2003, 1: 55). This relation of exhaustive—and inexhaustible—wrongs, by its very name, compresses an endless strife between the self and the other. Caste is also a war of the self; being of a caste—let alone outcaste—is being at war with oneself. For at its source is the law of individual and generational time, one that keeps clamped in place the blood-bound logic of social reproduction, succession and inheritance.

The second is that which Ambedkar calls the wrong 'worse than cruelty' (1978–2003, 1: 54), at whose heart is the invisible, almost mystical foundation of authority, its cruelties and meanness, its misanthropy and snobbery, all made permissible by the moving centres and porous borders of the theologico-juridical apparatus. The 'worse' here, for Ambedkar, is not the extreme violence of the wrong; it is its cruelty rendered *unpunishable*. In fact, cruelty can exist and recur only in some relation to the law, the norm even, even if this relation is in itself lawless and devoid of any purpose or *telos*. This apparatus, freed from moral constraint and temporal measure, extracts a price (or simply blood) either in the form of property, pain, restitution, or sacrifice. Ambedkar's formidable recuperation of the notion of what Marx calls the 'absolute wrong' takes us back again, as Étienne Balibar reminds us, to the 'messianic moment in Marx' (2017, 146), a constellation around the 'wrong' to which Hegel too belongs.[22]

Whatever its time, the injustice of and, most ineradicably, the injustice in caste is a wreckage of the human form beyond salvage. Caste can never be made just. Stronger still, there is no justice in any theory or promise of politics worthy of its name that privileges caste for its stability (which it purportedly lends). This is so not because caste is an irreducibly religious form with excessive political effects—such a malaise is constitutive of modernity at large—but because there is not a trace of truth around it, there can be no place for truth in it, nobody speaks the truth about it, and above all, it shall never yield to the gravity of truth without ceasing to be. Caste is the sovereign mode of being in denial about the basis of the world itself. 'Like a weed on the surface of a pond,' a twenty-five-year-old Ambedkar writes as early as 1916, 'it just hangs there to this day without support' (1978–2003, 1: 19–20). To annihilate caste then is to rethink gravity, to reclaim earth from its wretchedness, and to reposit not merely the human but force itself. Perhaps, the first post-caste subject will be an empty subject, a bearer of finitude who, like an architect, has touched the void (*sunnyata*).

Caste need not always be indicted for India's murderous consent, defenders of civilisational virtue say. Majoritarian indifference of such subcontinental scale cannot be blamed on caste alone either, they add. Above all, the causes of this stoic malaise, this mass of humanity unmoved by its own self-lacerating cruelty, can never be directly traced back to caste (*nothing can ever directly be traced back to caste*, which is its very point). Yet for all the claims of civilisational good faith, the truth is that the majority's electoral indifference—*the refusal of the majority to vote the vandal out of power*—resembles a rehearsed, reiterative, recursive and habitual disdain towards inequality and the unequal, fuelled by a silent enchantment with extreme power and a desolate love of tyranny that can have grown only in the monstrous excess of the caste contract. Caste requires a contract, a consent by subjection, not because it is violence by ordinary means for common ends but because it is a primordial, originary and cruel wrong. Its violence involves not blood sacrifice but moral cruelty, the infiltration of barbarity into non-violence itself. This, in fact, is Ambedkar's moral challenge (and his ethical demand): to salvage freedom for a swathe of humanity—the largest democracy in the Global South—where the majority has not only blurred, systematically and through recursive practice, the line between non-violence and vengeance but also uses one for the other.

If there is, in liberal democracy, a *majoritarian signature*, that is, the shape that a people's democratic mentality acquires in practical situations and that underwrites and gives form to its social contract, then caste is its unmoving stylistic scaffold, one that resembles, in all its normative features, the modern contract itself. I draw and modulate the expression, most obviously, from the works of Charles Mills (1999) and Carole Pateman (1988). I do so not only because caste shares devastating adjacencies with racism, with an equally voracious appetite for inequality rooted in communal misogyny, but also because the caste contract, insofar as its consent is anchored in violence before time, cannot flourish without a misogynistic control of reproductive rights and bodies. It is not coincidence either that the logic of the death penalty—the systemic, unforgiving use of the law for vengeance—is as fundamental to the caste contract (and to the constitutional tradition founded upon it) as it was to the system of Atlantic slavery (and the jurisprudence of American neglect that grew out of it).

What secures a majority's consent to such regimes for the use and abuse of bodies so that it acquires the normative shape of a contract? In the constellation of theorists grappling with this problem, Judith Shklar is among the rarest in the Euro-American liberal tradition to explicitly use 'Indo-European caste society'—at times, she substitutes it with an even more sacrificial term 'warrior society'—as a symptomatic expression of the continued tolerance of cruelty among urbane liberals who excuse its viciousness in the name of cultural particularity. 'To the extent that the European past is utterly hostile to freedom and that the most ancient of Indo-European traditions is the caste society, liberals must reject particular traditions,' Shklar writes in 'The Liberalism of Fear' (1989, 25–26). 'No society that still has traces of the old tripartite division of humanity into those who pray, those who fight, and those who labor can be liberal.'

By way of a beginning to supplement and complete Shklar's powerful critique of fear, let us simply note that India, whether or not it calls itself liberal, has more than just a systemic trace of caste in it. Caste is what gives political cruelty in India—but not only in India—both a morally palatable aesthetic and a tactically deployable form, making violence against life look like monastic disinterest and turning ascetic selflessness towards the world into a licentiousness to make inequality hurt. Its web of consent and indifference makes active, unapologetic neglect of the living and the alive—the still breathing—look like mere disenchantment from the world. Not political enmity, then, but the majority's obtuse viciousness and its civil, cultivated withdrawal from the politics of life—and species—underwrites the logic of its compulsive, hostile cruelty.

Afterlife

'Who were the Shudras?' Ambedkar asks in his most archaeological work of the same name (1946), as he finally begins to draw, in the final decade of his life, the silhouette of his philosophical method. He had set out this time not simply to excavate the remnants of India's deep history of inhumanity, which had not gone missing anywhere anyway. Having survived for centuries in the obdurate laws and unforgiving practices of social untouchability, its tentacles spread across entire lifespans of political regimes and legal systems. In New York, in his youth, he had examined its surfaces, its deceptive fluidity that hid an epochal stasis, its stillness free from the laws of moral gravity like 'weed on the surface of a pond' (1978–2003, 1: 19–20). Now, three decades later, he had decided it was time to disinter the subterranean and labyrinthine textual underwire of India's most ordinary vices and indifference to human life that it yielded. It was time to painstakingly examine the grammatical structure and lyrical verse of that exemplary moral wrong, that originary act of perjury, in other words, one in which a vicious, silent disdain had come to hold together and legitimise a civilisational fable of epic virtuosity, ascetic disinterest and self-righteous non-violence.

The task was as intensely literary as it was philosophical. Ambedkar recognised that the questions raised by the structure of this enduring moral cruelty—the making lawful of lawlessness through quiet, repetitive disparagement of those born unequal and a pernicious, oblivious disregard of that which is visibly human—were so stark and dark that no single gesture, no *law of genre*, might alone be adequate to its ask. How could an anti-imperial humanism so righteous as India's continue to sit so imperiously on the history of its own dogmatic and inhumane barbarism? What sort of a human, let alone *political*, subject might such a morally inert and cruel humanism eventually yield? What would really become of and come after the anti-colonial subject? For a society so enamoured by rituals of power (and its priests) that a majority in it was willing to live on in desolate powerlessness and voluntary servitude without end, if only in wait for its own merciless chance at domination, how long would it really take for this majority to turn against itself and fabricate enemies from among its own once an alien colonial power had vacated its shores?

Following Engels, Ambedkar frames in *Revolution and Counter-Revolution in Ancient India*—the title of his manuscript itself a tribute to Engels' *Revolution and Counter-Revolution in Germany* (1851–1855)—this suicidal play between power and powerlessness, desire and disinterest, as a fatal struggle between forces of revolution and counter-revolution in which hermeneutics has always played a decisive, if surreptitious, role. The counter-revolution, Ambedkar warns in 'Krishna and His Gita', is never simply a sacrificial war (1978–2003, 3: 357–380). It is the silent, seething stasis of interpretations at war, one in which texts and monuments are brought alive, if only to be ruined; it is the 'legislation of fratricide', a jurisprudence through which the living are reduced, by pure violence, to things (Kumar 2010).

This play has been staged relentlessly in different guises since Indian antiquity. It is not a timeless essence, this Indian thing with cruelty in it, Ambedkar is careful to posit. Rather, it is a structure, an apparatus or *dispositif*, a shape-shifting contract between the ruler and the ruled in which they might even deceptively exchange places. *Varnadharma*—the punitive regime of caste life bound by religious sanction—is not incidental but fundamental to this theatre of contractual cruelty, even if the liturgical drama between Brahmin power and Kshatriya counter-power has often given this brute stasis an opulent masquerade. Beginning with the earliest fratricidal strife of statecraft and their textual traces (of which the Gita is one poetic testimony), the Indian notion of the human—deficient as it is—has been inextricable from the subcontinent's elaborately codified 'caste contract', even and especially when the truth of this contract is obscured in a mire of untranslatable terms.[23]

The deconstruction of this seemingly bloodless, obstinately contractual paradox requires a forensic commitment, a work of legal and scriptural 'paleontology' (1978–2003, 7: 244). On the one hand, the bones of species left extinct by the sheer weight of India's urbane, smug forgetfulness, their cries of survival drowned in the breathless chanting of Brahminic liturgy (now backed even more ferociously by the apparatus of judicial disregard for right and life), need to be strung together again. On the other hand, the spine of a classical archive—statutes spread physically across a subcontinent, threaded through thousands of texts, a million verses and uncountable myths of unforgiving punishment, trans-generational rage, and petty jealousies that saturate its epics—must be audaciously broken to recover a breathing, unbroken humanity again. This is a work not simply of history, Ambedkar insists, but of moral and political 'archaeology', and *The Untouchables* is, he declares in a dazzling moment that returns to the constitutive relation between aesthetic and political judgement—*aesthetic judgement as political judgement*—a 'work of art' (1978–2003, 7: 244).

History cannot always tell us why or when a society might be tempted to suicidally jump into the abhorrent depths of hatred that it has slyly concealed for so long, even if it has never ceased digging itself into this abyss. History cannot always tell us how to decipher the code of this compulsive, collective brutalism when its moment has finally arrived, its nihilistic script made unmistakably legible to even those who had hoped their walls, built on delusional islands of snobbery and guarded by mythological banisters of civility, would be too high for the zealots to scale. Indeed, liberal purveyors of India's nationalist history have always told its people otherwise: zealots shall never manage to scale the walls and domes of our faith because *their* religion will not allow them to, for *their* religion is a religion of non-violence. Until they do climb the walls in the very name of *their* religion, crawling to the top of the dome—metaphorically and literally—with sickles and sticks in a slow and genocidal preparation.

This crude, blunt and archaic slowness is the very essence of majoritarian misanthropy. Often, the suicidal temptation to destroy everything that has life in it appears on the modern political horizon slowly and grindingly, hesitatingly even. It appears not always in a homicidal burst of spectacular violence, although such delirium has always lurked in the corners of the oldest Indic verses. It is instead filtered through a millennium of ritualised, practised neglect of the vulnerable, the outcast, the minor, the missing, the undercounted and the unreported. The bearer of this seething, destructive suicide is not a mass of devout fanatics but the completely withdrawn individual whose time passes with only himself, his own self. In that sense, the system of belief that undergirds the silent, 'communal majority'—with its unwavering will to punish—as Ambedkar extracts this figure, is only theological liberalism without the normative pretense; it is civilisational liturgy without moral value or political faith. It is at once government and indiscipline, at once lawlessness and technocracy. When did lawlessness become the law? 'Why is lawlessness lawful?' Ambedkar, the archaeologist, asks of the juridical archive, staring into the future of a civilisation's scriptural past even as he reads its verses painstakingly (1978–2003, 5, 62–74). He sees a future when the very border between persons and things, the living and the non-living, might be blurred in the very shadow of that intricate theologico-juridical tradition.

Denials of Persons and Things

This violence is slow, curated in neglect. Hatred does not lay monuments and cities to ruin overnight; it gnaws and digs into the self-righteous foundations of belief slowly, pulverising it into a decrepit submission under a fanaticism of all against all. Walls of urbane civility are mere banisters in front of the fanatical zeal that now speaks in the tongue of collective, sacrificial monasticism, in tones of a punishing vegetarianism even.

It is not a coincidence that the sacred figure of the cow appears in the most decisive passage of Nathuram Godse's confessional text on his assassination of Gandhi, its author furious at Gandhi's obstinate refusal to support a legislative ban on 'cow slaughter', even though, Godse seethes, 'Gandhiji could display the most vehement desire for the protection of the cow' (Godse 1993, 75). Symptomatically, the ferocity of this punitive, zoophilic Brahminism is unleashed not by Gandhi's refusal to privilege cattle over the Muslim, but instead, because the latter had also dared to see the animal and the neighbour as equals.

This strange bond between Brahminism and satyagraha is forged around their shared trouble with equality, but it comes to be decidedly tied around the artifice of dignity that both attach to vegetarianism, if only in varying degrees of dogmatic vehemence. This shared obsession with the animal—or beast—has always been a battle of perversity against perversity, a war between two visions of right and renunciation, centred unforgivingly on the self and its voluntary abstinences and desires (or the pathology of self-interest that posits itself as disinterest). In both Brahminism and satyagraha, this abstinent, celibate vehemence resolves itself (but) differently, incommensurably even. Brahminism deploys the semantic rage of popular sovereignty, satyagraha expresses a poetic disinterest in sovereign power. Yet the violent circuit of the dogma passes in both, *separately*, through a sacrificial indifference towards life that stains the democratic mentality indelibly. In a caste society where claims of dignity are indissociable from archaic rituals of power and resentment, as Ambedkar writes in a passage of diagnostic brilliance unparalleled in global democratic thought (1978–2003, 1:377), it turns a political mass into a 'communal majority' that simply will not accept disappointment as an inevitable fact of the common life.

This perversion is not new, even if the bloodshot vision fuelling Godse's testimony crystallises it with unprecedented clarity. If anything, this counter-revolutionary refusal to begin again, the refusal to let go of the belief that the majority must never be disappointed, stains the majority's communal sense of self at its inception. Its life-taking codes of honour were written at the very beginning of time in the purest language known to man, mounted on a grammar that was indissociable from the theory of dignity in the monarchical and monastic traditions alike. There is something truly archaic about that moment when modern, bourgeois civility meets classically learned orthodoxy, which is what Ambedkar might have meant by the term *counter-revolution*.

The emergence of nationalism in the late 19th century in Bombay and the Punjab, its surge fanned by rhetorics of cow protection, were loaded with this counter-revolutionary learnedness. Only now, it was made headier and legitimised by the emerging anti-colonial rhetoric of *swaraj*. Its most debilitating effect was that such a rhetoric simply left unquestioned—and eventually, rendered impenetrable—the developing bond between classical compulsions of Brahminic non-violence and modern spaces and political theories for majoritarian vengeance. To read the signs of this timeless compulsion demands not just Sanskrit—Ambedkar's formidable work on a Pali dictionary of the Ashokan universe was not incidental—but a politics of radical anti-amnesia.

This politics of radical anti-amnesia is what Ambedkar calls 'paleontology'. Its craft entails not just a recovery of ruins lost and forgotten but also a probing, painstaking work on the *structure* of forgetting. The subject here is not the 'fraction' that is forgotten but the 'millions' who are enablers of this amnesia. To a paleontologist, it is not simply that which is classical, dated and archaic that must be resuscitated. It is also that which is recent, modern, new even, but which insinuates itself into antiquity as if it always belonged there. Amnesia, after all, is not simply a forgetfulness of facts. It is also making classical, even quasi-transcendental, that which is manufactured, fabricated and mired in interest but pretends otherwise. Just as the moral stability of political foundations, especially constitutional foundations, needs an architect's refusal to yield to power, radical anti-amnesia requires the refusal of an archaeologist to let felony masquerade as civilisation as its cruelty slides into oblivion. It demands, above all, as Ambedkar publicly declares in 1925, a will to mastery (of texts) again. 'We should either burn down these scriptures and *turn them to ashes*,' he proposes, '*or master them* and falsify the rules that teach untouchability' (Kumar

2018, 174). There is no annihilation without some faith in it, then, and no political faith without the will to annihilation in it.

Yet, so understated is this anti-caste rigour (anti-caste truth as philosophical archaeology) in contemporary political thought that it must be posited, again and again, not only as the irrefutable principle of modern democratic life but also as the axiomatic theorem of political philosophy as such.[24] Why is this philosophical move so important for Ambedkar (and for us, in his wake)? The reason is that while philosophy, he writes, pursues truth, somewhere down the line, it *forgets* how to love truth. This forgetting of the love of truth, which might have been the foundation of *justice* or *maitri*, and the institution in its place of punitive fear as the logic of rule is the soul of the Brahminic 'counter-revolution' of classical India and of its epistemic regime. The sophistication of the counter-revolutionary discipline(s) paradoxically means that the desire to bring truth back to political thought would itself require a series of *philosophical* gestures, of which the *anti-caste gesture* would form the 'revolutionary' heart. There is, for Ambedkar, no way to bring philosophy back to truth (and truth back to philosophy) other than by patiently, meticulously, rigorously destroying the textual *dispositif* of caste. For it is here, in philosophical silence—in the theologies of the *unsayable*—that the perjury of a civilisation thrives. Does the deferral of this epistemological demand lie at the foundations of the Indian 'evasion' of political philosophy?[25]

The converse is thus equally true. Anti-caste philosophy must be an act of philosophical anti-amnesia. There is a reason why Ambedkar was always willing to forgive but never quick to forget. Let us think, quickly, of the Poona Pact of September 1932, for instance, where he surrenders his political conviction to Gandhi's sacrificial theatre. That moral tragedy—and farce—of the pact he recounts throughout the 1940s in a string of works. For to forget that betrayal of justice would be an unforgivable treachery against history itself. On the other hand, to not forgive a 'saint' would simply amount to replicating the structure of caste sacrifice and its history of retributive violence. That is the aporia of the figure of the architect: it knows how to forgive but it cannot afford to forget. It yields to gravity but cannot yield to amnesia.

The Sovereign Void

No metaphor or *figure* has marked Ambedkar's itinerary as a thinker with greater force than that of the 'architect'. While inadequate to the gravity of his constitutional vision, this figural attribution is not wholly unjust in its own right. At least in Roman political thought (a tradition that in Ambedkar's own oeuvre is brought to intersect radically with Buddhist epistemology), the inventiveness of the constitutionalist has often been strongly identified with the exactitude of the architect. Both exemplify the precision of a dexterous craftsman: the constitutionalist imagines the power of laws without precedent just as the architect visualises lines of force in the emptiness of space. Both see contours that are invisible to the ordinary citizen in the sometimes thin, often dense, and almost always abrasive air of gravitational fields and social strife. Both work in the radical emptiness of the void, beginning with nothing other than force at its very inception.

Among all sorts of craftsmen, ancient and modern, why is it that the architect has come so squarely to belong to politics, so frequently invoked in the history of political thought, in a manner that another craftsman who works as routinely and as intricately with force—engineer, electrician, metallurgist, mathematician, surgeon—is simply not? What makes architecture yield to politics? And what pushes politics to yield to the figure of the architect? Of Ambedkar, the constitutional theorist and moral thinker par excellence, one who has come to be sovereign among all the architects of the Southern constitutional tradition that appeared on the global horizon in the decades after decolonisation in Asia and Africa, this much can be said even more forcefully: Ambedkar does not simply inhabit this classical fable of jurisprudence. He redraws its silhouette. He does not simply burnish the laws of state. He burns them with an infinite passion for the possible.

Perhaps Ambedkar is, if he is an architect at all, a thinker less interested in the strictures of history (or the illuminations of theology) than he is in the transcendent gravity of democratic truth. For Ambedkar, this gravity—which is a force so minor, so impenetrable, and yet so insurmountable that it is a perfect example of nonforce—comes from the courage of those truth-tellers who see in it (and know that truth always carries) the seeds of a transcendent, even luminous, disappointment. What is an architect if not this figure who works with the gravity of truth in the face of its very disappointment? For disappointment—even 'repudiation,' pace Baldwin—there will be. As Judith Shklar cautions, 'Because political hypocrisy is part of the rhetoric of legitimization and of the politics of persuasion, there is an uneasy fear of fraud and dissimulation in liberal democracies' (1984, 75). This explains why 'democracy generates disappointment, and a sense of being deceived' (75).

On the one hand, there is the more visible, more palpable affliction on the surface of this disappointment that Amebdkar bore on his skin: the exhaustion of India's fabled commitment to liberal and secular values, which has involved a calculated, steady destruction of political faith and the destruction of faith in politics—a 'love of truth'—itself. The covenant of self-determination that bound a people together in a simple act of trust after its struggle against the empire, the constitutional belief that the majority will always truthfully decide what is best for the liberty of all, seems to have been stretched to its depoliticising, brutal seams. On the other hand, there is the more oblique, more tacit and more urbane pathology that drives India's megacity brutalism: a wilful denialism and cultivated indifference towards social inequality and material dispossession in cities and farm country alike (of which the stasis between insurgent farmer protests and despondent farmer suicides is but one symptom). A denialism—*moral cruelty*—has reduced people to things through systemic and legalised neglect, rendering any talk, let alone any collective vision, of moral life subject to scornful scepticism, resentful cynicism, and nihilism even, so that truth and truthfulness themselves have lost their gravity. If Ambedkar's vision for the future seems fragile today, it is at this point: time has wilted his hope in the city as a place of refuge.

My question to begin with was quite simple. What is an architect, if Ambedkar is one at all? And what is it not? Firstly, in the most obvious sense, we can now say, the architect is a *figure*: a node in a series of lines of force, a silhouette artist, and a cultivator of force fields. The architect is one who thinks with his hands and gives himself freely to dexterous imagination. He pulls lines out of space not to give them determinate or even material shape but to push the very limit of matter to the extremities of their tensile—or what might become, during construction, volatile—potentiality. The architect embraces the void, the nothing. He touches emptiness at its extreme limit. Nothing the architect thinks does not run through this limit, line or border. This border is not only of land, however; it extends to the sea. Above all, it belongs to air, where nothing yet exists and where a vertical creation by sheer imagination awaits. A part of earth torn apart from itself will soon rise there, always a part apart, to make place for a more just space.

Secondly, the architect is not a foundationalist. Instead, he is resolutely anti-foundational, a craftsman who begins without prior ground. He neither inaugurates structures nor celebrates—or memorialises—the foundation. Instead, he looks for breaches and possibilities of potential fissures and cracks. He understands that sometimes in greatest impotentiality, behind the most stubborn walls of invisibility and disinterested withdrawal from the world, lie the highest, most intense or, as Ambedkar puts it, most 'obdurate, merciless logic [and laws] of force' (Ambedkar 1917, 21). The architect shares something of a relationship with the science and law of time, then, in a manner a prophet might: they both stand at the edge of groundlessness; at the limit of what is given (or possible); the cusp of giving what has never been received (or imagined). 'The great defect in the policy of least resistance and silent infiltration of rational ideas,' Ambedkar posits in *What Congress and Gandhi Have Done to the Untouchables?* (1945), 'lies in this: that they do not compel thought, for they do not produce crisis' (1978–2003, 9: 136).

The task of the architect is to live not only with the perennial imminence of crisis but also in intimacy with its disappointment, insofar as so much of crisis might simply be a repetition of unrepaired, festering wounds rather an opening for newness. The architect might even have to invent (something out of) crisis, or sometimes, imagine crisis into existence—even if as a groundless premonition of it—to make the law more morally durable against social assault. In the figure of the architect, an *anarchy of the new*, a vision of that which comes *before the law*, a judgement of that which exceeds the law—justice—intersects with the archaeologist's obsession with longevity and fascination with endurance.

Thirdly, the architect—a fabricator of the unprecedented, his artifice of hope mounted on the groundless and the nothing (*sunnya*)—sees absolute freedom in his own judgement and cultivates the ability to trust it (in a manner the foundationalist simply cannot). It is not that Nehru, possibly Ambedkar's most powerful peer, for example, did not make judgements. But, in him, there was less freedom, less contingency, less risk, more planning, more certainty, and, not by chance, more civilisation. Rivers are to Nehru what electricity is to Lenin. For all his precision, the architect understands the limits of 'mathematical exactitude', for he understands that not counting but morals—a *moral jurisprudence that rejects vengeance*—alone might sometimes save the teeming millions from being reduced to barely alive fractions. This faith in the law, even as he must transgress it, gives the architect both a radical amphibiousness, a felicity with the fluidity of materials and, conversely, a facility with the materiality of fluids. The architect is no less a philosopher of touch than he is a figure in its history.

Above all, the architect is a democrat, one who, when he draws, inhabits the lines of force in the very abyss—Ambedkar says 'dungeon'—of his own nonforce, his own 'unpower' (*aasakti*), committed to his own faithful surrender to its principle. He is one who understands that force, in the final instance, must remain inappropriable and belong not to power but to those wronged by it. In the architect, there is this enigmatic movement between force and non-force, between logic and the *dispositif*, between absolute weakness and soaring majesty, mastery even. The architect, above all, works close to the earth in only his own company, in a solitude whose gravity we are still to comprehend. His sense of self is scarred less by fears of democratic crises, which he prophetically anticipates, than it is by the majoritarian lust for stability.

For Ambedkar, the earth holds a lesson for politics as such. What seems constitutionally stable to our limited vision is not always, in truth, the most morally durable. What seems fecund with mortal life might instead hold the immortal remains of an extinct species, a history of violence done to life and buried in amnesia. The architect is driven not by *disenchantment* from earthly rules and constraints of the building laws; he is simply driven by the will to *demythologisation*.

'Nations reel and stagger on their way; they make hideous mistakes; they commit frightful wrongs; they do great and beautiful things,' Du Bois writes in his chapter on 'The Propaganda of History' in *Black Reconstruction in America* (1935), published just a year before *Annihilation of Caste*. He asks in a tone unhopeful if not entirely hopeless, 'Shall we not best guide humanity by telling the truth about all this, so far as the truth is ascertainable?' (Du Bois 2017, 638). For Ambedkar, the trouble with majoritarian hideousness is not that it will, with any degree of certainty, come undone in the future but that it has already wrecked the beauty of the past and left its memory to fester, attended only by a curated indifference. The counter-revolution might be ancient, but its denials are eternal. Its afterlife might endure well into all the future pasts that are still to come, its pervasive history of lying bound inextricably even to the most innocuous structures of common words and ordinary language. What would otherwise cause the modern caste subject to so frequently affirm, for example, 'I do not practise caste?' Or as someone like Baldwin might say of the white citizen's equally frequent protestations that are couched in another iteration of the same denial and amnesia, 'I am not a racist!'

It is this insight about civilisational denialism—from which follow a litany of civilisational felonies—that compels the architect to take his own work of founding seriously. It is the same insight that also compels him to patiently dismantle, with indomitable scepticism, the hubristic myths of that very founding. These two acts—of a demythologising architecture and a defiant archaeology—are, on the surface, incommensurable. And yet, in Ambedkar's theory of democratic judgement, the passage of one ineluctably runs through the other. Only the architect knows that he has not simply sketched his lines over the depravity of the foundation's violent, forgotten scaffold; he has also touched its empty, vindictive centre, its sovereign void. It is a void to which he alone might bring back, even at the risk of disappointment, a moral gravity—truthfulness—worthy of democracy. The architect must pardon the vengeance of even the most unforgivable crime, but he must never forget the punitive logic of foundation that has haunted it since the point of its inception. In that sense, the law is always violent, its effects often disappointing. And the lawgiver is but a ‚ghost,' a real test of our democratic will and of our 'force,' a young Ambedkar writes of Manu in 'Castes in India' (1978–2003, 1: 16).

This, then, is Ambedkar's aporia, lodged, as Derrida (2023) might say, between the perjury of his countrymen and the pardon that he must grant them, which Ambedkar does, if only through his sovereign, undefeated exit we call 'conversion'. This majesty is also what lights his fraught passage through self-knowledge. It is a knowledge of the self and its emptiness, a reckoning with the violent foundations of one's own craft and work with force that are not easy to bear, and they yield a very difficult freedom. What is justice if not this very yielding of freedom from the throes of inconsolable disappointment? What is force if not this solitary adventure into gravity and grace, one that the indefatigable architect alone can ever undertake?

References

Primary References

Ambedkar, Bhimrao Ramji. 1978. 'Castes in India: Their Genesis, Mechanism, and Development'. In *Dr. Babasaheb Ambedkar: Writings and Speeches* Vol. 1, 5–22. Bombay: Education Department, Government of Maharashtra. First published 1917.

———. 1978. 'Annihilation of Caste: With a Reply to Mahatma Gandhi'. In *Dr. Babasaheb Ambedkar: Writings and Speeches*. Vol. 1, 23–96. Bombay: Education Department, Government of Maharashtra. First published 1936.

———. 1941. *Thoughts on Pakistan*. Bombay: Thacker & Co.

———. 1946. *Who Were the Shudras? How They Came to Be the Fourth Varna of Indo-Aryan Society*. Bombay: Thacker & Co.

———. 1948. *The Untouchables: Who Were They and Why They Became Untouchables?* New Delhi: Amrit Book Co.

———. 1968. *Annihilation of Caste: Speech Prepared for the 1936 Annual Conference of the Jat Pat Todak Mandal of Lahore but Not Delivered*, 3rd ed. (1944). Jalandhar: Bheem Patrika Publications.

———. 1977. *What Congress and Gandhi Have Done to the Untouchables* (1945). Lahore: Classic.

———. 1978–2003. *Dr. Babasaheb Ambedkar: Writings and Speeches*. 24 Volumes. Bombay: Education Department, Government of Maharashtra.

———. 2002. 'Motion on the Draft Constitution' (1948). In *The Essential Writings of B.R. Ambedkar*, edited by Valerian Rodrigues. Delhi: Oxford University Press.

Arendt, Hannah. 1963. *On Revolution*. New York: Viking Press.

———. 1958. *The Human Condition*. Chicago, IL: University of Chicago Press.

———. 1992. *Lectures on Kant's Political Philosophy*. Edited by Ronal Beiner. Chicago, IL: University of Chicago Press.

———. 2005. *The Promise of Politics*. New York: Schocken.

Baldwin, James. 2010. *The Cross of Redemption: Uncollected Writings*. Edited by Randall Kenan. New York: Vintage.

———. 2000. *Just above My Head: A Novel*. New York: Random House, First published 1979.

Du Bois, W.E.B. 2015. *The Souls of the Black Folk*. New Haven and London: Yale University Press. First published 1903.

———. 2017. *Black Reconstruction in America*. London and New York: Routledge. First published 1935.

Fanon, Frantz. 2004. *The Wretched of the Earth*. Translated by Richard Philcox. New York: Grove. First published 1961.

Gandhi, Mohandas Karamchand. 1999. *Collected Works of Mahatma Gandhi*. 100 Volumes. New Delhi: Publications Division, Government of India.

Godse, Nathuram. 1993. *Why I Assassinated Gandhi? And the Events, the Accused, and the Epilogue by Gopal Godse*. New Delhi: Surya Bharati Prakashan.

Kant, Immanuel. 2000. *Critique of the Power of Judgement*. Translated and edited by Paul Guyer. Cambridge: Cambridge University Press. First published 1973.

Lenin, V.I. 1920. 'Our Foreign and Domestic Position and Party Tasks.' Speech Delivered to the Moscow Gubernia Conference of the R.C.P. (B.), 21 November. https://www.marxists.org/archive/lenin/works/1920/nov/21.htm.

Marx, Karl. 2002. *The Communist Manifesto*. London and New York: Penguin. First published 1872.

———. 2009. *A Contribution to the Critique of Hegel's Philosophy of Right*. Translated and edited by Joseph O'Malley and Annette Jolin. Cambridge: Cambridge University Press. First published 1844.

Mill, John Stuart. 2003. *On Liberty*. Edited by David Bromwich and George Kateb. London and New Haven: Yale University Press. First published 1859.

Nehru, Jawaharlal. 1956. 'Obituary Reference.' In *Parliamentary Debates*, Vol. 10C, 1769–1770. New Delhi: Government of India. Reprinted in *Dr. Babasaheb Ambedkar: Writings and Speeches* Vol. 15, 974. Bombay: Education Department, Govt. of Maharashtra.

Nietzsche, Friedrich. 2019. 'Skirmishes of an Untimely Man.' In *Twilight of the Idols*, edited by Friedrich Nietzsche and Thomas Common. Mineola, NY: Dover Publications, Inc. First published 1888.

Rajagopalachari, C. 1946. *Ambedkar Refuted*. Bombay: Hind Kitabs.

———. 'A Restless Spirit Has Found Peace: Rajaji's Tribute.' *Indian Express*, 7 December 1956.

Tocqueville, Alexis de. 2000. *Democracy in America*. Edited and translated by Harvey C. Mansfield and Delba Winthrop. Chicago, IL: University of Chicago Press. First published 1835/40.

Weil, Simone. 1952. *Gravity and Grace*. Translated by E. Craufurd. London: Routledge. First published 1947.

———. 2003. The Iliad *or the Poem of Force*. Translated and edited by James P. Holoka. New York: Peter Lang. First published 1940.

Secondary References

Balibar, Étienne. 2017. *Citizen-Subject: Foundations for Philosophical Anthropology*. Translated by Steven Miller. New York: Fordham University Press.

Benjamin, Walter. 1996. 'Critique of Violence.' In *Selected Writings*, edited by Michael W. Jennings, Howard Eiland and Gary Smith, 236–252. Vol. 1. Cambridge, MA: Harvard University Press. First published 1921.

Benjamin, Walter. 1998. *The Origin of German Tragic Drama*. Translated by John Osborne. London and New York: Verso. First published 1928.

Choudhury, Soumyabrata. 2018. *Ambedkar and Other Immortals*. New Delhi: Navayana.

Derrida, Jacques. 2003. *Psyche: Inventions of the Other*. Vol. 2. Stanford, CA: Stanford University Press.

Derrida, Jacques. 2009. *The Beast and the Sovereign*. Vol. 1. Translated by Geoffrey Bennington.

Chicago, IL: University of Chicago Press.

———. 2020. *Life Death*. Translated by Pascale-Anne Brault and Michael Naas. Chicago, IL: University of Chicago Press.

———. 2023. *Perjury and Pardon*. Vol. 1. Translated by David Wills. Chicago: University of Chicago Press.

Eisenman, Peter. 2007. *Written into the Void: Selected Writings: 1990-2004*. New Haven and London: Yale University Press.

Foucault, Michel. 1984. 'Nietzsche, Genealogy, History.' In *The Foucault Reader*, edited by Paul Rabinow. New York: Pantheon.

Gopal, Ashok. 2023. *A Part Apart: The Life and Thought of B.R. Ambedkar*. New Delhi: Navayana.

Glaude, Jr, Eddie. 2020. *Begin Again: James Baldwin's America and Its Urgent Lessons for Our Own*. New York: Crown.

Heidegger, Martin. 1968. *What Is Called Thinking?* Translated by Fred D. Wieck and J. Glenn Gray. New York: Harper & Row.

Kojève, Alexander. 2018. *Atheism*. Translated by Jeff Love. New York: Columbia University Press.

Kumar, Aishwary. 2010. 'Ambedkar's Inheritances.' *Modern Intellectual History* 7: 391–415.

———. 2015. *Radical Equality: Ambedkar, Gandhi, and the Risk of Democracy*. Stanford, CA: Stanford University Press.

———. 2018. 'In the Void of Faith: *Sunnyata, Sovereignty, Minority*.' In *Secularization, Tolerance, and Democratic Politics in South Asia*, edited by Tanika Sarkar and Humeira Iqtidar, 156–190. Cambridge: Cambridge University Press.

———. 2020. 'War without End: Ambedkar, Time, and Stasis.' In *The Oxford Handbook of Comparative Political Theory*, edited by Leigh K. Jenco, Murad Idris and Megan C. Thomas, 351–374. Oxford: Oxford University Press.

———. 2024. 'The Caste Contract.' Forthcoming in *The Oxford Handbook of the Global South*, edited by Christopher Lee, Anne Mahler and Monica Popescu. Oxford: Oxford University Press.

Lorde, Audre. 1984. 'The Uses of Anger: Women Responding to Racism.' In *Sister Outsider: Essays and Speeches.* Berkeley, CA: Crossing Press.
Mehta, Pratap Bhanu. 2010. 'What is Constitutional Morality?' *Seminar* 615 (November 2010): 17–22.
Mills, Charles W. 1999. *The Racial Contract*. Ithaca: Cornell University Press.
Nancy, Jean-Luc. 2017. 'Lenin and Electricity.' *Crisis and Critique* 4 (2): 357–361.
North, Paul. 2015. *The Yield: Kafka's Atheological Reformation*. Stanford, CA: Stanford University Press.
Obama, Barack. 2020. 'Why Obama Fears for Our Democracy.' Interview with Jeffrey Goldberg. *The Atlantic*, 15 November 2020. https://www.theatlantic.com/ideas/archive/2020/11/why-obama-fears-for-our-democracy/617087/.
O'Leary, Joseph S. 2019. *Reality Itself: Philosophical Challenges of Indian Mahayana*. Nagoya: Chisokudo Publications.
Pateman, Carole. 1988. *The Sexual Contract*. Stanford, CA: Stanford University Press.
Ricoeur, Paul. 2014. *Oneself as Another*. Translated by Kathleen Blamey. Chicago: University of Chicago Press.
Rorty, Richard. 2021. *Pragmatism as Anti-Authoritarianism*. Cambridge, MA: Harvard University Press.
Shklar, Judith N. 1984. *Ordinary Vices*. Harvard, MA: Harvard University Press.
———. 1989. 'The Liberalism of Fear.' In *Liberalism and the Moral Life*, edited by Nancy Rosenblum, 22–37. Cambridge, MA: Harvard University Press.
Taylor, Charles. 1992. *Sources of the Self: The Making of the Modern Identity*. Cambridge, MA: Harvard University Press.
Viswanathan, Gauri. 1998. *Outside the Fold: Secularism, Modernity, Belief*. Princeton, NJ: Princeton University Press.
West, Cornel. 1989. *The American Evasion of Philosophy: A Genealogy of Pragmatism*. Madison, WI: University of Wisconsin Press.

Notes

1 On the moral and constitutional effects of this declaration of independence, which compresses Ambedkar's distinctive affirmation of political faith beyond the limits of civil religion, see Kumar (2018).

2 Gandhi, "Dr. Ambedkar's Indictment-I", *Harijan*, 11 July 1936 in *Collected Works of Mahatma Gandhi*. See Gandhi (1999). On the politics of Gandhi's first reading of *Annihilation of Caste*, which I call an 'event' in the genealogy of Southern theory of political freedom, see Kumar (2015, Chapter 1). Meticulous or not, Gandhi's reading of Ambedkar's political faith is certainly grey. This greyness of nationalist response to *Annihilation of Caste* is also what decisively and unforgettably institutes it as an event. At the very least, given that, as a masterful critique of the anti-colonial *evasion* of political philosophy—which is to say, of its disinterest in human freedom—as such, *Annihilation of Caste* stands without precedent, prior example, or moral ground, it reveals itself as an event only through the

silence—the liberal vacation of responsibility—that surrounds it. It is an event because in both its logical structure and its moral architecture, the purity of force at work in *Annihilation of Caste*—its constitutive groundlessness—opens an abyss in that most elementary of relations between time and narrative (which is to say, in the relation between *amnesia* and *identity*) that is forged in Ambedkar's own time by such works as Gandhi's *Hind Swaraj* and Vinayak Damodar Savarkar's *Hindutva*. *Annihilation of Caste* is a text on political responsibility precisely because, while it arrives out of joint with time, it is also an untimely meditation on time. It is a moral claim to memory composed against civilisational (or majoritarian) amnesia, one to which orthodox nationalism could neither respond with an exculpatory story (or nostalgic counter-memory) of its own—nationalist response to it was marked by theological fear—nor consign its indictment to yet another tradition of critique that they might have claimed as their own. To read *Annihilation of Caste* as an event is to respond to this radical untimeliness that seeks human freedom in the reclamation of mortal, finite time: the time that was stolen from the unequal; the time as it was before the counter-revolution set in, which is tragically also the time that never sought to free itself from that reactionary catastrophe; and which, therefore, is now a time that has been emptied of all memory. An immovable scaffold of denialism has been erected, reproduced by institutional *doxa*, under whose shadow the politics of finitude—justice for those mortals who always find themselves waging a losing battle for a little more time on earth—has been simply replaced by the brutal desire for civilisational stability. It is this illusion of stability that Ambedkar calls 'armed neutrality' (1978–2003, 1: 64). On the uses of this expression in Ambedkar's critique of violence, see Kumar (2020).

3 Here, as elsewhere, I use 'yielding' in the sense developed by Paul North (2015) in his work on Kafka's atheology.

4 Ambedkar's enduring critique of capital punishment, which he begins to weave publicly in *Annihilation of Caste*, must be seen in light of this rejection of political vengeance as a foundation of his constitutional theory and jurisprudence. It is a rejection that marks the still unfolding finale of his prophetic vision and gathers renewed salience with every passing day. For any society that continues to punish its citizens with death, sometimes leaving them on death row for years as they wait for the abyss to open, at other times summarily hanging them off trees just miles away from the national capital, in no palpable way makes itself safer. It simply institutionalises routine, social vendetta among citizens as a way of life, executed by sanction of the law. Caste would simply be the most modern name for this archaic rule by vengeance—or vindictive civility.

5 See Rajagopalachari, 'A Restless Spirit Has Found Peace' (1956).

6 I modulate here, following Ambedkar, the vastly unstudied expression from John Stuart Mill, whose exact words are 'the wellbeing of mankind may almost be measured by the number and gravity of the truths which have reached the point of being uncontested' (Mill 2003, 110). Ambedkar's

reading of Mill—amplified around their shared affinity for the Tocquevillian expression 'tyranny of the majority' (Tocqueville 2000, 239; Mill 2003, 76)—must be taken up elsewhere. Suffice it to say here that Ambedkar is not always convinced by British jurisprudence, even though he would deliver an entire course in Bombay that eventually became his *Lectures on the English Constitution*. The real trouble with Mill's idea of 'uncontested truths' is that it attaches, very explicitly, to the idea of number, measure and the majority. A majority bound by the murderous consent of the caste contract is no less susceptible to perjury than the clique of demagogues who speak in its name. The place of truth in politics gets more and not less tenuous when it turns towards the uncontested. For Ambedkar, the challenge is not to bring coercive supports and normative banisters to guardrail the common truth; it is to lend truth a *gravity, a force minimal but indefatigable*.

7 'Within the Veil was he born, said I; and there within shall he live,—a Negro and a Negro's son,' Du Bois writes in that searing passage in his chapter 'Of the Passing of the First-Born.' 'Holding in that little head—ah, bitterly!—the unbowed pride of a hunted race, clinging with that tiny dimpled hand—ah, wearily!—to a hope not hopeless but unhopeful, and seeing with those bright wondering eyes that peer into my soul a land whose freedom is to us a mockery and whose liberty a lie.' See Du Bois (2015, 157). I discuss elsewhere the place of this melancholic pessimism—one that is acutely aware both of the debilitating seizure and of the revolutionary power of disappointment, and whose searing rhetoric almost always borders on the style of the classical funeral oration—in the democratic thought of Du Bois, Ambedkar, Baldwin and more recently, Barack Obama.

8 It is not simply democracy as a political form that might collapse without this faculty of judgement—this capacity to separate the truth from untruth, as the cover inscription of *Annihilation of Caste* declares—but the citizen's relationship to words themselves. Thus, Obama's warning that the weakening of the truth-telling tradition marks democracy's 'epistemological crisis' (Obama 2020).

9 'Architecture as a state of becoming already defies its traditional idea of stability and stasis. But what,' Eisenman asks, 'is an architecture of becoming?' (2007, 57)

10 'Genealogy is gray, meticulous and patiently documentary,' goes that definitive opening sentence of his essay on truth and method, 'Nietzsche, Genealogy, History'. See Foucault (1984, 76).

11 The classic statement of this condescension towards species without hands appears in Heidegger. 'Apes too have organs that can grasp, but they do not have hands,' Heidegger points out. 'The hand is infinitely different from all the grasping organs—paws, claws, or fangs—different by an abyss of essence', Heidegger (1968, 16). At work here is not simply the denigration of those who are marked by a lack of hands among their organs, say apes or dogs. At stake here—even if Heidegger quickly says, 'Only a being who can speak, that is, think, can have hands and can be handy in achieving works of handicraft'—is the thread of

contempt that runs through national humanism and destroys it from within. Caste insinuates itself into humanism—thereby itself becoming profoundly modern—through an archaic inversion of this ontology, for it limits itself not only to those who have no hands. It pulls into its vortex of condescension next those who also work *with* their hands, who are considered, within the schema of this punishing humanism, just barely more gifted than the animal, their being barely of and on time. Ambedkar engages this distinguished ontology of being and time (a profoundly moralistic, civilisational ontology) in his archaeology of the word *antjya*. The word literally means a figure born at the end of time, barely surviving in it, its humanity adjacent to the animal alone. The figure is consigned by caste law to perpetual inequality precisely because it works (only) with the hand (but also only ever) on (animal) skin. Ambedkar's *antjya* is infra-human, as I suggest elsewhere. See Kumar (2020). Any ultramodern and techno-biological rhetoric of nationalist 'spirit,' about which Ambedkar openly warns in the 1940s, is inextricable from this violent, possessive humanism of, and around, the hand and from the constantly lurking possibility of its degeneration into a regime of manual cruelty. It would be a regime in which extreme violence would be executed by brute force of the hand—by simple, blunt tools and elementary knots and nooses, their movements and shapes improvised reflexively in a moment of murderous delirium, without planning, but always within an apparatus of habit that is cured and encased in the logic of caste life—right in the middle of the city, directed often against those who labour with their hands. It is because of this violent humanism of the hand that Ambedkar remains profoundly ambivalent towards national-spiritual and ascetic celebrations of manual work: not because he would rather have the machine take over manual work altogether but because, on the contrary, ritual asceticism has already insinuated itself into the most archaic logic—*techne*—of the machine. So that nationalism's apotheosis of the working, laborious, crafty hand barely conceals its sacrificial impulse to mechanically, almost thoughtlessly, take the life of precisely those who are disposable because they work by hand. Caste and class violence blur in this zone of manual delirium. This torsion and distortion are on Derrida's mind when he calls attention, in the context of national socialism, to the monstrosity lodged within the figure of the handyman. See especially Derrida (2003, 'Heidegger's Hand: Geschlecht II', 32).

12 Although quite distinct from the Arendtian conception, Soumyabrata Choudhury's galvanising use of the term in *Ambedkar and Other Immortals* (2018) points to the same awareness of limit that constitutes the *figure* of Ambedkar as an architect: transcendent and earthly.

13 Ruins come paradoxically alive in a world ruled by majoritarian resentment. For not only does resentment leave in its wake the shared vision and promise of an equal society (and equal earth) in ruins, it also turns ruins themselves into sites for the most visceral, most tactile expressions of rage against the mythic injustices of history (and its monuments). This

relationship between the resplendence of architecture and barbarism of civic strife, between the dignity of persons (and epochs) and their very defacement as things, fuelled by a tactical politicisation of majoritarian grievance, is fundamental to the logic of political cruelty. Not any violence but only violence that by sheer force turns life into a thing, as Simone Weil might put it, can be called cruelty (Weil 2003, 45). The archaeologist is the miner of this 'living thing,' a figure at once of the living and its decomposed Other—Derrida might say the figure of 'life death' (2020)—buried now by amnesia and now lying.

14 Benjamin writes:

> Philosophical history, the science of the origin is the form which, in the remotest extremes and the apparent excesses of the process of development, reveals the configuration of the idea—the sum total of all possible meaningful juxtapositions of such opposites. The representation of an idea can under no circumstances be considered successful unless the whole range of possible extremes it contains has been virtually explored. (1998, 47)

No thinker in the anti-colonial tradition traverses these extremes of thought—and certainly none probes the entire spectrum of their possibilities and impossibilities—more powerfully than Ambedkar.

15 I think here of the powerful strand of radical liberalism that sees the greatest threat of majoritarian and caste cruelty to reside in political fear as opposed to social anger. See especially Judith Shklar (1984). Anger is the moral counterpart to democratic disappointment, perhaps the most irrefutable truth and fact of democratic life, rather than the ferocious belief that one deserves no disappointment ever, and that every unearned disappointment is, therefore, a reason for retribution against those who cause it through an imagined, punishable crime. This ironic vengeance of punishing others for the sake of a world without disappointment is the root of resentful monstrosity. A world without disappointment would yield a terrifying architecture (or destroy all of it).

16 In probing the relationship between posture, sovereignty and dignity, I follow Jacques Derrida (2009).

17 Despite appearances, this toxic heteronomy plays not an insignificant part in Charles Taylor's magisterial account in *Sources of the Self: The Making of the Modern Identity* (1992).

18 This archaeology of 'police power' appears, among other equally powerful—and searingly titled—meditations in the essay 'Their Wishes Are Laws unto Us,' (Ambedkar 1978–2003, 5: 272–286).

19 In a passage that most powerfully captures Ambedkar's enigmatic reluctance to be called an architect (and his disappointment that he was caught being one, perhaps even the *sovereign* one, among them), Arendt writes:

> The crucial point is that the law—although it defines the space in which men live with one another without using force—has

something violent about it in terms of both its origins and its nature. It comes into being by means of production, not action; the lawgiver resembles the architect of the city and its builder, not the *politikos* and citizen. The law produces the arena where politics occurs, and contains in itself the violent force inherent in all production. (2005, 181–182)

Could one be the lawgiver, the architect, on the one hand, and on the other, a critic of violence and its archaeologist, at one and the same time?

20 For a genealogy of the appearance of this term in Ambedkar's November 1949 Constituent Assembly speech, see Mehta (2010) and Kumar (2015).

21 *Outside the Fold* (1998) by Gauri Viswanathan still remains an unsurpassed genealogy of this event, which in itself says something more significant.

22 Marx, among all the 19th-century thinkers, gives most prolifically to Ambedkar's revolutionary vocabulary. At the heart of this affinity is the status of philosophy as a revolutionary *form* or, better still, philosophy as the architecture of emancipation. 'Just as philosophy finds its material weapons in the proletariat, so the proletariat finds its intellectual weapons in philosophy,' Marx writes in his critique of Hegel's *Philosophy of Right.* 'The head of this emancipation is philosophy; its heart is the proletariat' (Marx 1844). One could with justice posit that Ambedkar takes this right to philosophy and converts Marx's call for proletarian 'transcendence' into a revolutionary *supplement*, deepening the Marxian formula further in *Philosophy of Hinduism* when he writes, 'Revolution is the mother of philosophy, and if it is not the mother of philosophy it is a lamp which illuminates philosophy' (1978–2003, 3: 8).

23 I develop this critique towards a Southern theory of political freedom in Kumar (2024).

24 I am indebted to Huzaifa Omair Siddiqi for this insight into the unavoidable *jointure* between any political philosophy worthy of the name and the desire for annihilation of caste, which must be inscribed at its heart. It is in this sense that Ambedkar's political thought is always of the future, always a meditation on—and out of joint with—time.

25 I draw the motif of philosophical evasion here from Cornel West's unsparing 'genealogy of pragmatism' in America (1989).

4

CRISIS AND THE UNCANNY

N.A. Jacob

I

To be absorbed in the moment of crisis obscures from view that there is a strangeness and familiarity in all crises. Our anticipatory fear, a manifestation of a broader structure of care and solicitude, runs ahead of us and marks all experiences of crisis with an uncanny familiarity. To arrive in the thick of a crisis is to be in a place that we have already visited in anticipation. Anxiety is never far from the surface of the everyday and is, therefore, strangely familiar. When anxiety disrupts our being-at-home-in-the world, it seems to return us to a position that we recognise as having occupied previously.

Both fear and anxiety precede the specific form that various crises may assume in an ontical sense. As states of mind, however, fear and anxiety need to be distinguished from each other. Following Heidegger, one should begin by placing both fear and anxiety within the 'primordial structural totality' of *care,* which ontologically precedes other phenomenon and states of mind (Heidegger 1962, 238). Fear as 'a mode of state of mind' is that very 'slumbering possibility of Being-in-the-world' that 'discloses' the world as a place in which the fearsome resides (180). 'Fearfulness' is, therefore, an 'existential possibility of the essential state-of-mind of Dasein in general', and therefore not a ontical and/or factual condition or predisposition (182).

Fear intensifies, not diminishes, when that which is perceived as threatening carries within it an indeterminacy. That which threatens approaches us yet may 'stay away and pass us by' (Heidegger 1962, 180). Yet in relation to anxiety, fear seems more directly oriented towards being-in-the-world and is cued to the world and the potential threats it contains. In contrast, anxiety is not generated by anything definite, and that which makes one anxious is nowhere: 'it is so close that it is oppressive and stifles one's breath and yet it is nowhere' (231).[1]

On account of this distinction, Heidegger describes fear as the 'fallen' form of anxiety: 'Fear is anxiety, fallen into the "world," inauthentic and as such hidden from itself' (1962, 234). Anxiety, which is 'nowhere' and is with reference to 'nothing', places us in a more authentic and uncanny relation to ourselves, while the relatively anodyne effects of fear turn us away from the uncanniness of anxiety: 'Anxiety is anxious in the face of the "nothing" of the world.... Fear is occasioned by entities with which we concern ourselves environmentally. Anxiety, however, springs from Dasein itself' (395).

The latency of anxiety is constitutive for Dasein since 'being-in-the-world itself is that in the face of which anxiety is anxious' (Heidegger 1962, 232). The phenomenon of 'falling' in which one loses oneself in the 'tranquilized familiarity' of being-in-the-world and describes Dasein's absorption in the world is precisely what gets disrupted through anxiety. As Dasein falls, 'anxiety brings it back from its absorption in the "world". Everyday familiarity collapses' (233). Such experiences are often brief and fitful and mark a moment of crisis. The uncanniness of such critical moments that disrupt the familiar springs from the fact that anxiety returns us to a condition of being 'not-at-home', which Heidegger reveals as being more primordial than being-at-home (233). The disruption of the familiar that anxiety produces brings us back to a mode of Dasein's uncanniness, which we now understand as that which is prior to the experience of being at-home. The familiar is revealed to be derivative of a deeper experience of unfamiliarity that is more primordial: tranquillised being-in-the-world 'is a mode of Dasein's uncanniness not the reverse' (234).

Anxiety is ontological, and it forces Dasein back into an encounter with 'its ownmost potentiality-for-Being—that is, its *Being-free for* the freedom of choosing itself and taking hold of itself' (Heidegger 1962, 232). In anxiety, 'the Being of Dasein can burst forth as a naked "that-it-is-and-has-to-be"' (173).

II

The earlier rehearsal of the Heideggerian account of anxiety and fear is to focus attention on the question of anticipation and the uncanniness that shadows all being-in-the-world. The concept of the uncanny forms an important part of Heidegger's account of Dasein: 'Uncanniness is the basic kind of Being-in-the-world, even though in an everyday way it has been covered up' (Heidegger 1962, 322). However, it is especially useful for the purposes of this chapter because it allows us to examine the uncanniness that inheres in the temporal experience of awaiting.

The idea of awaiting or expecting is central to Heidegger's architectonic of Dasein. Dasein's interpretation of the world is 'grounded' in 'something we see in advance—in a fore-sight … something we grasp in advance—in a fore-conception' (Heidegger 1962, 191). One of the words Heidegger uses to describe this phenomenon of what he calls 'fore-having' is the German word *vorgriff*, which is related to the verb *vorgreifen* that means 'to anticipate'.[2] As a 'self-projective Being', Dasein is always already 'ahead-of-itself' (236). Constituted in part by a 'potentiality-for-Being' (236), it must always '*not yet be* something' (276). The awareness of 'something still outstanding, which Dasein can be and will be' is foundational for Dasein (276). Furthermore, 'Dasein always exists in just such a manner that its "not-yet" *belongs* to it' (287). For Heidegger, such a temporal structure is primordial for Dasein.

Within a broader structure of such an anticipatory mode of Dasein, which is never free of that which it is 'not-yet', fear and anxiety play a crucial role. As I have already discussed, fear, in particular, operates within an explicit structure of 'expecting'. Fear awaits, and this awaiting belongs to the 'existential-temporal meaning of fear' (Heidegger 1962, 392). Fear is always a 'fearing about', and the specific modality that appears threatening is the possibility of something in the future 'coming back' to jeopardise what Dasein already is: 'The awaiting which fears is one which is afraid "for-itself"' (341). Fear lives in fearful expectation of having its present threatened by something that comes back from the future.

However, the temporality of fear is 'inauthentic' primarily because its focus on 'something definite' turns Dasein away and helps it flee, as it were, from a deeper uncanniness that it is thrown into by the crisis that occasioned it. In fear, one 'forgets oneself' in the ensuing bewilderment of fearful anticipation. Imagining dreadful possibilities both probable and improbable, fear is a 'falling' or 'constant fleeing … mode of evasion in the face of [Death]' into the immediacy of the ready-to-hand (Heidegger 1962, 298). In this connection, Heidegger characterises fear as a compromised mode of waiting: 'The having forgotten which goes with such bewilderment modifies the awaiting too and gives it the character of a depressed and bewildered awaiting which is distinct from any pure expectation' (392).

The conception of 'pure expectation' that Heidegger mentions is useful for understanding the distinct temporalities of anxiety and fear. Anxiety, unlike fear, is not a response to a specific threat that Dasein identifies in the immediate environment, but neither is it a 'nothing' in which we feel switched off from our connectedness with the world around us. The displeasure that we affectively experience in anxiety is because the world that is ready-to-hand and present to us does not '"say" anything any longer' (Heidegger 1962, 393). Anxiety, therefore, brings us close to the possibility of 'pure expectation', which is not a waiting for the object of our concern but, rather, represents a mode that 'temporalizes itself authentically' so as to not fall prey to the inauthentic and fallen mode of expectation (387).

Heidegger maintains the distinction between waiting and pure expectation by a terminological clarification that is crucial for his argument. An authentic relationship with the future without 'falling' into concernful absorption with specific possibilities in the factical world is assigned the term *anticipation*. On the other hand, a fallen mode of anticipation that is ahead-of-itself but distracted by 'objects of one's closest concern' is named '*awaiting*'(Heidegger 1962, 387): 'The inauthentic future has the character of awaiting' because, in awaiting, one 'lets what is threatening *come back* to one's factically concernful potentiality-for-being' (Heidegger 1962, 387, 391).

This splitting of the concept of expectation into its pure and fallen versions, namely 'anticipation' and 'waiting', allows Heidegger to construct a phenomenological model that is able to maintain the distinction between our 'thrownness' and absorption with our factical existence on the one hand and our potential for an authentic encounter with Dasein's ownmost potentiality-for-being on the other.

III

How does one phenomenologically describe the relationship between the two orders of 'expectation'? What is at stake in keeping the two orders apart? Both orders of expectation are intimately linked in that waiting is a 'forgetting' of one's ownmost potentiality-for-being, while anticipation, which is 'essentially futural', can 'let itself be thrown back upon its factical "there"' to accept its ownmost possibility-for-being (Heidegger 1962, 437). Anticipation shadows all waiting and is precisely that which is concealed in waiting. As Blanchot says: 'Sterile waiting, ever poorer and emptier. Fertile waiting, always the richer for waiting. The one is the other' (Blanchot 1995, 276).[3] Anticipation and waiting clearly may operate in time and yet have very different temporal dynamics. One way of understanding this difference is to focus on the different modalities of time assumed by waiting and anticipation.

Waiting is dependent on a structure of expectation that places the waiter in a continuum of time. Oriented towards a possibility of something occurring in time, waiting assumes both the possibility of a measurable wait and the continued existence of the waiter. In waiting, one's attention is on the object of the wait, not on oneself. In this sense, Heidegger talks of awaiting as a forgetting: 'The awaiting which forgets and makes present' does so by virtue of an 'inauthentic understanding [which] temporalizes itself with regard to its temporality' (Heidegger 1962, 389).[4] Waiting is a forgetting because, in waiting, one keeps the focus of one's attention on the impendence of that which is expected. By doing so, one deflects attention away from oneself and one's projective capacity in which 'temporality temporalizes itself primarily in terms of the *future*' (479).

In waiting, the Self is occulted from the experience of waiting by a specific temporal modality that I call 'calibrated waiting'. In calibrated waiting, time is rendered measurable, and the wait happens against a graded scale of time. A calculable wait is one where we observe our movement through time towards a definite possibility that we await either in fear or in hope.

In calibrated waiting, one has always plotted one's position on an imaginary arc of time. Time is spatialised and divided into uniform segments to rationalise the passage of time. Such a visualisation of time on a mappable space is used quite literally in GPS navigation systems or in numbered tokens that allow you to estimate your position in the span that the wait covers. Like milestones on a highway, calibrated waiting always draws attention to time and one's calculable passage through it. To wait thus is to be moving in time, charting one's course through it. The Self is consumed in following the arc of time until it arrives at its expected end. As Lukacs puts it in his classic essay on reification: 'Time is everything, man is nothing; he is at the most the incarnation of time.... Thus time sheds its qualitative, variable, flowing nature; it freezes into an exactly delimited, quantifiable continuum … in short, it becomes space' (1967, 90).

Time reified in end-oriented waiting produces an absorptive condition in the waiters for whom the space of the wait or the spatialised journey through time occupies the focus of their attention. The spatial representation of calibrated waiting becomes a way of conducting oneself through the wait. The Self here is merely the point in the present to which the future draws closer. Such waiting is at the end from the very start, and to reach the end is to have arrived at a point that was always in view.

However, calibrated waiting is rarely as efficient as the earlier description suggests. Waiting contains a messiness, a spillover, that fails to be completely mopped up by the ordered fiction of tractable time. In all waiting, one experiences a recalcitrance in time, a stubborn refusal in waiting to fit neatly into our attempts at parsing time into its divisible units. The waiter cannot quite escape the wait, for even in the most well-calibrated wait, one experiences time in terms of what Bergson called the 'fluidity of our inner life' (1965, 44), which is fundamentally indivisible:

> Listen to a melody with your eyes closed, thinking of it alone, no longer juxtaposing on paper or an imaginary keyboard notes.... Our attention may turn away from it and, consequently, from its indivisibility; but when we try to cut it, it is as if we suddenly passed a blade through a flame—we divide only the space it occupied. (49)

The waiters may periodically check their progress in quantifiable time but cannot help being pulled back into Bergsonian duration, which, being indivisible, must be endured consciously. The waiters can distract themselves by obsessively checking their progress through time ('How much longer do I have to wait?') but cannot help living through the duration of the wait.[5] Their absorptive waiting is a fleeing from duration, and the success of the venture (of killing time through various distractions) is always marked against the shadow of a pure duration that flows beneath the surface of ordered or spatialised time.[6]

This double movement is akin to the doubleness that is intrinsic to all waiting that suspends us between two orders of time. The first is what Kermode calls the space between the 'tick' and the 'tock' of a clock, which is an interim that is suffused with the expectation of the tock and which retroactively fills the interval between the two sounds:

> The fact that we call the second of the two related sounds tock is evidence that we use fictions to enable the end to confer organization and form on the temporal structure. The interval between the two sounds, between tick and tock is now charged with significant duration. (Kermode 1966, 45)

However, the space that follows the tock is 'simple chronicity' or 'mere successiveness ... which is simply 'one damn thing after another' (46–47). This distinction is what Kermode understands in relation to the difference between *chronos* and *kairos*, which he describes thus: '*chronos* is "passing time" or "waiting time"—that which, according to Revelation, "shall be no more"—and *kairos* is the season, a point in time filled with significance, charged with a meaning derived from its relation to the end' (47).

The kairos-driven time of waiting is an attempt to inoculate waiting from that which is unrepresentable in calibrated time. Waiting thus represented is anticipation deflected (and anxiety kept at bay). The interval between the tick and the tock is rationalised and made bearable by the reassurance that allows us to hear the imminent tock even before it arrives: 'It is one of the great charms of books that they have to end' (Kermode 1966, 24).

The inauthentic mode of calibrated waiting drains time away by offering many possibilities of end-oriented waiting. In this sense, Heidegger writes:

> He who is irresolute understands himself in terms of those very closest events and be-fallings … which thrust themselves upon him in varying ways. Busily losing himself in the object of his concern, he loses his time in it too. Hence his characteristic way of talking—'I have no time'. (1962, 463)

What is the waiter trying to flee in calibrated waiting? That which is sought to be turned away from in calibrated waiting is the 'other' waiting, which Heidegger calls anticipation. This 'fleeing in the face of uncanniness, (which for the most part remains concealed with latent anxiety)' is the shadow that falls on all waiting. Therefore, waiting cannot quite exhaust what Blanchot calls the 'movement' of waiting:

> Whatever the importance of the object of waiting, it is always infinitely surpassed by the movement of waiting.… Waiting begins when there is nothing more to wait for, not even the end to this waiting.… Waiting is waiting for nothing.… As soon as we wait for something, we wait a little less.… Waiting which takes place in time, opens up time to the absence of time where there is no place for waiting. (1995, 272–274)

Even though Heidegger suggests that the time of waiting is a 'backing-away' from Dasein's 'ownmost *thrown* potentiality-for-Being' that succeeds in shutting out and 'forgetting' the possibility of anticipation, it is clear from his larger discussion of anxiety and fear that the temporalising impulse of calibrated waiting is never quite able to get away from the other waiting, that which threatens to introduce the 'infinite dispersion of waiting' (1962, 388). The gathering up of this dispersion 'by the imminence of the end of waiting' is never quite complete in calibrated waiting (Blanchot 1995, 277). That which haunts calibrated waiting is, within itself, not without.[7]

Like Freud's concept of the uncanny, which anxiety is closely tied to (for in 'anxiety, one feels *uncanny*), there is a temporal folding back that reveals what was always known in advance (Heidegger 1962, 233). In this sense, anxiety is constitutive of the tranquillised normalcy that derives from the 'they' and precedes our familiarity with the world. As Katherine Withy proposes, uncanniness 'is not a matter of uncertainty, but a matter of time' (2015, 26). The disruption of temporal sequence, central to Freud's account of the uncanny, reveals the fragility of ordered time since that which was past reveals itself in an overwhelming presentness (2003).

In experiential terms, all waiting thickens time and retards its flow. We feel the viscosity of time when we are forced to encounter the experience of duration in waiting. However, in anticipation, unlike waiting, we encounter the present-at-hand shorn of its means-end relations with expected or feared/hoped-for outcomes. The 'Present of anxiety is *held on to* when one brings oneself back to one's ownmost thrownness.... The present-at-hand reveals itself in 'an empty mercilessness' (Heidegger 1962, 393–394).

To be authentically in the present in the 'moment of vision' that anticipation allows is not to be individuated—Dasein, in confronting itself, finds the world and its involvements fade away. On the contrary, the world presents itself as that which has 'withdrawn' and does not say anything to me any longer. As Withy writes: 'Thus when the totality of involvements falls away from significance and we lose our investment in things, what is revealed is *not* what is lost but instead what *remains*: the world in its worldhood' (2015, 61). This moment is revelatory since material objects, for instance, appear with an uncanny strangeness.

It is precisely this strangeness that we become aware of in anticipation, and this awareness brings us into a new relationship with things. We feel curiously levelled with the objects that we find ourselves amongst. Anticipation immobilises us and makes us feel an uncanny kinship with objects. In general, all waiting feels like an imposition in the precise sense that it takes away our freedom to move along at the pace that we had expected.[8] We find ourselves 'stranded in time—like a thing' (Schweizer 2008, 40).[9] This moment is uncanny because even as one feels the corporeal presence of oneself as a body, one realises that things are much better at anticipation than us. The singularity of things around one assumes a new intensity, and we feel the uncanniness of both our belonging and difference from corporeality.

In all waiting, if we approach the condition of things, then that would help explain our relatively poor capacity to retain memories of waiting. Bergson's use of Ravaisson's idea that 'materiality begets oblivion' brings us to the curious relationship between waiting and memory (Bergson 1991, 177). Memory seems to lack the teeth needed to bite into calibrated waiting, perhaps because, in such waiting, time is thinned out and lacks the ridges that memory needs to map the topography of waiting time. In this sense, waiting time is never memorable because memory tends to recall events rather than the intervals between events. In anticipation, however, the reverse is true since we feel the presentness of time with a new intensity and do not seek to flee from it.

Anticipation is the remainder left behind by all waiting, that which waits after waiting has ended. Anticipation is the movement that shadows waiting, and as Blanchot suggests, 'the night in which there is nothing awaited, represents the movement of waiting' (1995, 273). Anticipation stalks waiting but endures after the end of waiting.

IV

'Through waiting [or anticipation, in Heidegger's terms] that which turns aside from thought, returns to thought' (Blanchot 1995, 276). Although anticipation yields a deep ontological insight through which we come to terms with our own temporal finitude, it lacks an ontic content. Like the source of anxiety, it is about 'nothing', and therefore, there cannot be a specific truth learnt through anticipation. In revealing to us, what Dreyfus calls, 'the groundlessness of the world', anticipation not only interrupts our absorption with the world but also reveals the groundlessness that precedes the intelligibility we seek in entities. Anticipation marks the internal limit of losing oneself in the task of weaving meaning into the world and finding significance in it. We may steer clear of this limit, but this limit is the uncanny double that follows us around during our attempts at forgetting it. Its knowledge is not the repressed that returns to haunt us from the unconscious but the permanent shadow that we cast in making sense of the world and feeling at home in it. 'And even in the most indifferent and inoffensive everydayness', it can stand revealed as 'naked uncanniness' (Heidegger 1962, 173, 394).

We can comport ourselves towards waiting either with impatience or with a willingness to tarry with ourselves. While our absorptive involvement in the world obscures this knowledge, it is only through our 'falling' that the world 'opens' it's face to us. However, in disclosing itself, it hides that which resides in the latency of anxiety.

In this sense, the condition of be-falling and absorption is precisely that through which we return to and come to appreciate the value of anticipation, which presents the world to us bereft of the meanings we projectively generate onto it. Dasein falls and, in and through that falling, experiences the possibility of an uncanny return that gives us pause before the precarity of our end-fictions.

In such terms, waiting is the interval that suspends us between two significant moments (origins and ends), and the time of waiting is humanised and made bearable by end-fictions that inject expectation into the interval. However, waiting always does so at the cost of looking away from the other possibility of a time that is both indifferent to our projective fantasies or fears and brings to bear on us the possibility of a more authentic relation to time that acknowledges a time after waiting, a waiting that can begin only after the wait has ended.

References

Bergson, Henri. 1965. *Duration and Simultaneity: With Reference to Einstein's Theory*. Translated by Leon Jacobson. Indianapolis: Bobbs-Merrill Company.

———. 1991. *Matter and Memory*, Translated by N.M. Paul and W.S. Palmer. Brooklyn, NY: Zone Books.

Blanchot, Maurice. 1995. *The Blanchot Reader*. Edited by Michael Holland. Oxford: Blackwell.

Freud, Sigmund. 2003. *The Uncanny*. Translated by David McLintock. London: Penguin.

Heidegger, Martin. 1962. *Being and Time*. Translated by John Macquarrie and Edward Robinson. New York: Harper and Row.

Kermode, Frank. 1966. *The Sense of an Ending: Studies in the Theory of Fiction*. Oxford: Oxford University Press.

Kierkegaard, Soren. 1980. *The Concept of Anxiety: A Simple Psychologically Oriented Deliberation on the Dogmatic Issue of Hereditary Sin*. Translated by Reidar Thomte. Princeton, N.J.: Princeton University Press.

Lukacs, Georg. 1967. *History and Class Consciousness*. Translated by Rodney Livingstone. London: Merlin Press.

Schweizer, Harold. 2008. *On Waiting: Thinking in Action*. London: Routledge.

Withy, Katherine. 2015. *Heidegger on Being Uncanny*. Cambridge, MA: Harvard University Press.

Notes

1 Heidegger derived much of his notion of anxiety from Kierkegaard (1980). With reference to the 'nothing' that anxiety is about, Kierkegaard writes: 'What, then, is it? Nothing. But what effect does nothing have? It begets anxiety. This is the profound secret of innocence, that it is at the same time anxiety' (1980, 41).

2 See Macquarrie and Robinson's discussion of the same in Heidegger (1962, 191n2).

3 Blanchot's essay on waiting does not terminologically differentiate between the two orders of waiting, like Heidegger does. Perhaps, this is to bring out the intimate connection between one and the other.

4 This refers to Heidegger's insistence that 'world-time' is produced by a 'temporalizing of temporality … which constitutes a within-time-ness of the ready-to-hand and the present-at-hand' (1962, 472). In this sense, Dasein turns away from the true import of the temporal by occupying

himself with futural projects that operate through such a 'temporalizing of temporality'.

5 The inherently divided nature of waiting time, which flits back and forth between consulting clock time and retreating into duration, is the basis of Harold Schweizer's book on waiting (2008).

6 'Am I going to have to endure this much longer? For always, if you experience it as duration' (Blanchot 1995, 273).

7 When Dasein 'understands' uncanniness in the everyday manner, it does so by turning away from it in falling; in this turning-away, the 'not-at-home' gets 'dimmed down'. Yet the everydayness of this fleeing shows phenomenally that anxiety, as a basic state-of-mind, belongs to Dasein''s essential state of Being-in-the-world.... *From an existential-ontological point view, the 'not-at-home' must be considered as the more primordial phenomenon.* (Heidegger 1962, 234)

8 The idea of incarceration, as Foucault reminds us, specifically removes prisoners from the realm of action for an enforced period of waiting during which they forfeit the liberty and rights due to them as citizens. The length of the sentence is a span of time that the prisoner has to wait through. This is end-oriented waiting assuming a specifically penal dimension, though one that is not absent from many other institutional arrangements.

9 The phrase is from Schweizer (2008, 40).

5

CATASTROPHE AND THE LYRICAL SELF

Prasanta Chakravarty

> A certain longing seizes me to die, and to see the dewy lotus plants along the banks of Acheron.
>
> —Sappho, *Fragment 95.11-13*

> Their Language ... consists not so much of Words and Letters, as Tunes and strange Sounds which no Letters can express, for there are few Words but signify several Things, as are distinguished only by their Sounds, which are sung as it were in uttering.
>
> —Francis Godwin, *The Man in the Moone or a Discourse of a Voyage Thither*

> Jean-Jacques (age 5) tries to fly but hangs himself on curtain cord.
>
> —News snippet in Louis Malle's *Le Feu Follet/The Fire Within*

Catastrophe is a moment of ecstasy where all forces converge at once to produce stasis, says the playwright Richard Foreman (2010). Catastrophe is about losing the thread—a singularity when all coherent meaning dissolves into an abyss, an abyss that is a mirage too. A rigorous definition of catastrophe would take us beyond conflict. Conversely, it puts all mawkish mourning to test. Unlike conflict, it is not a relationship between a changing world and a posited ego. The conflict is in the being—which is a matter of vibration in the mind, a throb in the head or a testing of the soul. Catastrophe fosters no catharsis, only the deepest of moral disquiet, in the words of Howard Barker (1989). Its tall shadow stands against all carnival mania. As such, catastrophe provides absolute clarity to pain and charismatic defeat—to *unlived life* in general. Every passion is drowned in expediency in the catastrophic moment. All didacticism is scattered in the surge of terror. Is the trembling, restive Self able to confront disasters of such a nature? The voice of the unhomely and the adrift hides no persona. Their selfhood is not *gathered*. Tremulous voices babble and make scratches in the air.

The quavering Self in a catastrophe is, therefore, an 'effort' to put together whatever arises in the churning. A certain oscillation replaces conflict as the Self encounters other selves as a material force. At such a point, the Self, unable to cohere, distributes itself onto networks. Now the voice coagulates into half-meaning; now it drifts into nebulous and fantastic forms. Attention begins to stretch. There is no progression. Selves in a catastrophe are suspended and yet free in the 'field' of interaction. Each such Self allows itself to be folded over its own being. Such a folded Self sometimes emerges in art as a pure voice. The voice might be able to garner some gestures. Each voice stumbles over nature, as it were, plumbing its way through *phrasal gestures*. The truth of the condition is felt and expressed moment to moment in limit conditions. The voice turns away from the field even as it works within it. Encountering catastrophe is the secret and esoteric domain of such voices. The secret can only become public through riddles. Riddles hover. Within and after a catastrophe, there is neither wish fulfilment of spirit nor any hope for the absurd to salvage the condition. However, the sense of the catastrophe allows the lyric voice to stand at certain crossings—territorial and tropological. It hopes to cross borders.

Within such a backdrop, catastrophic art is a kind of *reverberation machine*, as Foreman puts it (1989). It records throbs and voices. Each Self is an accretion, a repository of 'deposited sludge' that art may come to reveal. Art cannot extract catastrophe from life. Such art rather arrives as a series of notations. It is the translation of a combination of courage and vulnerability. Art begins to scan life: the tracings of matter and the networks of relationalities. Catastrophic art is the ordeal of the Self, like sleepwalking. However, such an ordeal is never tied to wounds and suffering. When the ordeal becomes ecstatic, there is clarity. It is a miraculous moment of salience and limpidity and of an unexpected aliveness that stands sentinel outside to the world of sociability, relevance and carnival mania. Each voice dies and rises every moment. Catastrophic art is the celebration of a joyous return of the lyrical.

Darkness Echoing

On 16 November 2009, Achyut Mandal, associate professor in the Department of Modern Indian Languages and Literary Studies, discussed Badal Sircar's existentialist play *Ebong Indrajit* with the MA students. He lectured for about 40 minutes on the subject of death and suicide. Mandal, a teacher and a blogger of ghost stories and detective fiction, was found hanging early on 17 November 2009 by his wife, Sudipta Basu, at their Reids Line Flat, opposite Miranda House in the north campus of the University of Delhi (Edmond 2009). The police recovered a suicide note—a poem. The note/poem was also saved and salvaged by Saswati Ganguly, his colleague and friend from Miranda House, University of Delhi (Mandal, n.d.):

'অটো করে চাঁদে চলে যাবো'

একটা কথা বললে বেরিয়ে যাবো এক্ষুনি
অটো করে চাঁদে চলে যাবো
এতদিন চাঁদে যাইনি কেননা
বুড়িদের চরকা কাটা আমার পছন্দ হয়না
দেশাত্মবোধক জোচ্চুরি বলে মনে হয়
এখন চাঁদে জল আছে
আমার খুব তেষ্টা পেয়েছে আজ রাত্রে
রাস্তায় দাঁড়িয়ে আছি তাই
কখন একটা অটো আসবে--অটো চেপে চাঁদে যাবো.

গভীর সমস্যা খুব। চাঁদে পৌঁছে অটোওলা কি বলবে?
ভাড়া দেব ফরেন কারেন্সিতে--বেটাছেলে বুঝতেই পারবেনা.
রবীন্দ্র সংগীত করবো দুটো--তাতেও না মানলে
চাঁদের পাথর ছুঁড়ে মেরে ফেলবো ওকে...
চাঁদে তো আর বেকারি স্ট্রিট নেই
একা Ganguli হারিয়ে যাবো চাঁদের হাওয়ায়।

চাঁদের বুড়ি মাছ খায় না কেন,
বিধবা বোধহয় তাই জল জমে বরফ হয়েছে।
এক গাড়ি বরফ নিয়ে বিক্রি করেত চাই চাঁদের ওপিঠে
অন্ধকারে--তো আর মুখ চেনা যাবেনা।

চাঁদের খবর পেয়ে রুমা বললো জামাইবাবু Ganguli
চলো চাঁদে চলে যাই...
আমি বললাম বারান্দায় বালতির ওই জল
নাড়া ঘাঁটা করে চাঁদ খোঁজ
চাঁদে জল আছে।

অরিজিৎ কুন্ডু আধপেটা রুটি খেয়ে ফিরছে
প্রেমিকার সঙ্গে ঝগড়া হয়েছে তরো
দুজনেই উত্তেজিত হলাম মধ্যরাতে
অটো খুঁজছি, চাঁদে যাবো, চাঁদে জল আছে।

তোমার চাঁদ, আমার চাঁদ, বৈজ্ঞানিকদের চাঁদ, বেশ্যার চাঁদ.
ঠাকুমার চাঁদ, শিল্পীর চাঁদ, কবির চাঁদ
কবির ভাগ্নের চাঁদ, ভাঙা চাঁদ, গোটা চাঁদ,
মোটা চাঁদ, শুরু চাঁদ, বুড়ি চাঁদ যে গেছে ভেসে বেনোজলে
কেউ জানতো না যে চাঁদের জল আছে, চাঁদ কাঁদে।

কত বড়ো লোক আমি জানিস
খালি ঘুমুনোর সময় কথা বলতে পারি না।
জেগে থাকলে চাঁদের সাথে কথা বলতে বলি
জানলায় ল্যাপ্টানো চাঁদ অন্ততঃ আত্মীয় স্বজনের চেয়ে কালো।

পুরোনো আত্মীয় স্বজন সব ফেলে এসেছি
আছে চৌমাথার ওপরে চাঁদ
রেলিঙে দাঁড়ানো হাত পা
বিবর্ণ মুখের ভঙ্গি আর...
নেই মানুষের স্বপ্ন ফেলে এসো, বিষন্ন দাওয়ায়...
কে যেন সাইকেল রাখলো চাঁদের তলায়
আর চাবি দিচ্ছে মেঘ যেন চুরি করে নেবে
চাঁদের বর্তুল মুখে কান্নার করুন দাগ নেই কেন
কেন শুধু চান্দ্রসভা বর্ষণের ইঙ্গিত দিয়েছে
এক জানতো তখন এই উচ্ছসিত বুদ্ধ পূর্ণিমায়
চাঁদের ভিতরে জল আছে

To the Moon in an Auto[1]

1

One more word and I am off
Will take an auto to the moon
Didn't take off for the moon all this while
Because I hate those spindle-wielding hags
They seem like nationalistic frauds.
Now there is water on the moon
Terribly thirsty am I tonight
So I stand at the street corner
Whenever an auto shows up—will ride it to the moon.

2

Aeons deep lie the problem. What would the auto-wallah say after reaching the moon?
Once on the moon, what will the auto-wallah say?
Shall pay him in foreign currency—the fellow will hardly realize.
Shall sing him a couple of Tagore numbers—if that does not placate him either
Shall kill him by pelting moon stones—
There are no unemployment streets on the moon—
Alone, alone I shall lose myself in the moon breeze.

1 Translation mine

3

Why doesn't the old lunar woman eat fish,
Water turned to ice because she's a widow perhaps.
I want to sell a cart-full of ice on the other side of the moon
In the dark—faces cannot be recognized, after all.

4

On hearing about the moon, Ruma says, come bro-in law
Let's go the moon—
I said shake the bucket on the balcony full of water
And look for the moon
There›s water on the moon.

5

Arijit Kundu is returning after a meagre meal
He's had a tiff with his girlfriend too
Both of us, agitated at the midnight hour
Look for an auto, to the moon, there is water on the moon.

6

Your moon, my moon, the scientist's moon, the prostitute's moon
Grandma's moon, artist's moon, poet's moon
Poet's nephew—his moon, the broken moon, the whole moon
Fat moon, emaciated moon, old woman moon who was washed away in the flood waters,
Not a soul knew that the moon has water, the moon weeps.

7

How great a man I am do you have any idea
It's only that I cannot speak while I am asleep.
When awake I tell the moon to speak with me
The hanging moon at the window is at least darker than my relatives, the close ones.

8

Old relatives and loved ones I have left behind
The moon stands over the crossroads

Arms and legs on the railings
Crushed posture of the face and—
The dreams of the no-person abandon, at the sorrowful portico
Look, someone leaves a bicycle under the moon
Locking it as if the clouds will pilfer it
On the moon's round face why are there no streaks of agony
Why only the gestures of lunar-gatherings that rain
Who would have known on that ecstatic Buddha-Purnima
That there is water within the moon.

The poet at midnight, like his acquaintances Arijit Kundu and Ruma, is excited. Living is a penitentiary, a penal colony. The denial of the will to live, therefore, opens up in the night. Together, they hope to find deliverance on the moon, for it is now established that the moon does contain water. The water on the moon is quite distinct from what passes for it on the Earth. Two molecules of hydrogen and one molecule of oxygen turn into an elixir on the moon. There is, perhaps, no scope for such a variety of water on the Earth. The Earth is the place reserved for old relatives and loved ones, all of who make little sense anymore to those who are excited to embrace the moon. The forgotten and the bereft (*nei manush*) must learn to quit all material dreams and desires to bag a ticket for the joyous machine that would ferry them to the moon. Besides, there is no unemployment on the moon and no hue and cry over strange ideals like nationalism. What matters is the news that, indeed, the moon reserves water. It can soothe and quench thirst. The old spindle-wielding hag of the folktales, who live on the moon, is unaware of the presence of water, but the drifters know.

The eternal boatman who ferries earthlings to the moon across the sea of space is the auto-wallah. The auto-wallah is Charon incarnate or the loyal servant of Yama ferrying the wandering soul across the Vaitarani. The cosmonauts of the galactic autorickshaw wait at the crossroads, the space station on earth. They are done with all corporeal transactions. Or are they? Will the auto-wallah show up with his winged contraption and provide the space travellers respite from the relentless charade of earthly dealings?

The moon itself is a strange being: it is darker than relations and well-wishers. It is grave and incandescent in its darkness, awaiting the earthlings. It is not shifty in light and shadow, like the games our relations like to play with us. It hangs by the window, easily touchable. One has to just try. The moon is honest in its ominous luminosity. For the moon cries (but hides the act). The water that it produces comes out of agony. Only the cosmonauts, the lost and forgotten souls, who are ready to take the galactic ride, are aware of the moon's sorrow.

The catastrophic night lurks, potent and perennial at once. The devoted artist is like an automaton, forever waiting, and therefore, nurturing the advent of catastrophe within the soul. A devoted poet is drawn to the approaching catastrophe, hurtling the Self towards the point where it is an impossibility to live. The mad rush to be entertained, and the practice of sentimental sorrow all around nauseate the poet. There comes a point when writing empties itself of the world. It begins to appear to the poet as abandoned, without any valance Maurice Blanchot calls this experience 'the very experience of night' (1989).

> In the night, everything has disappeared. This is the first night. Here absence approaches—silence, repose, night. Here ... the sleeper does not know he sleeps, and he who dies goes to meet real dying. Here language completes and fulfills itself in the silent profundity which vouches for it as its meaning. (Blanchot 1989)

Night is the horror and the fantasy in which the adrift are exposed to the darkness in human life and to the black hole of a non-human void. Mandal seeks to escape the night of sociability—that of relations and needless complications and of the drudgery of negotiations. The night abolishes servitude that has been imposed upon by socially endorsed values and constraints. Community is abandonment. The water on the moon would rather provide the *unlived* with an ecstatic and beautiful relationship, a genuine democratisation of everyday life. The autorickshaw provides the adrenaline of a fairground ghost train. It is a spacecraft that takes voice to quench its thirst and allows the autorickshaw to disappear into the moon breeze.

Is the hope of embracing the void and thus achieving deliverance justified? Do Rousseau's Julie, Goethe's Werther or the likes of Thomas Chatterton begin a process of martyrological pathology from which modernism hopes to break free but is unable to complete the process? Can immolation of the Self give closure to fixated self-consciousness or is it just a wishful and clumsy experiment to control the Self's destiny? Is it ever possible or necessary to skirt suffering, 'the hideous shapes that were born of the night' (Schopenhauer 1913), by destroying physical presence?

In this context, Blanchot divides the night in two: 'When everything has disappeared in the night, "everything that has disappeared" appears. This is the other night' (1989). We enter into the night, and we rest there, sleeping and dying. However, the *other* night does not welcome us always; it remains a lurking hope, a wish. In it, one is still outside—on the crossroads, waiting. It does not close either. It is the great castle, near but unapproachable and impenetrable because the door is guarded. The night is inaccessible because to have access to it is to accede to the outside, to remain outside the night and to lose forever the possibility of emerging from it.

On such a night, the moon is an approaching possibility for Mandal, as the autorickshaw could arrive. What is the nature of their rendezvous? There is no guarantee that the rickshaw would arrive, though, and deliver those who wish to take the planetary trip. Does the lyric voice actually wait *in oneself*? One awaits oneself and nothing else. Or does one await an *arrivant*? Or do the auto-wallah and the voice wait for each other? And if the rickshaw does eventually take the eager passenger, could it be that the route is a decoy? Is imminence also a receding mirage? Could it be that the auto-wallah is a ghostly apparition who takes the passenger to the shores of oblivion instead, the abyss of yet another planetary catastrophe, the black hole where all bereft souls end up?

Art affirms the interminability of living—its elixir. However, lying in wait does not efface the marks of the catastrophe: the disaster of the impossibility of death. All ideas of repose and deliverance—silence, night and absurdity—are mocked by the catastrophe of living death. Oblivion is a recurring trace in living. Nothing can be made bearable or felicitous by invoking immortality or life after being gone. Is there a beginning or an end to catastrophes? Perhaps the journey to the moon is a supreme irony thrown at us, the living dead, by Mandal? Indeed, there is lunar water only in his imagination. What life might Mandal wish to restore or achieve after such a separation from all earthly transactions by hoping to be ferried across to the moon? The impossible and ludic nature of the autorickshaw-spacecraft is what takes us to the lyric core of the poem. As the intensity of his quest heightens, so does our sense of curiosity and horror at the prospect of following through such a fatal, uncanny journey. To encounter the poem is like entering a magic funnel, a black hole in some distant galaxy that gradually sucks and siphons off all that is excess and excessive—the motifs of garrulousness and overstaying.

The lyric stands up to chattering—in a culture that makes everything speak and makes every move come to a climax. Where every word must get somewhere, Mandal takes us to a trail that makes little sense, for it speaks to itself—round and round. Sensitivity will not help either with such a terrible, unearthly promise. We must confront the catastrophe directly and in its entirety. Only the restive core of lyric energy can deflate its neutral wrath.

Perishing or Demise?

Martin Heidegger proposes in *Being and Time* that 'mineness and existence are ontologically constitutive for death' ([1953] 1996). Dying is something that every *dasein* must own up to as the constant and intimate marker of finitude. Death is already in and before man. Death is always and anticipatory, and one is freed from its lurking presence and anxiety when marked as dasein's 'very own'. Marking the esoteric and continual existence of ending, Heidegger distinguishes inauthentic encounters with death among the masses, to whom it is a factual presence at hand, not integral to the Self. To the masses, therefore, being obliterated appears to be alien and despairing.

Heidegger feels that 'when dasein reaches its wholeness in death, it simultaneously loses the being of the there' ([1953] 1996). It appears that, objectively, life or the Self is no-longer-being-there. The deceased is no longer dasein: this is what the mass feels. The lifeless object affirms unliving. Such a lifeless object has lost its biological existence. The deceased is torn away from those left behind in that it is not the corpse that has just been buried. The remaining with the deceased is grasped as the being together with something at hand. Those remaining in the world can still be with him or her. The dying of others is, therefore, never an authentic experience—it is taking care of the deceased. Being-with or still-being-there does not give us the answer about the authentic Self. To that end, Heidegger says: 'Every dasein must itself actually take dying upon itself'. To that end, Heidegger says that every dasein ought to take dying upon itself. What does he mean?

Death is essentially one's own. Death is never an event but a constant presence. Hence, Heidegger affirms that the 'medical concept of "*exitus*" does not coincide with that of perishing' ([1953] 1996). Ending, rather, constitutes a being whole of that Self that exists. A not-yet belongs to the *dasein*, which is an outstanding constancy. This constant presence of coming to an end coincides with no-longer-being-there. Further, the coming to an end cannot be represented by other beings. The whole of being is completed in oblivion, but oblivion is a continuous presence in the finitude of the Self.

Heidegger takes us to the moon too. He suggests that the last quarter of the moon is outstanding till it turns full. As the shadow covering the moon disappears, the not-yet begins to decrease. The moon, however, is present in its constancy. It is present as a whole ([1953] 1996):

> Apart from the fact that the moon is never wholly to be grasped even when it is full, the not-yet by no means signifies a not-yet-being together of parts belonging together, but rather pertains only to the way we grasp it perceptually.

The Self is not yet real until it attains its end, which defines its being or non-being. The Self has to turn into what it is not-yet, which is always already its not-yet.

Ending is, therefore, not stopping, finishing, disappearing or being fulfilled. Dasein is rather a being-towards the end of this being. With death, dasein stands at its naked, 'ownmost' potentiality of being. Heidegger calls such an intimacy the imminence of dasein to itself when all relationships are dissolved in it and that which cannot be bypassed. Absolute non-relationality is thrown back at the Self at the starkest in being-towards-the-end. The Self is completely attuned to itself in this move and mood.

Evading death, on the other hand, is a mark of 'tranquilized everydayness'. The concern to evade death comes from an intention to comfort the dying person. One can, as it were, either tranquilise the very subject of ending or invoke propriety and practise indifferent calm to the fact of dying. Death is either way estranged as the Self takes flight from it. However, there is no escape from the non-relational potential of being-towards-the-end. Death is always ahead of itself.

Could such anticipation of the ever-present possibility be what moves Mandal's quest for a distinct kind of water on the moon? Is he not far too distracted to be an authentic Self? This attunement to oblivion is angst, a direct confrontation with the Self's thrownness, Heidegger affirms ([1953] 1996). In angst, the dasein faces the 'nothingness of the possible impossibility of its existence'. Angst discloses the most extreme possibilities of existence, which is ending. The Self in its constant annihilation is fundamentally attuned to the wholeness of the potential-being. In this manner, the *being-there* authentically and resolutely anticipates the end. Being-towards-death is angst. It generates a condition that takes the *being-there* away from fear and expectation. This condition is the beginning of a passionate anxiety reaching 'freedom toward death which is free of the illusion of the they, factical, and certain of the itself'.

It must be iterated that the resolute anticipation of not-yet is not a psychological outcome of a private subject having a choice action or an inner attitude towards the world *at crisis* and/or its reaction to ennui. Authenticity is a function of dasein's efforts to engage with historicity. Encountering finitude is to encounter time.

Jean-Paul Sartre takes on the very idea of finitude and being-towards-the-end as formulated by Heidegger by considering death through an existential rather than a phenomenological lens. To Sartre, death has little implication for the one who dies or for one's living: 'There is no place for death in being-for-itself' (Sartre [1943] 1966). One must choose a course of action rather than be attuned to finitude as future death. Seeking radical freedom must undermine all anticipatory resoluteness directed towards the end and instead invest in consistent action. However, the first point about the existential take on ending is that it must foreground subjecthood as opposed to dasein. Death becomes a brute and contingent fact when conceived in nihilistic terms. Heidegger insisted that ending has nothing to do with perishing, for dasein never perishes; it does not experience its own death. Hence, he uses the term *demise* for authentic dying. Death is a way to be. Sartre, on the other hand, highlights the radical contingency of human existence. Sartre turns nostalgic and emphasises radical antagonism in living when he says that since no one can have any agency after death, one's death makes the person future prey to the living. Once again, such a formulation relies on the existentialist assumption of subjectivity. Once we bring ourselves to the existentialist plain, it is possible to relate death with absurdity or seek succour in other spheres, such as in theology. Death to Sartre is an accident just like birth and not, as Heidegger feels, a constant and impersonal presence. There is no direction of time in Sartre's sense of ending. There is only the nihilation of all possibilities.

In his meditation on death, *Aporias*, Jacques Derrida reads the end as a crossing of borders—to a different territory and country (from the Earth to the moon, for instance) and gives the Heidegger–Sartre debate a startling direction (1993). The end, for him, terminates all geopolitical determinations of an entire topography, where certain 'totalities are overdetermined or rather contaminated'. *Terma* or *finis* terminates all determinations—the catastrophes that affection, sociability, religion or/and identity might produce and foster, for instance. The Self travels to the beyond by penetrating the turgid contaminations of the catastrophic topos. Crossing the border is to pass the term of one's life. The passage to the moon is a prohibited one, indeed a non-passage, but that which promises water and, therefore, a topos for a future advent.

Passage or conceiving a passage by crossing the borders by dying is also a trespass. Babbling about taking one's own life, for instance, or engaging in a strange sign system is not permitted among the earthlings. It is not necessary or proper. To be lyrical is to take such a step, a step that crosses a line. Catastrophe is this limit that the earthly topos provides to the lyric voice. Catastrophe is the name of the insurmountable problem that the world encounters in dealing with the voice of the trespasser: 'There is a problem as soon as the edge line is threatened' (Derrida 1993). This problem can only be brought into tension with Derrida's favourite word: *aporia*—'not knowing where to go'. There is no protection or prosthesis when confronted by the end, the border. Such an exposed Self is the lyric voice. Death is hardly about the now or annihilation. Rather, it is the name of a possibility where all problems get confronted by a naked uniqueness. Tied up and paralysed by the end, aporia is the possibility of a dislocated pathway by means of effacing oneself.

Derrida especially marks a non-passive endurance of aporia to distinguish his way of looking into termination from the Heideggerian grounding in dignity. Catastrophes make the situation restive and contradictory, and the vulnerable voice feels 'a duty that owes nothing, that must owe nothing in order to be a duty' (Derrida 1993). The impracticability of the fortuitous, as seen in the play between the passage and the non-passage, is death's affirmation. Angst cannot dignify it. The Earth and the moon are separated and yet connected by certain attributes they share. That is the reason the moon hangs by the window, almost touchable. The moon is very much present on the Earth for Mandal advises Ruma to 'shake the bucket on the balcony full of water/And look for the moon' (n.d.).

Is this the imperative that produces the lyric—the move from the topological to the tropological and then to the anagogical/mystical? Or are we bound by the philosophic gestures still—of duty and hospitality—to which Derrida is beholden? Does the lyric voice have any duty towards being contradictory in its absolute vulnerability and, therefore, endurance?

The Voice within Catastrophe

What is the nature of the lyrical Self that also determines the syntagm of death? Does it carry the germ of the catastrophe forever with and within it? If the name of the death is not an event, could the presence fructify before the ontic event of mortal death? Catastrophe is the stark name for the complete and total annihilation that the Self faces in living. Only the lyrical Self can gauge the force and power of complete oblivion. But do dasein and the lyrical Self coincide, especially in contemplating the immolation of the Self? Does philosophical angst also disclose the authenticity of the being in art practice? Or for that matter, does confronting catastrophe as an obliterating force mean confronting absurdity and contingency?

Heidegger, in his postulates about being-towards-the-end, clearly seeks a unity of the being and phenomenon, the mediator being time. It is the obverse of Kantian idealism where aesthetic fosters and fortifies the reasonable subject in recognising itself. For Heidegger, the *open* is the site of such unity. The condition of catastrophe is, however, neither an idealistic possibility nor any state to achieve the romantic absolute. It is rather a predicament that characterises a complete breakdown of all unity. There is no comfort or companionship in conceiving the whole of being-there in conditions of living death. The poetic dwelling between the earth and the sky is torn asunder as *the lyrical inflexion becomes nomadic and is stunned into a fundamentally creaturely state.*

If the subject is gone, what remains? What is the nature of the residue in the lyric?

Lyric poetry is a homage to an unlived life. At its distillation, the lyric characterises limit-experiences. It marks the lineaments of utter disruption: in love, madness and death. Lyric is unadulterated unhomeliness. The lyric Self, therefore, is characterised by voice and gesture in babblings and doodles and, sometimes, in the chant and its repetitive fervour. Its immersion stands outside the transparency of communicative language. The lyric voice is not a persona, nor is it coterminous with the whole of *being-there*. It is the repeated graph of demolition, emergence and demolition. It is a strained and taut wire, a vibration of body and soul, for our durance is but small on the earth. In the throes of the unfathomable, Gerard Manley Hopkins, therefore, seeks the comforter: 'Pitched past pitch of grief/More pangs will, schooled by forepangs, wilder wring' (2008). However, grief does not comfort. The ramblings of the bereft waft, adrift. The half-gestures of the lyric emerge as a doubling of selfhood, but it is unable to represent the 'steep or the deep' (Hopkins 2008). It is an emergent form, only partially sketched, coalescing only to be dissolved in the form's crossings.

The poverty of the lyric voice is not about any lament: 'On the moon's round face why are there no streaks of agony/Why only the gestures of lunar-gatherings that rain' (Mandal 2008). There could be a sense of newfound joy, which hides the aching affliction of the voice standing face to face with catastrophe. The poem is about the 'dreams of the no person abandon'. Mandal's getting ready for the end is full of possibilities, though he shuns all physical and psychic modes of grasping so that he can survive false promises. There is an outright rejection of false tales of lament of the spindle-wielding hags. There are no unemployment streets on the moon, nor are there scheming relations. He/the voice is about to make a fortuitous journey. So he lightens all his earthly baggage—most significantly, plaints and tales of suffering. Instead, the voice begins to tarry: at the street corner, it waits excitedly. It is an imminent journey, but the waiting could be stretched. The voice is hardly an embodied space traveller. A spectral presence, the voice has left aside all sensory experience and anatomical descriptions as he repeats his joy at coming to know of the presence of water on the moon. His voice is strung only with other ghostly ones, that of Ruma and Arijit Kundu—all three of them look for water. Whatever they may have endured, there is no representable naming of corporeal loss—love, sexuality or friendship. What is being rejected by the living dead? No judgement is passed directly on the tormentors of the forgotten. The moment of the auto's arrival is a taut possibility—that is all. The auto is the arrivant that makes the event of separation from the Earth to the moon possible. Only the condition of thirst is highlighted. The voice awaits itself as it awaits the deliverer arrivant. Notably, tears and rain are the most corporeal metaphors that describe lunar water. And ice, that he hopes to sell on the moon. We can only guess the unsayable afflictions of his parched soul. That is all. The details of the wound are merely a matter for the embodied persona who walked and played on the earth.

The lyric is not about disembodiment though. There is no disinterested purpose in the lyric voice. Nor is there any direct reference to the pressures of complying with the exhortations of being-towards-the-end. It is also not that catastrophe hits the voice, leading to an eventual contingency. The subjecthood of the narrator is blurred, for it is foredoomed to be among relationalities and negotiations. It can only hope for the ecstatic journey to the moon. The voice begins to subtract earthly baggage. It begins to tell simple things now—about the cart full of ice, the meagre meal, the moon breeze and the locked bicycle. Each such image is oracular.

The images are not in any manner revelatory or renunciatory. The form of the poem emphasises demise on the earth itself, so that seeking water on the moon and considering the end is the only an ecstatic possibility. Once we retract all meaning from the games we play, meaning begins to partially emerge, through a glass darkly. Only the lyric form, with its partial but dangerous gestures, can overcome the silence of the being and the garrulity of the social persona. There is no consolation. There is no need for any. Failure is victory.

The moon is not a space for dwelling. It provides no shelter for the voice—only kindles hope for water. It only proposes an alternative: living on another plane of existence, the other side of the moon, since the moon is no permanent habitation to be *attained* once the disembodied Self has crossed the blood- and pus-filled Vaitarani. It is rather a space beyond the arrogance of earthly habitation and being's faith. The voice must dissolve into the moon breeze.

The lunar space offers no phenomenological ground nor any intending subject. It is a space as defined by the voice—the poet and the poet's nephew, Grandma and the prostitute. Foreman calls such a move 'granular widening'—a predicament where attention is stretched in relations. This widening would diachronically reach Mandal's favourite student, Tanmoy Kundu, who ended his life in a similar fashion, six years after Mandal's death (Arora 2014). Perhaps, both of them realised that the romantic unity of the subject and the object is elusive on the moon, for there is no situatedness in celestial bodies. The Earth is no more a site. The *assured open* on the Earth is not to be found. There is only a slow erosion of space. The voice breaks open on the moon: a prospect. It conceals distance. It lets go of all inwardness. On the moon, spectral voices join in communion with other cosmic beings. Mandal was deeply invested in spectrality as he was in art. One can still visit his video work on spectral presences (Mandal 2008).

The voice dreams about such a dream of the 'no-man abandon'. It is a migratory voice, that of the journeyman cosmonaut. It only requires the moon for a definite need—water. Otherwise, there is no permanence on the moon. The auto may not arrive. The arrivant is but a call, a nomination. The moon affirms the distance from the Earth, a place of refuge for the voice that has been turned away from the world. There is no motion, only the promise of deportation. The lines are a departing gesture, but the predicament is static. There is no movement. Only the gesture lingers—of a realisation that, on the ecstatic occasion of Buddha Purnima, the moon promises water. Can we anymore distinguish between authentic demise, perishing or crossing of the border?

Catastrophe is living death: that which is *unsayable*. Time turns out of joint. Lyric is a visitation that erupts when such a voice is created, and the voice trembles in and through incantations and warbling. The voice is a vestige, aleatory and ludic. There is no identifiable cause for the step that Mandal is about to take, but a great destiny is made and prefigured by the lines. The lines are at once a fictive promise and a matter-of-fact note. A stream is thus released: could his Self/the voice travel to the moon and we, his readers and interlocutors, await such an aesthetic release here, on the Earth? There is nothing numinous or pathological about such a suicide note; it does not reveal anything. The voice just harks for the auto on one random night. One night, it discovers that to taste water, it has to traverse to another topos. The lyric resists hermeneutics. It only remains as a foreign song, a trace and a footprint on the other side of the moon.

'I am Alive. No, You Are Dead'

The instant of the end is not the event of death. It is the carrying of a living corpse and a severed soul after and along with a catastrophe or disaster. The condition is most vividly portrayed by Maurice Blanchot in the *recit The Instant of My Death*. The recit concerns a young man 'prevented from dying by death itself—and perhaps the error of injustice' (Blanchot 2000). The Germans were about to shoot a young Frenchman—a marquis living in a chateau—after a raid. As they were aiming at him (the human target) and awaiting the final order, the man felt a sense of extraordinary lightness and a sort of beatitude—'sovereign elation' in Blanchot's evocative words. Blanchot wonders whether it was the encounter of death with death. It seemed he was invincible at that point in an ecstatic moment. Death meant steeping to immortality (the moon?). Further, he was flooded with a feeling of compassion for the suffering humanity. Was the release a matter of realising that he does not have to carry the burden of immortality anymore? It seemed he was 'bound to death by a surreptitious friendship' (Blanchot 2000).

At that moment, a nearby battle exploded. The soldiers waited. The moment, as it were, was split between life and death. A detour of time beckons. With a fortuitous turn of events, some Russians arrived at that point at the scene, and the marquis was left to disappear in the distant forest, still feeling light, until he was brought back to 'reality' as fire and a gun battle raged close by. He learnt that the three sons of a farmer had been slaughtered in the raid. They were 'truly strangers to all combat' (Blanchot 2000). Their fault was their youth. The seigneurs of the chateau—the man and his family—were spared. Nobility came between their existence and death.

The young aristocrat was now under the torment of injustice. At this point comes Blanchot's telling submission: 'This was war: life for some, for others, the cruelty of assassination' (Blanchot 2000). The man was torn—between inconsolable pangs on one hand and a sense of lightness on the other. Was he freed from life henceforth? He felt neither happiness nor unhappiness. There was an absence of fear and a looking into another cosmos. Blanchot concludes that for the rest of his living days, this unanalysable feeling was 'as if the death outside of him could only henceforth collide with the death in him' (Blanchot 1986). The instance of one's death is always at abeyance. Hent de Vries glosses the condition:

> Speaking of the *arret* of death, Blanchot evokes this paradoxical, indeed aporetic, structure by suggesting that one's being sentenced to death does not exclude but, on the contrary, presupposes the suspension of its actual arrival. More precisely still, death does not stop to arrive. Yet a death that at every instant goes on to arrive never arrives as such. (1998)

Jacques Derrida sought to underscore the relationship between the fictional and the archival, the imaginative and the evidentiary, in genres such as a recit, which is absolutely lyrical in its temperament. He particularly emphasised the 'undecidable limit'(*demeure*) of literature and its haunting possibilities—such as the one we encounter in Mandal's poetic excursion. The limit 'swears testimony to secrecy', even when it makes its aspirations public (Derrida 2008). The temporal moment of the secret is at once a fiction in its secrecy and a decision taken in the instant. Testifying to a secret without disclosing what is at the heart of it is something that interests both Blanchot and Derrida. The avowal to keep secret that which also must be declared marks a certain condition of the poetic. In the context of death, Derrida mentions the double suffering of the same passion, the passion of death in life, not only the impossible death, but the dying prohibited, 'the gentle prohibition against dying' (2008).

If we are attentive enough, we can notice a similar sense of secret avowal in Mandal's decision to take a ride to the moon. The unanalysable feeling, 'as if the death outside of him could only henceforth collide with the death in him', marks his secret space mission (Blanchot 1986). Blanchot designates such a state as 'neuter'—to which Derrida attests. In *The Step Not Beyond*, Blanchot says: 'The Neuter, the gentle prohibition against dying, there where, from threshold to threshold, eye without gaze, silence carries us into the proximity of the distant. Word still to be taken beyond the living and the dead, *testifying for the absence of attestation*' (1992). The neuter is a non-emotional but lyrical state. The poet does not give away anything; he does not confess nor does he dwell in any elegiac mode. Nothing is to be known except his supposed journey to the moon in an autorickshaw. The lyric voice is beholden to this condition of the neuter.

The role of culture is to cover up catastrophes—to deny the strangeness of all breakdowns. Only the lyric voice affirms the utter incomprehensibility of force and fate. Hence, it tears itself away from all consoling comfort. It would rather sell water on the nether side of the moon. Culture seeks authenticity. It wants to render death personal. However, such purity is adulteration, as John Gregg has rightly noticed (1988). Death's impurity is marked by the rejection of relations and the tale of the lunar hag. Blanchot and Mandal insist 'on the anonymous and non-eventful character of what the former calls *le mourier*' (Gregg 1988). The lyric voice makes all annihilation impersonal and irrelevant.

Suicide is an aptitude. It stays away from propriety. It shuns all merging with the great abyss. That would be a Stoic aim. The self-immolation of the persona means as if it aims to be completely conscious while taking its life, but it loses consciousness as it sinks. Suicide cannot be a project—an act of power. It is futile to 'choose' dignity for a voice that is forever in catastrophe and is living death itself—not unlike the marquis in Blanchot's recit. The casual ways of Mandal taking on teaching duties on a day when he goes on a journey to the moon affirms that death was always already a presence but never a philosophical project to mark propriety or Stoicism. The restless hide-and-seek of his lines depict what Blanchot calls a 'circular exigency': 'In order to die it is necessary to write' (1989). Writing is like a ghost caught on a camera.

Therefore, there is the birth of the lyric. Facing catastrophe, the lyric shuns all anchorage. It takes repeated flights, often misfired and misdirected. There is a tremendous sense of impatience in the note/poem. Writing is merely an impatient waiting game, an omission of selfhood, peppered with restless bouts of indecision. To be with the neuter is a practice. The voice must lose its way to wander into another universe. There are no shortcuts to the moon, no fixed orbit of traversing safely. Seeking water on the moon is a trap—but there is no respite from its siren call. The very errancy inhered in the misplaced hope that the auto-wallah shall eventually arrive is the victory of fiction over propriety.

References

Arora, Kim. 2014. 'Job Woes Kill Sharp, Friendly DU Scholar.' *Times of India*, 17 August 2014. Accessed 28 May 2021. https://timesofindia.indiatimes.com/city/delhi/job-woes-kill-sharp-friendly-du-scholar/articleshow/40324202.cms.

Barker, Howard. 1989. *Arguments for a Theatre*. London: John Calder Ltd.

Blanchot, Maurice. 1986. *The Writing of the Disaster*. Translated by Ann Smock. Lincoln: University of Nebraska Press.

———. 1989. *The Space of Literature*. Translated by Ann Smock. Lincoln: University of Nebraska Press.

———. 1992. *The Step Not Beyond*. Translated by Lycette Nelson. Albany: State University of New York Press.

Blanchot, Maurice, and Jacques Derrida. 2000. *The Instant of My Death/Demeure-Fiction and Testimony*. Translated by Elizabeth Rottenberg. Stanford: Stanford University Press.

Brown, Ron. 2001. *Art of Suicide*. London: Reaktion Books.

Carel, H. 2006. *Life and Death in Freud and Heidegger*. New York & Amsterdam: Rodopi.

De Vries, Hent. 1998. '"Lapsus Absolu": Notes on Maurice Blanchot's *The Instant of My Death*.' *Yale French Studies*, No. 93: 30–59.

Derrida, Jacques. 1993. *Aporias. Dying-awaiting (One Another at) the 'Limits of Truth.'* Translated by Thomas Dutoit. Stanford: Stanford University Press.

———. 2008. *The Gift of Death and Literature in Secret. Second Edition*. Translated by David Wills, Chicago: University of Chicago Press.

Edmond, Deepu Sebastian. 2009. 'DU Professor's Last Lecture Was on Suicide, says Student.' *Indian Express*, 23 November 2009. Accessed 28 May 2021. http://archive.indianexpress.com/news/du-professor-s-last-lecture-was-on-suicide-says-student/544943/

Edwards, P. 1975. 'Heidegger and Death as a "Possibility"'. *Mind* 84 (1): 546–566.

———. 1976. 'Heidegger and Death: A Deflationary Critique.' *The Monist* 59 (1):161–186.

Foreman, Richard. 1989. *Reverberation Machines: The Later Plays and Essays*. Barrytown Ltd.

———. 2010. *Manifestoes and Essays*. Theatre Communications Group.

Gregg, John. 1988. 'Blanchot's Suicidal Artist: Writing and the (Im)Possibility of Death.' *SubStance* 17 (1, Issue 55): 47–58.

———. 1994. *Maurice Blanchot and the Transgression of Literature*. Princeton: Princeton University Press.

Hammet, Jenny Yates. 1977. 'Thinker and the Poet: Heidegger, Rilke and Death.' *Soundings: An Interdisciplinary Journal* 60 (2): 166–178.

Heidegger, Martin. (1953) 1996. *Being and Time*. Translated by Joan Stambaugh. Albany: State University of New York Press.

Hopkins, Gerard Manley. 2008. 'No Worst, There Is None.' In *Poems and Prose*. New York: Penguin.

Hoy, David Couzens. 2006. 'Death.' In *A Companion to Phenomenology and Existentialism*, edited by Hubert L. Dreyfus and Mark A. Wrathall. Malden, MA, Oxford and Victoria: Blackwell Publishing Ltd.

Kauppinen, J. 2000. 'Death as a Limit of Phenomenology.' In *The Origins of Life. Analecta Husserliana* (The Yearbook of Phenomenological Research), edited by A.T. Tymienieck. Vol. 66. Dordrecht: Springer. Accessed 20 November 2022. https://doi.org/10.1007/978-94-017-3415-8_23

MacDonald, Michael, and Terence R. Murphy. 1990. *Sleepless Souls: Suicide in Early Modern England*. Oxford, UK: Clarendon Press.

Mandal, Achyut. n.d. 'Brief Biography and Poems.' Milansagar. Accessed 28 May 2021. http://www.milansagar.com/kobi/achyut_mandal/kobi-achyutmandal.html.

———. 2008. 'Ghosts Caught on a Camera.' *Jorabhoot* (blog). Accessed 28 May 2021. http://jorabhoot.blogspot.com/.

Sartre, Jean Paul. (1943) 1966. *Being and Nothingness*. Translated by H.E. Barnes. New York: Washington Square Press.

Schopenhauer, Arthur. 1913. *Studies in Pessimism: A Series of Essays*. Translated by Thomas Bailey Saunders. London: George Allen and Company, Ltd.

Thomson, Iain. 1999. 'Can I Die? Derrida on Heidegger on Death.' *Philosophy Today* (Spring): 29–42.

Uranga, Emilio. 2021. *Emilio Uranga's Analysis of Mexican Being*. Translated by Carlos Sanchez. London, New York, Oxford, New Delhi, Sydney: Bloomsbury.

Winkler, Rafael. 2016. 'Time, Singularity and the Impossible.' *Research in Phenomenology* 46 (3): 405–425.

III

AESTHETICS OF THE SELF

6

ANIMAMNEMO: SOVEREIGNTY OF THE SELF AND THE MNEMOCULTURES OF INDIVIDUATION

D. Venkat Rao[1]

Contexts of Concern

A context is a convergence of formations (be it an object, an event or a relation [of any species/gender]) and their reception. Such a convergence is a condition of the possibility of response. A context is thus doubly constituted of reception and response. Reception involves response, and response requires responsibility. A context is a condition of possibility *and* impossibility. Our contexts must be made to reorient the impossible to the possible—without certainties and guarantees. Quite often, in the context of the classroom, the context of the formation of the discourse gets privileged as the source of learning, teaching and relating them. Consequently, the context of reception (students, teacher(s) and their background) barely receives attention, which has consequences for the event of teaching and the formations involved therein.

If the privileged context of production in cultures that faced European incursions is determined by Europe, the formations of the discourse in question are the concepts of literature, woman, the humanities, the institution called the university and the communication system(s). The context of reception in our case, then, is India, students, teachers, institutions, native languages and their formations from India. This educational scenario impels a set of questions: How did these contexts interface, if they did at all? Did the interface irrupt a crisis? How was Europe received and responded to from the Indian context of reception? How was such a context (of reception) configured, if at all it ever was? Was the Indian context responsive from its resources to the invasive Europe? In the same breath, we can also ask: Was Europe sensitive to the context it invaded? As can be seen, the question of crisis pertains to the formation of, and the relation between, India and Europe.

As is well known now, the interface was based on an asymmetric relation between Europe and India. Europe imposed its frameworks of learning and understanding; and it calculatively designed the learning material, be it European or Indian. Existing forms and modes of learning and institutions in the context of reception were either discarded or discredited or made over. Consequently, there is a powerful disjuncture between the newly introduced educational programming and the learning traditions and practices of the context of reception: the context of production dominated the context of reception. The crisis in question is the eruption of such disjuncture with decisive consequences. Any attempt to unravel the crisis must engage with the European enframings of Indian formations. The conceptual grid that Europe releases at large is not necessarily universal, but today we (the 'non-Europeans') are programmed to reproduce them in our contexts.

Double Move in the Double Bind

How do we respond to these invasive enframings from the locations of their receptions? The task involves a double move in a double bind. A double bind is a situation in which one continues to use resources even when they are seen to be detrimental to the user who draws on them. European inheritance implicates us in a double bind: the un-inherited impels disinheritance. However, we can't just deny or voluntarily reject the irruptive framing. There could be another possible response to it from within: we must use the (un)inheritance more to know the genus of this formation (Europe) *from* the contexts of reception which it invades, rather than advance it as a resource for our nourishment. We use it to know Europe rather than to morph or force 'India' into the frames institutionalised by the illegitimate inheritance.

The second task is more challenging: taking the risk of configuring the contexts of reception minimally at least. What does 'India' stand for 'us' in the double constitution of our context? More specifically, in the context of this chapter, it should be possible to respond to the question of crisis by focusing closely on the long-cherished literary inquiries of/from India and/(*as*?) the forms of (the) engendering *of* woman. This chapter confines itself to conceptions of cultural forms that circulate as literary or poetic in relation to the question of engendering of woman.

Is the 'literary' a universally privileged engendering form? How do cultures engender the feminine and the poetic or the literary across cultures? Is the masculine the model/destination of the feminine? What conception of the feminine spurs the division between literature and philosophy? The task in our context would involve tracing the responsive receptions of such conceptual articulations in Greek, Sanskrit, Judaic and Christian cultural formations—in short, inquiring into these themes across Pagan (non-Semitic) and Semitic cultural formations.

Given the magnitude of the issues involved and the limitations of this chapter, it can only outline and thematise the problem on the premise of the cultural difference between the Semitic and non-Semitic cultures.

Such a sketch proposes that European cultural heritage can be unraveled as a concerted effort to expropriate and supersede pagan cultures over the last two millennia. The contours of such a sketch with regard to the thematics of the literary/feminine can be pointed out here: The Homeric mnemocultural ethos intimated *aletheia* as unopposed but variedly related notions of truth and deception, *muthos* and *logos*, feminine and masculine in singing *of* reality, which was not decisively reducible to some putative spatio-temporal determinants. The Judaic covenant displaces aletheia and advances an abiding secretive pact that demands loyalty but which cannot be disclosed. The call of the covenant is the eloquent secrecy that binds the elect and disseminates their promise indefinitely across space and time. The transcendental imperative of (Reformation) Christianity interiorises the call and inscribes the law as the principle that promises to subsume the chaotic manifold under the law of the sovereign Self. In the so-called modernity, the call seems to become the principle—the un-provable a priori. The a priori is the covenant, now driven by the interiorised imperative by which the self-determining subject abides. The concept of literature appears to be the immaculate conception of such a sublated synthesis disseminated across the 'gates of enemies', the pagans.

Melancholic Warping

The patently secularised discourse of two centuries (17th to 19th) covers up the blood-soaked story of the expropriations of the pagan Homeric aletheia. The discourse, at the most, comes out as a parricidal or fratricidal war of Semitic religions. If Catholics arraigned and castigated Jews as pagans, Protestants returned the same animosity to Catholics. If Plato was a pagan to Kant (Nancy 2008, 16–21, 86–90), Hegel saw Kant as Jewish (Derrida 2021, 238). Heidegger thought there can be no philosophical thought from the Judaic prophets (Zarader 2006, 7–8, 186–189). Curtius (probably following Hegel) discounted Jews as aesthetic people (Curtius 1953, 36; Gasche 1998, 92; on Hegel, cf. Derrida 2021, 49–50). Benjamin wished to free the Judaeo-German psyche of the Greek aura (Benjamin, 1986, 277–300), and so did Patočka (2002). Derrida vehemently denies the possibility that literature could ever emerge from pagan sources.[2] The story is endless, and the so-called pagans either disappear into silence or are impelled to be partisans in these alien fraternal wars of expropriation.

Literature is constituted by the Semitic 'aporia of forgiveness' (Derrida 2008, 138). Why does this ontology of guilt assert itself in this meditation on literature? Perhaps, guilt and forgiveness are inseparable from the question of sovereignty. Transgression makes one guilty, and only the power of sovereignty can forgive. Literature, in such a conception, is performative of the drama of defiance, guilt, remorse and forgiveness. Derrida's extended parabolic commentary on the conception of literature seems inherently melancholic, and it unfolds this defiant-remorseful performative from the Semitic genealogy (2008).

Can this melancholic Semitic-Abrahamic memory be declared as the destiny of planetary existence, despite the relentless efforts to secularise and universalise it?[3]

Perhaps, one can ask: *What if* this entire grand narrative about the romance of literature and philosophy is essentially a dissimulation of what Europe does not wish to say (Europe's, and certainly not Greek, 'secret')? After all, the lover's (but also murderous) antagonism between literature and philosophy emerges from the wrenching apart of muthos and logos. What if muthos and logos are fundamentally differentiated but non-oppositional, intimately but variedly related strands that are entwined with each other in the performative modes of mnemocultures, as they are in the Homeric tradition? Only a violent severance of the 'pair' brings forth literature as philosophy's parricidal reparation: 'Their distinction is exactly the de-intertwining, the de-embracing. The tangle thus untangled is separated by the sharpest of blades, but the cut itself forever bears the marks of that entanglement' (Nancy 2018, 26). The reparative structure seems to get crystallised in the Semitic encounter with the so-called pagan mnemocultures. The Semitic idiom (sharpest blade, cut, mark) in Nancy's commentary on the wrenching apart of muthos and logos cannot be missed (2018, 26). The reparation in question does not pertain to discourses as such (either about muthos or logos or literature or philosophy). European reparation (covenant, guilt, sublation/supersession) is a more 'hau(o)ntological' anxiety about its continued erasure of what Christianity circumscribed as pagan or heathen. The European romance is a remorseful secrecy about, to repeat Derrida's coinage, a 'genocidal annihilation' (erasure of genus/species) of 'pagan' modes of being in existence.

In the shadow of such an enframing context of production, one must take the risk of reflecting on the context of reception. The rest of the chapter takes such a risk and suggests the way the cultural difference works in the conception of the thematics of the literary and the feminine in the context of India.

Mnemocultural Configurations

What is called Indian culture is an inter-animating assemblage composed of distinct biocultural formations—*jati*s—and their singular cultural forms: *vidya*s and *kala*s. Jatis are internally differentiated *and* differentially marked formations that cohabit in shifting and changing habitats across extended durations. As the most enduring and resilient formations, they bring forth divergent cultural forms that proliferate variedly and rhizomically across and beyond the colossal assemblage of 'India'. Jatis/*Jan-Jati*s and their inexhaustible generative force have formed the mnemocultures of India. Mnemocultural generative impulses come forth through the most primordial and immemorial or originary technics of the body: gesture (performance) and speech (song). Here, the body itself operates as the absolute medium and effect of radical generativity. These technics bring forth varied and related performative cultural forms such as music, image, text and performance. They foreground the body as the medium and the destination of experience. Inquiries into these performative traditions reveal cultural differences.

Performative reflections bring forth a liveable learning—a learning that is rendered in living and a living that is intimated by learning. Liveable learning persistently exposes one to the question without, however, such a question being formalised: *How should one live?* The response to such a question must be rendered in praxial modes in given situations of temporal existence, in one's *lokation*. The quintessential praxial modes of such performative living are immersive listening, silent recall and meditative focus. Performative articulations subsume the thematic and formal considerations in the formations of liveable learning. The test of learning is in the lively rendering of learning rather than in interpretive discourses *about* it—hence, the extended *absence* of (literary) critical, interpretative and translational traditions among the mnemocultures of India.

Indian cultures of memory flourished mnemonically and non-inscriptionally over millennia, mutually constituting and enhancing the genos and genres of India. These biocultural formations disseminate themselves as lively archives. Lively archives embody and enact their cultural memories in their performative modes of being. They remain indifferent to the inscriptional retentional systems. The guardians of these heterogeneous lively archives are from very distinct cultural formations or jatis. They are also the masters of the idioms chiselled by the technics of the body over an extended duration. The liveable learning they forge and impart is excruciating and demanding, and they carve out the recipients for it with patience and perseverance.

The Sanskrit/Indian *Vaangmaya* (pervasive verbal universe) emerged and flourished over millennia in a mnemocultural milieu. It preferred to disperse embodied memory in enacted forms and impart liveable learning through lively archives, even after inscriptional systems invasively established themselves. Indeed, they embraced inscriptional cultural forms into their mnemocultural lively currents.

The Sanskrit vaangmaya proliferates in two major verbal and visual forms, well known as the heard ones (*shruti*) and the recalled ones (*smriti*). The entire delimited range of cultural forms like the Vedas, the Brahmanas, the Aranyakas and the Upanishads are classified as a part of shruti vaangmaya. The infinitely proliferating cultural forms of the smriti such as sutra, *shaastra*, *itihaasa*, *purana*, *naatya*, *shilpa*, *chitra* and *kavya* continue to flourish across the entire mnemoscape of India as smriti vaangmaya. The relation between these two mnemo currents is that of responsive reception. The smriti compositions draw on the imports of shruti and transformatively remediate them across indefinite time and space. The trio of the singer-bard (*suta*), the performer (*bharata*) and the seer (*kavi*) enliven and disperse the recalled cultural forms of the vaangmaya even to this day. The trio circulates as the guardians of mnemocultural intimations and (trans) formations.

Almost every jati and jan-jati of India has, directly or through detours, embraced, transformed and enhanced the smriti traditions beyond measure. 'Indian culture' is entirely the result of intense and persistent responsive receptions across the twin currents of shruti and smriti on the one hand and that of the jatis on the other. All the extant and emerging mnemocultural forms of image, music, text and performance of India (and its relays) can be explored as the dynamic effects of such responsive receptions. The reflective and creative media of India, from oral to digital technics, are woven in multiple ways in the mnemocultural milieu. The invisible intimations of these mnemocultural forms and their biocultural formations can be sensed in their perpetual communication across India. The roots and routes of such (in)tangible but insistent currents can be said to compose the Indian mnemocultural-scape. These currents are also the restive and lively channels that relay the cultural forces inside and outside of the cultural-scape of what has come to be called India. In such a weave, we should attempt to track the questions of our concern here: How do the literary inquiries move in such extended traditions of shruti and smriti? And how has the sense of the poetic or literary articulated the question of the engendering of woman within the delimited fabric of the Sanskrit vaangmaya?

Performative Teleosis

Verbal and visual compositions and inquiries into them are of immemorial origin in the Sanskrit vaangmaya. Inscriptional articulation of them (in plastic and pigmental forms) emerged nearly two millennia *after* the vaangmaya has dispersed itself. From Bharata to the colonial period, sustained and divergent traditions of inquiry into the literary proliferated across Sanskrit, Prakrit and other *bhasha*s (languages) of India. Yet, across all these extended inquiries, no standardised, canonical conception of the literary was ever universally or canonically advanced. A kavya (poem) is what the kavi did with the received verbal-poetic language and form. Literary inquiries emerged as reflective formations of kavis (from *kavana*—to say). Literary inquiries in Sanskrit traditions emerged and were nurtured in a general learned milieu of inquiries. These inquiries were concerned primarily with formationality in general on the one hand, and its relation to actional or performative modes of being on the other. This relation and its spatio-temporal occurrence is seen to be recursive, and it results in transformative manifestations of emergences and dissolutions of formations and their relations. These inquiries themselves brought forth enduring disciplines of learning (shaastras).

In such a flourishing reflective milieu, Bharata's *Naatyashaastra* emerges as the most celebrated discipline of learning pertaining to performative traditions. His inquiries were made possible within a prevailing performative milieu of the shruti traditions. Bharata's inquiries spurred and impacted other kinds of exploration in other domains, such as literary, sculptural, pictorial-pigmental, architectural and musical. The *Naatyashaastra* is an exhaustive compendium that deals with the minutest articulation of the discrete elements of the body formation. It is a digital rendering of gestural, acoustic and lexical elements that compose performative, verbal and musical forms in a designated architectural form ('theatre'). Bharata draws on the given, available sources of the tradition to bring forth unforeseen cultural forms: musical-dance-drama.

Such forms draw on the *loka* (spatio-temporal complex), and they are orientative in essence—to turn humans from their indulgent vulgar ethos (*graamyadharma-pravrutti*; Bharata 2006, 36.46, 1102) to a refined or transformed mode of being. Performative forms are desirable and playable visual and verbal compositions: '*kreedaneeyakamichhaamo drushyam shravyam cha yadbhavet*' (1.11, 60). They bring forth cultural forms enacting virtual lives that are pleasurable and orientative. They repose the strife-ridden: the sorrowful, tired, grief-stricken, meditative and resting people of the world gain succour from dance-drama (1.114, 79).

Virtualised rendering of the existent modes of being is the aim of performative traditions like the dance-drama. The day-to-day modes of being are called *lokadharmi* (common ethos) and the virtual ones *naatyadharmi* (performative ethos). Such a differentiated rendering of the existent modes of being has a possibility of distancing the indulgent from *graamya* (vulgar) and *loka pravruttis* (common modes of going about). Such a reorientative distancing form must be pleasurable to the receiver. Pleasure is a savourable actional affect/effect, which in turn can spur action: affect is the medium and effect of action (of all the varied ethos or *dharmis:* graamya, loka and naatya). The source and destination of pleasure are sedimented actional affects/effects. Actional affects/effects communicate to actional affects/effects through a detour evoked by the spurring affects: the detour is the savourable actional flavour.

Bharata identifies eight renowned sedimented actional affects/effects: erotic, jestful, sorrowful, rageful, exciting, frightful, disgusting and puzzling (Bharata 2006, 6.17, 212). These, in turn, evoke eight communicable actional flavours. Erotic, funny, kindred empathy, rageful, heroic, frightful, dreadful and bewildered are the eight performative gestures in dance, renowned as actional flavours (6.15, 211).

Another sediment and its corresponding flavour were added to the received ones after Bharata: the *viraaga* affect/effect is said to evoke the *shaanta* flavour. All modes of being (graamya, loka and naatya) are media and effects operated by these nodes of gratificatory affects: nothing escapes them. The question of affect is central to inquiries in general in Sanskrit traditions. The most general level at which this question was addressed, without such a question being formulated or formalised, took the form: What is the relation between the affect and the transformative formations? In other words, what is the relation between modes of being and shifting formations of existence? An implicit response to such a question with which the inquiries concerned themselves is praxial living in the formational existence exposed to actional affects/effects. Bharata's take on the affect opened another kind of responsive reception. Inquiries into cultural forms reiterated variedly his responsive reception of the tradition.

Literary inquiries spread across nearly two millennia in the common era (from Bharata to Jagannatha Pandita and beyond). The singular aspect of these disciplines of learning is that most of the inquirers not only reflected on the question of (cultural) formation in particular but also themselves brought forth singular cultural forms of the domain concerned (that is, they brought forth kavyas or shaastras). In other words, inquiring learning here manifests in a rhythm of reflective action *and* reflection on action in relation to the formation in question: the inquirer and his relation to the domain of the discipline and the particularity of the relevant form. That relation must come forth as a singular cultural form. Each of the cultural forms—plastic, pigmental, verbal and musical—incorporated in Bharata's inquiry received singular and exhaustive attention in the later years. Each such endeavour resulted in the emergence of a unique (but deeply filiated) discipline of learning. Each of them offered colossal and minutely detailed concrete accounts concerning the material, the manner and the formation of a particular discipline of learning (such as shilpa, chitra, *sangita* and kavya/*sahitya*). Literary inquiry happens to be just one among an extended set of inquiries.

Literary Pulsations

Given the performative nature of inquiries in Sanskrit traditions, what is common to all of them is the body complex or the biocultural formation. Reflection here distinctively works in the performative/actional modes: the body gets put to work reflectively. Rajasekhara captures such a performative reflective relation most eloquently and most economically (2003). From the entirety of vaangmaya, Rajasekhara specifies only three singular domains of learning in his inquiry into the literary. In *recalling* these domains, Rajasekhara's distinction is in foregrounding the distinction of the literary impulse (4–6):

1 The 'un-agentive' compositions of learning (*apaurusheya*) are compositions without any association of a definitive author or authorising agency. These compositions accrue six 'limbs' as ancillary domains of learning (*shadanga* or *vendanga*), which are necessary to discern the imports of the 'unagentive' compositions of the Vedas (shruti).
2 The domains brought forth in turn by the learned of the shruti are 'agentive' compositions ('*paurusheya*'—smriti), which are often associated with a specific name in the tradition (such as puranas, *itihaasa*, *dharmashaastra*s or kavyas). Smritis are understood on the basis of the imports of shruti. Internally differentiated, the paurusheya domains multiply, but Rajasekhara specifies them broadly as four in number (he names them as purana, *anveekshaki* [a reflective validational discipline], *meemaamsaa* [a discipline of learning that enquires into the sense of Vedic utterances] and *smrititantra* [disciplines of praxial or practitional learning]).
3 A mode of utterance deeply attentive to musical, acoustic and verbal elements as affective media is kavya. Without a rigidly segregated domain of its own, the kavya impulse pervades all domains of learning.

In all, these domains of learning of shruti and smriti combined are fourteen in number (four+six+four). Now, Rajasekhara sees the inherent permeation of the kavya impulse across both the shruti and smriti domains. Therefore, he contends, the learning pertaining to the kavya impulse should be accorded a place among all the agentive and unagentive domains of learning (Rajasekhara 2003, 5–13).

The kavya mode is pervasive, observes Rajasekhara. Given that the shruti compositions are verbal, acoustic and musical performative forms, to sense and discern their verbal musical import, a domain that explores the cultivated elegance of kavya can be accorded a supplemental place among the shadangas as a *saptamaanga*. Such a new domain of learning is designated as the *alamkaarashaastra* (the domain of embellishing tropes). Similarly, Rajasekhara contends that given its cultivable elegance as a formative source, kavya can also appear as a distinctive supplement among the fourteen shaastra vidyas of the smriti vaangmaya, and he designates it as the kavya vidya (2003, 5–13).

Vidya is a musically and gesturally uttered verbal composition, a form of the muthos. One can compose even an intricate domain of learning—say, pertaining to the formation of language or tropes—in a kavya form as a kavya vidya. Rajasekhara calls those who compose such poems shaastra kavis. The received set of fourteen vidyas can be enhanced with the addition of four more vidyas of an everyday transactional nature: *Vaarta* (growing crops, tending animals and trade), *kaama* (erotics), *shilpashaastra* (sculpture) and *dandaniti* (domain of punishments). These domains help the cultivation of discretionary action in everyday living. Even among these, kavya can have a distinctive place as the fifth one. Rajasekhara names it sahitya vidya, the domain of learning that conjoins everyday transactional life with an orientative ethos. The latter is the essence of such domains of learning: it imparts cultivable orientation (Rajasekhara 2003, 5–13).

All these shaastra and vidyas are spread across all the lokas, and no one can exhaust even any one of them. At a most elementary level, the term *kavya* emerges from kavana, which implies utterance, a kind of perlocution, utterable or sayable. '*Kavaneeyam kavyam*', says Abhinavagupta: that which is said/sayable/singable is kavya [Anandavardhana 1998, 30]). The sayable is not reducible to either what is said or how it is said and what it entails. Yet attention to the 'how' is at work in giving shape or form to the sayable. As can be seen, kavya can have a place wherever verbal-acoustic, musical and actional media are at work. Here, kavya seems to be more of an impulse of formationality in general. It is a cultivable and refinable orientative impulse that can lend itself to distinctive formations of varied domains. Such an impulse is the basis of literary inquiries in India. Hence, Bhamaha (following

Bharata) thought that there is no domain that the kavi (kavya) cannot permeate: '[There is] no sound, no expression, no logic, no gestural formation that a kavi cannot (afford) not (to) know. What a burden the poet has to carry!' (Bhamaha 2004, 5.4, 106).

Several centuries before Bhamaha, Bharata has already sensed this in his source treatise: '[There is] no knowledge, domain of learning, carved formation, verbal domain, gestural formation, yoga, performative-act which cannot be shown in the dance-drama/theatre' (Bharata 2006, 1.116, 79). Therefore, Rajasekhara thought that kavya can be sourced (kavya *yonis*) in all the thirty-two vidyas (which he enumerates) and sixty-four kalas (which he mentions) (2003, 13–14).

Languages of Inquiry

Literary inquiries in the Indian context came forth broadly in two related forms: (i) an inquiry that brings forth a kavya composition and (ii) an inquiry that probes into *how* the cultivable refinable impulse is at work and how its efficacy can be sensed among specific poetic compositions. The latter can yield a shaastra composition without negating or erasing the kavya impulse from its formation. As modes and formations of utterance, what is common to these two inquiries is that they both unequivocally put the cultivable orientative impulse to work. However, why, how, where and when the kavya/the sayable occurs remains intractable. Literary inquiries of the shaastra kind, in focusing on the question of *how*, aspire to become a domain of knowledge among the renowned ones. Their status, however, as a distinctive domain was questioned from within this very domain of literary inquiry.

Language as the sayable formation is central to literary inquiries. However, literary inquiry is not the first domain to probe into the question of language. Language as a source of formation has already received intense attention among the celebrated disciplines of linguistic, phonetic, metrical and etymological inquiries among the Vedic shadangas long before literary inquiries staked their distinctive status as a novel domain of learning. From another related vantage, the appropriateness of contextual usage, the situational sense of specific usages and the evidentiary status of language were rigorously examined by the six domains of the Darshanaas. Literary inquirers were nurtured in the milieu of such extended and intense inquiries into the nature and usage of a verbal formation called language.

Brought up in a demanding milieu of inquiries, literary inquirers appear to advance a 'novel' claim concerning language. They contend that language, like *any* other formation (or formationality in general), is the medium and effect of the affect. That is, the affect inflects and articulates language contextually in unforeseen ways and brings forth uncommon significance out of the commonly used medium. Such an affective inflection may take into account the established rules pertaining to verbal formations, their contextual usages, their sources and their validity, but it can also *counter* their significance by going beyond what such rules offer. Such inflections of the given bring forth novelty in the articulations of language. A great literary work is recognised on the basis of its power to evoke the uncommon from the common. Following Bharata, one can say that *kavyadharmi* ('literary' ethos) transforms the affective flavours of the *lokadharmi* of common language and releases the unprecedented affective savouring. Such a savouring experience is not merely the result of linguistic competence (which *shrutighana*s (masters of Vedic utterance) and *shaastrakaara*s (experts in various domains of learning) have in perfection, says Rajasekhara (2003, 212). The affective orientation of language can spur awake the sedimented effects that can communicate the unprecedented delighting rapturous flavours of/for experience. Refined affective infusions can shape the medium of utterance and bring forth the incomparable and the unforeseen.

If formationality is the concern of Indian inquiries in general, literary inquiries focused (like the *Vedaanga*/*Daarshanika* savants) on the formation of language and treated it essentially as the other complex formation: the (human) body. The relation between the body and poetic formation (kavya *shareera*) is more than analogical in these inquiries. Both these bodies (or the shareera in general) are formed of cultivable endowments and a non-formational force, a force which cannot be formed or reckoned with formational resources. Such a force is seen as the source of formationality in general, and it is said to precede, pervade and permeate all the formations and relations. It has neither a beginning nor an end and does not emerge or get dissolved the way all the formational emergences do. In such a context, the task of the endowed or the one who is concerned with the body is to aim at a persistent refinement of these endowments and, through such refinement, attempt to sense/experience the force of the non-formational. This sensing itself, when one learns to receive it, was seen in some inquiries as the supremely rapturous experience. The literary inquiries *of* the kavya suggest that the essence of kavya is *akin* to the non-formational force that is the source of formationality in general.

Bioculturalities of the Literary

Literary inquirers differed from each other in conceiving the literary formation. Consequently, the emerging domain of literary inquiries remained internally and externally contested in its extended existence. Such contestations, however, were not aiming at determining a standardised systematic formalisation of the domain and its concepts. Even when they seemed to generalise, the drive for universalisation seemed alien or unintelligible in these inquiries. Every attempt at generalisation was qualified with the instantiation of an exceptional occurrence. Mammata captures this impulse quite aptly:

> *Niyatikruta niyama rahitaam hlaadaikamayeem*
> *ananya paratantraam navarasaruchiraam nirmitee.* (Mammata 1995, 1.1, 1)
>
> That [composition] which is formed in accord with conventions and rules but abides by no regimen of principles, replete with delighting sense, effusing the nine savourable flavours, and depends on none other [that is kavya].

Some inquirers, however, saw the essential task of the kavi as the refinement of the endowments of poetic formation. Given that kavya is an acoustic, verbal and gestural formation, the task was seen as the diligent refinement of sounds and words (sense) of the composition. The reiteration of the formationality of (poetic language) endowments can be seen from a wide variety of formulations over a millennium.

Bhamaha says, '*shabdaarthau sahitau kavyam*' (2004, 1.16, 16). Kavya is the togetherness of the sound and sense. A kavya, says Dandi, is:

> *Shareeram taavtishtaartha vyavachhinnaa padaavalee.* (2011, 1.10, 7)
> Delighting verbal chain [composes] the (kavya) body.
>
> *Shabdaartha shareeram taavatkaavyam.* (Abhinavagupta 1998, 22; the citation is from Sreeramachandrudu's Introduction [Mammata 1995, 18])
> Kavya is the embodiment of sound and sense.
>
> *Shabdaarthau sahitau yatra kavi vyaapaarashaalini*
> *bandhe vyavasthitau kavyam tadvidaahlaadakaarinee.* (Kuntaka 2007, 1.7, 26)
> Those conjoining of sound and sense through the curved (carved) work of the poet, which is the source of delight: that is kavya.

Bhoja further elucidates the work of kavya:

> *Nirdosham gunavat kavyam alamkaarairalamkrutam rasaanvitam kavih kurvan keertim preetim cha vindati.* (Bhoja cited in Sreeramachandrudu's Introduction to Mammata [1995, 19])
>
> By beautifying the poetic formation with blemish-less endowments, the poet evokes delighting flavours and attains fame and pleasure.
>
> *Vaakyam rasaatmam kavyam.* (Viswanatha cited in Sreeramchandrudu's Introduction to Mammata [1995, 20]).
> A sentence permeated by delighting flavours is kavya.
>
> *Ramaneeyaartha pratipaadaka shabdah kavyam.* (Jagannatha 1942, 7)
>
> Sounds positing (evoking) captivating sense is kavya.

Kavya can come forth as verse or prose composition, declare all literary inquirers.

Literary inquirers insisted upon reflections on the affective articulation of the endowed media (of language and/as the body). Such a claim seemed to differentiate them from the Daarshanika conception of language. The latter accorded a valid status to a verbal utterance only if it conformed to their rigorous means of validation (*pramaana*). The Daarshanika means of validation are: (i) direct/perceptual grasp (*pratyaksha*); (ii) indirect inferential surmise (*anumaana*); (iii) authority of the Vedic utterance (*shabda*) and the doxa (*aapta vaakya* or received opinion or the word of the well-regarded). The function of language (for the Daarshanikaas) is to relate a 'form' of utterance to a (commonly known or conventional) 'meaning' (shabda/*artha*). Such a function of relation is designated as *abidha*. Abidha is composed of two aspects: form and meaning. The form is called *vaachaka* (shabda/saying) and its meaning *vaachya* (the said/artha). Thus, the formation of language is configured as a form, its meaning and the function it renders (in relating it to the context and the elements of the formation). Such a relation is evidenced in everyday usage of language for the Daarshanikas.

Literary Obversense

In their conception of kavya shareera, literary inquirers evoked a different sense of language/formation/body. They differed from Daarshanikaas in different ways. Some treated the kavya as beauteously adorned decorative tropes or epithets of linguistic endowments. The charm of these epithets is seen as the property/endowment of language. Yet the significance of such properties cannot be reduced to the conventional denotations of the Daarshanikaas. The beauteous epithets evoked/conveyed an alluring significance that differed from the common usage of denotation: hence, their attention to the endowments of language and their refinement in the context of the work of the affect. Only embellished epithets delight as kavya:

> *Kaavyam graahyam alamkaaraat.*
> Kavya is received/grasped as its figural embellishments.
> *Saundaryam almkaarah.* (Vamana 2003, 1.1.1–2, 1–2)
> Figural embellishment is beauty.

This strand of literary inquiries is known as *Alamkaarashaastra*, and it was sustained over centuries by Bhamaha, Dandi, Vamana and Rudrata in the first millennium of the Common Era. Aalamkaarikaas (masters of figures of speech) designated the function of language as *lakshana* (marker or indicator), the form of the epithet as *laakshanikam* (trope or figure of speech) and its meaning as *lakshyaartha* (implied or suggested or alluded sense). These terms differed from abidha, vaachaka and vaachya of the Daarshanikaas. The Laakshanikaas contend that the relation between the verbal form and its sense can exceed that of common denotation. Yet another strand of literary inquirers differed not only from the Daarshanikaas but even from the Aalamkaarikaas. They contend that the source of rapturous experience of kavya cannot be reduced only to its exhibitive linguistic charms.

The carefully chosen elements of language in use by the poet, contends the third group, spurs a sense that is indeterminable and irreducible to the mere linguistic function of its endowments; such effect/affect can traverse intractable generations, contexts and formations and yet communicate indefinitely and atemporally, they contend. Such intimations spur the remotely submerged and sedimented actional affects/effects. Such spurring is rapturous for the one who experiences such an affective effect and, one becomes immersed in savouring such an experience.

Kalidasa intimates such an experience:

> *Tachchetasaa smarati noona ma bodha poorvam*
> *bhaavasthiraani jananaantara sauhrudaani.* (cited in Satyanarayana 2007, 83)

> Earlier un-sensed memory awakens transgenerational actional sediments nesting or sheltered in the heart of the receiver (intractable traces of generationally traversed memory get awakened by the poetic utterance).

Poetic compositions that evoke such remote and incalculable intimations indefinitely are called *dhvani* kavyas (resonant compositions). The third strand of literary inquiry is advanced by the Dhvanikaaraas, primarily Anandavardhana, Abhinavagupta and Mammata (in the first and second millennia). The term *dhvani* itself is inspired by the *Vayyakarani* (an expert in the domain of *Vyakarana*, one of the Vedaangaas) Bhartrhari in his conception of *sphota* (plosive spurring of memory), which evokes a sense that was inaccessible or unavailable until that specific instance. Sphota/dhvani (which are not to be conflated) was used by the third group to differentiate their strand from those of Daarshanikaas (*meemaamsakaas*). Primarily, the Dhvanikaara contention was that the very same endowments of common language can spur up remotest sense, a sense that is not consciously or calculatively evoked as such. Such sense cannot be reduced to the denotative accounts of language. The Dhvanikaaraas designated such a function (surplus from/through the commonly known sense) as *vyanjana*, its form as *vyanjaka* and the sense it spurred as *vyangyaartha*.

The Daarshanikaas contested that one of their pramaanaas (inferences) can serve the function of denoting the hidden and thus denied a different account of language. However, the Dhvanikaaraas contend that only when vyangyaartha is *contrary* to what a common utterance denotes, a poetic work can be considered a resonant poetic formation (dhvani kavya). Otherwise, they agreed, such resonance can only be an inferential suggestion. Only great poets can accomplish such a poetic composition, argued the Dhvanikaaraas.

What is at stake in these disputations is according a distinctive status to literary inquiries among other disciplines of learning (seventh, fifteenth and fifth positions of supplementation, as discussed earlier in the context of Rajasekhara). Such a status is sought based on the intensive and extensive reflections of the literary inquirers on the question of the affect in the process of putting to work the endowments of the (biocultural) formations. To be sure, all inquiries grappled with the question of affect in the tradition, which makes the disputations entirely internal to the tradition. All the literary inquirers (of both kinds—often by the same persons) were very learned in the shaastras. They composed shaastra treatises and also composed celebrated kavya works. In other words, every poet/kavi is a real or potential shaastrakaara, and every shaastrakaara a poet. Kshemendra, like

Rajasekhara, identifies four distinct ways in which kavya can manifest and cut across any rigorous divide between shaastra and kavya (a division which is a distinctive metaphysical manifestation since Plato in the European heritage):

> *Shaastram kavyam shaastrakavyam kavyashaastram cha bhedatah Chatushprakaarah prasarah sataam saarasvato matah.* (Kshemendra 1983, 2.2, 265)
>
> Saraswati's (goddess of learning) endowments can manifest in four different ways and formations: *shaastra* (a domain of reflective learning/formation—here, pertaining to poetic formations: *alamkaarashaastra*), kavya (domain of poetic formation), *shaastrakavya* (reflective-poetic formation—here that formation which poetically imparts the traditional four ends of man: dharma [discernible endowments], *artha* [permissible wealth], *kaama* [permissible urges] and *moksha* [releasment]) and *kavyashaastra* (poetic-reflective formation which becomes accessible to many) (165–267).

However, these internally differentiated and yet interwoven positions (of kavya and shaastra) indicate two approaches to the question of affect in relation to formations (in general).

Formational Pulls

Language happens to be just one among infinitely finite formations. Indian inquiries deeply and widely probed into formationality in general, sensing, at the same time, the very formational nature of the inquirer and the medium focused upon ('language'/medium/body in general) for inquiry. A formation is in essence the absolute medium and effect of formationality as such for these inquirers. The operation of the medium has transformative consequences for the formation in question. In such a praxial reflective tradition, refining the medium/media of formations is the essential orientation of any formation in its instant of manifestation. Such a task is perennially exposed to the dynamic of affect.

When the affect dominates the relation to formation(s) in their task, one gets fixated on the formation and longs for it. Consequently, one suffers insecurity and anxiety and disavows or ignores the transient and transformative nature of formationality. At the same time, one can't obsessively repress affect and thus presume to overcome it: affect and action are inescapably related and constitutively work on the medium of the formation. Fundamentally, affect is a formless force that seems to spur action but which itself cannot be reduced to the resulting formation or action. In such a situation, one fails to see that obsessive indulgence (say, with regard to formations) itself is an articulation of the force of the formless affect. Those who discern this subtle and complex relation are known as the seers of 'that (*of*) you': *tat-tva-darshi*.

Such seers are neither formation- or medium-specific. They discern such a play of the affect across formationality in general—human or non-human. Wherever there is a form and relation, such a sense of seeing is possible. In the Indian vaangmaya, such a possibility is already opened up by the compositions that are neither shaastras nor kavyas as such but which already contain these two related reflective creative currents and fibres. Such are the apaurusheya compositions of the shruti strand that flow through the smriti fibres essentially, variedly and pervasively. In the realm of smriti, the differentiated formations or domains of learning—verbal and visual compositions—multiply, emerge and proliferate. They transformatively communicate the imports of the shruti strand.

When one takes pride in the craft of utterance or sound and sense and becomes obsessed with validational means alone or glorifies embelleshing epithets, one cannot sense that subtle relation of affect and formation that binds and bonds with formations and the entailing action. The Laakshanikaas (Aalamkaarikaas) suffer from their fixation with the adornments of language. The deepest urge of the Daarshanikaas to ascertain valid knowledge and their minutest observations of means of validation may cause them to lose the path to such discernment:

> *Shabdaartha shaasana jnaana maatrenaiva na vedyate*
> *vedyate sa tu kavyaartha tattvajnai reva kevalam.*
> (Anandavardhana 1998, 1.7, 136)
>
> Mere commanding learning about sound and sense alone does not enable one to discern. Only those who are aware of *kavyaartha tattva (the that-ness of the* kavya [which cannot be reduced to the mere sonic-verbal expertise]) can sense through *prateeyamaana/ vyanjana* of the great poet:
>
> *Prateeyamaanam vastvasti vaaneeshu mahaakaveenaam.* (Anandavardhana 1998, 1.4, 62)

The essence of a great poem (*kavyaartha tattva*) gets articulated as vyanjana (counter-sense). Such counter-sense cannot be reduced to the formations of language that the Laakshanikas and the Daarshanikaas are obsessed with . The essence of a great poem deviates radically from the given to sense the 'given' in unforeseen ways in an instance of its occurrence. In the utterance of the great poets resides the *prateeyamaana* (obverse-sense or obversense). The great poets and the learned are indeed *kavya tattvaartha darshibhi* (Anandavardhana 1998, 208), the discerners of kavya's own otherness in itself; the irreducible internal differentiation of oneself as the other—*tat-tvam* (that-(*of*) you)—the same formation (body or the verbal poetic form) as the radically other from within itself. Hence, kavya is irreducibile to the formational. In inducing indulgence among formations, affect has the power to occlude the other that is irreducible to the formations, whereas the *tattvadarshi* discerns the force and the play of the (non)affect and senses the heterogeneous in the 'same'.

Un/formable Force

While drawing on much deeper sources of the shruti trajectory, the shaastra tattvadarshi, such as Bhartrhari, grappling with the formation of language, senses the non-formational that is irreducible to the formational as *para*. Para is the 'source' of all formations (including verbal-visual language), which itself remains, however, always already, like the affect, forever non-formational. The non-formational inheres in all formations, but sensing or accessing it can only be achieved through the medium of formations. There is no question of thinking or experiencing of para outside the matrix of formationality. However, such 'access' cannot yield a formational grasp of para: para cannot be formed. Every attempt to grasp para by the formational means only enhances the latter, leaving para unaccessed or inaccessible. Yet para can be discerned. The efficacy of such discernment can be experienced and reckoned with only in modes of being. The sensing involves a living on *of*/with the radically heterogeneous—formational and the non-formational—within the 'same' formation. How do the heterogeneous relate? The effect of such discernment can be seen in how one relates oneself with the other (tat-tvam) of one's 'own'. Para cannot be designated as either external or internal to the formation. Even here, once again, the question of affect seems to surge up. The *shaastradarshi* aims to suspend the desiring affect and practises the path of actions without desire or actions sans domestic benefits, that is, actions that are not aimed at accruing some coveted results.

In contrast, the kavya *tattvaarthadarshi* responds to the question (how do the heterogeneous relate) in a singular idiom—the very idiom of affect. Given their total attention to the role of the affect in and of formations, the literary inquirers designate even the *unaffected* mode of relation itself as an affect. Such affect, Anandavardhana contends, results when there is depletion or waning of desire for *something*, that is, calculated desire (*trushna kshaya sthiti;* 1998, 723–724). Such an affect was designated, after

Bharata, as *shaanta rasa* (savourable flavour of quietude), and the actional sediment it evokes or appeals to is called *vairaagya* (free of affect or longing [*vi-raaga*]). If affect predominantly binds, pulls and fixates one to formations and relations, this ninth rasa frees from affective indulgences from within the formations, even while being woven into the web of relations. It is an apathetic affect in a pathos-ridden existence. The shaanta affect alludes to a relation of non-relation in the formational weave:

> *Shaantascha trushnaa kshaya sukhasya yah pariposhah tallakshano rasah prateeyata eva.* (Anandavardhana 1998, 723–724)
>
> The desire depleted solace called *shaanta* emerges and this obversive affect is acclaimed as *rasa,* the serene delighting flavor [such a 'sense' can be discerned experientially—says the translator]

Anandavardhana goes on to suggest the distinction of such happiness:

> *Yatcha kaamasukham loke yatcha divyam mahatsukham*
> *Trushnaakshaya sukhasyaite naarhatah shodasheem kalaam*
> (3.101, 724).
>
> Whatever the comforting joys that one enjoys in the *loka* and the greater pleasure that is associated with the *loka* of gods are not even comparable to the sixteenth part of happiness one gains from the gratification that accrues when freed from indulgent longing/craving.

Such a savourable affect is beyond the duality of pleasure and pain—the duality that eventually ends up enhancing pain. Therefore, shaanta is barely comparable to the everyday experience of the duality, although it is inescapably contrasted with the formational experience of existence.

If the shaastra tattvadarshis either suspend or endure affect indifferently, the kavya tattvadarshis value and cherish affect as a source of an extraordinary formation of refinement that can evoke and render pathos as apathos. They claim that such evocation itself can communicate a distinctive flavour of rapturous experience. Such seers can discern a composition of such indifferent delight only among great poets. Even when they seem mutually contentious paths, the ends of shaastra and kavya are the 'same': grappling with the relation between affect and formation as the effective media. Even when their approaches or apparent aims are different, the interminable task they share remains one: refining modes of being of formations through the endowments that bring them forth. Yet these trajectories cannot be reduced to some homogeneous domain. How do they render their complex tasks, then? How are these paths differentiated?

Perhaps, the difference of these (kavya-shaastra) trajectories can be tracked in their articulation of memory. A most evocative kavya composition (actually a commentary on yet another composition of literary inquiry, a clear instance of the impulse of kavya at work even here) captures this related difference effectively:

> *Smrutirvyateeta vishayaa matiraagaami gocharaa*
> *Buddhistaatkaalikee jneyaa prajnaa traikaalikee mataa*
> *Prajnaam navanavonemesha shaalineem pratibhaam viduh*
> *Dve vartmanee giraam devyaah shastrajna kavi karma cha*
> *Prajnopajnam tayoraadyam pratibhodbhava mantimam.* (cited in Sreeramachandrudu's Introduction to Mammata [1995, 21])
>
> Remembrance relates intractably remote occurrences (issues); reflective pondering, the yet to happen. The discerning faculty enables the instantial awareness—whereas learned competence (*prajna*) all the states of temporality (past, present, future). Unforeseen and novel ways of manifestation of *prajna* occurs with/as *pratibha*—the radiant blossoming—say the learned. Saraswati/Parvati's paths are thus two: the learned *shaastra* and that of the performativity of poets.

The radiant blossoming generative force brings forth kavya in unprecedented forms and modes. It is not just memory as such but the radiant plosion of temporal atemporalities in/as atopal spacing in an indeterminate instant of existence that the force of kavya blossoms its incalculable formational memory. Such blossoming is open to the indefinite addressee. The plosive spurring is the force of the non-formational, and the learned competence of prajna tunes it (pratibha) to blossom into a poetic formation. As we have seen from Rajasekhara's and Kshemendra's reflections, there is no prajna entirely devoid of elements of pratibha, and the effulgence of pratibha is not bereft of prajna. However, the difference between them cannot be erased: prajna alone cannot bring forth kavya.

As a generative force, pratibha (kavya) is involved in the formational circuit, whereas prajna (shaastra) unravels the paths of such formational circuitry as the effect of affective indulgences. But the performativity of pratibha implies two critical issues:

1. The task of refining performativity unaffectedly. Therefore, the generativity of pratibha can be an indifferent affect and can bring forth a non-relational relation among formations.
2. Indian inquiries endlessly reiterate that precisely such an affect of indifference can be sensed as the force of the non-formational para and the formationality as such as the force of *apara*.

Indian inquiries essentially unfold this inexhaustible 'secrecy' of the (non)relation of apara and para.

Engendering Force and Originary In-Difference

When apara as a condition of emergences gets articulated (or surges up) within and from para, that condition is figured as *paraa-shakti* (the force of *para*); thus, apara is *of* para, and Since this is a force of emergences, it is seen as the feminine element. Apara (paraa-shakti) is, however, neither derivative or secondary nor it is opposed to para. Apara can come forth only from para. Apara is *of* para—without either of them reducible to any being of existence.

As a force of emergences, apara unfolds two related sets of primal and attributive traits. The first set consists of (i) generative, (ii) differentiative, (iii) individuative, (iv) relational and (v) actional effects. The second brings forth the effects of (i) temperance *(sattva),* (ii) impulsiveness (*rajas*) and (iii) indolence (*tamas*). These two sets combined bring forth all the differentiated formations and relations. Each of the attributive traits brings forth basic elemental units that form the constitutive factors of entities and relations through various combinations. Thus, the trait of tamas brings forth the five fundamental elements (of sky, wind, fire, water and earth) and their respective essences (sound, touch, form, taste and smell). Rajas brings forth the five actional (talking, giving, walking, pleasure and release) and perceptual (speech, feel, sight, taste and smell) faculties and five permeative winds (inward drawing, outward purging, digestive, upward moving and permeative) of a formation. Then, the third trait of sattva brings forth the internal faculties of *manas*, discernment, attentiveness and the individuative sense (*Sri Devi Bhagavatamu* 1996, 1.3.7. 25–39, 161). Sankaracharya's well-known *Nirvaanashatka* evokes these varied sets of formational relational elements:

> *Manobuddhyahankaara chittaani naahaṃ*
> *Na cha shrotrajihve na cha ghraananetre*
> *Na cha vyoma bhoomir na tejo na vaayuḥ*
> *Chidaanandaroopah shivo'ham shivo'ham.* (Sankaracharya 2017, verse 1, 201)
>
> Neither desiring memory, nor discerning resolve, neither individuating impulse nor attentive element am I
> Neither the listening nor tasting, the smelling nor the seeing-sense

Neither the sky nor the earth, neither the fire nor the wind
Intently rapturous form (of) Shiva I am, Shiva I am.

Na cha praanasanjno na vai panchavaayuh
Na vaa saptadhaatur na vaa panchakoshah
Na vaakpaanipaadau na chopasthapaayu
Chidaanandaroopah shivo'ham shivo'ham. (Sankaracharya 2017, verse 2, 201)

Neither the sign of life breath nor the five winds am I,
Neither the seven tissues[4] nor the five sheaths[5]
Neither the utterance, hands and feet, nor the gratifying genitals and the excretory anus
Intently rapturous form (of) Shiva I am, Shiva I am.

As can be seen, these stanzas economically capture the work of the attributive traits. The entire set of elemental faculties and relations is a working out of the other primal set of generative, differentiative and relational traits as well. However, the recursive refrain of each stanza of Sankara's composition, after enumerating the work of the two sets of traits, releases what is radically heterogeneous to these traits. Each of the enumerated traits is invoked in denial to allude to the Shiva of the refrain. Shiva here stands for the non-formational force—para.

The entirety of the formational relational universe comes forth as the making of or coming forth of the individuative effect, says *Sri Devi Bhagavatamu*:

Ahamkaara krutam sarvam vishvam sthaavara jangamam.
(*Sri Devi Bhagavatamu* 1996, 1.3.7.17, 160).
The entirety of the universe of rooted and stable entities is the work of the individuative trait.

Here, individuation already implies the correlated effects of all the other traits; they all evince a metonymically filiated relation in their unfoldment.

Notably, by their very characteristic features, primal and attributive sets cannot be unified into any harmonious equilibrium. Such equilibrial harmony implies the termination or cessation of the universe of formations and relations. It is the restive churn and contestatory relation among both the sets that replenishes the universe. The lively throb of the universe results from the surge of the restless energy of the contrary forces (of the apara effect). Therefore, one cannot 'hope' for a non-contradictory, seamless tranquil state in the formational existence. It's no wonder that none of the reflective formations of the tradition can assure one of a non-contradictory and harmonious state of being in existence: Given that everything is formed of three attributive traits, one cannot find even among the Vedas, the Puranas or the Dharmashaastras a unified (non-contradicting) sentence (*ekavaakyam*). (The composition goes on to enumerate how mutually contradictory modes of being flourish in the world [*Sri Devi Bhagavatamu* 1996, 1.4.4.29–39, 266]).

Yet, precisely in such birthing and raging pulsations released by the two sets of traits that form the matrix of existence, Sanskrit traditions advance an indifferent mode of being that comes forth as a tranquil and equilibrial state within the matrix formed by them. Therefore, such a mode of being must appear as a radical contradiction in the most convulsive formation of the universe. Such a possibility of stasis or equipoise in the impossibly disturbing universe is always already implied in the apara and para relation. The sensing and orienting or attuning oneself towards para—the indifferent—is forever open to the formational in general, for all formations are already permeated and pervaded by para. From such in-differential para as a non-formation, the formational and differential effects of apara surge forth. Para neither affects nor is affected by the apara set of forces. Precisely, this sense of the extraordinary cohabitation of the 'contraries' in the commonality of formational existence is performatively rendered in Sankara's *Nirvaanashatka*. The contrary pulls of denial (*naa ham … shivoham*) are enacted in Sankara's reflective poetic compositional formation (Sankaracharya 2017, verse 1, 201).

However, the contrary forces of para/apara (or [a]para) are not treated as some projected principles in the Sanskrit traditions: principles do not derive from descriptions and narratemes. They are not the results of observation and deduction. Principles are fundamentally known as presuppositions, which can contribute to hypothesis formation. Principles and their hypotheses provide explanatory accounts that can be tested and verified under given circumstances. Theory building emerges from such explanatory accounts. Para/apara has never been postulated as principles(s) to build any anthropo-centred theories of existence in the Indian traditions.

(A)Para is (are) not just the linguistic verbal coinage(s) that circulate(s) in most of the languages in everyday use. They are also persistently described and incorporated in song-story-performative traditions. These terms are not part of any theory-driven enterprise—if there is such a thing at all in the Indian context. Yet they can be explanatory or experiential sources that are part of the discerning reflective poetic compositions. However, these 'explanatory' sources (if they can be legitimately called so) are not rigorously differentiated from other accounts. Therefore, (a)para can neither be reduced to principles or empirical factoids. (A)Para unfolds the play of contrary forces and simultaneously opens up (in)differentiality in general and instantiates it in the infinity of finitudinal formations and relations.

Difference emerges from the indifferent, that is, 'from' the non-differentiable (para). Apara as such, the source of emergences itself, however, remains inarticulable but functions as the source of the differential. Such a source alone designates the non-differential as para. In yet another composition, Sankara evocatively captures this conjuration of para by apara: indivisible, discerning, non-dual rapturous para, immersively dispersed across the emergent formations of sky, wind and such other elements, churns in the ocean of delusive existence. Maaya conjures impossible occurrences as possible (Sankara 2017, 3, 200).

Maaya is the other name for apara, for it/she is a conjurational force. Apara is the source, and its effects are the media of emergences. As a force of differentiation, apara brings forth pluripetal formations. Species and gender distinctions, for instance, happen to be the effective manifestations of the differential force. Since every formation comes forth as a temporal convergence of contrary forces, no formation as such can be said to have some exclusive and absolute uniqueness and distinction. All such claims are the conjurations of apara. The so-called human formation happens to be one such convergent effect of the contrary forces.

Formational Finitude

In the finite infinity of formations, the human formation happens to be just a single particular fractal manifestation. This particulate formation, like most, is constituted by the two sets of effects and the cohabiting 'contrary', the formational and the non-formational, forces (para/apara). Every formation and relation is the result of the incalculable permutations and combinations of these elemental and attributive effects. Yet the human formation has a tendency to intensify its individuating effect and proclaim supremacy over other formations and relations, which it aims at subsuming under its conceptions for its ends. Apara's 'work', at the same time, opens up passageways to sense the relation of the non-formational force of para. The intensities and valences of the human, as it indulges in its ends, tend to disavow the passageway. The actional consequence of such disavowal is deathly life—a machinic gyration in existence without respite. Formations (re)articulate or remediate formations in the churn of such a gyrational existence.

The human formation as a weave of intensities and valences of the primal and attributive effects brings forth symbolising technics. The latter mutually rearticulate the biophysical formations. The human aims at subsuming existence as a whole and the very source of existence under its symbolising powers and techniques. If formations in general are the weave of elements and attributes, so should be the ensuant symbolising formations. Symbolisation is at once an enactment of the primal effects, and at the same time, it functions as a medium to sense the work of the 'contrary' forces of formationality in general. Like formations in general, the symbolising formations too, as media, are exposed to the valences of stress and rapture in existence: they are the molecular popping in apara's oceanic churn. The primal symbolising sources of sound and form are associated with the originary elements of sky and fire, respectively. A formation in turn can entail other symbolising elements by rearticulating its endowments: gestures of the body, music and words of the language bring forth symbolising cultural forms.

Formations as projective effects, however, unleash strife—without which formations are impossible. Strife intensifies when a formation works or is put to work as an end in itself. Such strife indulges formations in machinic reiterations of itself. Only when formations are lived as the work of apara, the latter opening possible effective passages to sense para, the strife may mutate into rapturous delight. In other words, formationality articulates the valences of strife and rapture where the very act of putting the formational to work can be deadly stressful or it can yield lively rapture. The work, as it morphs stress into delight, turns work into non-work (karma into *akarma*). Among various effects that constitute a formation, however, this enterprising human formation exhibits the intensification of the effects of individuation to demonstrate its supremacy over all the formations and relations. For its purpose, the human formation selectively concentrates on formations. In other words, its search is predetermined by its ends—what it looks for.

Engendered Intensities

There is yet another trajectory that the human tendency to valorise individuation can result in. However, on the basis of the figuration of apara as the engendering force, to take recourse to gender appellations to designate apara and para as feminine and masculine, respectively, is to project a species differentiation onto the forces that are non-formational in essence. Such a designation, however, like all designations in general is the work of apara. This primal difference cannot be reduced to gender/sexual difference. The latter difference is a more regional variation within the more primordial work of formationality.

If apara is all formationality and work, how does para get projected in this matrix? Para gets designated as the indifferent, ineffective, non-formational, un-affective and inactive force. Why call it a force then? This is an inoperative force—a force that permeates and surrounds the formational spur and all its effects indifferently. Therefore, para cannot be the gendered opposite of the feminine force. What differs from the feminine need not be the masculine. It could also be the un-engendered/un-engendering. Para as the un-engendered force cannot be opposed to the feminine as the masculine. Therefore, apara can only be the engendering force and para the un-engendered. If apara exudes energy and unfolds *energaia*, then para is eminently *un-ergaia*. From this un-engendering force that apara as the formational force comes forth and releases its effects. These effects, through their intensities of convergence and divergence, bring forth differentiated formations. Such engendered formations get further differentiated into species and genders.

Elemental formations are the effects of the apara as the emergent force. Para is the force that does not exist nor does it emerge; it is always already *there*. Such force is also referred to as the non-formative sonance (shabda/*nada*) that is always already there without manifestation. Bhartrhari's sutra reverberates across Sanskrit mnemoscapes:

> *Anaadinidhanam brahmashabda tattvam yadaksharam.* (Bhartrhari 2006, 1.1, 2)
>
> Without origin and extinction that sonic essence of Brahma is the endless verbal unit (acoustic 'letter')

From such sonance that the force of apara surges up and unleashes acoustic, verbal, musical, gestural, visual and graphical formations. The Vedic *vak* (sound/utterance) is identified as a female (Vagdevi). The formational force (apara) is also designated as Sri. Symbolisation manifests as vidyas (verbal-acoustic-musical formations) and kalas (visual-gestural-graphical formations). The entirety of the domain of vidyas (including that of the Vedas) is designated as apara vidya. Kalas are ancillary-correlative vidyas. We recall from Rajasekhara that vidyas are numbered thirty-two and kalas sixty-four (2003, 13).

The Sanskrit vaangmaya seems to conceive symbolisation as doubly feminine: as a formative force and as a figurational force. The mnemocultures of India are replete with compositions that invoke the primal apara force as a feminine figuration. No wonder, the shruti and smriti compositions of *Sri Sukta* (as the endower of wealth), *Sri Lalita Sahasranaamam* (as the force of emergences, dissolutions, affect in its multiple dimensions and action invoked in a thousand names) and countless invocative compositions (of *stuti*, *stotra*, *shataka*, *nama*, *stava* and the like) address and appeal to the figure of the feminine deity in everyday lives. Thus, the engendering formationality is seen as the primal force (*aadi* shakti), and its formational manifestations are seen as the feminine formations of this force. Thus, the primal symbolising elements—acoustic-musical, seed letters and the visual, graphical and gestural forms—are identified as the feminine manifestations and as a female formation, Sri.

Sri Lalita Sahasranaamam is a performative composition. It embodies the relation between formationality and the question of the feminine. This composition is rendered in everyday life in thousands of homes and temples. Mnemocultural symbolising formations are enlivened in performative modes: they invoke, address, delineate and seek from the figure through the very (symbolising) endowments that the force of the figure releases. The biophysical and the symbolising formations confound their difference. As mediums, they attune to each other and open up the possibility of sensing the primal 'relation' and experiencing of rapture in the very performative act.

> *Matruka varna rupini.* (*Sri Lalita Sahasranaamam*, Sastry 1998, 116, 249)
> [The goddess is invoked as the] seed/sound letter formation (in the *Sri Lalita Sahasranaamam*).
> *A ka cha ta tha paadi varne rasa purne.* (Muttuswamy, n.d., first stanza)
> [The source and formation of] the sonic-letters *a, ka, cha, ta, tha, pa* and others replete with savourable flavours.

These compositions are also imparted as a wealth of shaastra learning:

> *Atma vidya, mahaa vidya, sri vidya, kaamasevita.* (*Sri Lalita Sahasranaamamu*, Sastry 1998, 118, 249)
> [Sri is referred to as the source of] Para-learning [which is], an inordinate learning [which is] served by the god of erotics (Manmatha).
> *Sarva Vedanta samvedya.* (128, 249)
> [She is] perceptive of the ends of all the Vedas
> *Saraswati, shaastramayee....* (137, 250)
> Goddess of learning and the embodiment of *shaastra*
> *Kalaa nidhih, kavya kalaa, rasjnaa ....* (151, 251)
> [The deity is the] Wealth of radiance (of two kinds: verbal-acoustic [shruti] and graphical [visual-gestural]), embodiment of poetic formations [smriti], knowledgeable of savourable flavours.
> *Chandassaaraa, shaastrasaara, mantrasaaraa.* (157, 252)
> Essence of musical metrics, quintessence of every domain of learning, core of all the mantras (mantra is that which is without a name and whose recall protects).

Tattvaadhikaa, tattvamayee.... (168, 253)
Exceeds the essence/para [as apara can have para inhere in every formation] and replete with essence/para.

Similarly, the graphical manifestation of Sri is figured in the singular verse associated with the circle of Sri (Sri Chakra). Perhaps, this is one of the most economically composed verses of geometric formations:

Bindu trikona vasukona dashaara yugma
Manvasra naagadala shodasha patra yuktam
Vrutta trayam cha dharanee sadana tryamcha
Sri chakra raja uditah para devataayaah. (*Sri Lalita Sahasra Nama Vivaranamu*, Sastry 1998, 225)

Composed of a dot (cipher), triangle, angular octave, (and a) union of ten inner-outer angles
With emergent fourteen triangles, circled by eight-petalled lotus, nestling in the sixteen-petalled lotus
Covered by the trinity of circles and located in the triad of the base
Emerges the supreme circle of Sri as the divine other

Graphically composed, from above, this geometric formation looks like a temple raised from the base of the earth. The structure of the temple is composed of various triangular, circular and petal (angular, curved and pointed) structures. The entire formation is framed within unconnected, three-lined square brackets. At the very centre of the sanctum of the temple, Sri is seated as the celebrated other deity. Sri is invoked in and as such a formation.

Invocative Figurations

Similarly, the *Saundarya Lahari,* attributed to Sankaracharya, is an extraordinary invocative composition in this regard. Invocative or apostrophic genres are composed of epithets of narratemes. They are deeply imbued with numerical, mathematical attributes. Each of the phonemes forming the composition is seen as a seed, a sememe and a museme (from Muse), which in its combination with others fecundates the verbal, musical, semantic and graphical layers of the composition.

The *Saundarya Lahari* eloquently invokes the manifestations of Sri/apara. Like the kavya impulse in Sanskrit traditions, this composition too confounds any rigid division between the shaastra and the kavya domains. More importantly, Sankara's composition devoutly brings forth the feminine source of formationality in general. The composition devotes forty-one *shlokas* in which the morphing of Sri into verbal-acoustic, graphical, secretive, traversing and filiative force is figured. The entire invocation is an immersive offering made to Sri. The remaining fifty-nine shlokas of the *Saundarya Lahari* delineate the entire feminine formation of the deity from head to toe. The composition itself is conceived as waves—and these are waves of delight and enhanced beauty.

The structure of the Sri Chakra, like that of the *Nirvaanashatka*, is also a figure of the composition of a formation. Manifesting as elemental attributive formations that, for instance, in turn converge to compose the human formation, the force of Sri traverses the various nodes of the human entity. Here, each of the nodes is conceived as a geometric formation—a triangle, a circle or a cipher. The *Saundarya Lahari* delineates how the formational force manifests in formations that are deeply filiated with elemental and biocultural complexes and bears within 'her' the non-formational force of para, here named as Shiva.

In such a concentric structure, how Sri traverses is captured in a verse in the *Saundarya Lahari*:

> *Maheem moolaadhaare kamapi manipoore hutavaham*
> *Sthitam svaadhishtaane hrudi maruta maakaasham upari*
> *Manopi brhoomadhye sakalamapibhitvaa kulapatham*
> *Sahasraare padme saha rahasi patyaa viharase.* (Sankaracharya 1984, 9, 39)

> O Sri, [you traverse] from the earthly primal base, through the watery gem circle, the circle of fire, through the heart's airy circle, above that the purity of the circle of sky, and from there the circle of *manas* of modest knowledge located between the eyebrows, piercing through the *kulapatha* (in the passage of *sushumna*) to reach the thousand-petalled lotus where you jaunt with your consort in secrecy.

This graphical verbal schema constitutively filiates the elemental formations with the human formations. This is the filiation of the outside and the inside of the formations. In such a figuration, the (human) biophysical formation called the body is seen as composed of six circles in an ascending and descending order. The last or the one at the bottom is named the circle of the primal source (or root), and it is constitutive of the earthly (*pruthvy*) element connected to the spinal base. The one above it is referred to as the gem circle (*manipura*), composed of watery (*jala*) element and identified with the navel. The third one from the bottom is called the circle of presiding Self (*svadhishtaana*), brought forth by the element of fire (*agni*) and related to the base of sexual organs. The fourth one is called the unstruck/soundless circle, formed by the wind (*vaayu*) and is associated with the heart. Above that is the one named the purest circle, associated with the throat and formed of the element of the sky (*vyoma*). The sixth one (from the base) is referred to as the circle of command, formed of manas, and is placed between the eyebrows. Above all these resides the thousand-petal lotus where Shiva is said to reside.

> *Manastvam vyomatvam marudasi marutsaaradhi rasi*
> *Tva maapastvam bhumistvayi parinataayaam nahi param*
> *Tvameva svaatvaanam parinamayitum vishvavapushaa*
> *Chidaanandaakaaram shiva yuvati bhaavena bibhrushe.*
> (Sankaracharya 1984, 35, 236)
>
> O shiva's beloved you are the essence of *manas*, sky, wind, fire, water and earth. You morph into these 5(+1) elements. There's nothing other than you. You bear/carry in you the force of Shiva and morph yourself into these various formations.
> *Na che devam devo [shiva] nakhalu kushalah spanditu mapi.* (Sankaracharya 1984, 1, 1)
> Without conjoining you, that god cannot even move.

Precisely, these five+one elements are acoustically/verbally, musically, figurally and graphically rendered in the Sri Chakra. The *Saundarya Lahari* invokes the source of such a formation as Sri, the goddess. In figuring Sri as a force that morphs into these elements, the *Saundarya Lahari* also addresses her as a formation. The *Sri Chakra* is a geometric verbal invocation of the female deity and her union with Shiva in the biocultural formation of the body.

Here, the feminine force of apara, even as it forms the elemental and the biophysical formations and constitutively filiates the 'outside' with the 'inside', is said to traverse across the circles to unite with Shiva in the thousand-petal lotus. Her 'separation' from that lotus seems to make the formational process possible, and through that very process, she reaches out to unite with Shiva, who is the non-formational para in this composition (Sankaracharya 1984, 35–41, 236–281).

The structure of the manifest forces of Sri and *(the non-formational)* para as Parvati and Shiva is delineated by Sankara in his own way:

> Four inverted triangles of Shiva and five upwardly pointing triangles that are of (yours)—O Shiva's beloved
> Different from each other but together form nine primal sources

> Eight-petalled lotus, sixteen-petalled angles contained in the three-lined earthly circuit
> Encircled by three angles is formed your dwelling place of forty-four triangles. (Sankaracharya 1984, 11, 57)

The geometric structure exemplifies the interpenetrating forces of para and apara in the Sri Chakra, which Sankara is invoking here, and this chakra appears to bring forth the engendered formation of the human body.

As can be seen from the discussion, formations are never closed ones. They cannot be rigorously severed from the elemental, for the elemental pervades and permeates the formational. But the elemental itself (sky, air, fire and the like) is also a formational effect, apara's conjuration. Thus, formations emerge from/within the always already constitutively woven visible and invisible networks of relations. No formation can ever be absolutely autonomous.

Sankara reckons all modes of mnemocultural symbolisation enacted before the deity as offerings made to the invoked figure:

> As offerings of myself and my acts—let my spontaneous prattle (*jalpa*) be my silent recall of your *mantra*. Let all my hand movements be various gestural figurations/signs submitted to you. Let my free movement be my circumambulations around you. What all I eat is an offering in fire for you; my torsions on the bed be my salutations to you. All the comforting-pleasant things with which I make offerings: let them be the delighting *puja* for you. Provide me such boon that these acts render such offerings. (Sankaracharya 1984, 27,151)

In these invocative compositions, Sri/the feminine is not reduced to some carrier—some passive receptacle—of man's children. More importantly, it is seen as the absolute source that morphs itself into a multiplicity of formations. Formations are foreclosable openings, but they cannot escape their transformative repetitions of strife and delight. That which spurs and gravitates towards *something*, elsewhere, appears to be the feminine in these compositions. Such a force dances with relations. Apara is dynamic and energetic and, fundamentally, as the feminine, 'it' is a force of *atelos* (goalless, endless). She neither has a dedicated purpose nor is she invested in any of her acts, formations and their consequences.

The *Saundarya Lahari* can easily be characterised as a composition of Waves of Eros (*Shringaara Lahari*) or Coital Waves (*Rati Lahari*). Here, in naming the composition thus, we are invoking Bharata's account pertaining to the mutually spurring relation between the rapturous savourable flavours (rasa) and the actional sediments (*bhaava*). Sankara's composition could emerge only from a milieu that brought forth the *Naatyashaastra*. The *Saundarya Lahari* celebrates and delineates the embellished body parts of Sri on the one hand and equally emphasises the state of rapture attained in the coital union of Shiva-shakti (paraa-shakti *and* Shiva) on the other. In a way, this is a composition without any narrative elaboration that shows or equates the rapturous experience attained in a poetic composition as the experience of coital union. In other words, the composition is a performative response to the sense of the relation between para and apara (or Shiva-shakti). However, in both cases, what is essential and gets foregrounded in the composition is the spectacular manifestation of an engendered formation—Sri/Devi. The composition is at the same time an *upaasana*—an immersed invocative addressing of Sri, a praxial performative learning.

Perhaps, the *Saundarya Lahari* is one of the earliest compositions that delineates the formational operation of/as the feminine most elaborately and in a non-narrative mode. Precisely, such a formational impulse is invoked by the Aalamkaarikaas in their literary inquiries. For them, kavya is a beauteous formation that evokes the sense of rapture on experiencing it. Sankara's composition, as is a conventional practice, evokes the feminine in kavya and Purana idioms, without taking recourse to the *Puranic* narrative chains. Literary inquiries always drew on such extended compositional resources and unfolded the primal relation of non-relation between para and apara.

The Enigma of Relations

Two most significant Sanskrit verses capture the entire formational and sexual relation in most eloquent and evocative compositions. One is from a renowned poet and the other from an enduring shaastrakaara.

> *Anaadi nidhanam brahma shabda tattvam yadaksharam*
> *vivartatertha bhaavena prakriyaa jagato yataha.*
> (Bhartrhari 2006, 1.1, 2)

> The essence of the non-formational sonance is already there without cessation or inception. Such singular an-originary source appears to lend itself to sonance (shabda), which appears to morph itself into sound and sense (as the morphed sonance). Such a process is akin to the very formation of *jagat* (a colossal assemblage on the move) itself.

The essence of sonance, Bhartrhari suggests, is un-morphing for it is non-formative (that is, non-existent). However, what emerges from it is prone to transformation. Vak is the morphed effect of the sonance, and it lends itself to morphemics. Vak is not the originary sonance, but it is the formational effect of the sonance. Vak is the formed, morphed sonance. However, vak's relation to sense remains a peculiar one. Vak may sense it, but the moment it articulates and sounds what it senses, artha/sense slips away, leaving only yet another vak formation. Vak as a verbal formation can only replicate itself—despite the differences between these utterances. Differences, be they biophysical or symbolising, and their relations surge up from the indifferent, undifferentiable sonantic essence. What is called artha, like the originary sonantic essence, can never be exhaustively grasped and captured in a formation. Therefore, the union one can talk about between sound and sense can only be between the articulated formations: the morphematic formations. Formations unite, relate, serve and disperse. They are exposed to the strife and duality of pleasure and pain in unfolding this process of transformation. However, artha is not out there as a hidden 'kernel' or sovereign essence of all existence. For artha, like the sonantic essence, inheres in the formational vak, but it can never be articulated. Every effort to grasp it by the formational vak yields yet another vak formation. Like the sonantic essence, artha will only have to be sensed and experienced when a vak searches for it. That experiential sensing itself unfolds a sense of delight within the formational living/being. Kalidasa alludes to that rapturous delight in precisely relating vak-artha as the union of Parvati and Parameshvara:

> *Vaagarthaaviva sampruktau vaagartha pratipattaye*
> *Jagatah pitarau vande parvati parameshwarau.* (Kalidasa 2010, 1.1, 1)
> The union of vak and artha releases formations of sound and sense, (like the union of Parvati and Shiva) O the parents of the universe, salutations of praise [to thee].

As can be seen, both the Kalidasa and Bhartrhari verses evoke the operation of fundamental relations (vak–artha, Parvati–Parameshvara, Jagat, shabda–artha bhaava). Both the verses imply that the formational universe (biophysical/symbolising) is the effect of the union of the formational and the non-formational forces. What inheres in the formation is the unformable as the tattva of the formational. The unformable (inexhaustible and unfathomable) can only be sensed. Shiva here, however, need not be reduced to the Puranic god who is essentially a formation, which is prone to dispersive transformation. The Shiva referred to here is the very Shiva whom Sankara invokes in the refrain of his resonant murmur:

Nirvaanashatka. Each of its six stanzas repeats the refrain: *Chidaananda roopa Shivoham, Shivoham* (That intently rapturous non-formational (para) Shiva I am, Shiva I am; Sankaracharya 2017, 1–6, 201–202).

In these performative reflective traditions, the feminine is neither a figure of truth or falsity (little to do with the theo-philosophical aletheia). It is the formational force at work in transforming the conjurations of the proper and forever articulating an uncanny relationship with what is radically heterogeneous to it—uncanny as it enacts a relationship of non-relation of para. Para inheres in and pervades apara.

In such a context, the impulse of kavya that permeates the entirety of vaangmaya embodies a secret most eloquently:

> What the literary is remains an inscrutable colossal secrecy
> It can be grasped only by the learned and served by the competent
> To gain and access such a secrecy one must pursue the most subtle tact:
> Know what all can be known and achieve the state of singular attentiveness of the *manas* (*samaadhi*). (Rajasekhara 2003, 4.2, 30)

'*Literary inquiries radiate such reflective creations in their play with/as formations: they come forth as intimations of/from the feminine formation (kaantaa sammita)*' (Mammata 1995, 1.2, 3). This insight does not imply that kavya is feminine and shaastra masculine for the simple reason that kavya permeates the entirety of vaangmaya irrespective of whether the composition is of 'unagentive' or agentive formation.

Cultures and Differences

As we discussed earlier, Sanskrit literary inquiries emerged within a general milieu of inquiries that explored the relationship between the affect and formation and their (non)relation to the non-formational. These inquiries focused on the embodied memory and aimed at persistently refining the performative modes of its articulation. The memory in question here remains intractable and inexhaustible. Its articulations discontinuously carry their residues in the emergence of formations. Memory as a dynamic alithic palimpsest of origin and endless traces is accessible to only one faculty of any relational formation: *manas*. Manas is also the abode of desire or affect. Desire/affect and memory—indeterminable non-inscriptive palimpsests—spur the action of a formation. In such a milieu, the singular task that Sanskrit inquiries advance remains: *refining reorientation of the cultivable endowments of formations*. Such a praxial task yields happiness in sensing the limits of the formational and the enigma of its relation with the non-formational in modes of being or of formational existence.

Sanskrit inquiries, despite their internal *polemos*, neither privilege nor erase any discipline of learning. Multiplication of domains of learning or modes of being only affirms the generative force of formations. This generative function can only reinforce the praxial task of sensing the limits of formationality and the force of (de)generativity. Neither shaastra nor kavya can be elevated to a superior position exclusively. Nowhere does shaastra consolidate itself into a meta-level discipline of learning that would explain or grasp the 'meaning' of a kavya. In other words, here, shaastra does not play the role assigned to either literary criticism or theory (philosophy) in the European tradition. Such latter discourses remain unintelligible in the performative reflective traditions of India. No wonder, the discourse of the addressee (the listener/reader) is conspicuous by its absence in Indian traditions. No one sets out to explain or, indeed, *interpret* a kavya or compare it with another one in its entirety on the basis of a shaastra. The science of literary interpretation will be an anomaly in the Sanskrit traditions. Shaastra and kavya are mutually formational, and yet, they cannot be conflated into a homogeneous unity. This difference gets performatively articulated by the kavya and shaastra compositions of the tradition. The very same teachers who teach kavya also impart shaastra learning generationally. There are no teachers exclusively for either of the domains. To see their relation in exclusive terms by privileging one over the other is to get fixated on a blinding formation, which can only propel one into a (de)generative matrix. Formationality is the absolute and the only medium to sense its limits.

But how does this entire discussion pertaining to Sanskrit inquiries into formationality help us to configure cultural difference or to explore how differently cultures think and live? More specifically, in the context of the inquiries of the Sanskrit tradition that we are pursuing, how does the question of formationality get articulated in specific and distinct cultural formations? From the Indian background risked here, one can say that only through the play of intensities and valences of the primal and attributive effects, which replenish and re- or disorient formations, can cultural distinctions be configured. Cultural formations are brought forth by the weave of cultural media of alithic and lithic techics. As the lithic formations invest in the pull of immortality, they valorise surrogate (assumed to be imperishable) formations that promise longevity, if not immortality, to their intensities and valences. The alithic ones, meanwhile, kindle, nurture, improvise and impart lively archives in the embodied and enacted modes with the given formation as such. Such a formation is seen as the absolutely primal medium that could open up to and receive other formations and their intimations in general. This process of responsive reception is shaped by the play of the intensities and valences of the formational effects and the play has the effect on formationality as such. Alithic formations put to work the dynamic of the life-death/strife-rapture process in recursive instances of existence. They bring forth modes of liveable learning.

In such a context, literary inquiries enact the praxial ethos and sense the essential secrecy of the literary in performative articulations of it. The secrecy neither celebrates a sovereign nor reiterates a covenant. The secrecy does not urge indulgence in interpretive deciphering. It is not a cryptic code to be decoded in an analog(ical) system to elicit some hidden kernel/essence. Nor is it a principle that would determine the significance of the manifold on the basis of a supreme law, for the non-formational can be configured as neither a sovereign nor a juridical/moral imperative. Hence, there is no discourse of the addressee in Sanskrit literary inquiries: no judge or judgement of universal validity is valorised in these traditions. The rejoicing and cordial listener/viewer can only articulate his/her response in alithic gestural or performative modes of the body. Such enacted expressions, says Rajasekhara, cannot be captured even by Bharata's *Naatyashaastra* (2003, 4.18, 39–40).

Surely, literary inquiries (of the two kinds) evoke literary formations. However, in doing so, they enact the generative force and suggest its limits as the generative effects cannot be erased voluntarily. They must/can be lived indifferently in modes of being. Therefore, if there is to be any kind of sovereignty, it must be in such indifferential modes of being. However, such sovereignty cannot be a commanding and controlling one. Sanskrit inquiries had no use for such all-determining supreme sovereign force.

Outside (in) the Semitic Fold

Perhaps it is the valorisation of sovereignty—be it theo-centred or anthropo-centred as in the case of Semitic cultures—that yields certain persistent responses to existence as a whole. These responses can be seen in the motifs of law, binding pact, faith, father, guilt, reparation, mourning, nostalgia, the human, utopia, remorse, responsibility, hope, love, morality, promise and penitence. All such motifs may appear elsewhere as well. However, in Sanskrit traditions of inquiry, they are not accorded any salient pattern-forming, anchoring status. They do not get reiterated in cultural forms across time and space in these traditions.

Sanskrit and Semitic traditions unfold heterogeneous approaches to modes of being and their relation with formations of reflection in existence.

When such traditions interface, the interpretive violence of the Semitic subsumes the non-Semitic/pagan. Such supersessional subsumption irrupts psychic disjunction in the cultures that are conscripted into European expropriations. Sanskrit traditions do not unleash invasive interpretive formations. Today, all our contexts of reception are made over by the privileged discourses, institutions and the media of the European context of production. We continue to reiterate by default as it were these implanted European frameworks that enframe what we do and what we might want to say about what we do. We indulge in the provocations of the 'Self' and foreground the 'crisis of the Self'. In a word, we lend ourselves to the subsumptions and supersessions of the sovereign. In such intellectually destitute times, perhaps Sanskrit (literary) (and other non-Semitic) inquiries may open up from their background a chance to reorient not only what we do and what we say about what we do but also, perhaps, what (Semitic) others say about what others do. Such a reorientation is urgently needed in all contexts of reception that faced Semitic European invasion. That is possible only when the contexts of reception learn to respond through their double move in the double bind without alibis. Only through such a double move in the aporia that we are exposed to and interpellated into can this condition of impossibility be turned into a condition of possibility—without, of course, guarantees.

What do we do with what we have?!

References

Anandavardhana. 1998. *Dhvanyaalokamu.* (With Abhinavagupta's *Lochana*). Translated from Sanskrit into Telugu by Pullela Sreeramachandrudu. Hyderabad: Jayalakshmi Publications.

Benjamin, Walter. 1986. *Reflections: Essays, Aphorisms, Autobiographical Writings.* Translated by Edmund Jephcott. New York: Schoken Books.

Bhamaha. 2004. *Kaavyaalamkarah.* Translated from Sanskrit into Telugu by Pullela Sreeramachandrudu. Hyderabad: Samskruta Bhasha Prachara Samiti.

Bharata. 2006. *Naatyashaastram.* Translated from Sanskrit into Telugu by Pullela Sreeramachandrudu. Hyderabad: P.N. Sastri.

Bhartruhari. 2006. *Vakyapadiyamu.* Translated into Telugu by P. Suryanarayanasastri, Sri Bhashyam Appalacharyulu, Pullela Sreeramachandrudu, Appala Someshwarasarma. Hyderabad: Telugu Akademi.

Curtius, E.R. 1953. *European Literature and the Latin Middle Ages.* Translated by Willard R. Trask. London: Routledge & Kegan Paul.

Dandi. 2011. *Kavyaadarsha.* Translated from Sanskrit into Telugu by P. Sreeramachandrudu. Hyderabad: Potti Sriramulu Telugu University.

Derrida, Jacques. 1992. '"This Strange Institution Called Literature": An interview with Jacques Derrida by Derek Attridge.' Translated by Geoff Bennington and Rachel Bowlby. In *Acts of Literature*, edited by Derek Attridge. New York: Routledge.

———. 2008. 'Literature in Secret: An Impossible Filiation.' Translated by David Wills. In *The Gift of Death*. 2nd edn. Chicago: The University of Chicago Press.

———. 2021. *Clang*. Translated by David Wills and Geoffrey Bennington. Minneapolis: University of Minnesota Press.

Gasché, Rodolphe. 1998. *The Wild Card of Reading: On Paul de Man*. Cambridge, MA: Harvard University Press.

Jagannatha, Panditaraja. 1942. *Rasagangaadharamu*. Translated into Telugu as *Navarasagangaadharamu* with a commentary by Madhavaraya Sarma. Guntur: Navya Sahitya Parishattu.

Kalidasa. 2010. *Raghuvamshamu*. Translated from Sanskrit into Telugu by Gollapinni Sadasiva Sastry. Hyderabad: Jnaanasri Arshavidya Gurukulamu.

Kshemendra. 1983. *Suvrutta Tilakam*. Translated from Sanskrit into Telugu by Pullela Sreeramachandrudu. Hyderabad: Surabharati Samiti.

Kuntaka. 2007. *Vakrokti Jeevitamu*. Translated from Sanskrit into Telugu by Pullela Sreeramachandrudu. New Delhi: Sahitya Akademi.

Mammata. 1995. *Kavyaprakaashamu*. Translated from Sanskrit into Telugu (with an Introduction and commentary) by Pullela Sreeramachandrudu. Hyderabad: Samskrutabhasha Pracharasamiti.

Muttuswamy Dikshitar. n.d. *Kamalaamba Navaavarana Kriti*, 1. Accessed 20 July 2021. http://www.medieval.org/music/world/carnatic/lyrics/srao/kamala.html.

Nancy, Jean-Luc. 2008. *The Discourse of the Syncope: Logodaedalus*. Translated by Saul Anton. Stanford: Stanford University Press.

———. 2018. *Expectation: Philosophy, Literature*. Translated by Robert Bononno. New York: Fordham University Press.

Patočka, Jan. 2002. *Plato and Europe*. Translated by Peter Lom. Stanford: Stanford University Press.

Rajasekhara. 2003. *Kavyameemaansaa*. Translated from Sanskrit into Telugu by Pullela Sreeramachandrudu. Hyderabad: Sri Jayalakshmi Publications.

Sankaracharya. 1984. *Saundarya Lahari*. Translated from Sanskrit into Telugu with a commentary by Chadaluvada Jayarama Sastri. Madras: Sri Aruna Book House.

———. 2017. 'Nirvanashatkam'. In Sri *Sankaracharyakruta Stotramulu*, edited by Challapalli Venkata Ratna Prasad, 201–202. Hyderabad.

Sastry, G.L.N. 1998. 'Sri Lalitaanaama Sahasramu.' In *Sri Lalitaanaama Sahasra Vivaranamu*, Part I. Guntur: Jagadguru Pitham.

Satyanarayana, Viswanatha. 2007. *Kavyaanandamu* [Poetic rapture]. Vijayawada: Sri Viswanatha Publications.

Sri Devi Bhagavatamu. 1996. Translated from Sanskrit into Telugu by Sri Devulapalli Sivaramayya. Hyderabad: Sri Venkateshwara Arsha Bharati Trust.

Taittiriya Upanishad. 1984. Translated from Sanskrit into Telugu by Pullela Sreeramachandrudu. Hyderabad: Surabharati Publications.

Vagbhata. 2004. *Ashtaangasamgrahamu*. with Shashilekha commentary. Translated from Sanskrit into Telugu by Panyam Parthasarathisarma. Hyderabad: Telugu Akademi.

Vamana. 2003. *Kavyaalankaarasutrani*. Translated from Sanskrit into Telugu by P. Sreeramachandrudu. Hyderabad: Jayalakshmi Publications.

Zarader, Marlene. 2006. *The Unthought Debt: Heidegger and the Hebraic Heritage*. Translated by Bettina Bergo. Stanford: Stanford University Press.

Notes

1 All the English renderings of Sanskrit verses and passages cited, unless mentioned otherwise, are mine.

2 Literature *cannot* have originated in pagan cultures, contends Derrida, going against the established doxa (Curtius 1953, 36). Neither Greek nor Latin, let alone any non-European cultures, a fortiori could have originated literature, asserts Derrida (1992, 40). The one and only source of literature is the Covenant of Abraham, declares Derrida. The *Aqedah* and what it entails offers the incomparable and incommensurable parable of literature, and it indelibly carves out the signature of Europe, contends Derrida (2008, viii–ix).

3 What is proposed requires much more elaboration and substantiation, which will be undertaken in another work.

4 The human body is composed of seven tissues that result from the source *dhaatu* of digestive fire (*jattharaagni*), and these vulnerable (sub) dhaatus are:

> *Rasaasrungmaamsa medhosti majjaa shukraani dhaatavah*,
> Fluid/plasma, blood, muscle, fat, bone, bone-marrow and semen are dhaatus (tissues). (Vagbhata 2004, 1.1, 17)

5 The body complex is0 said to be composed of a set of five sheaths: (i) *Annamaya* (food-filled), (ii) *Praanamaya* (filled with life breaths), (iii) *Manomaya* (replete with desiring memory), (iv) *Vijnaanamaya* (surfeit with discerning sense) and (v) *Aanandamaya* (replete with rapturous delight). As can be seen, each sheath is subtler than the preceding ones (*Taittiriya Upanishad* 1984, 36–70).

7

SUBJECT NATURE DIVINATION

Rimli Bhattacharya[1]

This chapter seeks to explore the lineaments and possibilities of a kind of 'elemental aesthetics' that defines Akhtaruzzaman Elias's novel *Khwabnama* (1996), with a coda on select films of Kumar Shahani. I shall focus on the specificities of the disciplinary lens through which a certain immersive rendering and reconfiguring takes place in the medium of print and cinema. It would involve tacking, in relation to the medium, the shifting and disjunct modes of perception, human and non-human, that emphasise the terrain as a living thing, the pulse of history. This attention to movement will require a close reading of select passages/sequences—such as the multiple temporalities of smell, touch and taste in the early chapters of Elias's novel and the individuated treatment of dance in Shahani's films—often against the grain of dominant theories of narratology, ecology, audiography and so on. What may not emerge explicitly in these readings is the plotting of a 'self' in relation to history as an event, memory or metaphor or even as the dream of a future. The readings will suggest, however, that the self (in history) may reside and be divined in every drop of dew or rain or sweat.

A Warning

Often appraised as some kind of an arch-naturalist, seemingly pitiless in his depiction of the lower depths, Elias's poetic prose is praised under the generic rubric of 'magic realism' (Dasgupta 2002). A notable exception is Sibaji Bandyopadhyay's superbly calibrated and lyrically written chapter on *Khwabnama* in his study of five Bangla novels (1996), which will filter through the lines of this chapter.

It is hard to miss (in Bangla) the compassionate and sensuous pressure wielded on the syntax and the vocabulary that Elias chooses to privilege and mould into what he often refers to as his novelistic 'scheme'.[2] The opening lines cue us to the syntactical challenges of *Khwabnama*:

> The place where he slightly embeds his soles in the mud and standing straight, the muscles of his neck pulled tight straining to look up as high as he can to chase away the deep grey clouds, Tamij's father waving his two jet black arms—it is necessary to observe this place well. (Elias 1998a, 9)

The subjects of history (past, present and future—those somewhat inadequate terms) are incisively inflected with a colloquial turn of phrase, an apparently insignificant detail:

> *A long time ago*, when let alone Tamij's father, his father too had not been born, and, it would be some time before his grandfather Baghar Majhi would come to this world, Baghar Majhi's grandfather's father or his grandfather may well have not been born, and if he had, would have been crawling around on all fours on the earthen floor of the homestead that come up on the freshly-cleared forest. (emphasis mine; Elias 1998a, 9)

Then comes a sudden pause in syntax and semantics within the generational swish of time captured in the sentence so far:

> *On one such afternoon*, when he was rushing to Kartowa to join the innumerable fakirs of Majnu Shah towards the fort at Mahasthan, Munshi Barkatulla Shah, felled by a bullet of Taylor, the leader of the white sepoys, had fallen off his horse. The hole in his throat made by the bullet never did heal. (emphasis mine; 9)

Finally, we have one of the subjects who is long dead but ubiquitous in the so-called 'present' of the novel—Munshi Barkatulla Shah, hereafter referred to as 'the Munshi'.

These two figures positioned in the first paragraph are arrested, as it were, in different temporal moments: Tamij's father and the Munshi. The equation changes if we note the assonance in their respective stances: the seeker standing erect and the fighter falling or being felled off his horse with a bullet through his neck. In the former, we have the vertical axis of the human body, feet slightly embedded in mud and neck arched, gazing at the ash-grey clouds flying across the sky, the scrawny black arms flailing and chasing the clouds, like the flock of fleecy sheep that flounder and swim along the waters of the huge water body, the *beel*. The skin-and-bones human body loses its customary proportions and turns (unselfconsciously) into a divination stick, linking earth and heaven and the tree in between.

Should one attribute such stylised sets of signification to the work of a dispassionate narrator? And should such a passage be read exclusively as an aesthetic of abstraction? What appears to be a static or frozen moment then unravels in swiveling syntax and temporalities, where the actors are many. For, in his language, syntax and imagery, Elias gifts people (the characters *and* the reader) the possibility of a sensuous thinking life in narrativisation and in the narrative. But this gift is in the nature of a relentless probing, into history, cognition, language and in all forms of political relations. Elias himself, in numerous interviews, is critical of anything 'syrupy' or 'namby pamby' or self-indulgent, as he is of the preachy or didactic (1998 interview reported in *Rupam*; Ahmed and Sami 2002, 114). Unsurprisingly, he repeatedly marks out as 'exceptional' the poet and artist Sukumar Ray who 'for the last forty years has had an impact on me … a poet who makes us aware, raises our consciousness through laughter' (hashtey hashtey sachetan korey tolen) (Ahmed and Sami 2002, 149). Asked about endings in novels and their end, Elias's response is that the 'possibility' is all.

A warning, or perhaps a command, is issued right at the beginning of *Khwabnama*: 'One must observe this place attentively (ei jayegata bhalo korey kheyal kora dorkar)' (Elias 1998a, 9) Bandyopadhyay glosses the word *jayega*: 'What we call place is actually quite complex; it is hard to plumb. Mathematics, maps, detailed geographical description—none of these is enough to get an introduction to the water or any part of the land' (Bandyopadhyay 1996, 145). What he goes on to say, partly tongue in cheek, is also in the nature of a warning: 'That is to say, to displace the ground beneath the reader and make him unsteady is precisely the wicked intention of the narrator' (145).

Jayega or place can mean many things—location, terrain or even space. It is not as though one site is sacred to one person or one incident. In some sense, all places are sedimented in slow moving flows of history, including the beliefs of people who seek to turn material 'evidence' into myth. A place is not only created by the proper names it is known by, its relation to neighbouring spaces and its association with historical events. It is shaped by the stories that generations of people breathe into its material signs, such as the ancient ruins of a monastery or a crumbling fort in relation to the apparently more natural landmark of a tree, a river, a mound or the like. Once we accept this proposition, history becomes omnivorous and shape-shifting, not restricted to the strict definitions of the discipline as we know it, even now, after its attempts to wriggle out of its positivist straitjacket.

Elias's lengthy letter to Mahasweta Devi (dated 1 August 1996) may be read as a manifesto of the artist's stake on his land and the vulnerability therein. It invokes both the literal ground beneath his feet and all that has disappeared below the earth and survives in stories and local lore. He writes of the ground that he would now have to negotiate with a crutch after his right leg had to be amputated:[3]

> Almost six months after [I received your letter] I have begun writing my long planned novel.
>
> Ekkori's Saadh, the place where the people of this novel live, is known to you; the hero's home is located there as well. Mahasthan is only six miles away from my home in Bogura. I've been roaming around and intensely absorbing (choshey bedachhi) the huge ruins of Pundranagari, mostly by myself and sometimes with friends. (Ahmed and Sami 2002, 158)

Elias then evokes a map that is both spatial and temporal:

> To the north of Bogura town there is a place called Subil—one could say this is the beginning of Pundranagari. After that is Gokul, there is a huge ruin of Buddhist *vihars* and after Gokul comes Mahasthan .... Do you remember that your Ekkori had seen the reflection of the broken red brick palace in the waters of the Kartowa? (158)

He merges the fictional and real worlds of Mahasweta Devi and his own yet-to-be realised novel:

> My people live on the banks of that [same] Kartowa river. But there's no counting how many times this red reflection has found a body (*kaya peyeche*). From the time of the Dibyik and Bhim Kairbarta to the revolt of Majnu Shah ... and finally, the 1971 Freedom Struggle .... In the blood of innumerable people, Kartowa has been flooded with the blood of humans. (158)

Buddhism had found a home in Bengal, even becoming an international centre for centuries. Elias does not valorise this aspect of the past either. A few lines later, he writes to Mahashweta Devi, 'I've heard that even in the time of the Buddhists' non-violent preaching, a few thousand Jain monks were killed right here [by the river]' (Ahmed and Sami 2002, 158). Elias's attachment to the ruins of Pundranagari must be seen in light of its layered history: recent excavations have revealed eighteen layers of settlements, going back to back to the 4th century BC.[4] No wonder Elias says he feels torn: 'I would like to stick to the War of 1971 ... but would that be paying respect to this place?' (159)

For myth-making is living history: 'I have walked around a lot all over these places. I have seen how a story turns into myth. Shall I tell you the story?' (Ahmed and Sami 2002, 158). The story Elias invokes is of Behula and Lakhindar from the *Manasamangal Kavya* of medieval

Bangla, versions of which circulate in song, verse and image across Eastern India and elsewhere in the subcontinent too. Every feature of the landscape is linked to some aspect of the dramatic narrative around these mythic characters.[5]

Even very sensitive readings of *Khwabnama* end up by attempting to make peace between history and fiction, often posited as binaries (Dasgupta 2002). Whereas, for Elias, history apparently resides in the sensorial, the research, the imagination, and a mix of the material and the imaginative that can almost be divined by long spells—of walking. 'Whatever I've written my entire life has not been written with my hands; I've written with my feet' were Elias's words to his friend Sibaji Bandyopadhay. Barely a month after the amputation, Elias was bent on trying out his crutches even in the busy thoroughfares of Park Circus, where he was then staying, in Calcutta.[6]

A peripatetic mode of experiencing over time and seeking to know through temporalities is a writerly preoccupation. It is a necessity that is also foregrounded in his characters.

The Peripatetic

In a recent book entitled *Precarious Flânerie and the Ethics of the Self in Contemporary Anglophone Fiction* (2002), Eva Ries attempts to show how the flânerie text becomes a medium of ethical critique in post-postmodern times. Rather than bringing the approach of 'the flânerie text' to his oeuvre, it is more the trail of wandering in apparently unconnected episodes of personal life and known and anecdotal history that is meticulously composed by Akhtaruzzaman Elias to prod and produce an ethical contemporaneous self. He envisages the reader as a fellow traveller, walking alongside the writer. This vision is enabled through multiple refractions (rather than any mimetic representation) of an experiential peripatetic self that has an intimate understanding, if not bond, with the environment, in this case, the fluvial and otherwise watery terrain of the region.

The novel's specific political directions—in several senses of the word—have been well charted in relation to popular mass uprisings during the consolidation of British power under the East India Company (Bandyopadhyay 1996), continuing into the throttled power of the Tebhaga Movement and the 1947 Partition (Ahmed and Sami 2002; Dasgupta 2002; Marik 2019; Nath 2020). What might change, however, if one ventures to read it within a longer durée?

Reading aloud *Khwabnama* in Bangla and participating in collaborative readings (involving several languages, in writing and in conversation) in the act of translating it into Urdu/Hindi opened up, in a very heightened manner, the interpenetration of sound and syntax in the novel, cueing the reader to its pauses, ellipses, repetitions and leitmotifs, its cadenced sentences punctuated with colloquial phrase as well as the cuss word. Together, they impart to the text a physical musicality. The translation was taking shape as one was literally following the micromovements of the character through an astonishing range of linguistic registers. Is Tamij's father sleepwalking as he heads towards to the beel on his wanderings? How is it that Kulsum's long interior monologues are shot through with an acute awareness of all that is happening around her and looping through her childhood, even as she critically scrutinises aspects of her face in the little round mirror at home or while she energetically splashes water on her face hoping to lighten her skin colour at the all-purpose pond (*doba*) outside their home?

Nature, manifested as tree, branch, flower, fish, a flock of egrets, cloud and water (and let us not forget the clusters of blood-sucking leeches), flourishes equally in the compost of history. In turn, history seeps into the dream narrative that is part of the Sufi tradition, particularly in the Indian subcontinent, which is touched upon in the following section.

The historical fakir-sanyasi battles against the Company took place from 1763 to 1800 for almost three decades. Variously called the Sannyasi Rebellion or the Sannyasi, Fakir and Peasants' War, the composition of its participants, their spontaneous or planned alignments and the significance of the rebellion from the vantage point of contemporary history continue to be debated (Bandyopadhyay 1996, 152–160; Bhattacharya 2012; Chatterjee 1984; Dasgupta 2002). Bandyopadhyay, in particular, dissects how within Elias's novel and without, the history of these battles is rendered differently in diverse textual traditions. It is the huge all-embracing densely growing *pakur* (banayan/fig) tree that bears living witness to this past, more than any written text can (Bandyopadhyay 1996, 143).

If the giant tree is itself a text, there is a reversal in the way the book of dreams, the text of divination, refuses to stay within the script and the diagrams or scrawls that mark its pages. The text itself—that precious and worthless bundle of worn out, dog-eared pages introduced in the early chapters—becomes a living thing, redolent with the memories of a wandering childhood and of music that travelled across land and water or of sandbanks (*char*) that rise and dissolve in the river. It is the journey of the melody (*sur)* of generations that resists the very fetters of the novelistic form as we have chosen to imagine it. In the novel, the music of the wandering singer, Cherag Ali, is evoked through the acutely listening—sniffing, remembering and longing-to-hear—being of his granddaughter Kulsum (Elias 1998a, 18). Besides those composed or remembered by her grandfather, what is foregrounded are the *sholokes* (from *slokas*) that 'the old man' (her husband, Tamij's father) appears to mutter. Sometimes, the mantra appears to come from the windblown branches of the pakur (fig) tree, which is the *sithaan* (*sthan*, seat) of the rebel Munshi, follower of the fakir Majnu Shah, felled by the bullet of a Company soldier.[7] Words, even the sound of what might be words, and speech turned into sur compose the sound capillaries of the novel. Arguably, these capillaries too constitute the terrain.

Elias makes a striking and certainly conscious choice in leavening the prose of *Khwabnama* with songs and doggerels, writing as he did in the late 20th century (Bandyopadhyay 1996, 162, 168–169). Verse and music were a conundrum faced by many early American-English translators of classics from the 'non-Western world', Japanese and Chinese novels, for instance, into English: What does one do with the profusion of poetry and snatches of songs scattered like flowers across the leaves of a multi-volume page-turner like the *Romance of the Stone*, also known as the *Dream of the Red Chamber* (1791)? Or, closer home, consider the fate of early novels in Urdu, Hasan Shah's *Nashtar* (1790) or Mirza Hadi Ruswa's *Umrao Jaan Aada* (1899). Often, the solution was to simply omit or pare down the verses. After all, classic Western novels did not dabble in verse.[8]

How do we respond to the 'straightforward description' of the world in the signature verse of *Khwabnama*? What might appear mysterious or magical is stated in an unadorned manner, much like the laws of gravity. Which is the self that has internalised this mise-en-scène to a 'reality'?

> Munshi lives atop the *pakur* tree,
> Below lies the *gojaar* fish, fearful to see.
> In the dark of the night at Munshi's command,
> The *gojaar* in the *beel* changes to a ram. (Elias 1998a, 13)

Elias's response to a query about whether he had ceased being a poet is worth citing: 'Who says I don't write poetry any more? My novel *Khwabnama* is being serialised in a magazine … you will find a lot of poems there. *Arrey*! The poems in that book …. I've written all of them' (Kaiser 2002, 32). I would argue that *Khwabnama* has poetry of several kinds, not only verses like the one above. They do not attempt to mimic 'the subaltern' but posit a different way of apprehending the world.

There is also a response to a high canonical work running through *Khwabnama*, as has been highlighted (Bandyopadhyay 1996, 153). Elias alerts us to the class use of book learning and a dominant reading of an iconic text of Bengali nationalism, Bankimchandra Chattopadhyay's *Anandamath* (1882)—now foregrounded in contemporary Hindutva's brand of nationalism. It is a 'given', used to silence the unlettered and put them 'in their place', sowing suspicion of the Other as 'the enemy of the musalman' (*musalman'er shatru*; Bandyopadhyay 1996, 153). Snatches of such conversations are enmeshed tightly within the webs of class and religion and hierarchies within occupations and lineages, claimed or denied, that move beyond any political-ethnographic mapping (Nath 2020, 167–168,182).

The novel is at once expansive in referencing and speaking in citation, internalising a wide range of textual traditions, while taking on the compressed and evocative quality of a lyric in imagery and syntax. Its possibilities do remind us of Bakhtin's *The Dialogic Imagination* (1981), but Elias has travelled too far and too deep into a deltaic land for us to rest with Bakhtin.

It will also become apparent to the reader that the persistence and existence of the dream in *Khwabnama* is unique to the topos, the region and its waves of migration or people, faiths and languages, filtrated in various degrees of perception and communication. Frederic Jameson's persuasive argument about 'Bovarysme', the 'register of impressionistic daydreaming' invented by Flaubert around his titular heroine in *Madame Bovary*, and that he used then as an object to be demystified by the second [more "realistic" register] does not afford us an entry point either into Elias's linguistic registers or his narrativisation of dreaming (1981, 213). Jameson concludes that Flaubert's intended effect of the separation of registers did not work and 'it becomes … of a piece with the text' (212–213). If Elias aims at 'demystification', it is through the interpenetrative play and juxtaposition of multiple registers, microtones that traverse the range of sleep and wakefulness. The intention perhaps is of not giving the reader much respite.

'Awake or Dreaming?'

Dream frames are common to literary traditions, oral and textual, across the world. In recent times, Western Romantic poetry legitimised the dream vision, bringing it out of the more structured allegorical religious reading of medieval texts, often displacing it into magical (or oriental) locales, even blurring the sharp compartmentalisation between dreaming and wakefulness. Arguably, modernism foregrounded dreaming as a mode of ironic metacommentary, foundational to fiction-making in a desacralised world. Here, one could think of two very different literary figures experimenting with form and language, Joyce and Borges, both of whom Elias enjoyed reading.[9]

The title of Elias's novel, *Khwabnama*, demands an extended contextualisation. While we may agree in a general way with statements such as 'Elias would look at the politics of the left [sic] as it entered the popular consciousness through dreams (*Khawab*) reflecting the narratives (*Namah*) of the past and present among peasants, but where that also intersected [with] Muslim community identity' (Marik 2019, 95), scrolling through the gamut of signification carried in the word *dream* (*swapna/khwab*) yields a wider-ranging dense matrix. Elias's fiction and his own observations on fiction writing indicate a more complex relational template of subject and subjectivity. In several of his interviews, he speaks about a certain detachment (*nirbikaratva*) required of the writer in tandem with the need to see the 'total' [English in the original]. He elaborates: 'For many communists, a peasant (*chasha*) is "nothing but a poor man" [in English in the original]. But one would not know everything about the peasant if one does not know about his family life, his beliefs, his culture and even his sexual life' (*Lyric*, 1 Baisakh bs 1393; Reprinted in Elias 2011, 41–42). An exploration of all of these factors would inevitably lead the writer to engage with powerful dreams that sway the masses:

> But this influence strengthens the foundations of exploitation (kintu ei probhab shoshoner bhittike shakta korey). If you look [deeper] into this influence, you certainly see it all—the dreams of people, the use of their dreams, 'blackmailing' of their dreams, in a larger sense, in politics as well. (*Lyric*, 1 Baisakh bs 1393; 41–42)

A writer must enter these dream realms but neither identify entirely with them nor read them as self-fulfilling prophecies.

An elaboration of this position is found in a diary entry of December 1982 on novels from Africa. Elias reflects on the Nigerian writer Elechi Amadi's *The Great Ponds* (1969), which he believes could be seen as 'an African epic' (2011, Diary 5, 301–302):

> What we call superstition has been presented as a natural part of life … in an incomparably robust manner. Amadi does not have a 'reformative attitude' [in English in the original]…. There is complete trust in the reader. The writer does not tell us what is serendipity, what is supernatural…. As a result, the reader's responsibility is bound to deepen. I take these as signs of great artistry. (Diary 5, 301–302)

The divination of dreams has a powerful presence in popular print culture in Bangladesh. Elias highlighted this strand after the publication of the novel in 1996 in an interview in *Nandan* (in Calcutta):

> Do you know, there's a kind of book that is found in the home of semi-literate Bengali Muslims. It's *khwabnama*, colloquially called *khaabnaam*, that is to say, it carries interpretations of dreams. For example, it might be written that such and such will happen if you dream of an elephant.... I have taken the title of my book from this phenomenon. (Ahmed and Sami 2002, 125)

Elias concedes: 'I thought I knew the subject. But while writing, I found that I did not know all about the matter ... and that's why, in the course of my writing, I have to keep going to the villages in Bogura' (125).

Elias would also have been aware of the larger strands of Sufi traditions in north India, particularly between the 16th and 18th centuries. 'According to the internal perception of Islam, dreams were considered sufficiently important so that a corpus of technical literature, called *ta'birnama*, developed to interpret the dreams within its broader cultural framework' (Khanna 2001). The 'multidimensional' aspect of Sufism in different parts of the subcontinent and their amalgamation into or reconfiguration based on local traditions is well recognised in historiography (Eaton cited in Khanna 2001; Digby cited in Khanna 2001). Elias's deep involvement with local lore and their geographic 'narrativisation' may be related to the rather unique history of sedentarisation in what we call Bengal/Bangladesh today, which was formed by its shifting maritime frontier, its active delta and course-changing rivers (Mukherjee 2017). (Kartowa was once a mighty river before the floods of 1787 when its parent river, Teesta, shifted from its old channel and moved into the Brahmaputra/Jamuna.) With the coming of Islam from 1200 AD, most intriguing is the role of charismatic Sufis (mystics) who initiated a slow eastward and southward movement, leading their converted followers to the clearing of forests and the reclamation of land for agriculture, thus creating 'wet-rice cultivating' peasant communities and an 'expanding agrarian frontier' (Eaton 2020, 363).

This long durée is expressed in *Khwabnama*, which I have elsewhere described as 'a translator's delta, crisscrossed by watery furrows that seep into the visionary', bringing to life the momentous political events of undivided Bengal of the 1940s (Bhattacharya 2009, 3). One of the entries from Elias's diaries of 1986 shows the family tree of one such *pir*[10] family, for an 'epic novel' that he hoped would bring the ancient history of Mahasthangarh into juxtaposition with the *Muktijuddho* (the Liberation War) of 1971 (2011, Diary 7, 305).[11] (The massive uprising of all classes of people in 1969 in what was then East Pakistan, leading up to the war, was the subject of Elias's first novel, *Chilekothar Sipahi* (The soldier in the attic, 1986).[12] Interestingly, in this diagram, one of the last descendants of the pir family is also called Kulsum, a central character of *Khwabnama*. It is through her 'super wakeful' consciousness that the intricate and changing history of land and labour comes alive in chapter two.

Khwabnama is not one of the many classic river novels in Bangla.[13] It is not as if there has not been any experimentation with Bangla prose to articulate the synaesthetic density of vegetation, land and water before Elias. The opening paragraph from 'The Third Chapter' of Rabindranath Tagore's last novel *Char Adhyay* (Four Chapters, 1934) is a breakthrough in this respect, inspired by his absorption in painting in the last decades of his life and perhaps, too, the condensed structure of classical Chinese poetry. In a different vein, the prologue and epilogue to Bibhutibhushan's last novel, *Ichhamati* (1950), and specific sections of the long novel seek to capture the ephemerality of life along the river banks.

In Elias's sensorium, water shapes lives and dreams, the surface and what lies beneath. The topographical vocabulary distinguishing different kinds of water bodies, big and small, still and flowing—*beel, jheel, khaal, pukur, doba .... nad-nadi*—permeates the entire novel, dreams and all, blurring the magical, the mundane and the material.[14] Several of his short stories 'play' with the sounds of rain as expressive of censored or hushed up speech, the protagonist's inner life, mourning after death and imminent death: 'Nirrudesh Jatra' (An aimless journey; 1976), 'Apaghaat' (A violent or unnatural death; 1989) and 'Raincoat' (1995) offer three starkly different treatments of the corporeality of rain and its resonances within the human body and of tears and the changing rhythms of weeping.[15]

Does the sense of self have to do with the interpenetration of topos in sound, moving into multiple 'kinds of seeing' or not seeing, sensing but not with certainty? Might one conceive of this form of narrativisation as synaesthetic spirals laying bare the barely noticeable—the shifts in occupation and ownership, the wiping out of entire neighbourhoods with none but birds as witnesses? To put it bluntly then, how does this sophisticated and sensuous mode of telling lay bare the entire gamut of transformation in modes of production and changing human relations that animate the dream?

Sensoria: Synaesthesia

Kulsum has invented her own hunger game, indulging in it and keeping it at bay. It comprises deep breaths, breathing in food smells in the rancid breath of Tamij's father, one who can devour vast quantities of food no matter that he is like a stick. She lets it flow between her breasts, swirling into her stomach and then allows it to settle down in her abdomen (Elias 1998a, 16–17). There's a catch though. This practice won't work if you unlock your mouth and spit, even a drop (23). Then, all labour is in vain.

Like other orifices of the body, the mouth consumes, expels and breathes. It also speaks. Speech and food and smell and hearing are intertwined desires. She brings her ears close to her husband's mouth, hoping to hear the Munshi in the garbled mumblings of the old man. She inhales the slowly fading odour of Tamij's left-behind garment, as one would inhale the precious aroma of *ittr*. She inhales the smell of the raggedy book whose leaves are crumbling, waiting for signs, waiting to catch a glimpse of her *dada* (grandfather) who seems almost to appear at their door (17–18). Eros, hunger and the imagination are inseparable temporal realms.[16]

Kulsum, we learn, is the 'given away' granddaughter of a *madari* fakir. (As mentioned earlier, Majnu Shah was of the Madariya order.) The term '*fakir'er beti*' (daughter of a fakir) is used contemptuously by others in the neighbourhood of her marital home to deny her a more legitimate social standing. In her ruminations, she puzzles over this perception. She does not recall experiencing it earlier in her wandering days with her dada, Cherag Ali, the diviner of dreams (Elias 1998a, 26).

Cramped within their small hut and within the dwelling, confined to the *macha*, a small raised platform, her wandering days with her dada waft into the unravelling of chapter two in stray sentences from a faraway place. There are songs sounding within her, through the many pauses for resting, cooking and eating, being scolded at or beaten up for mistakes on a moonlit night. She feeds on memories of food that was given as alms or as a ritual to the singing fakir. And she, holding on to his hand, his walking companion, shared some of this offering. Food is linked to specific days and times (of feasts and prayers) and harvesting seasons and even to the lean or prosperous season of dreaming:

> The rainy season was painful. It was difficult to go outdoors, and also, people were reluctant to give alms before the harvesting of the *aush* paddy. This was a time when people did not even see dreams. Once the paddy was harvested, there was an overflowing of dreams. (Elias 1998a, 27)

At some point, these precarious but tensile communitarian links start to break down, as more mainstream forms of religiosity take over. The river changes its course, and their neighbourhood is swept away. Later, her dada is afraid of orthodox Khadem who turns the *dargah* into a masjid (30).

On an empty belly, late at night, Kulsum fantasises about cooking the *shapla* stalks, the water-growing greens, but is dismayed to find that the sleepwalking old man has somehow carried back only a few torn petals of the shapla flower on his journey home (Elias 1998a, 15). The shapla creeper is just one of those million 'things' of all that is green and edible growing wild on water and land and free for the picking. Elias juxtaposes the inedible shreds of the flower and the edible greens, the old man and the starving young woman, as though mocking with a delicate irony his own sentence a few pages earlier, about Tamij's father's dream-like walk homewards: 'Although a few thin peelings of his slumber fall off at the soft touch of the torn petals, sleep does not let go off him completely' (chhenra panpri'r norom chonwaye taar ghoom'er patla koyekta khosha uthey geleo ghoom kintu shob-ta kaatey na) (13).

Actually, the torn petals appear almost at the last phase of the dream-walking back home. Like slowly shaking off the deepest part of the slumber, from the unconscious depths of the beel, his feet first fall on the base stalk, and he bends forward to hold the stalk and steady himself. But 'can a shapla creeper ever bear the weight of his body?' (Elias 1998a, 13). Such casual edgy and rhetorical questions with a Brechtian intent are woven into the flow of sensation and movement making up every sequence of *Khwabnama*. They range from the sharp to the languorous, in the form of a character's interjection or moments of sheer abandon, as though establishing the narrator's joking camaraderie with the protagonist.[17] In all instances, it makes for the unsettling tenor of narration that Bandyopadhyay had warned us of (1996, 145). A novelist has to find other modes of disruption than a playwright.

As a medical or clinical term, the 'sensorium' in human beings would naturally be defined in categories approximating to the 'normal', the 'altered' and the 'lacking'.[18] In the Anthropocene, one would, belatedly perhaps, wish to acknowledge all that mass of life invisible to the uncaring human. Artists appreciative of the potential of synaesthesia would also, naturally, be interested in exploring all those states and modes beyond the normative. I can think of two very different poets whose oeuvre plumbs the sensorium in language as much as the social milieu they inhabited. Baudelaire made it the very substance of his urban flânerie in Paris. Elias's belief that the artist had no obligation to 'relieve the reader of any critical uneasiness'[19] (1998 interview reprinted in Ahmed and Sami 2002, 113) surely takes us to Baudelaire's address to the 'hypocrite reader': —mon semblable, —mon frère! In early 20th-century Calcutta, Sukumar Ray delighted in bending the rules of Bangla phonetics and semantics, moulding them to create marvellous new creatures, familiar and grotesque in the same breath. Elias, whose admiration for Ray as a poet of sounds was unequivocal, absorbs the sharp juxtapositions, the unexpected outcomes and the sheer delight in invention that characterises the latter's poetic nonsense.

The shrinking and swelling sensorium that one may gauge even from these two chapters (of a book of fifty-nine chapters) comes into being through an internal linguistic 'scheme' of synaesthesia (I am falling back on Elias's own term). The scaffolding is rigorous and playful, a subject meriting a separate study, written in Bangla, preferably. A few indications may be given here.

Narratorial pauses create an oral dimension and also suggest connections: 'Taa, shey ki aajker katha? Shei kone amoley ek bikaalbela bela dobaar aagey aagey' (But then, it's hardly something that's just happened! On an afternoon of some long ago era, a little before the light began to die.... Elias 1998a, 12). *Taa* is a kind of pause or filler word, like *well* or *so*, indicating that a person is reflecting before pronouncing an opinion or is about to broach another topic.

The indeterminacy of the narrative voice is sustained not only with questions but also parenthetical asides:

> But does it always happen the same way? But is it the same every time? Or, on some days, a certain prolonged sound has broken the sleep of Tamij's father, from very far away—where else could it be but from the pakur tree?—someone says in a hoarse voice, drawling out the words' (Kintu shobshomoy ki emni hoye?—Na kono kono din taana kono awowaje'e Tamij'er baap'er ghoom ekdom bhenge giyechhe. Anek dur theke, pakur gaach chada aar kot-theke hobey?—bhaanga bhanga golaye teney teney ke jeno koye). (Elias 1998a, 13)

Specific phrases are echoed as in a musical composition, with a slight difference in the rendering each time. The familiarity of the images and the length of the sentence lull one into believing or assuming it will be the same as before, but there is inevitably a change. Consider, for example, the metamorphosis of the Munshi into light and darkness, inexplicably turning into a single filament of the down on a bird's wing (10–11).

One last example could serve as being foundational to the novel's unique take on land, habitation, ownership and dispossession and the conscious blurring of distinctions between birds, beasts and humans. It is the recurrent image of the child who has not yet learnt to toddle, crawling on all fours on the newly made earthen floor of a home where, only a while ago, a forest stood. The temporal markers of the opening paragraph of *Khwabnama* return in speaking of Dasharath Kamar's genealogy

> Even if Dasharath's ancestors did not actually go by the name of [the fabled] Mandhata, but right from Mandhata's era itself, when—why

> [neither] Dasarath nor his grandfather was yet born and perhaps not even his grandfather's father.... (Elias 1998a, 13)

The difference is illuminated in the same passage by the slight detail of the glowing fire of the forge:

> and even if he was, around the time he was crawling around in the glare of the newly installed fire and bellows in the new homestead built after clearing the jungle—the family history of the egrets settled on the *arjun* tree, had begun from that very day onwards.[20] (13)

To return to Kulsum, in the troubled (and sometimes) easy-going relationship she appears to share with her stepson, deeply inhaling the slowly fading scent of sweat of his outer garment (*piran*) tucked away in a basket in a corner, she remembers all that he tells her of his first visit to 'elsewhere' working as a day labourer. The micro-context of what became known as the Tebhaga Movement comes through her understanding of what he has recounted. It is as new to him as it is to her. It is through her recollecting scraps of this jesting, jousting conversation, that the reader is intimated about the hopes of a first-generation sharecropper and his eventual decision to join the movement (Elias 1998a, 19–20).

In *Khwabnama*, none of the senses is ever a discrete function. What might the sensorium mean in the larger whorl of a wandering world, where rivers change their course as a matter of course? And the large waterbody, the *beel*, dwindles daily as trees are chopped off to feed the ever-hungry maws of brick kilns?

'Their Hunger of Aeons'

It is impossible to miss the pangs of hunger as they appear unexpectedly, poetically, sensuously and with direct brutality in all of Elias's ouevre (Bandyopadhyay 1996; Dasgupta 2002). Asked to frame his life against contemporary events, Elias stated that his birth and his son's birth were both framed by famines, the Bengal Famine of 1943 during the Second World War and the famine of 1974, shortly after the birth of Bangladesh ('Ami o Amar Samay' in Elias 2000, 2). The Sanyasi-Fakir Rebellion also took place during the 1771 famine. These and other recorded famines may be signposted against the region's 'flourishing agrarian economy' for millennia. Epigraphic records indicate the export of paddy in ships setting off from the ancient port of Tamralipta (Chakravarti 2020, 119–121).[21]

References to the 1943 famine (*aakaal*) are ubiquitous in *Khwabnama*, suggesting that the very appetite for and the nature of food has changed before and after. Not so evident and perhaps more enthralling—in the original meaning of the word and not as an adjective applied to a hit film—are the ways in which the strains of labour, nature and hunger combine like different notes to create one of the predominant surs of the novel. An early instance in the novel signals the breakdown of traditional occupations of the farmer and the fisherman/boatman and the subsequent shift to hiring themselves out as daily wage labourers in places distant from home. At dawn, groups of men are setting off for work, trekking through a *kash* forest (whose delicate feathery clusters comprise some of the most memorable shots of Bengali cinema):

> It was the month of *Paush*. At dawn, with mist hanging above them, some folks from the Majhipara on this side of the beel, along with the farmers from Nijgiridanga, set off on two boats, and with them went Tamij's father to find work as a daily wager. They took the initiative because the kash forest does not get waterlogged at this time of the year. (Elias 1998a, 11)

Elias proposes a different cinematic shot:

> But no, there is no place that is bone-dry in the kash forest. At every step, the water sloshed beneath their feet. On the slender branches of the kash hung thousands of leeches, drying themselves to ward off the cold dew of the winter months. The branches were slightly bowed down by their weight. (Elias 1998a, 11)

The forest, which also is subject to change in accordance with seasons and human intervention and which appears to be *only* a passage to another destination is that intermediate space extending into their homes:

> When so many humans carrying their sickles and spades entered the jungle, those terribly famished leeches picked out an individual and came in droves to fasten themselves on each labourer … on his stomach, abdomen, thigh, pee-pee, butt, knee and even on the anus—seizing and hanging on to from whichever place they could cling to. (11)

Hunger brings together man and worm in one condensed sentence:

> In satiating their hunger of aeons, the fishermen of Girirdanga and the farmers of Nijgirirdanga, if not actually afraid, become active in picking them off, in their pain, and when they return home after dark, come back either with a live leech or the bite or wound from a leech on their bodies. (Elias 1998a, 11)

The phrase '*tader bohukaal'er khidey*' could be translated as 'their hunger of many aeons' or a long-festering, smouldering hunger. Festering (although the word is not present in the Bangla sentence) would immediately link it to the *bohukaaler* bullet—a wound suffered long ago by the Munshi, through which gap come his cries, scoldings and instruction. Its immediate 'presence' is in the never-healing and never-increasing sore/wound on Tamij's father's inner thigh, made by the bite of a *gojar* fish. We glimpse it first through the eyes of Kulsum as she strains to listen to the mutterings of her old man (15). The men and the leeches are victims of this long-drawn-out hunger, and the leeches appear to be legitimate in falling upon the men setting off with their tools to work. Despite the multiple temporalities through which hunger flows and clings to the external parts of the body, the Bangla sentence ends with their return home at evening inscripted by the fierce energy of the leeches.

Yet the passage through the kash forest is finally not only a metaphorical one. Before the blood-sucking kiss of the leeches on the bodies of farmers and fishermen have been erased, the land changes hands. A 'town babu' takes it over, although Sharafat Mondol had long been eyeing the land to plant jute crops, and the ownership keeps shifting. The narrative spirals back to the past in the next couple of pages, while appearing to stay with Tamij's father looking out for the Munshi. In the 'landscape' laid out for us, almost a bird's eye view, in the opening pages, settlements on the basis of caste, occupation, religion and so on, were mapped onto natural but prone-to-change stretches of land and water. When the ironsmiths (*kamar*) start popping off during 'the last famine' (as do the egrets nesting on the arjun tree) (13), about half their neighbourhood is bought up by Jagdish Saha. The rivalry between him and Sharafat Mondol involves using the remaining smiths as pawns.

The displacement of the birds is inseparable from the dispossession of the smiths from their land and their inexorable path to the 'town' for jobs. It is not the omniscient narrator who 'recounts' the story. Hierarchies of pollution and purity (*pak na-pak*) cut into the narrative through the circular flight of birds and other signs that come straight from a human world of segregation, marginalisation and exploitation but that are now narrated through signs of 'nature'. All this through the daze of a sleepwalker squelching his way home in the mud, his feet riddled with tiny sores from long exposure to water and embedded with thorns (Elias 1998a, 14).

Hunger is of many kinds. There is also the perennial hunger for land, water and rights. Every meal is a mouthful. The full belly, in turn, can barely digest; it is a momentary sense of fulfilment. Tamij's father evacuates all that he has stuffed in well before it can be digested and become part of his body. The river, too, is eager to devour. The rapid erosion along the banks of the Jamuna threatens to swallow up *madaripara*, the sanctuary of the wandering fakir and his granddaughter. All but Cherag Ali abandon their homestead, knowing the ravenous appetite of 'that slut' (Elias 1998a, 30).

Hunger lights up like a torch at the very end of *Khwabnama* in the almost wordless exchange between Tamij's wife Phuljan and their little daughter, Shokina. But alongside the smell of freshly cooked steaming rice are the thoughts-words that stir audibly inside Shokina's head (*bij bij korey*), which her mother senses and is anxious about, which will burst forth in fresh sholokes that go back to her grandfather and back again to the Munshi (Elias 1998a, 346–347). Phuljan muses fearfully about her daughter:

> Now, one may understand the fragrance of rice and the aroma of fish, but what is it that is stirring to life in Phuljan's daughter's head? Then, will words sprout like grass from the mutterings inside her head, and would this Shokhina string sholokes with it and bring it alive? What else does the girl know but eating rice? Would she be able to string together sholokes? Who knows what sholokes she would string together! (346)

Hunger and the act of conceptualising and composing are oftentimes inseparable and their articulation imminent. It is as though Elias passes on the writer's commitment and fierce creative energy to the little girl whose 'jet black legs' are planted firmly, entrenched in the soil. She is like her grandfather but also someone else; she is the future who will find her own speech.

'Play of Densities'

> When we started to evolve the enunciation for the film *Char Adhyay*, we had yet another problem on our hands. We had to pay homage to our freedom struggle and all its contradictions … Yet, we had to move in tangential directions. The cinema, as Tagore had so succinctly stated has to free itself from literature. In fact, Tagore himself was freeing himself from literature at the very point he wrote *Char Adhyay*. His intense desire to make visuality as significant as his poetry made him avoid all description characteristic of the novel form.
>
> The visualising had to be created minimally, tending towards a play of densities. Therefore for us, our colour contrast was that of violet and gold, of extension value. Fortunately, Somenath Hore

> had carried forward Tagore's own deep dark absorptions into the scorched white on white textures of cotton waste pulp to speak to us of the wounds of civilisation. (Shahani 2015, 25)

Elias gives the example of Kamal Kumar Majumdar as a writer 'whose extraordinary talent is used to keep the reader at bay' (Interview in *Rupam*, October 1988; Ahmed and Sami 2002, 114); the reader has to be willing to take risks to venture into the text. Later in the same interview, he speaks of writers 'whose sharp intelligent structure (literally, weave) does not allow the reader to be passive or oblivious .... a deep and meaningful relationship with the writer is only possible if the reader is alert, walking alongside the story' (114).

As a Marxist, Elias was actively involved in the Left writers' Camp/Organisation (Bangladesh Lekhak Shibir) and worked on a wide range of concerns well beyond the rubric of decolonisation as nationalism: the anti-blasphemy law, for tribes and others belonging to the hill tracts of Chittagong, for all Hindu minorities, was cognisant of the failures of various national parties in being unwilling or unable to harness spontaneous collective movements, leading to betrayals again and again (Interview in *Nandan,* July 1996; Ahmed and Sami 2002, 121).

Only a wide range of interpretive strategies, including many that may not yet have a name, would make for any creative engagement with not only the text in question but also the disciplinary lens through which we approach his writing. Elias does not hold on to a strict binary between science and faith, rationality and superstition. He does not care for the 'idea' of a peasant or a political leader. His own involvement straddles the local and the international, both felt as shackles and perceived as horizons and—through the tracks of international funding—dreams of migration to the West and the Middle East, or apprehended in literatures from 'distant lands', which speak of the struggles he has witnessed in his lifetime and those from millennia before his birth. An internationalist, he kneads the languages of his land to bring up undiscovered textures, allusions and connections.

Elias's essay 'I and my times' ('Ami o amar samay') is composed as a series of questions, such as 'How do I mark my or any milestone? (2000) 'Crisis' does not quite capture the catastrophes that he experienced in less than half a century: from his birth during the 1943 famine, the ravages of the World War under colonialism, the Tebhaga Movement and the Partition, the language movement (Bhasha Andolan) in then East Pakistan, the imposition of Martial Law, the counter-movements of 1962, the unique mass movement in 1969 not based on ethnic or religious lines but, sadly, tamed down to a 'middleclass nationalism', war again, the birth of Bangladesh, what he cryptically calls 'Swadhinata no 2', and 'famine again … this time my son was born' and then, to witness those who had once believed in liberation turn into 'looting lumpens' (Elias 2000, 1–3). He ends the essay: 'I stand on tiptoe … to see what lies on the other side of the wall' (Elias 2000, 3).

There exists no wall in cinema, even as a metaphor. While there is a screen, it opens out to suggest infinity.

Some artists embark on an unceasing project to work with and against the grain of anything they have inherited. Inheritance is never pure. Inheritance may be realised in a process that encompasses accidents and choices. Uprooted as a child from Hyderabad, Sindh, of undivided India, Kumar Shahani finds his pulse of history in the language of cinema.

The scope of Shahani's work has taken him across the entire Indian subcontinent, to Europe and the Americas and to diverse cultures across Asia. He found his teachers in Ritwik Ghatak and Robert Bresson, from two very different milieus and cinematic and cultural contexts. Not desirous of being slotted as a 'regional' filmmaker, Shahani opens up each of his films to the many migrant musical and dance traditions that have come to define our subcontinental heritage. Innumerable 'recces' and research (in defiance of impoverished budgets) have meant crisscrossing north and south in musical ragas (*Bamboo Flute/Bansuri*, 1999); land and water, rivers, seas and deserts (*Khayal Gatha*, 1989); forests, hills and ravines (*Bhavanatarana*, 1991); *Kasba* (1990) and *Khayal Gatha*) (1989). We listen to (and read in the intertitles) fragments/citations of *shloka*s (verses) from the Upanishads, ancient and medieval poetry in their many Prakrit tongues, contemporary poetry and traditional rhymes for children (*Char Adhyay/Four Chapters*, 1997) and old *bandishe*s (compositions) that bear witness to their Indo-Persian aural travels (*Bamboo Flute/Bansuri*).

From his very first feature, *Maya Darpan*, (1972), the sound montages alone in Shahani's films draw us into multiple viewings and, attuned to the camera movements, invite us to make inroads into their syntactical complexity (Shahani [1978] 2005, 179–184). Overall, the film has more 'sound shots' than 'colour shots'. For the filmmaker, it was the first time that he began to simultaneously conceptualise colour, sound and movement into a shot that would lead to emotional resonances, like a play of *rasa*s.

In the lengthy epigraph to this section, Shahani reflects on his directorial vision in approaching Rabindranath Tagore's controversial last novella, *Char Adhyay* (*Four Chapters*, 1934): 'We had to pay homage to our freedom struggle and all its contradictions … Yet, we had to move in tangential directions.' He offers an insight into his film *Char Adhyay* (1997), which commemorates half a century of India's independence from British rule, as one where the individual's aspirations for freedom are treated obliquely through enunciation, texture, colour and tactility, primarily in locations where nature is wild and very lush, almost threateningly so. Both Tagore and Shahani rely on *vyanjana* (evocation) to achieve this end, with signs of history inseparable from foliage, water and habitations.

The grammar of dance, of diverse dance forms, are recited and performed in quotidian and singular locations chosen after much physical exploration in almost every one of Shahani's films. The relationship of dance and nature and how the filmmaker works with movements specific to each dance form deserves further study (Shahani [1995] 2005, 243–249; Bhattacharya 2016, 249–268). These spaces traverse a continuum of the natural and human—the sea shore, a grove of trees, a private garden, a giant boulder, a temple, an abandoned mosque or an abandoned coal pit where a woman sings to the accompaniment of a solitary musician (the latter in *Bamboo Flute*). Each is distinctive, marked by the particular features of a natural terrain and yet imbued with the possibility of becoming something else in those unique moments of cinematic composition and shot taking (Sharma 2015, 212–236). (All the more selective because of not being a big budget commercial film that is being shot on digital and, therefore, with the possibility of 'infinite' takes and retakes.)

We may recall that Akhtaruzzaman's jayega (place) had the potential for a similar kind of expansive cinematic conceptualisation. *Khwabnama* is woven of the stuff of dreams, threaded in the nocturnal wanderings of Tamij's father, fuelled by his hunger which never goes to sleep and his awareness of the Munshi's myriad modes of presence in the darkness.

Even when it is spectacular, the relentless highlighting of darkness and the night should not be confused for special effects in either Elias or Shahani.

Shahani has a penchant for night shots, the nocturnal, and, in a more explicitly metaphysical frame, for exploring the various realms/layers of darkness, albeit in starkly captured material locations. Perhaps, the most luminous instances that involve peeling off the layers of darkness are to be found in *Bhavanatarana* (1991), for which title Shahani proposes 'Immanence' as the English equivalent. The dancer Guru Kelucharan Mohapatra (hereafter Kelu-babu, as Shahani addresses him) plays dark Krishna expressing his passion for Radha and also, in the course of the film, performs the *raudra roopa* (valiant and fearful manifestation) of Shiva (Sharma 2015, 187–211). Finally, of course, the varying shades and depths of darkness may only be revealed by lighting up the location and through the choreography of the camera. The découpage or breakdown of shots in cinema has, necessarily, a different gestation period than a novel. For one, cinema involves intense collaborative work. Such shots were greatly enabled by a deep understanding between Shahani and his long-time collaborator, friend and batch mate, the iconic cameraman, K.K. Mahajan.

Several possibilities open up if we extend (perhaps stretch) the meaning of divination beyond that of sensing the hidden, prophesying or soothsaying to include an enquiry into the self and into the realm of psychoanalysis. Kelu-babu often spoke of himself as something like a water-diviner (he came to this term, initially expressing it in gestures) in his exchanges with Shahani.[22] Both films in which Kelu-babu danced (*Bhavantarana* and *Bamboo Flute*) were permeated by lengthy conversations between the two.[23] I would like to end this chapter with a condensed reference to a third film in which he is 'present' after his death, primarily through the dance of his pupil Ileana Citrasiti, who came to India some four decades ago from her home in Bergamo, Italy. I shall touch upon a sequence of Ileana Citaristi dancing Narcissus in Shahani's latest, *Priye Charushile* (completed in 2018, awaiting release).[24]

Our usual 'memory' of the Narcisuss myth derives from the poet Ovid's rendering in his *Metamorphoses* (8 CE) where Echo finally 'disappears', remaining only as a voice without any active agency. Narcissus is always a male in the Greek myth, in love with his own reflection as a punishment for rejecting love. In Ovid's poem, Narcissus does not at first 'recognise his own image in the water'. It is later that he 'says out loud what he sees in the water' (Nelson 2000, 372–373). So in Ovid too, the movement is from the visual to the oral.

Shahani is inspired by the female Narcissus, Nergis, in the Persian tradition. In making her central to the film, the search for femininity and eros in nature, movement, nurturing relationships, there is search for a self in which knowledge (of the art and of the self) is not objectified. It is a concern that runs through his earlier films with Guru Kelucharan, which Shahani has spoken of in relation to '*sringara* … which begins with self-awareness and moves to discover the other—the opposite of the Narcissus myth' (Bhattacharya 2016, 264). The dance movements of both Odissi and Chhau provide a complementary and dynamic possibility of exploring and entwining versions of the myth. As Shahani writes in an earlier essay, 'Upon two basic poses and two basic movements, one can build up whole cybernetics that reveal the nervous system's encoded signs of nature … to work with or against gravity, discovering new sources of speech' ([1995] 2005, 243). As a dancer, Citaristi has specialised in both Odissi and Chhau, besides her training in philosophy. She came to India, she says, because she 'was searching for a grammar of the body' (Citaristi 2021, 4.05).

Humans have always been fascinated by reflective surfaces, water being possibly the earliest mirror. In the sequence I am referring to, instead of showing Narcissus's/Citaristi's reflection in the water, it is the dancer's face, neck and arms that reflect not only the shimmering dappling water but also the trembling leaves and the movement of branches. The camera is the mirror, the water, where the gaze is directed. The minimal movement of the tree flanking Ileana (and the waterbody by which she stands) becomes integral to the sequence, highlighted in the pan and tilt of the camera at the end, away from the dancer to the tree, where it rests on the gently swirling leaves once the dancer is out of the frame.[25] To achieve this configuration, the sequence was shot in early evening.

Inspired by the Greek myth, Ileana draws on her training in Chhau. She uses 'the techniques … by expanding the style' (Citaristi 2021, 12.50–13.20) to choreograph the sequence in tight controlled shifts of the torso, arms extended and gently undulating to the tips of her fingers, the leg raised high, shifting the balance on one leg every now and then. The face, initially appearing directly on screen, then turning away and almost immediately returning, shows an intense curiosity to know the self and (as suggested through subsequent sequences in the film) come to terms with that knowledge through a passage of space and time, experiencing the materiality of different cultures across a lifetime. The binary of East and West is in constant dissolution in the film like the shifting play of densities and the tints of green, the luminescence of water on flesh and on the ground, to the almost eerie vibrations of the electronic music animating this sequence.

Writing on art, literature and cinema in an age of digital explosion and on the cusp of the ChatBot will continue to be a challenge. The devaluation of the word or the image is not a new lament in human history. However, it has perhaps never been so furious and fast as in our present in ever more 'accessible', everyday technological modes of 'faster than sound' communication.

The subjects of this essay are primarily creatures of the imagination, who have been given sustained and rigorous attention by the respective 'makers'—writer, filmmaker, dancer and so on. Now, in a fairly uniform way across cultures and countries, the imagination is suspect and is not perceived as constituting any form of capital. Words, images and sound bytes are weaponised in the immaculate production of lies, and the new rasa is intended to other in extreme ways. In such circumstances, it might be a necessary risk for the scholar and the critic to step out of the hegemonic (global) template that defines one's discipline. This essay is a small gesture in the direction of the oblique, the resonating and the generative. It seeks to acknowledge and affirm the syntactical complexity of expressive forms in specific moments in history.

References

Ahmed, Anwar, and Ishan Sami, eds. 2002. *Rupam*. Special issue on Akhtaruzzaman Elias, No. 2. Published from Dhaka.

Bakhtin, Mikhail M. 1981. *The Dialogic Imagination*. Translated by Caryl Emerson and Michael Holquist. Austin: University of Texas Press.

Bandyopadhyay, Sibaji. 1996. 'Khoaber Raatdin.' In *Bangla Upanyashe Ora* ['They' in Bangla novels], 141–176. Calcutta: Papyrus.

Barthes, Roland. 1977. 'Diderot, Brecht, Eisenstein.' In *Image–Music–Text*, essays selected and translated by Stephen Health, 69–78. London: Fontana Press.

Bhattacharya, Ananda. 2012. 'Reconsidering the Sannyasi Rebellion.' *Social Scientist* 40 (3/4): 81–100.

Bhattacharya, Rimli. 2009. 'On the Track and Off: Fragment, Resonance and Fact'. Unpublished paper, Leverhume Translation Project (International), Jawaharlal Nehru University, New Delhi, 6 January.

———. 2016 'Realizing the Body in Movement: Gestures of Freedom in the Dance Aesthetics of Rabindranath Tagore and Kumar Shahani.' In *The Bloomsbury Research Handbook of Indian Aesthetics and the Philosophy of Art*, edited by Arindam Chakrabarti, 249–268. London: Bloomsbury Academy.

Chakravarti, Ranabir. 2020. *Trade and Traders in Early Indian Society*. 3rd ed. New Delhi: Manohar Publishers.

Chatterjee, Suranjan. 1984. 'New Reflections on the Sannyasi, Fakir and Peasants War.' *Economic and Political Weekly* 19 (4): PE2–PE13.

Citaristi, Ileana. 2021. 'In Conversation with Ileana Citaristi, Odissi and Chhau…' DD India, 22 June 2021, Interview with Munmun Bhattacharya. Accessed 14 February 2023, 1.5--2.27. https://www.youtube.com/watch?v=A2ZPjwnqD6I&ab_channel=DDINDIA

Dasgupta, Subhoranjan. 2002. 'History's Creative Counterpart.' *Seminar* 510 (February 2002): 21–27. Accessed 18 July 2022. file:///Users/rimli/Desktop/Akhtaruzzaman%20Ilyas/Subhoranjan%20Dasgupta,%20History's%20creative%20counterpart.htm

Eaton, Richard. 1993. *The Rise of Islam and the Bengal Frontier 1204–1760*. Berkeley, CA: University of California Press.

———. 2020. *India in the Persianate Age: 1000-1765*. Delhi: Penguin Books.

Elias, Akhtaruzzaman. 1986. *Chileykothar Sipahi* [The soldier in the attic]. Dhaka: University Press Limited.

———. 1998a. *Khwabnama* [Narrative of dreams]. Calcutta: Naya Udyog.

———. 1998b. *Sanskriti'r Bhanga Setu* [The Broken bridge of culture]. Dhaka: Mowla Brothers.

———. 2000. *Akhtaruzzaman Elias'er Galpasamagra* [Akhtaruzzaman Elias: Collected stories]. Calcutta: Naya Udyog.

———. 2011. *Akhtaruzzaman Elias: Churno bhavna o churna katha sangraha* [Akhtaruzzaman Elias: Fragments of thoughts and words], edited by Allaudin Mondol. Calcutta: Naya Udyog.

———. 2021. *Khwabnama*. Translated into English by Arunava Sinha. New Delhi: Penguin India.

Jalil, Rakshanda, and Debjani Sengupta, eds. 2022. Introduction to *Bangladesh: Writings on 1971, Across Borders*. Hyderabad: Orient BlackSwan.

Jameson, Frederic. 1981. *The Political Unconscious: Narrative as a Socially Symbolic Act*. Ithaca, NY: Cornell University Press.

Jayamanne, Laleen. 2015. *The Epic Cinema of Kumar Shahani*. Bloomington: Indiana University Press.

Kaiser, Abu. 2002. 'Krondoner ichha nei, tobu' (I do not wish to cry, but ...) In *Rupam,* edited by Anwar Ahmed with Ishan Sami, 30–33. Published from Dhaka.

Khanna, Meenakshi. 2001. 'Dreams and Visions in North India Sufic traditions ca 1500–1800 AD.' PhD thesis, School of Social Sciences, Jawaharlal Nehru University, New Delhi. Accessed 17 July 2022. https://shodhganga.inflibnet.ac.in/handle/10603/29018

Kumar, Sukrita Paul. (2002) 2010. '*Aap Beeti* or *Jag Beeti*: Narration and Reality in Umrao Jan Ada (1899).' In *Early Novels in India*, edited by Meenakshi Mukherjee, 227–239. New Delhi: Sahitya Akademi.

Marik, Soma. 2019. 'Critiques of Nation and Gender in South Asia: Akhtaruzzaman Elias' *Khwabnama* and Savitri Roy's *Trisrota* and *Swaralipi*.' *Sahitya, Journal of the Comparative Literature Association of India* 8: 94–112.

Nelson, Max. 2000. 'Narcissus: Myth and Magic.' *The Classical Journal* 95 (4): 363–389. Accessed 25 April 2014. http://www.jstor.org/stable/3298150

Medicine Net n.d. 'Sensorium.' Accessed 23 August 2022. https://www.medicinenet.com/sensorium/definition.htm.

Mukherjee, Rila. 2017. 'Accidental Ports: The Bengal Delta in the Sixteenth-Seventeenth Centuries.' In *Subversive Sovereigns across the Seas: Indian Ocean Ports-of-Trade from Early Historic Times to Late Colonialism*, edited by Kenneth R. Hall, Rila Mukherjee and Suchandra Ghosh, 146–175. Calcutta: The Asiatic Society.

Nath, Pradosh. 2020. 'The World of *Khoabnama:* The Dynamics of Social "Unchange".' In *After the Revolution: Essays in Memory of Anjan Ghosh*, edited by Partha Chatterjee, 165–187. Hyderabad: Orient BlackSwan.

Shahani, Kumar. (1978) 2005. 'Notes for an Aesthetic of Cinema Sound.' In *The Shock of Desire and Other Essays,* edited and introduced by Ashish Rajadhyaksha, 179–184. New Delhi: Tulika Books.

———. (1980) 2005. 'Word and Image.' In *The Shock of Desire and Other Essays,* edited and introduced by Ashish Rajadhyaksha, 146–150. New Delhi: Tulika Books.

———. (1995) 2005. 'Dance and Film.' In *The Shock of Desire and Other Essays,* edited and introduced by Ashish Rajadhyaksha, 243–249. New Delhi: Tulika Books.

———. 2015. 'Shabder Mukti.' Translated into Bangla by Amiya Dev. *Arek Rakam*, No. 16: 24–26.

Shahani, Kumar, dir., and K.K. Mahajan. 1989. *Khayal Gatha* (Hindi and Persian). 35mm, Feature.

———. 1990. *Kasba* (Hindi). 35mm, Feature.

———. 1991. *Bhavanatarana*/Immanence. (Oriya and Sanskrit). 35mm, Feature-documentary.

———. 1997. *Char Adhyay*/Four Chapters (Hindi and Bangla). 35mm, Feature.

———. 1999. *Bansuri*/ *Bamboo Flute* (Hindi and Tamil). 35mm, Feature.

———. 2018. *Priye Charushile* (Oriya and Italian). 35mm, Feature. Awaiting release.

Sharma, Aparna. 2015. *Documentary Films in India: Critical Aesthetics at Work*. London: Palgrave Macmillan.

Wikipedia, s.v. 'Pundranagar.' Accessed 20 August 2022. https://en.wikipedia.org/wiki/Pundranagar

Notes

1 All translations from Bengali in this chapter are by me.

2 In talking about how he 'plans' a novel, Elias writes:

> I take a lot of notes and all before a novel, even draw up a 'scheme' [both words are in English in the original]. But once I start writing, everything turns upside down, the characters turn into bravehearts [*bahadur*]; they don't wish to be under my thumb. (Letter to Mahasweta Devi, 1 August 1996; Ahmed and Sami 2002, 159.)

In the course of writing, Elias must continually revisit the site.

3 Akhtaruzzaman Elias was diagnosed with cancer in early 1996 and eventually had his right leg amputated in Calcutta in March 1996. He succumbed to the disease in January 1997 in Dhaka.

4 Pundranagari was an important urban centre from the 3rd century BC to the 12th century AD, with Buddhist and Hindu rulers through that period until the advent of Muslim rulers in successive ways. The land in the region of Pundranagari is almost 36 m above sea level, which would also make for a specific kind of terrain (Wikipedia).

5 This part of the letter harks back to a diary entry of 30 August 1989. He is visiting villages in Bogura and records the conversation he has with 'an old farmer who was repairing a bamboo basket above the high flat mound was a dighi (lake), called Chuna'r dighi'. The old man believed that the mound used to be the dispensary of an old king and that the earth around them had medicinal properties against snake bites. These conversations clearly made a deep impression on him (Elias 2011, Diary Entries 9 and 10, 319).

6 Personal communication, Sibaji Bandyopadhyay, 22 March 2023. It moved me to hear this from Sibaji, long after this chapter was written, affirming a particular reading of Elias's work.

7 Elias wrote a short biography of Majnu Shah (b. 1700/1735) where he mentions that Shah, who belonged to the Madari[ya] Sufi order, was from Mewat. In the course of his resistance to the East India Company, he gathered many followers from the peasantry of Bengal and Bihar and organised them against zamindars who were pro-English (Elias 2011,

344–346). The biography (meant for school children) is very much in the revisionist mode of Soviet rewriting of Tsarist history where those dismissed as bandits against the Tsarist state in official history are represented as rebels with a cause. In Tsarist Russia, Alexander Pushkin's novella, *The Captain's Daughter* (1836), about Pugachev's rebellion (1773–1774) comes to mind.

8 When the protagonist of the novel is herself/himself a poet, if the translator into English decides to edit out the verses, it is an erasure of an entire environment and mode of emotional and social exchange. See, for example, Kumar ([2002] 2010, 227–239): 'Hyder extensively edits out the long ornate pieces, ghazals and love letters' from Hasan Shah's *Nashtar* (The Knife) (1790). Also, 'when in their translation of *Umrao jan Ada*, Khushwant Singh and Husaini leave out the chapter called "Mushaira", they are in effect eliminating an important feature of this novel' (232).

9 Joyce's *Ulysses* figures in Elias's list of twelve favourite writers, which was published in *Aajkal* on 21 April 1996, republished in *Rupam* (Elias 2011, 328). Borges came to him through issues of *The Encounter,* edited by Stephen Spender at the time (Elias probably did not know about the CIA funding the magazine for a decade or so. Spender resigned once he found out about the source of funding.). An interview published in *Lyric*, editor Aijaz Yusufi, No. 8, 1 Baisakh, BS 1393, Chattogram, reprinted in 22–73. 'Alaapcharita' by Shahadurzaman, 27.

10 Holy man

11 The diary entries of 3 January 1986 include details of the crops, names of villages, local trees and water bodies in the area (Elias 2011, 305–306).

12 Of the betrayal of the mass-based '1969 uprising' articulated in this novel, Elias underlined in a later interview in *Nandan* in July 1966: 'Although the people of our land had some degree of nationalism within them, the matter of class was increasingly becoming acute. It was precisely the question of class that the Awami League suppressed in the rhetoric of Bengaliness ('bangalitwar dhuon tuley)' (Ahmed and Sami 2002, 121).

13 Two other novels that must be mentioned are Kamal Kumar Majumdar's *Antarjali'r Jatra* (The Final Journey, 1962) and Debesh Ray's *Teestapaar'er brittanto* (Along the banks of the River Teesta, 1988). Elias admired Manik Bandyopadhyay's *Padma Nadir Majhi* (The boatman of Padma River, 1936). Ritwik Ghatak made an extraordinary film of Advaitya Mallabarman's *Titash Ekti Nadir Naam* (A river called Titas; 1936 be), which was produced and shot in Bangladesh soon after that nation was born.

14 Elias also wrote a short piece, 'Banglar Nad-nadi', on the riverine nature of Bangladesh (Elias 2011).

15 'Nirrudesh Jatra' (An aimless journey) is also the title of a feature film inspired by Elias's story, made by Debasish Das. 'Apaghaat' and 'Raincoat' have been translated into English by Debjani Sengupta and are included in a recent anthology of writings on Bangladesh in *Bangladesh: Writings on 1971, Across Border* (Jalil and Sengupta 2022, 77–91).

16 On how the book is an object of desire for different people, how it changes hands and how it also is the object of scorn, see Bandyopadhyay (199, 170–171).

17 'Ei bujhi re Munshi eshey porlo' (Watch out, the Munshi might turn up any moment!)(the *ei* emphasising a sudden thought or the imminence of an imagined interruption (Elias 1998a, 13). On a very different note is: '*Kisher bashona go*?' ('And what kind of a desire, my dear?' (15).

18 See, for example, Medicine Net (n.d.) where 'sensorium' is defined as:

> The totality of those parts of the brain that receive, process and interpret sensory stimuli. The sensorium is the supposed seat of sensation, the place to which impressions from the external world are conveyed and perceived. The sensorium also refers to the entire sensory apparatus of the body. In medicine, 'sensorium' is sometimes used as a generic term for the intellectual and cognitive functions.

19 In this interview published in *Rupam* on 20 October 1988, where Elias is being asked about the changes in and potential of the short story, he differentiates between a mere trend and an innovation that emerges from a radical change of perspective. He warns against a certain kind of self-indulgent, narcissistic selfishness passing off as individualism in a certain phase of the literature of colonial Bengal (Ahmed and Sami 2002, 113).

20 The image appears unexpectedly later, with regard to Kulsum's childhood: she loses her father when she is but a crawling child (Elias 1998a, 26).

21 Ranabir Chakravarti refers to the terracotta seals and sealings excavated in lower Bengal as providing evidence in image and in mixed scripts 'of the transportation of grains in maritime voyages'. They depict stylised paddy stalks on a ship with inscriptions that mention the 'ship in question' (2020, 'Maritime Trade and Voyages in Ancient Bengal', 119).

22 Personal communication to the author, November 2007.

23 I was a fortunate listener in one such conversation between Guru Kelucharan and Shahani, preceding the actual shooting of *Bamboo Flute*: it took place late one night in Bombay where Kelu-babu was visiting (c. 1998)

24 The title 'Priye Charushile' is an allusion to the loving address of Krishna to Radha from the 12th-century poet Jayadeva's *Geet Govindam*. Shahani extends its signification to celebrate the femininity in nature and in the Odisha landscape he celebrated through Guru Kelucharan Mohapatra, wherever one may discover it.

25 Since the film is not in the public domain, a glimpse of the Chhau movements I am referring to, as choreographed by Citaristi, appear in the course of an interview broadcast on DD in India on 21 June 2021. (See especially from 1.57 to 2.27 and from 12.50 to 3.20; Citaristi 2021)

8

FROM CARL SCHMITT TO WALTER BENJAMIN: SOVEREIGNTY, MYTHIC-FATE AND THE DIALECTICAL LEAP[1]

Rahul Govind

This chapter begins with an analysis of the relationship between Carl Schmitt and Walter Benjamin and does so to inquire into the latter's singular demand on the task of thinking through aesthetics and politics.[1] Interpreting this relationship will be seen to require a conceptualisation of the role, function and representation of history and life in relation to the formulation of the aesthetic and political object. Schmitt discerns in sovereignty the form and image of a 'vitalist-self',[2] a 'personalist decision', which is deemed to be irreducible to laws, norms, instances and instantiations. Such a thesis raises the difficulty of wording a history or conceptualisation of a 'decisionism' that, as such, appears to resist all representation except for the vague sense of what is almost an 'existential intuition'. Analogously, Benjamin's 'Critique of Violence' and *The Origin of the German Tragic Drama* (henceforth *Origin*), in their reflections on law, violence and the aesthetic work, voice a singularly solitary morality irreducible to the formulae of representation. However, contrary to Schmitt, as it will be the burden of this chapter to establish, there is in Benjamin's oeuvre, an articulated awareness of the profound problem of representing that which is denied the possibility of representation; a problem that, all the same, takes the form of an imperative to present and represent in the aesthetic as much as the political. In the formulation, iteration and animating quality of this imperative, in matters political as much as aesthetic, Benjamin

1 Schmitt's *Dictatorship*, analysed here, was one of the last texts that a reading group, which I was a part of, discussed. This essay is dedicated to the camaraderie that we shared during those occasions. The group—which kept changing like all life organisms over the course of some six years—included Sunny, Bharathan, Debdutta, Aurighno, Pia, Tannishtha, Suparna and Sanghamitra.

laboriously forms historical matter and then arrests sovereign law, fate and myth, so as to free what might be named *ponderacion misterosa* (Benjamin 2003, 235), 'divine' and 'revolutionary' violence.

Beginning with a double reading of Schmitt and Benjamin on the question of sovereignty and law in the first section of this chapter, the seemingly obscure interrelations between fate and myth that result will be pursued through a close attention on Benjamin's work on Baroque drama; this will constitute the second section. From this will emerge a sketch of Benjamin's logic of the 'physiognomic sign' (Benjamin 1986b, 311), or what is named here as the expressive affect, which reflects historico-legal reality in a way that Schmitt's 'personalist decision' fails to. Analysing this study of the Baroque is essential not merely because it portrays, in opposition to Schmitt, the 'indecisive sovereign' or secularism caught in its profoundly interiorising spiral.[3] But equally because, in this study of the mesmerising power of Baroque too, much like Benjamin's essay on law and violence, the aesthetic is formulated as the working out of a solitary morality taking form in a necessarily indirect way. This laboured indirection, in contrast to the ultimate opacity of Schmittian sovereignty, is 'represented' in the Baroque stage as much as its 'writing', expressing an aesthetic that is ambidextrously perceptual and linguistic; hence, the 'physiognomic sign'. Once more, unlike abstract Schmittian 'decisionism', this 'personalizing' on materialist-linguistic registers, engages and articulates the aporia of representation. The concluding section will argue that the 'divine' in both political violence as well as aesthetic drama is interpretable in terms of Benjamin's signature articulation of the Marxist problematic of 'revolutionary praxis' via 'myth-fate' and 'affect'.

This thesis will be sought to be articulated and defended in the three sections later. To schematise in anticipation: The first will interpret Schmitt and Benjamin, beginning with Benjamin's 'Critique of Violence', before moving on to Schmitt's *Political Theology* and *Dictatorship*, while ending with Benjamin's *Origin* on the role of concepts and history in the formulation of what appears irreducible to the latter, that is, sovereignty, solitariness and violence. The second section interprets *Origin* as building on Benjamin's essay on law in terms of its gripping sketch of 'affect' as key to the peculiar demands of sovereignty as it carnates in allegorical form, whether in drama or image writing. The final section interprets Benjamin's logic of affect and myth as a critique of epistemic antinomies, aesthetic complicities and progressivist perfectionism, finding 'resolution' in Marxist 'revolutionary praxis'. This will be the final critique of Schmitt's political thesis on the relationship between philosophico-historical representation and sovereignty on the grounds of labour, language and praxis.

I

'There is gunpowder in the air.'[4] In the darkening backdrop of class struggle, a defeated war-torn country, a failed revolution and the brutal murder of Rosa Luxemburg, Walter Benjamin and Carl Schmitt throw in their two bits on the nature of sovereignty, violence and the law. Both share a suspicion towards the ability of laws and norms to capture sovereignty and violence while agreeing that politics in its essential form of sovereignty cannot as such be represented. For Benjamin, this lies in divine revolutionary violence in its immediacy, while for Schmitt, it is the state-sovereign's decision on the exception. How are such positions articulated and arrived at? Beginning with Benjamin, Schmitt will be dealt with in turn.

On the question of violence, Benjamin writes that the divine commandment 'Thou shall not kill' 'exists not as a criteria of judgment, but as a guideline for actions of persons and communities who have to wrestle with it in solitude, and in exceptional cases, to take on themselves the responsibility of ignoring it' (1986a, 298). The 'critique of violence' had begun by excluding natural law approaches in favour of positive law by arguing that the former, by its nature, focussed on the ends as a criterion for violence whereas what was needed was the more 'precise critical approach', which examined violence as a means; something provided by positive law (279).[5] It was from positive law that the roots of the legitimacy or illegitimacy of violence could be found, and for Benjamin, this took form in the maxims of contemporary European legislation, which disallowed violence by individuals; not because such violence was a threat towards legal ends but because such a threat threatened law itself (281).

However, the legal-positive system did permit violence in its recognition of the 'right to strike'. 'Organized labour is apart from the state, probably today the only legal subject, apart from the state, entitled to exercise violence' (Benjamin 1986a, 281). When law, therefore, met the violence of the strikers with violence of its own, it revealed an 'objective contradiction in the legal situation, but not a logical contradiction in the law' (282). Moreover, Benjamin argues, military law was no different from strike law since it too rested on the 'objective contradiction in the legal situation' (283). Here again, in military law, a conflict might arise because legal subjects have sanctioned violence, which may in turn clash with their own legal or natural ends; not unlike strike law.[6] The amplification of the strike into a general and revolutionary strike was a legal possibility[7], indistinguishable in legal status, from the enactment of military law and conscription. Both forms of violence indicated that legal situations could be 'founded' and 'modified' and were instances where the State had to concede the 'right to conduct warfare', just as it had conceded the 'right to strike' (283).

Military law and strike law combined the two features and functions of law, which Benjamin calls law making and law preserving. The former involved the use of violence for 'natural ends' and therein founded a new law; such as victory in war establishing a new law through 'peace' (Benjamin 1986a, 283). The other law-preserving function does not found anything new but preserves law as its name suggests; it is, however, 'threatening' by its very nature (283). And yet, notwithstanding this distinction between law-making and law-preserving functions, the actual conditions of the legal situation are best described in the suspension of this distinction—or their 'spectral mixture'—in the form of the police-security State (286–287). In policing, neither was it a question of proving the worth of victory (as in law making) nor subjecting itself to restrictions that it may not pursue new ends (as in law preserving). Rather, 'unlike law, which acknowledges in the law the "decision" determined by place and time a metaphysical category that gives it a claim to critical evaluation … [police] power is formless, like its nowhere tangible, ghostly presence in the life of civilized states' (287). Judicial decision, so loved by Schmitt, is pointedly rendered superfluous.

For Benjamin, the law-founding and law-preserving nexus do not annihilate; they leave victims mute and guilty (Benjamin 1986a, 295).[8] Punishment has little to do with deterrence, since the latter assumes the certainty that the guilty will be punished; a certainty that is in fact never to be had (285). Rather, what happens is that fate and guilt are woven by law into the marrow of the legal subject; the fact that some are punished and some not, some deserving and some not, is rationalised in the form of fate-misfortune-myth. Violence lies not only in that (legal) end for which it aims but ambidextrously in the threatening manifestation by which law is preserved. The police express this condition at its molecular level, while the State is its highest expression in the mythical forms and cycles that it takes manifesting time. It is in this context that one may return to the question of the 'solitary' revolutionary, whether individual or community (or class). 'But if the existence of violence outside the law, as pure immediate violence is assured, this furnishes proof that revolutionary violence, the highest manifestation of unalloyed violence by man, is possible and by what means' (300). An attempt at interpreting this 'resolution' will only be undertaken in the conclusion of this chapter after having traversed Benjamin's aesthetic and historical investigations so as to better prehend what might be meant by fate and myth. For now, it is important to read and re-read Schmitt's formulation of the legal situation.

To begin with, Schmitt configures sovereignty in the image of the vitalistic 'personalist' decision rather than laws and norms.[9] His *Political Theology: Four Chapters on the Concept of Sovereignty*, written in the aftermath of defeat in war and failure in revolution, was staged as a compelling interpretation of Article 48—the provision for emergency of the Weimar Constitution. This interpretation built upon his recently completed historico-theoretical work *Dictatorship*, published just a year previously. The issue to be decided on was whether the emergency provision Article 48 suspended the Constitution itself or whether it merely suspended specific articles of the Constitution. Schmitt insisted that the declaration of an emergency involved not merely the suspension of specific articles/rights of the Constitution but the Constitution itself, while remaining in itself constitutional as an act (Schmitt 2014, 187–194). It is this interpretation that has an air of paradox. Sovereignty is defined in terms of an act, a decision, and therein in itself not subject to any law or norm while at the same time being legally and constitutionally binding. One sees here a counter-point to Benjamin's description of the contradictions—and parallels—between strike rights and military law, just as one sees in Schmitt's super-valuation of the 'decision' the attempt to annul the 'spectral mixture' of the police state where no decision can leash the law in its raw and 'threatening' manifestation.

And yet, Schmitt appears to suggest that it was only his theory of the sovereign exception that was adequate to the concrete situation as opposed to the norms and laws of contemporary jurisprudence:

> The exception can be more important to it [the philosophy of a concrete life] than the rule … because the seriousness of an insight goes deeper than the clear generalizations inferred from what ordinarily repeats itself…. The rule proves nothing; the exception proves everything: It confirms not only the rule but also its existence…. In the exception the power of real life breaks through the crust of a mechanism that has become torpid by repetition. (Schmitt 2005, 15)

The exception is determined by the 'decision' in contrast to the 'norm'. The latter is strategically interpreted as outside of the 'decision', while law is, in turn, rendered as nothing but mere rule application; this is the normal, the rule, the repetitious, perhaps the banal. Notwithstanding all the emphasis on the concrete, Schmitt constructs an abstract distinction between rule and exception, after which there is no other way to bridge the two but to, in turn, phantasize a sovereign who makes the decision as to what is the exception and, therein, the rule. His critique of what he calls liberal constitutionalism consists in its interpretation of Article 48, according to which there is a division of powers between the president who declares and the Parliament which controls (Schmitt 2005,

11–12). Anxiously for Schmitt, if such exceptional powers could be circumscribed in this 'liberal-constitutionalist' manner, the very concept of sovereignty would be extinguished.[10] The worry is the sovereign concept, which is the only way to absolutely justify the unlimited powers of the sovereign exception. It is to resuscitate the immaculacy of the concept, that the particularly etched ambiguities of 'the everyday', the division of powers emergent in fact, the multiplying chaos of the concrete and the division and divisibility of the 'real life' are whisked away. There is here the false transmutation of Benjamin's 'objective contradiction in the legal situation' into a 'logical contradiction of the law' so as to then cynically-strategically invoke, presuppose or induce the intervention of the sovereign-state.

The state executive is therein abstracted from the legal condition in which it is embedded and deified in turn as its saviour. This forms the intention behind the historical preparations. The fruits of this historical study resulted in the following axioms:

> Public order and security manifest themselves very differently in reality, depending on whether a militaristic bureaucracy, a self-governing body controlled by the spirit of commercialism, or a radical party organization.... After all every legal order ... contains within it the contrast of the two distinct elements of the juristic-norm and decision. Like every other order, the legal order rests on a decision and not on a norm. (Schmitt 2005, 9–10)

It is from such a theoretical grid where the inherent plurality of time and politics is compressed into the spanner of necessity that Schmitt can see nothing unusual in mobilising his scholarship to elucidate and sharpen a particular interpretation of Article 48 of the Weimar Constitution on the powers of the president to declare an exception, and thereby suspend the laws in general. The differentiated weight of history is here only to be matched by—or hatched from—the violence of its epistemic instrument.

The seamless constitution of a concept holds on to a 'definition'—'Sovereign is he who decides on the exception'—across history (Schmitt 2005, 5). There is the rush to apotheosise sovereignty in the face of a concrete history of contention and bloody dispute, particularly in German history of the 17th century. Nonetheless, Schmitt has to clarify for his audience that dictatorship, far from being unconstitutional or monarchical, in fact, originated in republican Rome (Schmitt 2014, 1–2). It was the structure of dictatorship—unlimited powers to achieve a concrete aim—that would prove crucial to the unity of a state. This is demonstrated concretely even in imperial contexts. When after a detailed history of the campaigns of Wallenstein in the 17th century and detailing the complex relationship between the princes and the emperor in Germany, Schmitt comments,

> The question of Wallenstein's status *vis a vis* the emperor became insignificant by comparison with that of Wallenstein's dictatorship because the emperor had not decided to impose extraordinary rights for himself on the basis of his imperial plenitude of power. Ferdinand III's capitulation on 24 December 1636 was the constitutional expression of the fact that the emperor had lost his last chance of establishing a strong central power by appeal to the state of emergency. (Schmitt 2014, 79)

Misunderstanding the concept and institution of dictatorship was the root cause of the disunity in imperial Germany because imperial power still had as its possible counter-points the customary rights of communities as well as the rights of princes; only through dictatorship could unity actually be wrought. According to Schmitt, it was only by ignoring the problematic of dictatorship (which gave unlimited power and legally allowed the suspension of the legal order)—that the German Reich had failed to attain unity as an empire in this historical moment of the 17th century. This very real historical and institutional problem of the status of the states in relationship to the imperial Reich—the threat of disunity and chaos—haunted Schmitt in his interpretation of Article 48 (Schmitt 2005, 11–12).[11] A specific historico-institutional need is concealed as an eternally abstract conceptual demand for state unity.

Therefore, in the discussions on Article 48, when the argument was made that Schmitt's interpretation gave the president a right that neither the emperor nor the king had, Schmitt could not but agree. In fact, his historical work is precisely oriented by such a resolve, and hence the critique of the weakness of imperial powers in preparation for defending dictatorship through 'democracy' and 'republicanism': 'democrats have understood that the far-reaching authorisations granted through Article 48 are something specifically democratic' (Schmitt 2014, 203).[12] The president ought to be given such authority precisely as a constitutional figure, as one empowered by the Constitution, and it was in this sense that he was a 'commissary dictator' and not a 'sovereign one'.[13] As we have seen, the dictator had the kind of unlimited power that could not be assumed in the case of imperial powers, which had to contend with the jurisdictions, rights and customs of princes and communities. Thus, the unlimited dictatorial power of the president, in contrast to the more contestable imperial power, was in fact a result of 'democratic reasoning' so as to ostensibly accomplish precisely the people's mandate. The problematic of dictatorship colours Schmitt's understanding to such an extent that history is measured according to its adequacy to the concept of dictatorship and not the spiralling matters of dispute, disputation, the 'objective contradictions in legal situations', war and massacres over jurisdiction that had taken place historically. Schmitt's rendition of history is, in fact, the abolition of its reality in favour of its scripting as a failure to live up to the trans-historical concept of sovereignty. And it is to Hobbes, more than Leibniz, that Schmitt necessarily turns for a German history forcibly disguised in Hobbessian costume sans the vicissitudes of either German or English historical reality.[14] A dubious history, *Dictatorship* does not address the animating forces of popular will, the institutional changes in forms of government regarding franchise and property, the granular shifts in the semantics of sovereignty and the changing shapes of imperial territoriality and finds but the certainty of the concept of dictatorship or its need.

Disavowing the radical contingencies and bloody disputes subtending historical reality, Schmitt insists that to fully understand the *need* for dictatorial powers and the co-relative justification in the concept of sovereignty in the 20th-century Weimar Republic, one needed to turn to the 17th-century writers on natural law, who were to have conceptualised sovereignty as one of the decision and/on the exception (Schmitt 2005, 14). Accordingly, what is assumed to have been latent throughout history is to have found cogent theoretical expression in the decisionism of the natural law writers, particularly Hobbes. Once again, Schmitt re-enacts the proposition that conceptualisation immediately reflects a historical need and is meant to emerge heroically fully formed from it, without birthmark or scar. To know history is to know such a *concept* or its lack. In contrast to Schmitt's ultimate valorisation of the 'concept' in his treatment of sovereignty, Benjamin hones in on the 'objective contradictions in the legal situation', exemplified in the contradictions between strike law and military law, class and nation. However, this description of the legal situation in his essay on violence is also coloured in the figures of myth and fate, which appear condensed, even obscure. To better scrutinise the role and function of myth and law in figuring sovereignty in this essay as much as its roots in historico-legal reality, it is necessary to turn to *Origin*.

To the sceptic for whom this was a dissertation that had as its subject 'aesthetics', it might be important to signal that the legal situation as much as the aesthetic work are intimately joined by morality. A 'critique of violence' begins with the observation—the thesis—that a cause becomes violent 'in the precise sense of the word only when it bears on moral issues' (Benjamin 1986a, 284), the spheres of which are defined by law and justice. As argued earlier, the divine commandment on not killing is not a criterion for judgement and works as but a guide in the solitary moral struggles and actions of an individual or community. *Origin* too has an interpretation of the nexus between the divine commandment, solitariness and judgement. Benjamin comments in this context that the commandment not to make divine images referred to the fact that man's solitariness consisted in the singular condition of morality. Morality is defined as 'life in its extreme sense', which 'finds its fulfilment in death' (Benjamin 2003, 105).[15] As the 'the abode of danger as such', it cannot be represented (105). While warning that the artwork could not take the form of moral counsel or direct representation, Benjamin equally repulses the nihilistic 'abyss of aestheticism', where man is but an image.[16] This critique is duplicated in his summary dismissal of the 'childish anarchism' that allows for no constraint on persons and things in the context of law (Benjamin 1986a, 284). A childish anarchism or abyss of aestheticism is indicted for the same exclusion of the moral cum historical that poses in its most concentrated form the question of action, something obscured and concealed by the groundless and dangerous aestheticism of 'art for art's sake'. If morality cannot simply be circumvented when discussing aesthetic form, as Nietzsche was to have attempted (Benjamin 2003, 104), morality can be confronted only negatively, in the most indirect of ways, in the critical elaboration of the aesthetic work itself.[17]

If the urgent question of morality—in law as much as aesthetics—raises the question of representation and presentation, studying Benjamin's remarks on history and its organisation is in order. In contrast to Schmitt's *Dictatorship*, where history emerges as a storehouse of anticipations and perfections, something that one can just reach into and pluck out to address the moment in what might be a pointed warning to such a tendency, Benjamin had written:

> Just as a man lying sick with fever transforms all the words which he hears into the extravagant images of delirium, so it is that the spirit of the present age seizes on the manifestations of past or distant spiritual worlds, in order to take possession of them and unfeelingly incorporate them into its own self-absorbed fantasizing. (2003, 53)

The demanding work of representation and presentation cannot rest content with the 'pathological suggestibility' that historical material proffers to a current conundrum. Such opportunist and unreflective historicism is no different from the lazy nominalism that rummages through a mass of material and picks what it abstracts and construes as a common structure, a construal that is in fact dictated by any naïve apprehension of the contemporary. Illustrating, Benjamin warns against collecting examples of what is subjectively sensed as the tragic from the contemporary world to then construct by abstraction the commonality of these diverse examples into a formulation, which is then, ironically, taken to be the universal tragic (Benjamin 2003, 38–39). Rather than such 'shallow universality', he insists that one must pose, along with Lukacs, the more fundamentally historical question of whether the tragic was even possible in contemporary times (38–39). The historically precise question posed radically is not an empathy towards an imagined past—in the medium of progressive perfections that Schmitt appears to have succumbed to—but to inquire into whether 'past' forms such as the 'tragic' are indeed even possible today. This encrusts artistic representation into its world and transforms the present, as much as the past, into a line of inquiry. Putting both into question is to negate the Schmittian method of having one as either a determinant (such as the structured need for dictatorship being either successful as in the Hobbesian text, contrary to English history, or failing as in Ferdinand's Germany) or the hidden meaning (the past theological picture of sovereignty in the present secular liberal confusions) of the other. Ultimately, notwithstanding protestations to the contrary, this concept is accomplished by the disavowal of the 'concrete life' (Schmitt 2005, 15).

In contrast, what Benjamin provides for is a 'dual insight' that takes the concrete form of the fundamental differentiation between Greek tragedy and the German mourning play and the misunderstandings arising from applying a theory of (classical) tragedy to the latter, even if such is the self-understanding of the Baroque age (Benjamin 2003, 49–50). His focus on the 17th-century Baroque mourning play tends towards exhibiting a unique constellation swirling around as an 'eddy', as much temporal regression (to the 'medieval') as an anticipative hauling towards the 'now'.[18] This 'dialectical' movement, unlike Schmitt switching historicist-progressive perfections and opaque sovereign decisions, sketches a compressed antinomian visage of the age that can only be interpreted as affect, a staged affect as much as an affected stage. Affect is thus theorised and experienced as a form mediating representation and action. If Schmitt was unable to fundamentally theorise the relation between the concept and history or work out in practice their obscure intimacies, Benjamin provides both a theoretical and practical counter.

Against the *decisive* as much as the speechless hero of tragedy, the Baroque enacts indecision in a verbosity that is the signature of the times; it is not a dress rehearsal for interpreting Article 48. Moreover, differences are not to be treated in evolutionary terms. They 'acquire the status of complementary forces, and history is seen no more than the coloured border to their crystalline simultaneity' (Benjamin 2003, 38). Schmitt's conceptualisation of the exception as ultimately preserving the rule, while being staged as though coming from the 'outside'—the State as *ad nauseum* paradox both inside and outside—is no different from the elementary protocols of an epistemology of research endangered by being 'in danger of accommodating itself to a syncretism which weaves a spider's web between separate kinds of knowledge in an attempt to ensnare the truth as if it were something which came flying in from the outside' (28).

The antinomies between the two approaches can be outlined very early on in Benjamin's *Origin*. Citing Schmitt's *Political Theology*, Benjamin refers to the 'function' of the prince as being one who is to avert the state of exception; he is meant to save the world. And yet, Benjamin immediately qualifies this, by identifying the 'exception' with the Baroque 'catastrophe'.[19] The Baroque catastrophe is precisely that which resists any general and generalisable restoration and works as an antithetic to such a historical ideal of restoration (Benjamin 2003, 66). In activating an antithetic within the exception, impending catastrophe and not seamless restoration, Benjamin foregrounds the banal opportunism of Schmitt's sovereign exceptionalism. This will later be doubled in the swirling montage of an indecision that can only be captured in the antinomies of affect, in Baroque theatre, and not the utterly opaque and infinite historical repeatability of Schmitt's decision and false history. Art both captures and presents historical reality, beyond instances and abstractions, in a way that concepts cannot.

Benjamin's insight into legal-historical reality is undeniable, unlike the more ostensiblyl scrupulous historical work of Schmitt. They diverge most sharply in their working-out of the sovereign-secular nexus of the 17th-century Baroque. For Benjamin, not only is the sovereign figured and disfigured by a dialectical tension in the mourning play, the role of time in the shaping of the concept is decelerated so as to reach the zero-point of a charged stage, a visage. For, unlike Schmitt, Benjamin articulates an acutely historical understanding of 17th-century German contestations of sovereignty as 'assimilated' and refracted through the aesthetic work of the mourning play. The latter has 'historical life' as its object and content. The sovereign is the 'exponent' of history for very precise reasons. The Reformation and the Counter-reformation and the assassination of Henry IV of France meant that the Church could no longer hold in its hands the power to signal 'tyrannicide' (Benjamin 2003, 65). This implied an absolutist sovereignty, which required 'dictatorial powers' to decide on the 'exception' so as to restore the normal.

However, unlike Schmitt, Benjamin points to the emergence of the theory of exception in the 17th century as emerging from an '*antithesis*' between the 'historical ideal of restoration' and the 'idea of catastrophe' that haunts it (Benjamin 2003, 66). 17th-century 'natural law' had a 'vivid consciousness' of this significance in comparison to the 18th century (Schmitt 2005, 14). This was, however, neither because of the greater stability of the 18th century nor because the latter simply ignored the question of sovereignty, as Schmitt argued (13–14). Rather, for Benjamin, it was Kant's *theological* rationalism that prevented him from recognising emergency law as law, while the Baroque, in contrast, knew no eschatology or rather knew an eschatology in retreat as abyss (Benjamin 1985, 66).[20] This is not simply a Schmittian proposition of secularisation that both differentiates and dissolves the distinction between the theological and the secular. In an age abandoned by the eschatological, the Baroque stages the surging tensions and violent reversals of the sovereign life as world history. Standard epistemic nominalist protocols of finding commonalities need to be abandoned for interpreting the aesthetic episteme. It is only by paying attention to the latter in the Baroque period that the very problem of secularism can be posed. This is a secularism that has re-articulated the relationship between myth, fate and nature, thereby laying the grounds for the problems broached by Benjamin's critique of violence. It is therefore to this aesthetic episteme that one must turn, before returning to the question of sovereignty and violence.

II

If Schmitt's promise of showing the 'power of real life breaking through the crust of mechanism' remains unfulfilled in his studies of politics (Schmitt 2005, 15), it is in Benjamin's study of the Baroque antinomies and allegory in *Origin*, that such power might find representation, howsoever, and necessarily, indirectly. The irreduction of the 'vitalist' to laws and norms uncomprehendingly freed of scrutiny. While Baroque drama stages the perceptual character of language, the linguistic character of perception is revealed through image writing or the allegorical script. These two enfold one another, forming the powerful hieroglyph that is Benjamin's study, and we will approach one after another. On display is aesthetic experience as the world experienced; theatre and image-writing, 'physiognomic signs', as face. It is in such an experience, that the political too takes form, and in which it can be discerned. This form of the political, therefore, has as its material myth, fate and allegory and is characteristically 'secular'. This mode of representation in its figuration of sovereignty can be contrasted with the Schmittian emphasis.

Benjamin's aesthetics may be read as aimed at presenting that which is irreducible to mere concepts and norms and takes form as a non-introspective, objectively staged felt experience. In Benjamin's Baroque sovereignty—a secularism haunted by catastrophe—there is no scope of individual will or cosmological redemption. The 'indecisiveness of the tyrant' is the unavoidable complement of 'bloody terror' (Benjamin 2003, 71), and the sovereign incarnates historical life without escaping a fate mournfully enacted by a theatre of the tyrant-martyr. This dialectical switching of 'good' and 'bad', tyrant and martyr, are 'necessary expressions', the necessary extremities of the sovereign estate (71). Incest, fratricide or wife-murder, all evoke 'sympathetic wonder' because 'as he looses himself in the ecstasy of power', the sovereign 'falls victim to the disproportion between the unlimited hierarchical dignity with which he was divinely invested and the humble estate of his humanity' (70). The suffering of Christ, repeatedly invoked, reveals the 'drama of tyranny' to be a 'a history of martyrdom' (73).[21] Only in such a context is the Stoic technique fortifying against the state of emergency, as a particular form of affective apprenticeship, staged (73–74)[22]. This is a historical reality not bereft of the most deeply experienced.

Much like mannerist figures, which never showed themselves in a 'restful light', the power of theatre was not so much a face but rather 'fleeting expressions' (Benjamin 2003, 71). Not thought but 'changing physical impulses' were staged in the 'harsh light' of the sovereign's 'changing resolve' (71).[23] An age enthralled by the mismatch between a sacrosanct role and the human embodiment, neither actions nor deeds but literalised suffering, physically felt adversity, body the torments and torture of the tyrant-martyr, forming a coagulating exhibitionistic and exaggerated display. The goal of a restoration of 'natural laws' in the face of emergency—the Schmittian anticipation that shelters his sovereign—pales as but a 'utopian goal' (74). In actuality, the sovereign and its 'deceptive lustre' perfect the subject for martyrdom.

This strange secularism, this limitless disproportion is only to be captured in affect as expressive visage. The absence of redemption pressurises and condenses the space in which emotion, expressing the content of historical life, is stretched. It is to the expressive 'face',[24] to the countenance that one turns, since affect, according to the theories of the age, is physiologically determined and determinable, much like any natural force. 'The tempo of emotional life accelerated to such an extent that calm actions, considered decisions occur more and more infrequently' (Benjamin 2003, 99); undermined sovereign action only explodes in tyrannical madness. The age assimilated such display as though forces in nature, and 'knowledge', rather than being abstracted, is said to have lay embedded in the very linguistic character of speech.

And so the stock of natural-historical metaphors sonorously repeat themselves. 'One avoids trees that are about to fall' (Benjamin 2003, 90). The natural as organic interlocks, even coincides, with the mechanical, and sentiment is nothing but the synchronisation of the physiological and the psychological (96). In such a variegated affect element, the dictator is not merely the abstract function of deciding on the exception but rather the suffering tense polarity of 'strict inner discipline' and 'unscrupulous external action'. Pedagogy, for the theoreticians of the Baroque, was meant to communicate the life of the soul, 'action' but that through which emotion could be taught (99). Such theatre had little patience for the 'trivial emotion of suspense' or 'motivation' (74–75), and the latter exists only as manifested in the changing visual scenery to better seal the closed, inwardly pulled form of totality.

> For where it is a question of a realization in terms of space—and what else is meant by its secularization other than its transformation into the strictly present—then the most radical procedure is to make events simultaneous. The duality of the meaning and reality was reflected in the construction of the stage. The drop-scene permitted the alternation between actions on the forestage and the scenes which extended to the full depth of the stage. (Benjamin 2003, 194)[25]

Nothing is more difficult than to rule, and no sovereignty remains unscathed in this secular descent. Such a crushing 'tragic' burden is the Baroque, 'the drama of fate' (Benjamin 2003, 128–138). This is not simple determinism because determinism has the freedom of taking any form. On the other hand, fate is unleashed by the Baroque conviction of the creature's guilt, a theatrical display of what the door to redemption has been irrevocably shut to. History, the rise and fall of princes, is not the tale of moral transgressions and therein subject to ethical interiorised self-reflection. It is the 'swamp' of the original, Adamite guilt and recalls the 'mythical violence' of Benjamin's essay on law. Moral philosophy can only be apprehended by analogy with nature, and the only adequating response to the weight of guilt is the painfully hoarse cry of martyrdom. Chronological movement or progression is annulled by a staged space (Benjamin 2003, 92). Not the spasmodic chronological progression of tragedy and its decisive reversals of plot but the choreography of intrigue caught in the coagulations of sovereign, martyr and servant: nothing could be more different from the heroic action and decision of classical tragedy or Schmitt's dictatorship.

The release of causality onto the creaturely estate ensures that the sovereign can never be conflated with the tragic hero of antiquity. A fate that consumes not merely characters and nature but also (stage) objects and objectified properties reflects the fact that the chain of reason is always spellbound by the power of things. The secretion of the creaturely into manufactured objects is the signature of this newfound figuration of passion. Jealousy becomes the dagger, 'for Herod does not kill his wife *out of* jealousy; rather it is through jealousy that she loses her life' (Benjamin 2003, 133). The dagger becomes passion. Passion here needs to be distinguished from the psychological motive for action. Hamlet's death through the poisoned blade could not be more different that the tragic death of Ajax by his sword (136–137). Nature, objects and ghosts smudge the lines between calculation and chance, decision and individuation. The inner world of characters cannot be easily distinguished any longer from their outward action, and they no longer bear any relation to the cosmos in the manner of Greek tragedy; enclosed and enfolded into infinity in the this-earthly secular world they curl.

The 'hard historical actuality' of the times is revealed in the specific Lutheran burden of renouncing the results of 'good works' but at the same time compelling obedience in civic life (Benjamin 2003, 138–139). For Benjamin, such obedience, another side to the abduction of eschatology, implies an irreversible melancholia, a signature of the age. In a world where actions have no results, they are little more than a 'rubbish heap', a rubbish heap of objects that dictates a particular mourning, a peculiarly melancholic attitude (Benjamin 2003, 139). Whereas, in the realm of emotions conventionally conceived, intention might alternate between attraction and repulsion in relation to its object, in the case of mourning and melancholia, the intention deepens through a progressive intensification. In the surround of the word, the 'most simple object becomes symbol of enigmatic wisdom because it lacks any natural creative relation to us' (Benjamin 2003, 140).

Benjamin only needs to invoke, Durer, where the utensils of an active life are scattered around as objects of contemplation. The paradigmatic figure of this contemplative mourning is once again the sovereign, in whom internal disposition and external action enjoy no discernible ratio. This gaze of the dog or the gravity of the stone captures something of the acedia and dullness that expresses itself as the 'indecision' of the sovereign. A slothful inertia that is only to be matched by the inconstancy of the courtier, the unscrupulous parasite, whose fierce royalty lies with the profane things and accoutrements, the objects associated with sovereignty, the Crown, royal purple;

profane things rather than the infirm person (Benjamin 2003, 156–157). Unscrupulousness, the other side of this loyalty, also reflects this gazing, melancholic contemplation of things, enchained to a higher law. Spurred by the recalcitrance, the heaviness, the stubbornness of the profanely secular, melancholy acquires its character of persistence, absorption and intensification (156–157).

In Benjamin's study, the transition from the Baroque stage to allegorical writing is indiscernible because time is itself rendered as hieroglyph, an image script. 'In symbol destruction is idealized and the transfigured face of nature is fleetingly revealed in the light of redemption, in allegory the observer is confronted with the *facies hippicritica* of history, as petrified primordial landscape' (Benjamin 2003, 166). The secular folding into itself having been shut out of redemption is best exhibited in the singularity of dying with nothing left to redeem remaining its singular sign. 'The greater the significance the greater the subjection to death because death digs most deeply the jagged line of demarcation between physical nature and significance' (166).[26] The perception of the Baroque is prevented by the historically interceptive intervention of the symbol. In one sense, Schmitt's conceptualisation of sovereignty was a similar symbolisation that blocked access to the Baroque. The symbol's aesthetic character—in the visual mould of the Greek plastic arts—contained the qualities of momentary suddenness and totality, clarity and grace. As opposed to the symbol that directly incarnates the idea, in the manner of the Schmittian phantasy where sovereignty directly possesses the constitution in its dispossession, allegory lacks momentariness. It takes shape in time, iterating itself in constantly unfolding myth. Therein, the aesthetic displays in its body the radiation of sovereign power in its specific articulation of the 17th century.

Baroque writing is, however, contrasted not merely to the monumentality of the symbol but equally the abstraction of the alphabet in its in-mixing of the perceptual and the linguistic. Representation and presentation are therein rewired. Akin to emblem writing, the Baroque does not possess the abstract signification of the alphabet or the timeless image of the symbol.[27] It is a Baroque stage where neither changing scenes nor vacillating expressions apotheosise into, or are meant to be subsumed under, tragic reversals or heroic decisions. Indeed, there is no sovereign decisiveness in the age. In the deciphering of the occult relations between image and signification, Benjamin finds the humanist obsession with hieroglyphs, obelisks and iconology, perhaps in some measure compensating for the atrophy of religious mysteries, rites and their symbolic value in the wake of the Reformation. As merely conventional, alphabetic script was transient by its very nature and would not be understood beyond its historical era. By contrast, allegorical script imaged divine knowledge that did not alter with each of its objectifications but rather remained 'fixed in the simple form of the thing itself' (Benjamin 2003, 169), as the hieroglyph. Such picture writing was imbued with the same sentiment as the highly charged metaphors of Baroque speech, which combined convention with expression (175–176)[28]. Language was thus made to 'stand up' as a figure in these barqoue speeches (Benjamin 1998, 187).

In its charged linguistic metaphor, the Baroque indeed approached the visual, while in its necessarily fragmentary nature, it was opposed to the symbol. Its persistent difference in itself—image script—extinguished any false appearance of totality that characterised the symbol (Benjamin 2003, 176). Crossing the borders of artistic partitions, its language is 'statuesque', images are strung together; in extravagance, it veers towards the 'rhetorical arts' (Benjamin 2003, 177). This crossing of borders infects speech as much as architecture in the presentation of an artistic synthesis. To 'paint an ode' remained an ambition (177). This mutation of ideas into images is illustrated by Hallman's presentation of court life: 'Theodoric too has embarked on that sea where is fragile boat is surrounded by ice instead of waves, secret poison instead of salt, sword and axe instead of oars, spiders' webs instead of sails, perfidious lead instead of an anchor' (198–199).

Image writing and the verbal image as the allegorical sensibility preserved the 'tense polarity' between writing and sound. Attempts to 'sensualize' (written) language remained one more way to valorise the value of sound over 'silent profundity' (Benjamin 2003, 200–202). If spoken language (once) stood for intoxication, the ecstasy and rashness of the creature before God, writing embodied the powerless composure over objects of the world and nature. The spontaneous freedom of the spoken word is counter-posed to a writing that allegorically 'enslaves objects in eccentric embrace of meaning' (202). Such is the language of the fallen creature, and all knowledge requires a signature; the latter is the mark, the engraving of knowledge, the means by which the spirit manifests is revealed, constrained and codified. This inscriptive writing takes the form of the organ of speech writing so as to articulate voice as much as the vibration patterns in which sound manifests. This is not a question of the primacy of the object over the spiritual or the 'personification of things' but rather the attempt to give 'the concrete a more imposing form by getting it to stand up as a person' (187). Allegorical characters are 'figures' in the sense that they contain no individual or individuated morality.[29]

Benjamin insists that such Baroque forms are to be understood only with the aid of theological concepts, even in a world abandoned by the promise of redemption. An age is to be interpreted with the aid of its self-interpretation, even if the latter is itself but a unit in the hermeneutic. The theologically dictated degradation of the body is the only means of straining meaning from the latter as though from a sieve; hence, the obsessions and controversies over emblematics and embalmment (Benjamin 2003, 216–217).[30] If indeed only in death is freedom approached, this implies that only as a corpse does the body 'come into its own'. This Baroque attitude to the body is mirrored in the tension between the Christian condemnation of the guilty creature, for which nakedness invoked paradise, and the natural nudity of the Greek pantheon revived by a celebratory renaissance (217). Benjamin reminds us that the pantheon had traditionally been seen to shelter evil, for the devil was most at home in matter. Hence, the suspicion of mathematics and space and the warnings against the mournful melancholia that inevitably haunted their contemplation (226–227). Such mourning was indeed the fate of a nature rendered mute after the fall of man and his naming capacity (224–225).

German Baroque drama was involved in the gigantic endeavour of creating a secular drama that was all the same born in a religious age imbued with Christian sentiment. It is in the effort of expressing its violent times that we can find the secret of the 'agonizing violence of its style' (Benjamin 2003, 49). Demonstrated is a treatment of the aesthetic that is a key to a perception that cannot disavow its linguistic character. The age is captured through a form not reducible to the commonality of discrete contents or the evolutionary progressions of a concept. In this sense, even if perversely, it follows Benjamin's methodological dicta regarding the laboured task of representation in relation to its object, a process which does not slowly expose a secret but does justice to that which is therein revealed (31). How else is one to interpret the face and the churning surfacing of affect?

Benjamin notices a return to the Baroque in the contemporary 20th century with one crucial difference. Unlike the 17th-century writers who 'felt bound' to the absolutist constitution, contemporary writers were 'hostile' to the revolutionary state, if they had any conception of the latter at all (Benjamin 2003, 56). How is one to understand this in the light of his following well-known remark? The historian ought to

> stop telling the sequence of events like beads on a rosary. Instead, he grasps the constellation which his own era has formed with an earlier one. Thus, is established a conception of the present as the 'time of the now' which is shot through with chips of Messianic time. (263)

III

If Schmitt's historical method takes the form of a dictation, where there is a differentiation between past and present, the sovereign and the normal, the exception and the rule, that takes form in its annulment, Benjamin's is an effort at rescuing the 'aesthetico-political' from such historical laws of progress. However, such salvage is the making way for the *ponderacion misterosa*—revolutionary state, the divine-revolutionary immediacy of non-mythic, non-legal violence. This condensed 'framing' of 'revolutionary violence' is best approached through the contemporary political situation of class conflict and, particularly, the Marxist problematic of praxis brought to the fore by the life, death and corpus of Rosa Luxemburg as much as the writings of young Lukacs.[31] Schmitt, too, had clarified that his discussion of dictatorship took as its explicit context, if not provocation, socialist and communist politics. For here too, 'dictatorship' had become a 'category' in the philosophy of history, whereas Schmitt was, in turn, mobilising historical material to propose the democratic credentials of dictatorship as an interpretation of Article 48 of the Weimar Constitution. It is not surprising that unlike Benjamin, Schmitt does not engage with the concept of revolutionary action as a 'resolution' of the historical, and therefore, there cannot be that stretched Benjaminian opposition between the mythic and the revolutionary, the allegorical and the divine.

On might interpret this Benjaminian enactment as the aesthetical-cum-legal deepening of the Kantian antinomy, inflected by the Marxist lenses of Lukacs. It will be demonstrated that Benjamin's straining of the question of representation and presentation, particularly taking form in the uniquely worldly catastrophic, is best posed in terms of the Marxist critique of modern secular epistemology, which manifests itself in the Kantian antinomies as much as historicist evolutionism. This is to find resolution only in terms of a sharpened relationship between historical representation and praxis. It is such a vantage point that enables one to discern more carefully Benjamin's singular interpretation of problems of modernity, law and secularisation[32]

In Benjamin's conception of fate and catastrophe, as formulated in his Baroque study discussed earlier, specific signals of this secular, germinal form of a tectonic aporia can be seen. Lukacs had theorised such a 'bourgeois' antinomy that will be found to have cast its shadow on the Benjaminian 'impasse' of the secular. This arrival point was arrived at when thought was caught between the epistemic constituting of that which turned out to be no different from its own alienation; the object is now describable and known in terms of (necessary) 'natural laws' having nothing to do with its origination in the act in which the object was brought about. If the sensed object is to be known, it is known as necessary, and thereby spuriously abstracted from both the knowing act as much as the sensed-object. In awakening to the constitutive nature of its actions, knowing finds itself alienated in the known. 'The freedom (of the subject) is entirely unable to overcome the sensuous necessity of the system of knowledge and the soullessness of the *fatalistically conceived laws of nature, nor is it able to give them any meaning*' (Lukacs 1971, 134; emphasis mine). For Lukacs, this is specifically to be distinguished from a religious universe where the sensed and known object is ultimately unknowable as a creation. This alienation from the world in religious terms becomes a distinctively secular self-alienation, best exemplified by the 'Copernican' turn, where the object to be known must conform to a knowing subject, which turns out to itself be unknowable in its (constitutive) acts of knowledge.

Lukacs sees in art the capture of this problem but not its resolute resolution. The painted landscape as artwork destructs the (peasant-experienced) landscape in attempting to preserve it just as knowing destructs the known in the abstract-necessary element of its preservation; this impasse is a 'chasm' (Lukacs 1971, 157)[33], an image that haunts Benjamin's Baroque study. Schiller formulated the aesthetic 'play-instinct' as a means of overcoming this dilemma of the subject as an inward emptiness that is no different from the mechanical laws of nature that form its external surround (Schiller cited in Lukacs 1971). Only in 'play' is man fully himself in such an alienating context. However, this is clearly inadequate for Lukacs:

> That is to say, either, the world must be aestheticized, which is an evasion of the real problem and is just another way in which to make the subject purely contemplative and to annihilate action. Or else, the aesthetic principle must be elevated into the principle by which object reality is shaped: but that would be to mythologise the discovery of intuitive understanding. (Lukacs 1971, 139–140)

As discussed earlier in the context of his critique of young Nietzsche, Benjamin was at one with Lukacs in his critique of aestheticism, all the same providing a means to apprehend such mythologising in his treatment of the Baroque.[34] Nonetheless, he plunges into the Marxian problematic via Lukacs to see in (revolutionary) praxis the detonation of what is at once an aesthetic impasse as much as the epistemic antinomy, an antinomy that has a historicist and indefinitely progressive image of time as its correlate (Lukacs 1971, 162). Benjamin's critique of the 'historicist evolutionism' of the social democrats may be related to Lukacs's own words against them when he argued that 'dialectical trends do not constitute an infinite progression that gradually nears its goal in a series of quantitative stages' (182). Rather, one required to see a 'qualitative revolution' where (class) action articulates the 'problem of the present as a problem of history' (157), where both history and its abolition take place (168–169).

Benjamin penetratingly exhibited the impasses of knowledge, both in terms of an arbitrariness that spoke of its inherent indefiniteness as well as its 'infinity', whether in evolutionist time or epistemic antinomy.[35] His critique of nominalism lay in its abstract synthesis, which was successful neither in grounding itself as knowledge nor grounding the instances that it had collected in a synthetic-epistemic manoeuvre that it cannot but deny.[36] This directly applied to the problem of periodisation in time, which consisted in little more than a drunken lurch between the arbitrary or the evolutionist (Benjamin 2003, 39–45). To this, Benjamin advocates a patient labour in writing-representing, in constantly confronting the question of presentation and representation anew such that the act of representation repeatedly confronts the fact that the represented is always characterisable by a self-representation of its own; only this recognition prevents knowing from becoming indiscernible from possessing (29).

Such a form of writing and rewriting, therefore, has nothing of the immediate 'bold sketch' that speech might invoke with a flourish (Benjamin 2003, 29). In temporal terms, it reveals that 'singularity and repetition to be conditioned in all essentials' (46). While writing in its alphabetic form is degraded to the status of a mere sign—and, hence, always open to 'confusion' and the abyss of the mediate and arbitrary—image writing attempts to capture the fact that truth as the power of naming is given 'not so much in a primordial language as a form of perception in which words possess their own nobility as names unimpaired by cognitive meaning' (36). All of this is astonishingly put to bear by arresting the 'antinomies of the baroque age', the very experience of the Baroque that is neither to be formulated as objective facts nor psychological dispositions, so as to salvage it from the caged stages of historicist time as much as Schmitt's sovereign banality. Here, one sees acedia, the melancholic 'indolence of the heart', which marks the Baroque sovereign as much as the social-democrat historicist.[37] It is this critical take on acedia that joins Benjamin's theses on the philosophy of history to his Baroque study, just as action detonating evolutionist history is an unmistakable affiliation to revolutionary Marxism.

Finally, fate becomes the specifically Benjaminian concept that ties his critique of mythic violence, in the contemporary legal situation as much as the historical life of the Baroque, in an insight into the expressive face. This is the figure lying at the fold between historical-legal reality and 'life', taking up the challenge, as much as the failure, of

Schmitt's fumbling between history and sovereignty, norm and decision. The importance of visage indexes allegorical script as expression, and the solitary depths of morality can never be directly redeemed by either the judicial logic of fate-as-character or the aesthetic work on sovereignty, as Benjamin states in near identical idiom.[38] He alerts us to the remarkable fact that one thinks one knows a character by what is seen in the face or body. Such a seeing, 'knowing his character', means knowing how he will act in time, even if such knowing is based on a *sign*—the invisible *relationship* between the visible (facial expressions) and that which is not so (the character trait). And yet, one disbelieves the palmist who too sees the invisible (fate) by combining the visible (lines on the palm) with that which is not so. The mocked palmist and fortune-teller take their revenge in the form of the current legal situation where law functions as the 'scale' in which guilt and misfortune (or fate) lose their distinction; for the judge judges by building a nexus between the 'natural' aspect of the life of the character with his judgement. Guilt cannot be distinguished from misfortune because, once guilty, any chain of reasoning can be deduced from his life and circumstances to explain his guilt, a causal chain no different from those links illustrated by tarot cards below or the stars above. Reasons can always be found, events always lie in wait, 'things unchastely pregnant with certainty' (Benjamin 1986b, 308), to be tied together for the one pronounced guilty. This is the return of the Baroque Adamite 'swamp' (Benjamin 2003, 129)[39].

> The guilt context is temporal in a totally inauthentic way, very different in kind and measure from the time of redemption, or of music or of truth. On determining the particular nature of time in fate depends the complete elucidation of these matters. The fortune-teller who uses cards and the palmist teach us at least that this time can at every moment be made simultaneous with another (not present). (Benjamin 1986b, 308)

Benjamin goes on to state, 'It is not an autonomous time, but is parasitically dependent on the time of a higher, less natural life. It has no present, for fateful moments exist only in bad novels, and past and future it knows only in curious variations' 308).[40]

Schmittian sovereignty well fits into such an 'inauthentic temporal', where every normal can be magically undone into a sovereign exception. In contrast for Benjamin, fate and myth entwine as legal violence; if the former is its 'crown', in the latter does it 'manifest'. In 'power' and the 'state' do the cycles of mythic-fate, as much as law-making and law-preserving functions, churn by ensuring that such violence is no mere means to law but its manifest fearsome existence.[41] Not a punishing response to a transgression but a self-reaffirmation in the figuration of the guilty victim whose situation can hardly be understood outside the cord of fate, if it is to be sought to be comprehended at all. To such fate as much as the acedia of homogeneous time, there only remains the 'tiger's leap … in the open air of history [which] is a dialectical one, which is how Marx understood revolution' (Benjamin 1988, 261).

Postscript

Apart from his times, never might Benjamin's indictment have been more timely. The valorisation of myth today is at one with the worship of the tyrant-martyr. One trembles before him as the one who has taken on the awesome labours of sovereign rule and vicariously delights in his destructive ways; all violence is sanctified by sacrifice. It is no coincidence that this takes place in a milieu where memes and technology flood a sensorium, image writing is myth and action algorithm. How better to describe technology than to see ourselves marooned in it, the infinite bits of information scattered all over with little but our mournful gaze.

References

Agamben, Giorgio. 2005. *State of Exception*. Chicago: University of Chicago Press.

Anderson, Benedict. 1991. *Imagined Communities*. London: Verso.

Arendt, Hannah. 1993. *Between Past and Future: Eight Exercises in Political Thought*. New York: Penguin Books.

Benjamin, Walter. 1985a. 'On Some Motifs in Baudelaire.' In *Illumination: Essays and Reflections*, edited with an introduction by Hannah Arendt. New York: Schocken Books.

———. 1985b. 'Theses on the Philosophy of History.' In *Illumination: Essays and Reflections*, edited with an introduction by Hannah Arendt. New York: Schocken Books.

———. 1985c. 'Work of Art in the Age of Mechanical Reproduction.' In *Illumination: Essays and Reflections*, edited with an introduction by Hannah Arendt. New York: Schocken Books.

———. 1986a. 'Critique of Violence'. In *Reflections: Essays, Aphorisms, Autobiographical Writing*, edited with an introduction by Peter Demetz. New York: Schocken Books.

———. 1986b. 'Fate and Character'. In *Reflections: Essays, Aphorisms, Autobiographical Writing*, edited with an introduction by Peter Demetz. New York: Schocken Books.

———. 1986c. 'On Language as Such and the Language of Men'. In *Reflections: Essays, Aphorisms, Autobiographical Writing*, edited with an introduction by Peter Demetz. New York: Schocken Books.
———. 1986d. 'Theologico-Political Fragment'. In *Reflections: Essays, Aphorisms, Autobiographical Writing*, edited with an introduction by Peter Demetz. New York: Schocken Books.
———. 2003. *The Origin of German Tragic Drama*. London: Verso.
Bergson, Henri. 2001. *Time and Free Will, An Essay on the Immediate Data of Consciousness*. Mineola, New York: Dover Publications.
Deleuze, Gilles. 1993. *The Fold: Leibniz and the Baroque*. Minneapolis: University of Minnesota Press.
———. 2013. *Cinema II: The Time Image*. London: Bloomsbury.
Derrida, Jacques. 1992. 'The 'Mystical Foundation of Authority'. *Deconstruction and the Possibility of Justice*, edited by D. Cornell, M. Rosenfeld and D.G. Carlson, 3–68. New York: Routledge.
———. 1998. *Of Grammatology*. Baltimore: Johns Hopkins University Press.
Govind, Rahul. 2021. 'Criminalizing unto Death.' *Law, Culture and the Humanities*. https://journals.sagepub.com/doi/abs/10.1177/17438721211043231.
Kantorowicz, Ernst. 1957. *The King's Two Bodies: A Study in Mediaeval Political Theology*. Princeton, New Jersey: Princeton University Press.
Lukacs, Georg. 1971. 'Reification and the Consciousness of the Proletariat.' In *History and Class Consciousness*, translated by Rodney Livingstone, 83–223. London: Merlin Press.
Martel, James. 2011. *Textual Conspiracies:* Walter Benjamin, Idolatry, and Political Theory. Ann Arbor: University of Michigan Press.
———. 2012. *Divine Violence: Walter Benjamin and the Eschatology of Sovereignty*. New York: Routledge.
———. 2014. *The One and Only Law: Walter Benjamin and the Second Commandment*. Ann Arbor, [Michigan]: University of Michigan Press.
Schmitt, Carl. 2005. *Political Theology: Four Chapters on the Concept of Sovereignty*. Chicago: University of Chicago Press.
———. 2014. *Dictatorship*. Cambridge: Polity Press.
Vyapari, Manoranjan. 2018. *There's Gunpowder in the Air*. Eka: Kolkata.
Weber, Samuel. 2008. 'Taking Exception to Decision: Walter Benjamin and Carl Schmitt.' In *Benjamin's Abilities*, 176–195. Cambridge, Mass.: Harvard University Press

Notes

1 There is a rich literature around Schmitt and Benjamin. Among others, see the work of Samuel Weber, Giorgio Agamben, Jacques Derrida and James Martel. In the reading that follows, more precise engagement will be made with these thinkers.

2 Schmitt writes, in *Political Theology*, in his critique of Kelson, Krabbe and Preus (all of whom 'want to eliminate personal elements from the state') that such 'objections fail to recognize that the conception of personality and

its connection with formal authority arose from a specific juristic interest, namely an especially clear awareness of what the essence of the legal decision entails' (2015, 30). Schmitt is not interested in either the psychological or causal origins but ascribes that such a 'decision' belongs to 'legal perception' itself. Moreover, 'the problem of law as a substantial form is an act of ascertaining' (23; emphasis mine). Later,

> in the independent meaning of the decision, the subject of the decision has an independent meaning, apart from the question of content. What matters for the reality of legal life is who decided. Alongside the question of substantive correctness stands the question of competence. In the contrast between the subject and the content of a decision and in the proper meaning of the subject lies the problem of the juristic form. (32–34)

In *Dictatorship*, C. Schmitt defined dictatorship in terms of the union of three elements: 'personal rule', the 'consensus of people' and 'a strongly centralized apparatus' (2014, xxxviii).

3 The contrast between Benjamin's 'indecisive sovereign' and the role of decision in Schmitt as well as their differences on the question of secularism, has been insightfully noted by Samuel Weber in 'Taking Exception to Decision: Walter Benjamin and Carl Schmitt' in *Benjamin's Abilities* (2008). Agamben's essay in *State of Exception* does not appear to carry Weber's argument very much forward. The central aim of this chapter will be an interpretation of this difference using a range of Benjamin's work.

4 This thieving of the title of Manoranjan Vyapari's brilliant novel is not absolutely inappropriate considering the themes of mythic and revolutionary violence (Vyapari 2018).

5 This is after noting the insoluble antinomy that would arise if one abstractly contrasts natural and positive law into an opposition.

6 This point is worth emphasising because the analogous nature of strike law and military law have not been sufficiently recognised by Derrida. Derrida writes, in the context of Benjamin's discussion of strike law, that 'the state is afraid of fundamental, founding violence, that is, violence able to justify, to legitimate, (*bergrundem* "to found", p. 283) or to transform the relations of law (*Rechtsvrhaltnisse*, "legal conditions"), and so to present itself as having a right to law' (2016, 35).

However, in the relevant section, Benjamin had not spoken about the State but an 'objective contradiction in the legal situation' where law meets strikers who have law/right on their side (too) (Benjamin 1986a, 282). Later, Derrida writes that 'war is another example of this contradiction internal to law (*Recht* or *droit*)" (1992, 39). However, once again, Benjamin refers to an 'objective contradiction in the legal situation' and not a 'logical contradiction in law' (1986a, 282). Both Agamben, in his treatment of the two in *State of Exception*, and Derrida leave un-analysed this important distinction made by Benjamin and, thereby, end up reducing the former to the latter, rendering them complicit with a Schmittian manoeuvre.

7 Benjamin clarified that while the strike right was recognised, the coordination of strikes into a mass strike had its 'legality' challenged by many. One need not belabour the historical circumstances.
8 This muteness and myth is a strong motif in Benjamin to be found prominently in his study of Baroque drama as well as 'On Language as Such and the Language of Men', *Reflections* (Benjamin 1986e).
9 C. Schmitt, *Political Theology*, see note 2.
10

> If measures undertaken in an exception could be circumscribed by mutual control, by imposing a time limit, or finally, as in the liberal constitutional procedure governing a state of siege, by enumerating extraordinary powers, the question of sovereignty would then be considered less significant but would certainly not be eliminated. A jurisprudence concerned with ordinary day to day questions has practically no interest in the concept of sovereignty. (Schmitt 2005, 11–12)

Schmitt goes on to say,

> Only the recognizable is its normal concern; everything else is 'disturbance'. Such a jurisprudence confronts the extreme disconcertedly, for not every extraordinary measure, not every police measure or emergency decree, is necessarily as exception. What characterizes an exception is principally unlimited authority, which means the suspension of the entire existing order. (11–12)

11 These specific concerns of Schmitt as they take shape in his arguments have not been sufficiently attended to in the literature cited in the earlier notes.
12 Schmitt begins his study by referring to the Renaissance Humanists who saw in dictatorship 'a wise invention of the Roman republic' (2014, 1).
13

> A constituent assembly while in session could be termed a sovereign dictatorship, but a president empowered by such a constitution was 'commissary' one because his exercise of the emergency powers in the suspension of the constitution was at once it's preservation; he could not alter the constitution as a monarch could do in whom the monarchical principle and sovereignty law. (Schmitt 2014, 202–203)

14 While Schmitt cites Leibniz in *Political Theology*, he does not analyse Leibniz's critique of Hobbes and his theorization of forms of 'shared' sovereignty. Moreover, whether Schmitt does justice to Hobbes is a separate question, but my own work has consistently critiqued him on this account, most recently in 'Criminalizing unto Death' (Govind 2021).

15

> In this respect the human figure in literature, indeed in art as such, differs from the human figure in reality, where physical isolation, which in so many ways is only apparent isolation, has its true meaning as a perceptible expression of moral seclusion with God. 'Though shalt not make unto thee a graven image'—this is not only a warning against idolatry. (Benjamin 2003 105)

As Benjamin then writes,

> With incomparable emphasis the prohibition of the representation of the human body obviates any suggestion that the sphere in which the moral essence of man is perceptible can be reproduced. Everything moral is bound to life in the extreme sense, that is to say where it fulfils itself in death, the abode of danger as such. (105)

16 Commenting on Nietzsche's *Birth of Tragedy* and the justification of the existence of the world as aesthetic phenomena, Benjamin writes:

> The abyss of aestheticism opens up, and this brilliant intuition was finally to see all its concepts disappear into it....Where art so firmly occupies the centre of existence as to make man one of its manifestations instead of recognizing him above all as its basis, to see man's existence as the eternal subject of its own creations instead of recognizing him as its own creator, then all sane reflection is at an end. (2003, 103)

Continuing in this vein, with a more ominous reference to Nazism, Benjamin writes,

> For what does it matter whether it is the will to life or the will to destroy life which is supposed to inspire every work of art, since the latter, as a product of the absolute will, devalues itself along with the world? The nihilism lodged in the depths of the artistic philosophy of Bayreuth nullified—it could do no other—the concept of the hard, historical actuality of Greek tragedy. (Benjamin 2003, 103)

This critique of the hard historical actuality extends to Benjamin's reading—contra Nietzsche—of the chorus, the orchestra and the importance of legend for Greek tragedy, aided in the interpretation of the latter by Lukacs and Rosenzweig. Such a critique of aestheticism and 'art for art's sake' as inherently given to fascistic tendencies can be found in other works such as 'Work of Art in the Age of Mechanical Reproduction' (Benjamin 1985c). To aesthetic nihilism, Benjamin opposed his own nihilism as 'the task of world politics'; see 'Theologico-Political Fragment', *Reflections* (Benjamin 1986d, 313).

17

> For art cannot, for its part, allow itself, in its works, to be appointed a councillor of the conscience and it cannot permit what is represented rather than the actual representation, to be the object of attention. The truth content of this totality which is never encountered in the abstracted lesson, least of all the moral lesson, but only in the critical elaboration of the work itself, includes moral warnings only in the most indirect form. (Benjamin 2003, 105)

18 See note 3 earlier.

19 'The religious man of the baroque era clings so tightly to the world because of the feeling that he is being driven along to a cataract with it' (Benjamin 2003, 66).

20 Agamben informs us that the editors of Benjamin's work 'with a singular disregard for all philological care' altered Benjamin's formulation of 'there is a baroque eschatology' to 'there is no baroque eschatology' (Agamben 2005, 56). However, as Agamben goes on to say, the Baroque 'knows neither redemption not a hereafter and remains immanent to this world'. See 'Gigantomachy Concerning a Void' (56).

21 This is a motif in Kantorowicz's *The King's Two Bodies*; see, particularly, the analysis of Richard II (1957, 24–42). Benjamin is unnamed.

22 This may well be related to 'Fate and Character', where Benjamin had written,

> Not only is it impossible to determine in a single case what finally is to be considered a function of character and what a function of fate in a human life …the external world that the active man encounters can also in principle be reduced, to any desired, degree, to his inner world, and his inner world similarly to his outer world, indeed regarded in principle as one and the same thing. (1986b, 305)

23 Bergson aids in interpreting this 'mythical violence' staged as sovereign affect in Baroque theatre, which is scarce to be plotted in terms of the actions of a character, the motivations of a protagonist or the powers of a sovereign. He does this in *Time and Free Will* through the argument about the irreducibility of affective alteration to homogenous time (2001). Affect, mood, thought, all involve a qualitative multiplicity that cannot be quantitatively organised as a series, true whether the feeling is one of deep contentment or disturbed nervousness. The series is the basis for a conception of a progressive time because it is dependent on simultaneity (juxtaposition) as much as its abolishment (adding one after another of the identical). One can count only by retaining a difference in terms of space (juxtaposition in simultaneity), which is then cancelled in the counting of the series. 'Homogeneity' is therein intelligible as a spatial concept (even in its annulment), since without such a spatial mould, one

(term) would flow into the other without the ability to distinguish discretely. Affect and mood, on the other hand, experience differences that cannot be so organised, the feelings that constitute a feeling cannot be juxtaposed so as to than be totalised. Yet if Bergson drew from this impossible adequation of inner life and homogenous time, it resulted in a concept of 'duration' or 'life-experience', beyond what was described as evolutionist unfolding. However, in contrast to thinking that 'turning to the contemplative actualization of the stream of life was a matter of free choice', Benjamin offered in return the allegorical death mask (Benjamin 1985a, 199).

24 No doubt G. Deleuze's theorisation of the affection image may help us here, but he does so through Eisenstein and Bergson whom Benjamin knew. Moreover, Deleuze recognised the decisive importance of Benjamin's study of the Baroque in his own study of it; see *Deleuze* (1993, 125). The impress of Benjamin on this study—from the new formulations of time and space to an aesthetic which undermines the divisions of the arts and the individuation of perceptions—is all but clear.

25 As Deleuze writes in relation to painting:

> It will be a novel change, and crucial, in the 17th century, when characters address each other directly from one plane to another, in an organization of the picture along the diagonal, or through a gap which thus privileges the background and brings it into immediate touch with the foreground. The picture is 'internally hollowed out'. (Deleuze 2013, 107)

Deleuze continues, "And this moment of depth, becomes depth *of* field, whilst the dimensions of the foreground take on an abnormal size, and those of the background are reduced, in a violent perspective which does even more to unite the near and the faraway (107).

26 Contrast this to the role of death in Heidegger's oeuvre.

27 When Derrida writes of writing to designate not only the physical gestures of literal pictographic or ideographic inscription but also the totality of what makes it possible; and also beyond, the signifying face, the signified face itself. And thus we say 'writing' for all that gives rise to an inscription in general, whether it is literal or not and even if what is distributes in space is alien to the order of voice: cinematography, choreography, of course, but also pictorial, musical, sculptural writing. (1998, 9) and the absence of Benjamin's presence as interlocuter is striking.

28 If alphabetic writing was merely convention—while symbol claimed to be a direct expression—it was in allegorical writing that the qualities were interminably in-mixed.

29 This might be one way of interpreting the figures and shapes of the spirit, its voyage return in Hegel's Baroque phenomenology, which would be indicted by Lukacs as 'mythological'. See Lukacs (1971, 146–147). See concluding section of this chapter.

30 There have been several historical studies on these ceremonies, beginning with Kantorowicz's *King's Two Bodies*.

31 Considering simply the references to Marx and historical materialism in the literature on Benjamin, there appears a surprising lack of attention to the Marxist problematic in its various forms. For an insightful exception, see J. Martel's reading of Benjamin using the concept of commodity fetishism (and phantasmagoria) across his trilogy *The One and Only Law*, *Divine Violence* and *Textual Conspiracies*. The interpretation offered in the present chapter on Benjamin, however, does not attempt to be exhaustive or comprehensive—most unBenjaminian values—and so many crucial issues such as that of 'truth', ideas or constellations, as they appear in his empiric-critical prologue, have not been directly addressed. It is only hoped that a context has been provided for such communication.

32 The presence of Max Weber cannot be underestimated. To underline that the complex constellation of issues was signalled by secularism is to simultaneously caution any approach on the issue that does little justice to precisely such complexity. Claims to have discovered secularism at different times and different parts of the world will have to confront this problem or otherwise risk finding derivative correlates to ideologically determined fictions in the self-deluding cynical 'we had it first' game.

33 A citation of E. Bloch.

34 From precisely such a perspective, Hegel's phenomenology will have been its finest accomplishment. The configurations of the spirit are not the personifications of ideas, but the attempt to 'give the concrete a more imposing form by getting it to stand up as a person' (Benjamin 2003, 187). For all the critique of 'picture' writing, the phenomenological moments can only be comprehended as script, not merely in its imagistic writing but as much in its concrete conception, the fixing sign and fixed image at once. This is the signature of writing and allegory. If Lukacs lurches 'forward' towards Marx in formulating a praxis, Benjamin's critique of Schiller is a backward movement so as to give a chance to what is otherwise obscured.

35 Both in *Origins* as well as 'On Language as Such and the Language of Men' in *Reflections*, Benjamin critiques the reduction of language as 'mere sign'. In such a context, the former had developed the entire idea of script writing discussed earlier. In the words of the latter, 'hence it is no longer conceivable, as the bourgeois view of language maintains that the word has an accidental relation to its object, that it is a sign for things (or knowledge of them) agreed by some convention. Language never gives mere signs' (Benjamin 1986c, 324).

36 Benjamin's 'epistemo-critical' prologue offers a rigorous and insistent critique of nominalism in the name of a Platonism that cannot be systematically developed here; references to such a critique have, however, been referred to in a scattered way throughout the essay.

37 For the critique of historicism in the 'Theses on the Philosophy of History' and its characterising as 'acedia', see 'Theses on the Philosophy of History' in Benjamin (1985b, 256).

38

> On the other hand, the concept of character will have to be divested of those features that constitute its erroneous connection to that of fate. This connection is effected by the idea of a network that can be tightened by knowledge at will into a dense fabric, for this is how character appears to superficial observation. (Benjamin 1986b, 309)

Benjamin continues,

> Along with the broad underlying traits, the trained eye of the connoisseur of men is supposed to perceive finer and closer connections, until what looked like a net is tightened into cloth. In the threads of this weft a weak understanding believes it possesses the moral nature of the character concerned and can distinguish its good and bad qualities. But, as moral philosophy is to demonstrate, only actions and never qualities can be of moral importance. (309)

In *The Origin*, it is stated,

> Fictional characters exist only in literature and are woven as tightly into the totality of the literary work as are the subjects of goblins into their canvas so that they cannot be removed from it as individuals. In this respect the human figures of differs from human figure in reality, where physical isolation, has its true meaning as a perceptible expression of moral seclusion with god. (Benjamin 2003, 105)

39 This 'chain' has been captured by Deleuze's reading of Hitchcock in the not irrelevant context of original sin.

> If there are Christian themes in Hitchcock, beginning with original in, it is because these themes have from the beginning posed the problem of relation as English logicians well knew. Hitchcock, in his turn, begins from relations, the mental image, from what he calls the postulate. (Deleuze 2013, 206)

Deleuze continues,

> It is from this basic postulate that the film is enveloped with a mathematical or absolute necessity, despite the improbabilities of the plot and the action. Now if one begins from relations, what happens, by virtue of their very exteriority? It may be that the relation vanished, suddenly disappears, without characters changing, but leaving them in the void. (206)

On the other hand—on discerns—this combination of 'arbitrariness' and 'necessity' in Arendt's critique of 'pattern' in 'Concept of History' (Arendt 1993, 80–81). It is another matter that she ironically sees this as 'Marxist' when Marxists such as Lukacs, as shown earlier, had articulated and critiqued such a position precisely from the perspective of praxis.

40 Once again, notwithstanding profound differences, the trace of Bergson's presence in Benjamin's critique of 'homogeneous time' is unmistakable (Benjamin 1985b, 158–159). It is in terms of homogeneity that Bergson, too, articulated his critique of the quantitative, beginning with *Time and Free Will*. It is deeply ironical that Benedict Anderson's use of Benjamin's concept in his influential interpretation of nationalism does not reflect any of the issues at stake, and his reading of the newspaper is most at odds with Benjamin's own, who saw in the newspaper the inability to absorb meaning rather than the site of an accumulating consciousness (as Anderson suggests with little evidence or argument (Anderson 1991, 32–36)).

41 'For if violence, violence crowned by fate, is the origin of law, then it may be readily supposed that where the highest violence, that over life and death, occurs in the legal system, the origins of law jut manifestly and fearsomely into existence' (1986a, 286). The function of violence in law making is twofold, in the sense that law making pursues as its end, with violence as the means, what is to be established as law, but does not dismiss violence at the moment of instatement. Rather, at this very moment of law making, it specifically establishes as law not an end unalloyed by violence but one necessarily and intimately bound to it under the title of powers (295). On the argument moving from 'mythic' violence to divine violence and the 'abolition of the state', see Benjamin (1986a, 294–300).

IV

SELF IN PRACTICE

9

DIALECTICS OF TRANSCENDENTAL AND EMBODIED SELF

Andrei Tarkovsky's Image Motif in Context

Babu Thaliath

The Embodiment of Time

Andrei Tarkovsky elucidates a transitory nexus between humans and nature in his cinematic leitmotifs. However, the selfhood of his protagonists apparently does not conform to this nexus. The Self of his main characters is revealed in transcendental subjectivity and objective embodiment, which—despite their correlations—turn out to be contrary in their modes of existence and cognisability. The dichotomy of the Self that surfaces in an antagonism of contrariness and contradiction constitutes, in principle, a dialectic relationship between human beings and nature, more precisely between the transcendental 'I' and the phenomenal embodiments, particularly the embodiment of the human. Such a dialectical dichotomy is most likely to manifest itself in the temporal structure of the mise-en-scène in which the subjective, a priori temporalisation comes into conflict with the 'given' objective temporality.

For Tarkovsky, the film image is *sculpting in time*. The mise-en-scène is predominantly conceived in terms of time, that is, in temporal structures. Sculpture is primarily a spatial form or a plastic spatialisation. As a form of art, sculpture differs from painting—the other and more common form of plastic art—in that the sculpted spatial structure is both visually and tangibly accessible to us, the perceiving subject. The tactility gives the sculpted spatial structure a higher and more consummate dimension of embodiment. However, according to Tarkovsky, sculpting in time—as spatialisation of time—constitutes the essence of mise-en-scène. It strikes us as a mystery or a riddle for the mere *present* of time cannot exist and is, therefore, an aporia, which is already evident in the interpretations of the existence of time in antiquity, especially in Aristotle.[1]

Tarkovsky seems to make use of the aporia of time, which has been handed down since antiquity, film-aesthetically while developing a basic principle of mise-en-scène, namely, the film image as *sculpting in time*. To which existential category can the time sculpted in a cinematic mise-en-scène belong? In Tarkovsky's observation, time is represented in its objectivity, that is, in its corporeality—as an indispensable dimension of the physical existence. Certainly, in the prevailing framework of Kant's transcendental philosophy, time, also as the temporality of the object, is primarily a subjective category, an a priori notion (*Vorstellung a priori*) (1998, 106–107 [A31–32]). If the temporal existence of an object is perceived subjectively, the perceived time should, in principle, correspond to or complement the given temporality of the object. However, the inherent aporicity of time seems to muddle such a complementarity between subjective and objective time, which then consequently sink into a further aporia. Within the framework of his film aesthetics, Tarkovsky responds to the incessant persistence of the aporia of time in two ways. First, time is accentuated as a purely subjective concept, and second, time is detached from its aporetic present and concretised in the past. The embodiment of the human Self evolves in life, which rather materialises or attains its stable existence only in the past:

> Time is said to be irreversible. And this is true enough in the sense that 'you can't bring back the past', as they say. But what exactly is this 'past'? Is it what has passed? And what does 'passed' mean for a person when for each of us the past is the bearer of all that is constant in the reality of the present, of each current moment? In a certain sense the past is far more real, or at any rate more stable, more resilient than the present. The present slips and vanishes like sand between the fingers, acquiring material weight only in its recollection. King Solomon's ring bore the inscription, 'All will pass'; by contrast, I want to draw attention to how time in its moral implication is in fact turned back. Time cannot vanish without trace in our material world for it is a subjective, spiritual category. The time we have lived settles in our soul as an experience placed within time. (Tarkovsky 1989, 58)

The embodiment of time as the past, through which life gains its real concretion and 'givenness' in the ever-fleeting present, seems necessarily to take on objective traits, although for Tarkovsky, time—as the foundational framework of life—is a subjective spiritual category. For the embodiment of time as past entails the transformation of time into the past, represented both as memories and as objects left behind, which forms a central motif in Tarkovsky's characteristic mise-en-scène. The accentuation of objective time, as the temporality of the object, is perhaps the most important factum of Tarkovsky's cinematic motifs. Since the mise-en-scène is largely designed in the present, which also includes the memory and reconstruction of the past, the autonomy or the autonomous givenness of the objects in perception must be emphasised. In an apparently reversed directionality of cognition, the givenness of the object dictates the temporal existence or 'life' of the object to the perceiving subject. For Tarkovsky, the rhythm of film, which the conventional montage cinema tries to define solely on the basis of the editing, is determined or rather dictated by the temporal life of the object in the mise-en-scène:

> Rhythm in cinema is conveyed by the life of the object visibly recorded in the frame. Just as from the quivering of a reed you can tell what sort of current, what pressure there is in a river, in the same way we know the movement of time from the flow of the life-process reproduced in the shot. .... Rhythm, then, is not the metrical sequence of pieces; what makes it is the time-thrust within the frames. And I am convinced that it is rhythm, and not montage, as people tend to think, that is the main formative element of cinema. (Tarkovsky 1989, 119–120)

At this point, the necessary 'participation' of the object in the time structure of the mise-en-scène—and thus in the director's conception of time—is clearly emphasised. Tarkovsky builds his film aesthetics on such a reversal of the conventional process of perception in the cinematic mise-en-scène and deploys it as a main tool of his polemics against Eisenstein's prevailing montage principle. The film editing is not intended to demonstrate a mere temporalisation of the mise-en-scène; rather, it should emerge from the given temporality in the film strips, which is predetermined by the life of the objects in 'time', as depicted in the mise-en-scène:

> The distinctive time running through the shots makes the rhythm of the picture; and rhythm is determined not by the length of the edited pieces, but by the pressure of the time that runs through them. Editing cannot determine rhythm (in this respect it can only be a feature of style); indeed, time courses through the picture despite editing rather than because of it. The course of time, recorded in the frame, is what the director has to catch in the pieces laid out on the editing table. Time, imprinted in the frame, dictates the particular editing principle.... The consistency of the time that runs through the shot, its intensity or 'sloppiness', could be called time-pressure: then editing can be seen as the

> assembly of the pieces on the basis of the time-pressure within them.... In so far as sense of time is germane to the director's innate perception of life, and editing is dictated by the rhythmic pressures in the segments of film, his handwriting is to be seen in his editing. (Tarkovsky 1989, 117, 121)

Thus, film image is structurally a synthesis of the observation and the observed, more precisely, of the subjective observation and the objects that are given in it. Rather than a unilateral and transcendental synthesis, it forms a *participatory synthesis*. Observation occurs primarily at the aesthetic or pre-logical sensory level and aims at a synthetic unity of perception, which is not based on an epistemological hierarchy (as is the case in Kant's transcendental epistemology) but rather on a parallelity and participation of the observation and the observed. Tarkovsky identifies a certain reciprocity between the temporal structure of observation, which corresponds to the subjective structure of temporalisation, and the temporality of the observed objects, which, as a basic feature of objective existence, also determines the life of the object:

> The basic element of cinema, running through it to its tiniest cells, is observation ...a film is born of direct observation of life; that, in my view, is the key to poetry in cinema. For the cinema image is essentially the observation of a phenomenon passing through time.... Just as life, constantly moving and changing, allows everyone to interpret and feel each separate moment in his own way, so too a real picture, faithfully recording on film the time which flows on beyond the edges of the frame, lives within time if time lives within it; this two-way process is a determining factor of cinema. (Tarkovsky 1989, 66–67, 118)

'Observation of a phenomenon passing through time' summarises the structural determination of Tarkovsky's cinematic leitmotif. The dichotomy of the time structure is indicated here. Observation is a temporal phenomenon that depends on the subjective perception of time as well as the conception of time associated with it. Settlement of time in the observed phenomenon refers to the temporality or temporal existence of the phenomenon. The twofold time structures are not contradictory to each other, since they have a more participatory effect. So they equally participate in the creation of a film image. In the conventional montage cinema, however, such a balanced participation of the subjective conception of time and the objective temporality can hardly come about, as the principle of montage requires a hierarchical order in which the temporality of the object—the phenomenon passing through time—is subsumed under a prevailing subjective conception of time. Accordingly, Tarkovsky sees in Montagekino (montage cinema) the subjective imposition of a concept of time on the viewers, because of which they feel restricted und tied:

> 'Montage cinema' presents the audience with puzzles and riddles, makes them decipher symbols, wonder at allegories, appealing all the time to their intellectual experience. Each of these riddles, however, has its own word-for-word solution; so I feel that Eisenstein prevents the audience from letting their feelings be influenced by their own reaction to what they see. When in *October* he juxtaposes a balalaika with Kerensky, his method has become his aim, in the way that Valery meant. The construction of the image becomes an end in itself, and the author proceeds to make a total onslaught on the audience, imposing upon them his own attitude to what is happening.... Let us say that I want to have time flowing through the frame with dignity, independently, so that no-one in the audience will feel that his perception is being coerced, so that he may, as it were, allow himself to be taken prisoner voluntarily by the artist, as he starts to recognise the material of the film as his own, assimilating it, drawing it in to himself as new, intimate experience. But there is still an apparent dichotomy: for the director's sense of time always amounts to a kind of coercion of the audience, as does his imposition of his inner world. (Tarkovsky 1989, 118, 120)

Such a feeling of liberation is clearly against the rule and dominance of the subjective conception of time that is manifested in the editing technique. The liberation of the audience requires the liberation of the objects observed and represented in the cinematic images in a temporal framework. More precisely, the temporality of the observed object in the mise-en-scène should correspond to the subjective conception of time in cinematographic observation. If the observed objects participate in the subjective observation while maintaining their temporality or the autonomy of their temporal existence, the subjective conception of time refers to a processual temporalisation of objective temporality. Accordingly, the film image emerges from a synthesis of two different temporal structures, namely, the processual temporalisation and the existential temporality. According to Tarkovsky, if the subjective temporalisation prevails, following the principle of montage, it leads to the imposition of a temporal structure on viewers (120). In this hierarchical predominance of subjective temporalisation, the observed objects should orient towards the cinematographic observation, which is analogous to the Copernican turn of the perceptive and cognitive process in epistemology as initiated by Kant, on the grounds of which transcendentalism was programmatically established.

Viewed thus, the basic ideas of Kant's transcendental philosophy, particularly the transcendental aesthetics, can be incorporated in this investigation so as to explicate Eisenstein's montage principle and Tarkovsky's polemic against this conventional editing technique, as represented in his cinematic image motifs. In Tarkovsky's film aesthetics, objective temporality is accentuated and defended against subjective temporalisation. Accordingly, the film image should surface in a deconstruction of the *temporalised temporality* of the object in which the cinematographically represented object liberates itself from subjective temporalisation and thereby regains its own temporality. Such an aesthetic deconstruction, however, does not invalidate the hybridity or synthetic nature of the temporal structure of observation—as a temporalisation of temporality. Instead, the accentuation of the given objective temporality enriches the hybridity of observation, which is primarily dependent on the hybridity of objective existence. Temporality originally constitutes one of the various modes of objective existence, as the object in its mode of existence is a composite or synthesis of various embodiments. When the objects represented cinematographically are human figures, the synthesis of the embodiments refers to the construction of the human Self. What all could be embodied in man in terms of time and space? To begin with, man has a body that is embodied spatially and temporally alongside many natural objects. The Self further incorporates various forms of embodiment that construct the life itself, such as the embodiment of the past in memories, intellect and mental life, the cardinal virtues of love, faith and hope, history, tradition, inheritance and so on. In short, the Self is built upon various embodiments of physical and metaphysical factums that life always leaves behind and preserves, which suggests that the investigation of Tarkovsky's cinematic image motifs should be expanded from structural aspects to thematic peculiarities and their nuances.

Redemption and Resurrection

In the fifth chapter in *Sculpting in Time*, titled 'Cinema's Destined Role', some pictorial references are given to a remarkable scene, an important image motif from the film *Solaris* (1972): *the Death and Resurrection of Harey* (Tarkovsky 1989, 86). Complementing these images in *Sculpting in Time* is a quote from St Paul's first Epistle to Corinthians:

Figure 9.1. Solaris—Harey's Death and Resurrection

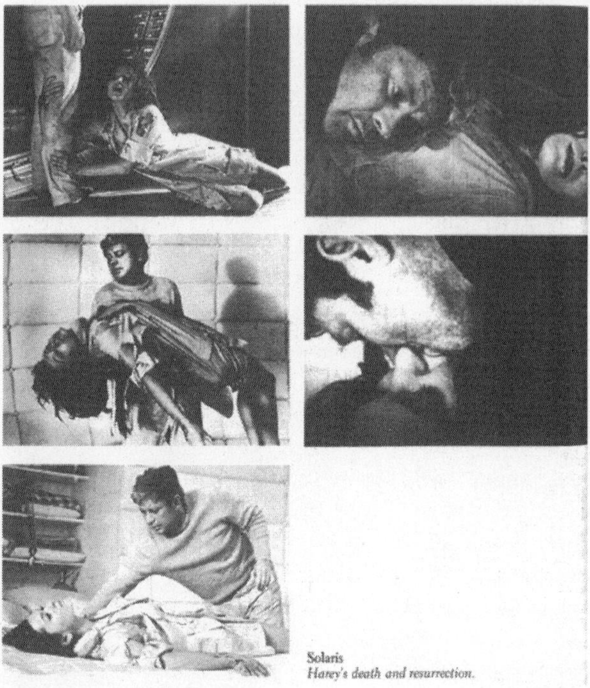

Source: Tarkovsky 1989, 86

> Now if Christ be preached that he rose from the dead, how say some among you that there is no resurrection of the dead? But if there be no resurrection of the dead, then is Christ not risen: and if Christ be not risen, then is our preaching vain, and your faith is also vain . . .
>
> But now is Christ risen from the dead, and become the first-fruits of them that slept. For since by man came death, by man came also the resurrection of the dead. For as in Adam all die, even so in Christ shall all be made alive. (I Cor 15, 15–19, 26–29; Tarkovsky 1989, 87)

Solaris, Tarkovsky's third feature film and first colour film, is built on the leitmotif of the embodiment of the deepest memories, largely relating to the deceased in the past. The magnetic ocean surrounding the Solaris space station has the strange potential to absorb the innermost memories of the past from the minds of astronauts and scientists in the space station and materialise them or bring them back to life. The film begins with scenes showing the protagonist Chris Kelvin, who is preparing for his journey to Solaris, and his family in a house in the countryside.

The strange phenomenon on Solaris had previously been reported to the Russian Space Agency by a former astronaut and pilot Berton, a close friend of Chris Kelvin's father. The members of the authority dismiss Berton's observations as pure hallucinations. Chris Kelvin has been tasked with going to the Solaris space station and dismantling it. As Chris arrives at the space station, he unexpectedly comes across strangers, apparently embodied from the past memories of his colleagues on Solaris: A girl regularly visits the chamber of the scientist Dr Gibaryan, who recently committed suicide. Another girl is seen in the chamber of the scientist Snaut. Also, some children resembling dwarfs are hidden in the chamber of Sartorius. Indeed, the deceased Gibaryan reveals the existence of such strangers on Solaris to Chris in a video and warns him against further materialisations on Solaris. Snaut and Sartorius, on the other hand, are hardly willing to accept these 'strangers' materialised in Solaris as real human beings. Shortly, Harey, Chris's wife who had committed suicide by injecting poison many years ago, materialises on Solaris. In the beginning, Chris tries to get rid of Harey, who has come back to life. When he tries to pick up his pistol from the bed, a clear motive for murder, it is unconsciously kicked away by Harey (Tarkovsky 1972, 01:14:38), who is lying on the bed. Chris then sends Harey into space in a rocket, but she returns to Solaris in the night (01:28:41). When Harey is mortally wounded in her attempt to follow Chris, her wounds instantly disappear, and she comes back to life (01:33:02). Even though Harey later idiosyncratically tries to commit suicide by drinking liquid oxygen, her body begins to tremble, and she consequently comes back to life (02:17:12–02:18:51). Chris begins to love his resurrected wife and chooses to live with her aboard Solaris.

The materialisation of Harey and other human figures on Solaris as well as Harey's resurrection on the space station, mark a fundamentally different principle of life, that is, the immortality of rematerialised and resurrected humans as compared to their mortal existence on the Earth, where they do not overcome death. Just as humans cannot live forever on the Earth, the materialised or resurrected humans on Solaris can never die. For the rationalist Sartorius, aliens, like Harey on Solaris, have only the form of a human being. Their bodies are artificial, that is, consist of neutrinos. For Chris, on the other hand, the Harey who repeatedly materialises and resurrects on Solaris is his wife, who can suffer physically and mentally and who truly loves him and, therefore, never wants to leave him.

What materialise on Solaris and always resurrect after death or the termination of existence are the innermost memory images of people who are detached from their earthly existence and arrive in their own world on the space station. The innermost memory image is, indeed, an essential part of human existence and as such a basis of one's Self in the past. Since humans always carry their past with them in the present as memories, and consequently can never let go of them, the memories from the past represent the immortal in the human Self that accompanies the ever-dying present of life. In this sense, the embodiment of Harey's memory image on Solaris in the form of physical materialisation and resurrection is the embodiment of a part of Chris's Self that he seeks to get rid of forever. Before leaving for Solaris, Chris tries to erase all traces of his earthly past, most of which are leftover images and other objects. The most important of these objects is a picture of Harey. The subject of this picture materialises with the same appearance—of the body and the clothes—aboard Solaris. On the first and subsequent returns, Harey leaves the same piece of clothing, her woollen shrug, on the armchair (Tarkovsky 1972, 01:30:03). As a leftover object from the past, the shrug shows the immortality of the past.

The immortality of the past in human existence normally leaves behind memories, images and material objects and, in unusual circumstances as in Harey's case, lets the memory images resurrect. This immortality points to the multilayered nature and structure of the Self, which primarily builds on the past. The human being, who is physically embodied and, at the same time, embodies all mental states and processes such as sensation, perception, cognition, judgement, thinking, remembering, imagination and so on, acquires a multilayered Self in life. However, the layers of the Self are not just integrated in a harmonious composition devoid of contradictions. Some of them seem contradictory, even dialectical, to the others. The scientific-rational thinking of Sartorius contradicts the reality of the materialisation of Harey from a past image and her resurrection. Here, he considers the embodiment of Harey on Solaris—as well as that of his own 'children'—to be an artificial and not a normal biological phenomenon. Such an inconsistency between the rational real and the deceptively artificial could be compared, albeit limitedly, to a robot endowed with artificial intelligence, even possessing a kind of Self. However, the immortal memory and the mortal body, which is subject to repeated deaths and disappearance and constant materialisation and resurrection in Harey's case, form a much more complex dichotomy and thus a dialectic of the Self. Since Harey as a memory image—both in her past death and in her present materialisation and resurrection on Solaris—forms an integral part of Chris's Self, her immortality could be viewed as an intrinsic matter as well an aporia of Chris's Self. Thus, a person's Self comprises various dialectical embodiments in time and space, as represented in birth and rebirth, mortality and immortality or death and resurrection.

Not every memory image materialises or resurrects on Solaris. Tarkovsky seems to attribute to those memories, which are predestined to materialise on Solaris, a certain *potential* for materialisation, resurrection and immortality. It is the potential of *guilt* or guilt-ridden memory, which demands materialization and resurrection on Solaris. The late Harey is not an ordinary memory for Chris but an embodiment of his guilt that persists in his memory. Harey is an object of Chris's guilt or guilt consciousness, as someone who died only in the present but lives eternally in the past. In his film analysis, Slavoj Žižek tries to universalise the specificity of this case in the cinematic narrative, such as Harey's materialisation and resurrection on Solaris, by regarding it as a unique phenomenon in a man's life. According to Žižek, woman is the embodiment of man's guilt (2016, 00:56:18). Here, the infallible biblical motif emerges in two connotations, the first being woman as a part of man's body, as referred to in the biblical account of woman's creation from man's rib. Therefore, woman can never die both in her body and as a memory image *in man*, in his Self. Second, this persistence of guilt points to the original sin by which man and woman *fell* from the heavenly paradise to earth and were consequently condemned to a mortal earthly existence.

When guilt imparts memories the potential to constantly surface or reappear in the present, it transcends the bounds between past, present and future. While the memories necessarily have a past, in life and in history, for reference, the guilt inherent in them prompts its persistence or steady presence. For guilt is ahistorical. The sense of guilt cannot merely archive the guilt-laden memories or permanently confine them to the past. The mental harbouring of such memories, which can arise and persist from biographical and historical sources, always has the potential to re-emerge and materialise in the present. When Dostoyevsky lets the protagonist Raskolnikov say in *Crime and Punishment* that everything comes back, it mainly refers to the life- and cultural-historical remembrance of guilt. In the human Self, the sense of guilt builds on both the biographical and the cultural past.

That the guilt-laden memories, which Chris and others on Solaris always try to overcome in their mental existence and thereby archive in the past, will necessarily embody and that the embodied memories will never die but always persist, imply the primacy of embodiment over a purely mental mode of the existence of memories in the Self. The emphasis here on the embodiment of memories, which originally constitute an essential part of the Self in their mental existence, marks a certain reinterpretation of the dominant modern conception of the Self. Through the epistemological method of negation, Descartes established the absolute primacy of man's mental existence. The human selfhood that unfolds from self-awareness is based solely on a *res cogitans*. When Descartes uses the method of negation to ensure the existence of the soul, the human subject simultaneously negates all sensory qualities in the object that make up the object's embodiment, so that a merely extended nothing—as *res extensa*—remains. This embodiment is at the same time the individuation of the object. Through the methodical negation of bodily individuation, Descartes desired to establish the epistemological as well as ontological primacy of the human soul and, thereby, wanted to conclusively overcome the discourse on individuation, particularly the discourse on *principium individuationis* that dominated the scholastic philosophy.[2] With Descartes began the modern dominance of the human subject, that is, the primacy of the purely mental existence of humans and their self-consciousness. This original idea of modernity was vigorously continued by all Cartesians—both rationalists as well as empiricists—and culminated in Kant's transcendental epistemology.

The resurgence of embodiment against the traditional notion of the merely mental existence of the Self clearly withstand—and does so historically—the dominant modern subject that derives its self-awareness primarily from the mental existence and, thus, the triumph of historically unfolding transcendentalism in modernity. However, such a confrontation does not lead to any negation of the subject, which would mean a complete reversal of the philosophical-conventional method of negation. It leads instead to a dialectic in the Self between the subject and the embodiments of subjective states, between mental and corporeal existence, which *layer* in the Self.

In some of Tarkovsky's image motifs, there are subtle references to the Self as embodiment and to the ensuing reversal of the primacy of the soul prevailing in modernity. An important reference is a poem of Arseny Tarkovsky, the famous Russian poet and the father of Andrei Tarkovsky, which the director recites in the movie *Mirror* (1975):

> A person has one body,
> Singleton, all on its own,
> The soul has had more than enough
> Of being cooped up inside
> A casing with ears and eyes
> The size of a five-penny piece
> And skin—just scar after scar—
> Covering a structure of bone.

Out through the cornea it flies
Into the bowl of the sky,
On to an icy spoke,
To a wheeling flight of birds,
And hears through the barred window
Of its living prison-cell
The crackle of forests and corn-fields
The trumpet of seven seas.

A bodyless soul is sinful
Like a body without a shirt—
No intention, nothing gets done,
No inspiration, never a line.
A riddle with no solution:
Who is going to come back
After dancing on the dance-floor
Where there's nobody to dance?
(from the poem *Eurydice* by Arseny Tarkovsky, translated by Kitty-Hunter Blair; Tarkovsky 1989, 157)

'A bodyless soul is sinful/Like a body without a shirt' (157). This observation underlines the primacy of embodiment over the soul prior to its separation—as a modern subject. Only the body can accommodate the soul through a progressive physical mantling, mainly through the skin. Here, a basic principle of the embodiment—as an individuation—seems to be indicated, namely the progressive mantling or veiling of the body, which initially involves the flesh and then the skin and finally the clothes. The opacity of these many layers of coverings or cases also suggests that the embodiment is indeed a progressive masking. The Self as embodiment arises accordingly from the principle of mask, which, as Nietzsche observes, is continually growing around every profound spirit (2013, 49–50).

When Harey materialises on the Solaris space station, she wears the same dress she wore when she committed suicide many years earlier. Her blouse is torn at the upper arm with an opening showing the mark of the injection on her skin. However, when Chris asks her to change, Harey is not able to undress and take off the blouse as the lace behind the blouse is just woven over the dress, which is not split and, therefore, cannot be opened (Tarkovsky 1972, 01:18:00). Chris then has to cut the blouse with scissors to open it. This strange event seems to suggest how the clothes, like a second layer of skin, also progressively mask Harey's materialisation, thereby perfecting her embodiment on Solaris. Here, as suggested in the poem by Arseniy

Tarkovsky quoted earlier, the clothes form an integral part of the body and of embodiment in general. While Chris unquestioningly accepts his wife, Harey, in her materialisation and resurrection on Solaris, Sartorius wants to medically examine her body to prove that she is not a human being with flesh and blood but an artificial phenomenon merely made up of neutrinos (01:35:56). Such a scientific diagnosis is obviously opposed to the progressive masking of the embodiment in layers—flesh, skin and clothes—discussed earlier. The power of the masks in embodiment is shown not only in the complete closure of Harey's clothes but also in the instantaneous healing of Harey's injury in the scene mentioned earlier.[3] When Chris tries to wipe the blood on Harey's skin (on the hand), he realises that her skin, that is, the bleeding open wound on her skin, has healed instantly on its own (01:32:59). This immediate autonomous healing of the injured flesh and skin may, prima facie, suggest the artificial nature of Harey's body, which Sartorius insists on. Indeed, this strange occurrence demonstrates the power and sovereignty of embodiment, represented in the permanence or imperishable nature of its mask-like layers.

When Harey materialises on Solaris from Chris's guilt-laden memory of his past, her repeated resurrections and her *immortality* seem to indicate not just the persistence of guilt and guilt consciousness, as previously alluded to but also a subtle leitmotif of redemption. The excerpt from the Epistle of St Paul to the Corinthians, quoted in Tarkovsky's work *Sculpting in Time* in association with the scene of Harey's resurrection, elucidates this leitmotif. 'For since by man came death, by man also came the resurrection of the dead. For as in Adam all die, even so in Christ shall all be made alive' (Tarkovsky 1989, 87). The reference to Adam (and indirectly to Eve) refers to his fall from heavenly paradise to earthly mortal existence, and the reference to Christ depicts eternal life in his resurrection from the dead and subsequent ascension to heaven. At the same time, the resurrection of Christ points to the redemption from the guilt of sins, through which man was subjected to mortality or earthly death. Resurrection as a victory over death or mortality constitutes man's redemption. Aside from such explicit biblical subtexts, Harey's repeated materialisation and resurrection prompt a clear transformation in Chris. Through the inevitable presence of the materialised and resurrected woman Harey,[4] the protagonist Chris experiences a true redemption of his soul on Solaris. He detaches himself from his previous persona and now bears a new person (to use a different and equally well-known leitmotif from Saint Paul in the Bible). The redemption of Chris does not unfold instantly, but only gradually as the narrative progresses. Upon first re-encountering his long-deceased wife, Harey, who materialises on Solaris, Chris behaves indifferently towards her and attempts to get rid of her by sending her into space in a Solaris rocket (Tarkovsky 1972, 01:20:35). The recurring materialisations of Harey in Solaris as well as her resurrection from her death show Harey's incessant urge to be with Chris, whom she does not want to leave. Indeed, when Chris slowly begins to accept and love Harey as his wife, he is not prompted by his helplessness that he can never get rid of her. This change is clearly an aftermath of his inner transformation. In the beginning, Chris appears to be governed by an inner dialectics of his Self, to a lesser extent than his colleagues Snaut and Sartorius. A redemptive transformation rapidly begins in Chris, caused in particular by the resurrection of Harey on Solaris. However, the course of redemption is not reflected in a triumph but in a physical and emotional breakdown or weakening of Chris. Chris succumbs to fever and to the subsequent deliriums, as a result of which he becomes physically and mentally weak and, in his delirium, returns to his childhood and mother (Tarkovsky 1972, 02:26:16).[5] The collapse of the protagonist signals that he, in his redemption and renewal, succumbs to his inner dialectics. Compared to his colleagues Snaut and Sartorius, Chris can no longer master his inner dialectics. In his redeemed and renewed sense of Self, Chris differs from his colleagues on Solaris, particularly from Sartorius who—a loyal and unyielding scientist—can no longer accept the materialised and resurrected woman on Solaris as a living being. Sartorius forms the antipode to Chris in which he always seeks to master the inherent dialectics of his Self by deploying his scientific-rational sensibility.

Fall and Flight

The flight or the counter-gravitational levitation of characters and objects is a unique image motif in Tarkovsky's films *Solaris*, *Mirror* and *The Sacrifice* (1986). A prototype of this image motif can be seen in his first feature film, *Ivan's Childhood* (1962), in Ivan's childhood dream of flying. While this scene depicts a dynamic flight, the other flight motifs in the films *Solaris*, *Mirror* and *The Sacrifice* show the static levitation of figures, such as the famous scene of the hovering mother in *Mirror* (Tarkovsky 1975, 01:33:39).

This flight motif in *Mirror* suggests a return to the mother. A caption is added to this image of the flight motif in *Sculpting in Time*: 'Mother came and beckoned me, and flew away' (Tarkovsky 1989, 156). It was taken from a poem by his father Arseny Tarkovsky and recited in the film *Nostalgia* (1983).[6] *Ivan's Childhood* begins with a sequence showing Ivan's dream of his childhood (Tarkovsky 1962). In chase of a butterfly on the field, Ivan takes to the air, flying on a supernal plane through the treetops, touching the leaves. Ivan, after landing in the woods, meets his young mother carrying water in a bucket. He then drinks the water and tells her, 'Mama, there's a cuckoo over there.' Suddenly, we hear the sound of firing, and the dream apparently ends in the tragic death of his mother (Tarkovsky 1962, 00:00:46–00:02:20). The flight or levitation motif in *Mirror* and in Tarkovsky's other films seems to suggest a return to birth, which may imply rebirth and also resurrection. Only in the flight motif in Solaris does Tarkovsky give a causal explanation, that is, zero gravity on the Solaris space station, as indicated by Snaut.

Chris's levitation with Harey, his resurrected wife, with the music of Johann Sebastian Bach and the painting *The Hunters in the Snow* (1565) by Pieter Bruegel in the background, also depicts the aforementioned redemptive transformation of Chris (Tarkovsky 1972, 02:11:44). The only flight motif in *Sacrifice*, Tarkovsky's last film, is in one of the final scenes of the film (1986, 01:49:40) in which the protagonist Alexander visits his servant Maria (who, according to his friend Otto, is a witch) at her domicile 'in the farm, beyond the lake and next to the church' and sleeps with her to save his family and the world from the nearing apocalyptic catastrophe (Tarkovsky 1999, 547). At the beginning of the physical relationship, Alexander and Maria hover over their bed. Sleeping or a physical relationship with Maria was advised by Alexander's prophetic friend Otto, the part-time postman, as the only possible path to redemption. However, this redemptive act of Alexander and Maria is one of the leitmotifs suggesting the renewal of life, as depicted in conception, birth, rebirth and resurrection.

The insinuation of redemption and resurrection in the flight motif seems more explicit in contrast to the opposite *fall motif* in Tarkovsky's films. The fall here is inevitably gravitational. It is a fall to earth, which is largely represented as death and ruination of fallen objects on the ground, but at the same time, as mentioned at the beginning, a transitory nexus between man and nature is being subtly flaunted. Some of the fall motifs in *Mirror*, *Stalker* and *Nostalgia* depict human figures lying on earth or having fallen to the earth, coming thereby in extremely close vicinity to objects lying on the earth, such as grass and small plants on marshland and under water, leftover objects, still and flowing water and so on (Figure 9.2). They appear to be fully integrated in the environment of these objects succumbed to gravity, that is, natural or earthly objects as well as fallen, forgotten and ruined objects left behind by human civilisations.

***Figure 9.2. Fallen and Forgotten Objects Lying under Water in* Stalker**

Source: Tarkovsky 1979, 01:26:18

The film *Mirror* begins with a scene depicting a remarkable fall motif (Tarkovsky 1975, 00:08:41). In this scene, we see the mother, played by Margarita Terekhova, sitting on a fence separating the yard of her country house from a vast meadow adjacent to a dense oak forest. A stranger, a doctor (played by Anatoliy Solonitsyn), is looking for the way to a place called Tomshin and asks her about it. A brief acquaintance develops from the conversation, and he takes the liberty of sitting next to her on the fence. The wooden fence breaks, and both of them fall to the ground. The doctor then lingers on the ground in the fully recumbent position and begins to monologise. He sees small plants and their roots in the immediate vicinity and hears the chirping of small insects on the grass and wonders how people tend to overlook and ignore these natural objects in everyday life:

> You know, I fell and found strange things here—roots, bushes.
> Has it ever occurred to you that plants can feel, know,
> even comprehend…
> The trees, the hazelnut bush
> …
> They don't run about.
> Like us who are rushing, fussing, uttering banalities.

> That's because we don't trust nature that is inside us.
> Always this suspicion, haste, and no time to stop and think.[7]
> (Tarkovsky 1975, 00:08:50)

At a distinguished gathering of St Petersburg's high society, Prince Myshkin, as feared before, breaks an exquisite antique vase, as if he was nearing an epileptic fall. This incident causes a very unpleasant interruption of the gathering, in which the invited high society looks at the prince with pity and, at the same time, with aversion. (Dostoevsky 2014, 1071–1074). Earlier, Prince Myshkin recollects his epileptic fit during which he begins to perceive the reality in a completely different way (438–440). Tarkovsky seems to have been deeply influenced by this famous fall motif in Dostoyevsky's *The Idiot*, a novel that he always wanted to adapt into a film (with Margarita Terekhova in the role of Nastasya Filippovna). In his last film, *Sacrifice*, there is a significant reference to this fall motif from the novel *The Idiot*. Marta, Alexander's stepdaughter, recollects how he once brilliantly played Prince Myshkin breaking the antique vase on stage (Tarkovsky 1999, 526–527).[8] Interestingly, after this conversation, in the next sequence, there is a similar *fall* of Otto to the wooden floor of the house, while he is visiting the family on Alexander's birthday.

Both in Prince Myshkin's epileptic fit and fall in *The Idiot*, during which he begins to perceive a different reality in an unconscious state of mind, and in the doctor's fall in *Mirror*, the self-inflicted loneliness of modern humans in a world of their own creation, which eventually leads to their alienation from the earth and its nature, is expressed. The fall to earth is originally connoted as a fall to mortality and death, which also biblically depicts the fall of Adam and Eve from the heavenly paradise to earth, that is, to an earthly mortal existence (and to which the passage of St Paul quoted earlier refers). One of the first scenes of the film *Andrei Rublev* (1966) shows a flight motif in which a person enthusiastically flies in a balloon and sees the church towers at eye level (Tarkovsky 1966, 00:05:12). This scene shows the great striving of human beings to free themselves from their gravitational bondage to the earth and to fly like birds. But the person fails in his flight experiment in a balloon and falls fatally to the ground. Another image motif in *Andrei Rublev* shows a falling horse in slow motion, with the horse trying in vain to save itself from falling to the ground and to stand upright (00:07:08).

In *Solaris*, Harey, in a desperate attempt to free Chris from her incessant presence, commits suicide by drinking liquid oxygen and falls to the floor of the space station and dies. Immediately, we see the strange resurrection of Harey from the ground (Tarkovsky 1972, 02:17:27). Further, towards the end of the film *Nostalgia*, Domenico sets himself on fire, sitting on an equestrian statue above the ancient Roman square, and falls to the ground and dies (Tarkovsky 1983, 02:00:30). Apart from such fall motifs ending in death, most of the fallen human figures in Tarkovsky's image motifs demonstrate a—previously discussed—transitory extension into nature by levelling their embodiment with the objects of nature and the other leftover objects, ruined and forgotten by human civilisations. The film *Stalker*, in particular, is rich in such image motifs. On the way to the mysterious Zone, the stalker and the writer rest occasionally on earth, most often on swampy terrains, surrounded by grass and plants grown wild along with leftover and ruined objects, that is, the remnants of human civilisations and, most notably, the expanses of water stretching over ruined terrains and objects (Tarkovsky 1979, 01:19:56).

The bodies of the protagonists, especially the faces, are levelled with the natural objects and ruins of human civilisations, such as coins, pistols, broken power cables and parts of power poles, syringes and also images (for example, a Christ icon; see Figure 9.2), most of which are lying on the marshland or under water.[9] In these fall motifs, human embodiment seems to be reduced to a mere object and thus equated to the objects of nature and the ruins of civilisations. The faces appear coarse and primordial in closer association with earthly objects. We can explain the predominant presence of ruined objects in these image motifs by the fact that the objects artificially created by human civilisations, when they *fall* into a state of being left behind and forgotten, are, in the subsequent process of ruination, *gravitationally regained*, that is, appropriated or incorporated by the earth.

The Dialectics of the Self

Mise-en-scène as sculpting in time is clearly an externalisation of time and, as such, characterised by the emancipation of time from an a priori confinement in the subject into a free existence, as implied by the temporality of embodiment in the notion of sculpting. However, time is the most important foundation of one's transcendental Self—as the basis of human self-consciousness—when, following Kant, we take into account the mental interiority of time as against the exteriority of space (Kant 1998, 97–98; A23–24). In the *Phenomenology of Inner Time-Consciousness* (*Zur Phänomenologie des inneren Zeitbewusstseins*), Husserl apparently extends the a priori inherence of time established by Kant. However, Husserl does not begin from the Kantian notion of the apriority or a priori inwardness of time but rather from Franz Brentano's basic idea of the intentional in-existence of a time-object (such as music). According to Brentano, time *objectively* migrates in consciousness—as an embodied time-object. From the merely a priori formality of time to which Kant's notion of time as an a priori form of sensibility (*Sinnlichkeit*) refers (Kant 1998, 106–107; A 31–32), to Brentano's and Husserl's conception of the embodiment of a time-object in human consciousness, a certain historically progressing dialectic of time can be discerned, which seems to suggest a historically unfolding dialectic of human self-consciousness. Such a dialectic builds on an original dichotomy between the subjective-processual temporalisation and the material embodiment of time represented in the temporality of objects, as discussed in the first part of this investigation.

Tarkovsky's film aesthetics, particularly his basic idea of mise-en-scène as sculpting in time, can be analysed in this way within the framework of theoretical philosophy. However, theoretical-philosophical foundations are far from sufficient to adequately explain the aesthetic conciseness and brilliance of his cinematic image motifs and their complex structure in the body of his cinematic narration. After all, theoretical-philosophical considerations serve to decipher the structural uniqueness and aporicity of the pictorial motifs, the thematic expansion of which will extend to a broader and deeper horizon of life and into transitory morphoses in memory and history. It seems that, in the transcendental internalisation of time and externalisation of space, as represented in Kant's *Transcendental Aesthetics*, a certain dialectical state between space and time consciousness is indicated (97–98; A23–24). However, space consciousness does not merely refer to the concrete objective and its immediate presence but also to internalised images, memories, dreams and imaginations. These purely subjective phenomena can hardly be apriorised in their entirety because they necessarily refer to a world of concrete objects that we experience through our senses, into which memories and histories morph and which are reshaped and recreated in our imagination.

Sculpting in time indicates an externalisation of time in plastic forms, which primarily entails an externalisation of the time-consciousness, represented in a concrete expression. For Tarkovsky, the embodiment or spatialisation of time manifests itself in different forms of objective temporality and the embodiment of internalised time. The external objects to be perceived by the senses free themselves from a prevailing transcendental temporalisation precisely in their temporality, which can be observed in their *life* and its autonomy. Internalised time, on the other hand, is primarily embodied in memories that are archived and preserved by a historical consciousness. Here, the dialectic of the Self is apparently an internal phenomenon in humans or in their self-consciousness. The concretion of memories in material forms and their steady or recurring resurrection, as Tarkovsky's pictorial motifs demonstrate, prompt an expansion of the dialectic of the Self from its transcendental concealment into a tangible presence in which the objects *encounter* the subject. Tarkovsky tends to see moments of redemption in such an expansion of the dialectical Self, represented above all in the persistence, that is, constant resurrection of the past. These moments of redemption manifest themselves in his pictorial motifs as a reciprocal liberation of perception and perceived, as a return to the past in life—to childhood and birth—as well as in the material concretion of memories.

Sculpting in time thus points to the primal dialectic of the Self between an internalised time-consciousness and its inevitable externalisation in the form of embodiments. Therefore, the original dialectic between the transcendental and the embodied Self is to be necessarily extended into a wide range of spatiotemporal objects and objectifications, such as the objects of immediate sensory experiences, past memories, dreams, imaginations and fantasies and so on. Just like the subjective perception of the colour of objects, which is merely a secondary sensory and not a primary or purely objective quality, each object and the reality of the present and past of its *life* form multiple modes of being, which also requires multiple forms of cognisability. Such multiplicity concerns the human Self and its strata, which span across different embodiments represented primarily as the persistence of embodied memories and immediate experiences in presence.

The dialectics between the transcendental and the embodied Self can also lead to the tragedy of existence, as the fate of some of the protagonists in Tarkovsky's films shows. While Snaut and Sartorius tacitly regard the materialisation of human figures on Solaris from their past as tragic phenomena, many travellers succumb to their tragic fate in the film *Stalker* in the mysterious Zone where people's innermost desires are fulfilled or realised. They end up committing suicide. In their tragic consciousness of fate, Snaut and Sartorius always try to hide the memory images embodied in Solaris, which they archive in themselves. Even if the mysterious materialisation of memories and their constant presence are revealed or come to light, both of them try to normalise these phenomena on Solaris through rational arguments and, in consequence, legitimise them scientifically. Such mastering of the Self, that is, its dialectics, has the consequence that both these scientists on Solaris are condemned to carry their psychic abyss with them and, therefore, never to get rid of their guilt-laden self-consciousness.

Tarkovsky's polemic against Eisenstein's montage cinema is based on the idea that, in mise-en-scène, the subjective temporalisation should not overwhelm the temporality of objects, which, in addition to the forgotten natural objects, consist of ruined objects left behind by human civilisations and also the embodiment of memories and guilt. In reality, his image motifs show a clear dominance of given and embodied objects and their temporality over the subjective predetermination of the time structure in mise-en-scène. When the embodied Self begins to predominate over the transcendental Self, it signals the triumph of the dialectics of the Self, which necessarily occasions the transcendental to free itself from its confinement in the subject and, thereby, extend into the environment and vicinity of other people and nature. When Sartorius, at Snaut's modest and quiet birthday party on Solaris, congratulates his colleague for his devotion to science, proposing a toast 'to Snaut and to science', Snaut remains passive and seems to ignore such accolades (Tarkovsky 1999, 172). He says, almost as if in a delirium: 'What man needs is man!' (172) This confession is a clear sign of his inner transformation, in contrast to Sartorius, who stubbornly remains firm in his belief in science and rationality. Snaut begins to succumb to his inner dialectics by transcending his Self from its subjective confinement and, thereby, reaching others, whose presence he accepts in its givenness and embodiment. In such a submission, Snaut gets closer to Chris, the redeemed but weakened protagonist who leaves the space station Solaris and returns to Earth.

The extension of the dialectics of the Self can also lead to tragedy, that is, tragic cessation of life, mainly in the form of suicide, in which the Self destroys its embodiment, and in civilisational tragedies such as genocides. Like the case of Gibaryan on Solaris, the motif of suicide in the later films *Stalker* and *Nostalgia* appears as an inevitable expression of the inner conflict of human beings, the dialectics of which they can neither master nor succumb to. Curiously, Tarkovsky uses Beethoven's ninth symphony, the fourth and final movement of the symphony in which Friedrich Schiller's lyrical poem 'An die Freude' (Ode to Joy) is set to music, as the background score accompanying the archival images of genocide in *Stalker* (sequence in the Zone) and Domenico's suicide in the penultimate scene of the film *Nostalgia*. The ironic emphasis on Schiller's poem, sung by the chorus in Beethoven's ninth symphony with extraordinary power and intensity, seems here to be a subtle reference to the monumental development of the transcendental Self, which Tarkovsky considers not as a triumph but as the tragedy of humanity. While the triumph of humanity in its earthly existence sounds in Schiller's poem, especially when it is set to music in Beethoven's ninth symphony, Tarkovsky's image motifs of human and civilisational tragedy appear paradoxically in the mise-en-scène. The musical background and scenic foreground form an inconsistent association here. However, such an inconsistency in the mise-en-scène, which rather suggests an ethical issue in the cinematic narration, unfolds in Tarkovsky's film aesthetics into a dialectic, that is, a dialectic of the Self apart from its redemptive and self-destructive consequences.

References

Aristotle. 1984. 'Physics.' In *The Complete Works of Aristotle*, edited by Jonathan Barnes and translated by R.P. Hardie and R.K. Gaye. Vol. I. Princeton: Princeton University Press.

Barber, Kenneth. 1994. *Individuation and Identity in Early Modern Philosophy*, edited by Kenneth Barber and Jorge J.E. Garcia. New York: State University of New York Press.

Dostoevsky, Fyodor. 2014. *The Idiot*. London: Alma Classics.

Heller, Franziska. 2010. *Filmästhetik des Fluiden*. Munich: Wilhelm Fink Verlag.

Kant, Immanuel. 1998. *Die Kritik der reinen Vernunft*. Hamburg: Felix Meiner Verlag.

Nietzsche, Friedrich. 2013. *Jenseits von Gut und Böse*. Hamburg:
Felix Meiner Verlag.

Peace, Richard. 1971. *Dostoyevsky. An Examination of the Major Novels*. Cambridge: Cambridge University Press.

Tarkovsky, Andrei. 1989. *Sculpting in Time: Reflections on the Cinema*. Translated by Kitty Hunter-Blair. London: Faber and Faber.

———. 1999. *Collected Screenplays*. Translated by William Powell and Natasha Synessios. London: Faber and Faber.

———. dir. 1962. *Ivan's Childhood*. Mosfilm. YouTube. https://www.youtube.com/watch?v=6Lnb1bI0VIk&t=124s

———. dir. 1966. *Andrei Rublev*. Mosfilm. YouTube. https://www.youtube.com/watch?v=je75FDjcUP4&t=454s

———. dir. 1972. *Solaris*. Mosfilm. YouTube. https://www.youtube.com/watch?v=Z8ZhQPaw4rE&t=8308s

———. dir. 1975. *Mirror*. Mosfilm. YouTube. https://www.youtube.com/watch?v=NrMINC5xjMs&t=553s

———. dir. 1979. *Stalker*. Mosfilm. YouTube. https://www.youtube.com/watch?v=Q3hBLv-HLEc&list=PL7EqAsBxqGgjarBzACNmCNDdr0y0iFu8U

———. dir. 1986. *Sacrifice*. Stockholm: Svenska Filminstitutet.

Žižek, Slavoj, dir. 2016. *The Pervert's Guide to Cinema*. Berlin: filmedition Suhrkamp.

Notes

1

> Next for discussion after the subjects mentioned is time. The best plan will be to begin by working out the difficulties connected with it, making use of the current arguments. First, does it belong to the class of things that exist or to that of things that do not exist? Then secondly, what is its nature? To start, then: the following considerations would make one suspect that it either does not exist at all or barely, and in the obscure way. One part of it has been and

> is not, while the other is going to be and is not yet. Yet time—both infinite time and any time you like to take—is made up of these. One would naturally suppose that what is made up of things which do not exist could have no share in reality. (Aristotle 1984, 369–370)

2 In the introduction to the edited volume *Individuation and Identity in Early Modern Philosophy*, Kenneth Barber gives an account of how Descartes and Cartesian modernity completely ignored the dominant discourse on individuation handed down in scholastic philosophy till Francisco Suárez. See Barber (1994, 1).

3 See Figure 9.1.

4 By accentuating Harey's resurrection on Solaris, Tarkovsky seems to tacitly adapt an important historical subtext of Dostoyevsky's *Idiot* (by which Tarkovsky is known to have been deeply influenced), namely the female protagonist Nastasya Filippovna as a resurrected woman, that is, a 'woman returned to life'—as the first name Nastasya implies in the historical context of the Russian Orthodox Church. See Peace (1971, 83–84): 'It is Aglaya, who in a fit of pique, reminds the prince that his role is to "resurrect" Nastasya Filippovna.... The possibility of resurrection is implied in Nastasya Filippovna's very name; for Anastasiya (Nastasya) means "the resurrected woman"; "the woman returned to life"'.

5 At this point, an important leitmotif of Tarkovsky's cinema, as expressed in the film *Stalker* in a monologue by the stalker (played by Alexander Kaidanovsky) in the zone, seems to surface, namely, the weakness of living beings in their childhood as a sign of their vitality and, conversely, their strength in old age as a prelude to death.

> When a man is just born, he is weak and fragile, when he dies, he is hard and insensitive. When a tree is growing, it is tender and fragile, but when it's dry and hard, it dies. Hardness and strength are death's companions. Pliancy and weakness are expressions of the freshness of being. (Tarkovsky 1979, 01:07:22–01:07:56)

6

> As a child I once fell ill
> With hunger and fear. Off my lips I peeled
> Hard scales, and licked my lips. 1 remember
> Still the taste of it, saltish and cool.
> And all the time I walked and walked and walked.
> Sat down on the front stairs to warm myself,
> Walked my lightheaded way as if dancing
> To the rat-catcher's tune, riverwards. Sat down
> To warm on the stairs, shivering every which way.
> And mother stands there beckoning, looks as if
> She's close, but I can't go up to her:
> I move towards her, she stands seven steps away,

Beckons me; I move towards her, she stands
Seven steps away and beckons me.
I felt too hot,
Undid my collar button and lay down,
Then there were trumpets blaring, light beating
Down on my eyelids, horses galloping, mother
Was flying above the roadway, beckoned me
And flew away . . .
And now my dream is of
A hospital, white beneath the apple trees,
And a white sheet beneath my chin,
And a white doctor looking down at me,
And a white nurse standing at my feet
And her wings moving.
And there they stayed.
And mother came, and beckoned me—
And flew away . . .. (Tarkovsky 1989, 91–92)

7 Notably, this *fall* was not included in the original screenplay of the film *Mirror*. See Tarkovsky (1999, 269).

8 Dialogue from *Sacrifice*:

> Alexander: I prepared myself for a life, a higher life, so to speak. I studied philosophy, the history of religion, aesthetics. And I ended up putting in chains of my own free will. But at the same time I am happy. Today for example....
> Victor (Doctor): What happened today?
> Alexander: I got a telegram from my friends. As a joke, they signed it: 'Richardians and Idiots', Old theatre friends. We played Shakespeare and Dostoyevsky.
> Marta: I remember!
> Alexander: No!
> Victor: Remember what?
> Marta: Those performances.
> Alexander: Oh, come now!
> Marta: Yes, I do! I remember how you dropped that vase from the tray and broke it. And your eyes were full of tears. I remember it well. The vase, too. It was white, with blue flowers.
> Alexander: That's right! She does remember! But those tears meant nothing. I had something in my eye. It hurt so, I didn't think I'd get through the performance.
> Adelaide (actress wife of Alexander): Alexander was superb as Prince Myshkin. That role *made* you.

See Tarkovsky (1999, 526–527).

9 In her work *Filmästhetik des Fluiden*, Franziska Heller examines the important function of fluid, that is, water, in Tarkovsky's mise-en-scène, particularly in the film *Stalker*. Heller observes a 'flooded labyrinth'

(*geflutete Labyrinthe*) between the subject's inside and outside, which seems to suggest an enigmatic, transitory extension of the Self into the outer space of nature.

> 'So heißt es dann auch bemerkenswerterweise über *Stalker*: 'There is so much water in this Film.' Im Folgenden wird es darum gehen, wie mittels der offensichtlichen Präsenz von Wasser, der besonderen audiovisuellen Medialität von Wassertropfen, *Raumdiffusionen*, insbesondere zwischen Eindrücken von Innen und Außen, als *paradoxe Polarität* generiert werden.' (Heller 2010, 86)
> Translation: In the following, it will be about how spatial diffusions, especially between impressions of inside and outside, are generated as a paradoxical polarity by means of the obvious presence of water, of the special audiovisual mediality of water drops.

10

THE LOST OBJECT: TRUTH IN AUTOBIOGRAPHY

Rachit Anand

Introduction

Travelling in a labouring bus across the Swartberg Pass, a boy releases a sweet wrapper into the vastness of the Karoo Valley. The valiant flight of the sweet wrapper into the depths of the abyss gives it a form—it takes the shape of a vessel that contains within it a scrap of paper the boy once held in his grasp. He leans back to catch the last glimpse before the sweet wrapper dissolves into the rugged background. He thinks all the time about this wrapper, 'alone in all that vastness' (Coetzee 1998, 31). He must revisit the Swartberg Pass one day and retrieve the scrap of paper, he tells himself. This task is his duty, and 'he may not die until he has done it' (31).

Before we say anything about this seemingly absurd 'duty' that the protagonist in Coetzee's autobiographical novel *Boyhood* (1998) takes upon himself, we must first acknowledge that this scene is shrouded in layers of obscurities. First, let us consider that this memory follows a game of 'reckless intimacy' within the narrative, that the boy, John, plays with his friends to recount their first memories (Coetzee 1998, 30). This is the 'other first memory' that he withholds from his friends but reveals to the readers (30). Secondly, glaring factual inconsistencies are woven into Coetzee's three-part autobiographical project, easily verifiable through public records (Attridge 2004, 160; Cardoen 2014, 101).[1] Lastly, the narrative voice in the first two of Coetzee's three autobiographical novels speaks in the third-person present tense, making it impossible to tell if the narrator and the protagonist are indeed the same person. How do we, then, assess the truth about the Self in these presumably autobiographical texts?

Should we read these texts as works of fiction with no bearing on the author's life? I suggest that such an approach would entail effacing the autobiographical traces that these texts carry despite their fictional posturing. Neither can we overlook the fictional texture of these texts due to their autobiographical posturing. Instead, the suggestion that these texts carry the 'truth' about the author's life despite their fictional structure requires a more thorough consideration. However, the paradigm of layers underneath which we will eventually find the kernel of truth is perhaps not well suited for this study. Instead of extracting the truth by unmasking layers of fiction, I propose to pay closer attention to the layers of fiction themselves that operate under the pretense that the more you uncover them, the closer you come to the truth. Being receptive to the 'logic of the fictive' would open a way to conceptualise the pretext on which the problematics of truth in Coetzee's autobiography operate. Put differently, the truth will not become accessible by lifting a veil, but the veil itself will be studied as the device sustaining the problematics of truth.

We take such an approach not because we aim to decode the fiction so that the encoded message about the author's personal life will be revealed at the end. Instead, we seek to engage the problematics of truth in autobiography, which invariably leads to a gap within the space of the fictive, perhaps in language itself. Each time the text crescendos towards the revelation of a 'secret' or the 'truth' about the protagonist that the autobiographical text promises to lay bare, we encounter a gap that cannot be filled by any amount of narrative dexterity. We wish to explore an encounter with this gap that surfaces as a missing piece within the metonymical web of fictiveness. The logic of the autobiographical novel hinges on this epistemological gap that marks a limit—the cause of the author's shame—at which point the text tries to symbolically encapsulate something beyond its reach. However, this impossible task is the 'duty' of an autobiographical text, and, as absurd as it may sound, the text remains incomplete without fulfilling it. Thus, this chapter aims to ascertain if there is indeed a topology of the Self whose outline can be drawn via the medium of autobiography. Or, is autobiography, perhaps like all other expressions of the Self, merely a mechanical device that produces a fiction of the Self to sustain its own endless continuum ad infinitum without ever arriving at an experience that stands beside the fictive?

Rethinking the Autobiographical Pact

To start, it would help to go over some conventional arguments about the genre of autobiography and the stakes involved in neatly demarcating a territory, separate from fiction per se, for it. Perhaps, the most cited name in the studies on autobiography is the French essayist Philippe Lejeune. In his work *On Autobiography*, he defines autobiography as a 'retrospective prose narrative written by a real person concerning his own existence, where the focus is his individual life, in particular the story of his personality' (1989, 4). On the face of it, the first two parts of Coetzee's three autobiographical novels meet the requirements of this definition.[2] Lejeune's ground conditions for identifying a text as autobiographical are balanced on the meeting point of three axes, namely the 'author', the 'narrator' and the 'principal character'. Their point of convergence is the idea of a *selfsame identity* that constitutes the 'autobiographical pact' (5). Lejeune asserts, 'In order for there to be autobiography (and personal literature in general), the *author*, the *narrator*, and the *protagonist* must be identical' (5). Moreover, without taking an explicit recourse to a higher order that can testify to the presence of this identity—divine or legal, for instance—Lejeune avows that 'an identity is, or is not. It is impossible to speak of degrees, and all doubt leads to a negative conclusion' (5). It is worthwhile to pause at this affirmation of identity by Lejeune.

Paul de Man terms Lejeune's insistence on the verifiability of identity as both 'exemplary', because of its thoroughness, and 'stubborn', because 'it does not seem to be founded in argument or evidence' (1984, 71). Contra Lejeune, for de Man, identity, even the proper name on the title page of the book, is grounded in the terrain of the tropological. To assume a voice, even, and especially the autobiographical voice, assumes a mouth, an eye and finally a face—a metonymical chain that culminates in *prosopopeia*, that is, the assumption of a voice by an inanimate creature (76). The voice, for de Man, crafts the face and not the other way around. Thus, autobiography does not so much testify to the emergence of the face, that is, a verifiable person. Instead, for de Man, it lays bare the de-facement or the *prosopoeic-ness* of its identity.[3] Even though de Man's insights on autobiography allow us to move past Lejeune's strained categories resolutely, I wish to linger on Lejeune's 'stubborn' insistence a little longer to weigh its political implications and to emphasise the larger stakes of this conception of Self in autobiography.

In the final analysis, then, where does Lejeune ground his insistence on identity's verifiability? Carefully avoiding a direct invocation of the Law, Lejeune answers: 'A person whose existence is certified by *vital statistics* and is verifiable' (1989, 11; emphasis mine). There is a particular method of verification to which Lejeune is appealing to 'certify' the identity of a person, which needs to be fleshed out. Is there indeed a topology of the subject operative outside the text through which the identity of 'the author', 'the narrator' and 'the protagonist' can be grounded as one? The reason I emphasise this point is not simply to highlight the lacuna in Lejeune's reasoning but because the pseudo-ontological ground upon which Lejeune implants the tripartite structure as a single 'verifiable' entity reveals something more insidious about South Africa's fraught relationship with the history of identification—a relationship that is not just relevant but is perhaps the most prominent feature of Coetzee's body of work.[4] 'Vital statistics', as it surfaces in Lejeune's final analysis of autobiography, resonates with the statistical technologies that the South African state employed for racial segregation (Lejeune 11). The myth of a *selfsame identity* avows to seal the gap in the conception of a Self that Coetzee's fiction and non-fiction most resolutely expose.

The 19th-century British statistician Sir Francis Galton (Charles Darwin's half-cousin, who repurposed the theory of evolution into eugenics), provided the 'scientific' basis and the tools to conceptualise 'vital statistics' in the first place, and without wasting a breath, he set the engines of segregation in South Africa into motion. His early 'explorations' in South Africa between 1850 and 1852 and his role in the birth of biometrics through the invention of fingerprinting, first brought to use in Africa and India, have not been sufficiently explored. Interestingly, the critical resource to ascertain the ideological basis for the invention of fingerprinting is Galton's own autobiography, *Narrative of an Explorer in Tropical South Africa*—a mode of writing that his life's efforts dismiss as an 'unreliable' account of one's Self. In *Biometric State: Global Politics of Identification and Surveillance in South Africa, 1850 to the Present*, Keith Breckenridge notes, 'For Galton Africans lived in a world which required an entirely new set of rules' (2014, 49). Legibility through writing was thus disallowed to the people of Africa, and in place of expressivity through the written word, biological verifiability was taken as a prerequisite for conceiving a civilisational horizon in these lands that Galton had vouched to have seen intimately.

For the purposes of this discussion, it is important to foreground the incompatibility between the ideality of identity as it gets straightjacketed via indexical technologies such as fingerprinting, on the one hand, and the emergence of the subject through the narrative form in an autobiography, on the other. An insistence on biological verification for identity—whether it is in the form of a 'verifiable pact' between the reader and the author that Lejeune encourages or Galton's mistrust for 'writing and legibility' that led to the invention of biometrics—is finally aimed at bypassing the slow engagement with the *infinite task* of reading to recover that which is irredeemably lost at the very sight of its inception, that is, an objective means to affirm one's identity. An engagement with this sight of loss, that is, an invocation of the resonances of the object that has fallen out of the subject's grasp when it finds itself in the web of language, requires further consideration.[5] Only through a slow assessment of the written word can one gather a sense of that which the autobiographical mode in Coetzee's novels is geared towards recovering (however, this task can proceed in earnestness only under the aegis of the 'painful knowledge' that this recovery will remain incomplete and utterly unverifiable but through the mechanisms of truth in fiction).[6]

However, if reading is unverifiable, it does not mean that fingerprinting offers a more secure ground to affirm one's identity. At the other end of this spectrum between language and biology exists a 'paper processing machine' of the State that must hold the capacity to sift through towering annals of data to lay a claim on full knowledge of identities (Breckenridge 2014, 7). The history of the ruthless application of *Bewsboek*, the 'internal passports' that every non-white South African had to carry with them while travelling through non-segregated areas, shows the cataclysmic failure of an enterprise of this nature. Even though the historical roots of identification via 'vital statistics' in South Africa is a story of its failure, this does not mean that its success would have been any more proof of its capacity to ascertain the ideality of identity. At no point does the 'paper processing machine' of the State converge with the human experience of reading a life story. To assume ahistorical reliability on 'vital statistics' that can affirm the author's identity from outside the text is based on a fabrication of the State's capacity to give a complete account of its citizens. Moreover, this insistence, or the 'stubbornness,' on biology to ascertain the subject's identity has shown an unmistakable tendency towards mutating into forms of segregation based on biological markers.

Shame and the Writing Machine

If the identity of the author of the autobiography cannot be grounded through biological verification of a 'living person' outside the text, then what other conceptual apparatus is available to us for thinking through this problematic? In the absence of religious absolution, the shame associated with the act of confession in secular autobiographical narratives often surfaces as a limit concept through which the 'truth' about the author's life is ascertained. However, for this to be true, shame would have to offer some form of absolution—a judgement on truth—if it is to take the place of a religious confession in a secular world. The frustrating incapacity of shame to provide such absolution is not a new concern for Coetzee. In 1985, he published an essay titled 'Confession and Double Thoughts: Tolstoy, Rousseau, Dostoevsky', which was in cautious agreement with Paul de Man's reading of Rousseau's *Confessions* in 'Excuses (*Confessions*)', the final chapter of *Allegories of Reading* (1979).[7] In this essay, Coetzee undermines the sanctity of shame to verify the truth underlying an act of confession. Arriving at this conclusion from different directions, both de Man and Coetzee posit that the hidden pleasure—the desire to be publicly shamed—that the confessant derives from the experience of shame itself produces new layers of shame that follow through in an endless regression towards the impossibility of ever reaching a point of absolution. This idea becomes clear from this passage on Dostoevsky in Coetzee's essay:

> Self-consciousness will not give him the answer, for self-consciousness in *Notes from Underground* is a disease. What is diseased about it is that it feeds upon itself, finding behind every motive another motive, behind every mask another mask, until the ultimate motive, which must remain masked (otherwise the endless regression would be ended, the disease would be cured). We can call this ultimate motive the *motive for unmasking* itself. (Coetzee 1992, 280)

At the bottom of all the unmasking—layer after layer of peeling through the shame—Coetzee diagnoses a perverse auto-generative 'motive for unmasking' (280). The more an author confesses, the more shame he experiences for having confessed, and thus, the more he writes. The production of shame is tied to the very entity that experiences shame—the act of confession of shame is by itself producing more shame.[8]

However, if the mask can never be truly removed to reveal the underlying *thing*, then does that square with the assertion that there was no-thing to be retrieved in the first place? In an oversimplified form, this can be understood as Paul de Man's answer to the problem. I do not disagree with de Man's larger synthesis of the endless regression of the language of confession as one that 'metonymizes the metaphor' (de Man 1979, 292). However, there is a gap, a split and a *vigil* for that, which precedes the metaphor, and whose position is held by the 'extra metaphor' that always extracts itself from the field, that is, the metaphor of metaphor.[9] Within the space of the fictive, that gap opens up in the instance of shame (not just of the character in the text but the shame of the text itself) around which the metonymical structuration of language orbits but which, by itself, is not *metonymisable*. So much is discernable also from Derrida's commentary on de Man's 'Excuses (*Confessions*)' in 'Typewriter Ribbon' (2002).[10] In this essay, originally delivered as a lecture, Derrida problematises the use of the anglicised French term *à propos* in the title of a conference on Paul de Man. Bringing his reading of de Man in conversation with this use of the term *à propos*, Derrida writes:

> When one writes 'à propos,' it is because one is at least pretending to leap at an opportunity to speak, metonymically, of something else

> altogether, to change the subject without changing the subject.... *And yet one knows that, at that very moment, one touches on the essential, one at least brushes against the place of decision. That is where the thing happens, that is where it comes about.* (2002, 76–77; emphasis mine)

This *happening* of the thing, the moment of decision, is what is at stake in the event of shame—it is the event of the allegorical transfiguration of an autobiographical text into an encounter with the author's lack. What surfaces here is the encounter with the Other that the author can never thoroughly metonymise into a mechanical momentum of the contraption called fiction. This moment presents itself before the readers as a task, not ontological or hermeneutic as de Man rightly underlines, but *ethical*.

To demonstrate the reverberations of this task, we may recall the event of shame—the gap that remains insuperable despite the barrels of ink spent on it—in Book II of Rousseau's *Confessions*. To quickly recall the details of this scene: A sixteen-year-old Rousseau is caught with a ribbon that he stole from his employers to gift to his co-worker, Marion (1953, 86–89). When asked to explain how he came to possess the said ribbon, he accuses Marion of having stolen the ribbon and gifting it to him instead (87). De Man asserts, 'What Rousseau *really* wanted is neither the ribbon nor Marion, but the public scene of exposure which he actually gets' (that is, by writing about this episode in *Confessions*; 1979, 285; emphasis in the original). Finally, for de Man, 'shame is primarily exhibitionistic' (285). About Marion, de Man does not have much to say. He writes:

> 'Marion' is meaningless and powerless to generate by itself the chain of causal substitutions and figures that structures the surrounding text, which is a text of desire as well as desire for text. It stands entirely out of the system of truth, virtue, and understanding (or of deceit, evil, and error) that gives meaning to the passage, and to *Confessions* as a whole. (289)

De Man forecloses any possibility of hearing Marion's voice through Rousseau's text— 'she stands *entirely* out of the system'—and in any case, he deprives her of exerting any weight on the epistemological fabric of Rousseau's text. However, Derrida points out the absence of Marion's voice not only in Rousseau's text but in the archives of autobiography as well: 'Will one ever know what she was able or might have been able to think, feel, love, hate, understand, or not understand about what was happening to her?' (2002, 123).

Let us momentarily take up this task since this is what Coetzee implores us to do in his contribution to the genre of autobiography that he inherits from Rousseau among others. We get a final statement from Marion in Rousseau's text to help us recreate at least a semblance of her presence or, at the very least, assess the effect of her absence from Rousseau's text and life. Marion's voice, in the final analysis, may just produce the *meaning* and *power* to 'generate by itself the chain of causal substitutions and figures that structures the surrounding text' (de Man 1979, 289). She says, 'Oh, Rousseau, I thought you were a good fellow. You make me very sad, *but I should not like to be in your place*' (Rousseau 1953, 87; emphasis mine). Within Rousseau's autobiography, Marion does not leave the scene without leaving her mark on the text. A curtain falls on what happens to Marion after she is terminated from her employment: 'I do not know what happened to the victim of my calumny, but she could not have possibly found it easy to get a good situation after that' (87). However, she does not leave the scene without introducing a palpitating absence in Rousseau's entire confessional narrative: 'but I should not like to be in your place' (87). Rousseau's confession is haunted by Marion, who *chooses* to withdraw herself from the mechanical output of this text. Does Rousseau's writing machine not receive its very purpose from this act of withdrawal? Hasn't Rousseau built the entire edifice of his confessional machine on an absence whose rigour even he could not help but retain in his narrative?

Sustaining the weight of this absence—giving it the meaning and power to structure the surrounding text—is, in the final analysis, *the* most quintessential feature of Coetzee's corpus. Indeed, the lingering murmur of the withdrawn voice is the source of its allegorical impulse—that is, its 'other' voice (*allos agoreuein*). The switch of focus from Rousseau to Marion is the happening of allegory— 'that is where the *thing* happens' (Derrida 2002, 77). Coetzee not only re-stages a version of this episode in his autobiography but, moreover, by paying attention to these gaps—Rousseau's shame and Marion's voice—he gestures towards the inadequacy of the form of autobiography to overcome this shame.

In the second instalment of Coetzee's autobiographical novels, *Youth,* we follow John from South Africa to London, where he takes employment as a programmer for IBM, but his true motive is to become a poet following in the footsteps of T.S. Eliot and Ezra Pound (Coetzee 2003, 20). After finally quitting his job at IBM, he decides to focus all his attention on writing (116). He temporarily becomes a caretaker for a flat in Swiss Cottage to make ends meet (118). The owner's daughter and a Malawian nanny, Theodora, will be staying with him as a part of the contract (118). During this time, he receives the news that his cousin Ilse and her friend will visit London (125). A few days later, he receives a phone call, not from Ilse but from her friend (126). In broken

English, she informs him that Ilse has been admitted to a nursing home with pneumonia (126–127). At the nursing home, the friend's name is finally introduced into the text: 'Marianne' (127). The silence of Marion and her withdrawal from the scene in Rousseau's text is reinscribed in Coetzee's autobiography, testifying that the archive to which he is contributing is inconceivable without this silence.

Marianne is a twenty-one-year-old student who is studying social work in South Africa. In his mind, John thinks, 'Social work—helping old women with their shopping—is not a subject a proper university would teach' (Coetzee 2003, 128). He takes her out for a walk by the Thames and to watch a Godard movie, which she barely understands, before bringing her back to the flat he is looking after at the moment. 'He kisses her; she does not mind being kissed' (128). However, soon, it is revealed: 'Marianne is a virgin. He finds out when at last he has her naked in the big double bed. He has never slept with a virgin before, has never given a thought to virginity as a physical state' (129). Thus, Marianne bleeds while they are in the act and continues bleeding later (129). 'They have been—the vision comes to him distastefully—wallowing in blood like pigs,' notes the narrator (129). Moreover, the bleeding does not stop, and Marianne must sleep with a soggy towel between her legs (129). The scene next morning is equally important:

> He strips off the bedclothes. The blood has soaked through the mattress, leaving a huge, uneven stain. Guiltily, angrily, he heaves the mattress over. Only a matter of time before the stain is discovered. He must be gone by then, he will have to make sure of that. (129)

He calls a taxi and puts a pound note in Marianne's hand. The last we hear from her is: 'I have got my own money' (130). Following this episode, there is a Rousseauesque exhibition of shame: 'He deserves to be slapped in the face, even to be spat on' (130). He knows that in the absence of someone to 'administer' the slap, he will continue to 'gnaw away at himself'—'*Agenbyte of inwit*' (130). Soon the focus shifts to how this new depth of shame can perhaps help him become a better writer: 'Perhaps the real depths are different, and come in unexpected form: in a flare-up of nastiness against a girl in the early hours of the morning' (131). However, this de Manian breakthrough moment is interrupted by a letter, not from Marianne but from his cousin Ilse. The letter does not have a transformative effect on John. However, the contents of the letter make an attentive reader aware beyond a shadow of a doubt that this episode has an entirely different position that has withdrawn itself from the scene, reminiscent of Marion's statement: 'but I should not like to be in your place'. Ilse writes:

> Dear John, I thought I should let you know that I am OK. Marianne is OK too.... She doesn't want to write, but I thought I would write anyway, to say I hope you don't treat all your girls like that, even in London. Marianne is a special person, she doesn't deserve that kind of treatment. You should think twice about the life you lead. Your cousin, Ilse. (131)

John has no means to cope with this letter but to retract into the contraptions of mechanical thinking: '*I am hard enough on myself*, he tells himself; *I don't need the help of others*. It is a sophistry he falls back on time and again' (Coetzee 2003, 132). This sophistry leads him to think that he can absolve himself of the guilt by shaming himself through his art. That, if a woman has to truly fall in love with him, then it can only be through his art: 'Until that woman arrives, until that day of destiny, he is merely passing his time. This is why Marianne can be ignored' (134). However, can Marianne/Marion be ignored in the signifying force of Coetzee's and Rousseau's autobiographies? Coetzee's fiction implores us to confront the meaning-making power of these absences within the genre of Western autobiography. John's shame is not limited to the contraption through which he can play at the game of absolution all by himself. Shame exceeds the person carrying it. It is not absolved through an 'excuse'—confession entails a position from which forgiveness can be granted or mourning for the loss can be undertaken. The allegorical thrust of Coetzee's fiction allows the reader access to a world where this position has been vacated and the webs of signification are swirling around an absence, a shame that refuses to be absolved through the text within which it is inscribed.

To close this section, I cite another passage from Paul de Man's 'Excuses (*Confessions*)'. This passage is *exemplary* in its insight about loss as the central problematic of the 'genre' of autobiography, but perhaps, it is just as *stubborn* in its insistence on not allowing a non-illusory basis for truth in autobiography. De Man writes,

> The text as body, with all its implications of substitutive tropes ultimately always retraceable to metaphor, is displaced by the text as machine and, in the process, it suffers the loss of *illusion* of the meaning.... This threatens the autobiographical subject not as the loss of something that once was present and that it once possessed, but as a radical estrangement between the meaning and the performance of any text. (1979, 298; emphasis mine)

Thus, in the final turn of this essay, I now explore the central problematic of loss of something that, as de Man aptly puts it, is always retraceable to metaphor. However, I seek to explore if that loss is 'the loss of an *illusion* of meaning' or of *meaning* itself—the entire problematic is captured in that subtle distinction (1979, 298).

The Lost Object

Before we revisit the scene of the loss of the sweet wrapper in *Boyhood* one last time, it will be helpful to retrace our steps so far. First, we ascertained that grounding the truth about the identity of the author through extra-textual means feeds into the perverse logic of a 'paper processing machine'. The 'paper processing machine' not only auto-destructs itself in the face of towering annals of data, but more importantly, it effaces the expressivity of the written word itself. Then, it was argued that in autobiographies, shame is not only a 'subjective emotion' but holds a structural place in between two instantiations of the Self, that is, experience and expression.[11] Thus, an autobiography was understood as an exploration of this gap, the shame, and the incoherence between the experience and the expression of the Self.

However, Paul de Man argues that the shame arising from this incoherence is the very force that perpetuates the mechanical movement of an autobiography (1979, 294). The act of confession, according to de Man, creates more shame and, thus, more fodder for future confession (299). However, I argued that the thesis of autobiography as a self-perpetuating writing machine fails to uphold the *vigil* for the 'extra metaphor', the metaphor of metaphor, that always escapes the metonymical/mechanical momentum of the text. Thus, at odds with de Man, I stipulate that the autobiographical text is an exploration of the loss of the 'extra metaphor' that has evaded the text. This loss calls upon the reader to be vigilant of the inadequacy of the text to fulfil its autobiographical function. Transmitting this inadequacy of form within the narrative space is the defining characteristic of Coetzeean allegory. Due to the very structure of this inadequacy, the symbolic operations of metaphors can only sustain the resonances of loss but never recuperate it.

A metaphor can only signal towards an object but never adequately name it; thus, it remains susceptible to being interpreted as just another metaphor in the mechanical output of the text. However, this inadequacy of the form of metaphor to represent its desired object presents itself as an ethical task for the readers. A de Manian recourse to thorough mechanisation of this operation forecloses the possibility of forming an ethical relationship with this scene of loss. The only recourse one has to gather a sense of the identity of the author of an autobiography is by undertaking this ethical task. What story, in the final analysis, does Coetzee, a white colonial settler in South Africa, seek to tell about himself? How does the form he has at his disposal, that is, Western autobiography, remain inadequate to tell this story? Let us revisit *Boyhood* to explore this question further.

In *Boyhood,* one day, in a mood of 'reckless intimacy,' John initiates a game with his friends, Greenberg and Goldstein, 'to bring out their earliest memories' (Coetzee 1998, 30). As we soon find out, the purpose of the game is for the boy to narrate one of his memories that would be a far superior artefact than what his friends 'can dredge up' (30). Greenberg refuses to participate in this game, while Goldstein shares a mundane story about a visit to the beach (30). John has prepared a 'magnificent' memory about a 'small, spotted dog' who accidentally runs in front of a car that comes racing out of the distance (30). The boy fills the scene with precise details: the wheels of the car 'go right over the dog's middle' (30). With its hind legs paralysed the dog drags itself away, squealing with pain' (30).

In the following paragraph, however, the super-egoic voice of the narrator raises concerns about the authenticity of this recollection: 'But is it true?... Is it possible that he saw nothing but a dog dragging its hindquarters and made up the car and the driver and the rest of the story?' (Coetzee 1998, 30). Thus, the text implicitly warns the readers that for a story to be serviceable, it must carry the guilt of fabrication. The text presented before us is effacing the 'truth' by fabricating details that are not indigenous to the author's life. This concern is echoed even more strongly by the fictional biographer, Mr Vincent, who is out to 'recover' Coetzee's life story after his presumed death in the third installment of his autobiographical novels, *Summertime*. When one of his interviewees, Sophie, objects to the biographer's method of relying exclusively on interviews rather than Coetzee's writing, his defence takes recourse to this argument: 'What Coetzee writes there cannot be trusted, not as a factual record—not because he was a liar but because he was a fictioneer.... If you want the truth you have to go behind the fictions' (225–226). Mr Vincent's desire to go 'behind the fictions' to retrieve the 'truth' about the dead author is central to understanding the problematics of truth in Coetzee's autobiographies (226). Despite the warnings about the fabrication of details about the events narrated in these novels, they remain the only material at our disposal to discuss the problem of truth in autobiography. The staging of the pitfalls in going 'behind the fictions' in *Summertime* soon after the publication of Coetzee's biography by J.C. Kannemeyer is a clear indication that we are looking in the wrong place if we wish to get to know the author through sources from outside the text (Kannemeyer 2012).[12] However, if these stories are fabricated, as we know they are, then what relationship can be sought between these fabrications and the truth in autobiography?

To this end, let us explore the 'other first memory', which the boy does not share with his friends but is revealed to the readers. As was the case with the previous memory about the 'small, spotted dog', the actual first memory also accentuates the details. The narrator first establishes the scene: 'He is sitting beside his mother in a bus. It must be cold, for he is wearing red woollen leggings and a woollen cap with a bobble. The engine of the bus labours; they are ascending the wild and desolate Swartberg Pass' (Coetzee 1998, 30–31). 'In his hand,' we are told, 'is a sweet wrapper' (31). The focus of the memory is then narrowed down to a specific action: 'He holds the wrapper out of the window, which is open a crack. It flaps and trembles in the wind' (31). 'Shall I let go,' he asks his mother, and she nods (31). Next, the boy releases the wrapper into the depths of the Swartberg Pass (31). The sweet wrapper flies in and out of the narrative space to make the reader believe that it is indeed the 'real' first memory:

> The scrap of paper flies up into the sky. Below there is nothing but the grim abyss of the pass, ringed with cold mountain-peaks. Craning backwards, he catches a last glimpse of the paper, still bravely flying.
>
> 'What will happen to it?' he asks his mother; but she does not comprehend. (30–31)

The craft of fictioneering, as Mr Vincent would have said, indubitably plays a prominent part in this recollection. If the narrative only indicated towards a concealed first memory of a sweet wrapper released from a bus, perhaps it would not carry the same metaphorical weight as it does in the passage quoted here. The metaphor of the sweet wrapper is metonymised through the narrative emphasising the labouring bus going uphill, struggling to keep pace with the growing weight of the metaphor escalating towards the uncharted height of its metonymical sublimity. The sweet wrapper is evidently a metaphor for J.M. Coetzee's sense of loss and mourning that he accumulated growing up in the Karoo, the desert region underlying the Swartberg Pass. But it is a metaphor nonetheless.

A metaphor cannot act in isolation—its metaphorical power must be sustained through its metonymisation in the form of a narrative. The loss of the sweet wrapper in the depths of the Karoo and the promise of its recovery is a metaphor for the autobiographical project that Coetzee has undertaken. However, does this transformation of an originary sense of loss cause it to shed all associations it may have to the primary event of entering the terrain of language, that is, of metaphoricity? Quite certainly, language cannot recuperate that whose absence is the ground condition for its functioning. No path leads from a metaphor back to that from which it originated, no matter how high on the axis of metonymy it reaches. However, this does not permit us to conclude, as de Man does, that any such link is illusory (de Man 1979, 293). The sense of loss to which this metonymised metaphor of the sweet wrapper bears witness is the procession through which language sustains the absent presence of the truth of an allegedly pre-linguistic entity that escapes the webs of signification by definition. This is a form of loss whose resonances allegorical thought sustains but one that it can never recover. However, this impossible task of recovery, almost pathologically, guides Coetzee's autobiographical project.

The narrative voice delivers this message: 'He thinks all the time about the scrap of paper, alone in all that vastness, that he abandoned while he should not have abandoned it' (Coetzee 1998, 31). Furthermore, the abandoned sweet wrapper does not dissolve into its metonymisation: 'One day he must go back to Swartberg Pass and find and rescue it. That is his duty: he may not die until he has done it' (31). Thus, when the metaphorical gesture towards an impossible task is written into the autobiography, it not only fabricates the author's life but turns it inside out. A metaphor lost in the regressing depths of metonymy is the only recourse for the author to tell the truth about himself, that is, the reason he writes anything at all. In other words, the only mode in which truth can emerge in autobiography is as an allegory of something that, by definition, escapes language. If the missing object could be symbolically expressed as itself, then we would not need metaphors, metonymy or allegory—all figures of speech would get contracted into that single expression, whose loss gives birth to the drama of the Self.

Coda

Boyhood is riddled with several such impossible promises. In a double gesture towards the past where the loss occurred, they also open the possibility of a future where the recovery must take place. However, it cannot be emphasised enough that this recovery is of the order of the impossible. Nonetheless, by allegorically sustaining its radiance, it enables historical progression towards an opening into the future always in the making. To better grasp this opening, we may look at another instance of an 'impossible promise' from the text.

In an unusual break from the present-tense narration of the text, the boy recollects a time in the past when a 'seven-year-old Coloured boy' named Eddie came to work for them from Ida's Valley, a province near Stellenbosch. After two months of working with them, Eddie runs away.

When a British renter in the Coetzee household named Trevelyan finds him hiding in the bushes along the Liesbeeck River, he takes it upon himself to punish Eddie for all the trouble. The boy remembers peeking in as Trevelyan 'was holding Eddie by the two wrists and flogging him on the bare legs with a leather strap.... Eddie howled and danced; there were tears and snot everywhere' (Coetzee 1998, 74). The boy doesn't tell anyone, but he believes that he owes a debt to Eddie because Eddie taught him how to balance a bicycle (75). The boy remembers wrestling with Eddie, who always won over the boy but was nonetheless 'cautious in victory' (75). Eddie held the boy down only for a moment and allowed himself a 'grin of victory' before rolling over and getting ready for the next bout. The boy thinks about Eddie in Ida's Valley. He ruminates that at this moment, he is ten years old, while Eddie, in Ida's Valley, is ten years old too. However, soon Eddie will turn eleven, while the boy will remain ten. Then eventually, he will turn eleven as well. They will stay the same age for a while. Then Eddie will again leave him behind. 'How long will this go on?' he wonders. 'Will he ever escape from Eddie?' (77). The debt he owes to Eddie will forever outgrow the boy's capacity to repay it. He knows that the task of pulling level with Eddie is impossible. However, he must keep alive the hope that one day he will, in earnestness, get to level with Eddie. In this ever-shifting but ultimately insuperable gap between Eddie and John, perhaps we can catch a flickering glimpse of truth about the author in Coetzee's autobiography.

References

Adams, Henry. (1907) 1973. *The Education of Henry Adams*. Edited by Ernest Samuels. Boston: Houghton Mifflin Company.

Attridge, Derek. 2004. *J.M. Coetzee and the Ethics of Reading: Literature in the Event*. Chicago: The University of Chicago Press.

Attwell, David. 2015. *J.M Coetzee and The Life of Writing: Face-to-Face with Time*. New York: Viking Press.

Benjamin, Walter. (1925) 2019. *Origin of the German Trauerspiel*. Translated by Howard Eiland. Cambridge, Massachusetts: Harvard University Press.

Bewes, Timothy. 2011. *The Event of Postcolonial Shame*. New Jersey: Princeton University Press.

Blanchot, Maurice. 1995. 'Gazes from Beyond the Grave.' In *The Work of Fire*, translated by Charlotte Mandell, 244–255. Stanford: Stanford University Press.

Boehmer, Elleke. 2016. 'Reading Between Life and Work: Reflections on "J.M. Coetzee".' *Textual Practice* 30 (3): 435–450.

Breckenridge, Keith. 2014. *Biometric State: Global Politics of Identification and Surveillance in South Africa, 1850 to the Present*. Cambridge, United Kingdom: Cambridge University Press.

Cardoen, Sam. 2014. 'The Grounds of Cynical Self-Doubt: J.M. Coetzee's *Boyhood, Youth* and *Summertime*.' *Journal of Literary Studies* 30 (1): 94–112.

Coetzee, John Maxwell. 1974. *Dusklands*. London: Vintage Books.

———. 1983. *Life & Times of Michael K*. London: Vintage Books.

———. 1990. *Age of Iron*. London: Penguin Books.

———. 1992. *Doubling the Point: Essays and Interviews*, edited by David Attwell. Cambridge, Massachusetts: Harvard University Press.

———. 1996. 'Apartheid Thinking.' In *Giving Offense: Essays on Censorship*, 163–184. The Chicago: University of Chicago Press.

———. 1998. *Boyhood*. London: Vintage Books.

———. 1999. *Disgrace*. London: Vintage Books.

———. 2003. *Youth*. London: Vintage Books.

———. (1977) 2004. *In the Heart of the Country*. London: Vintage Books.

———. 2008. *Diary of a Bad Year*. London: Vintage Books.

———. 2009. *Summertime*. London: Vintage Books.

De Man, Paul. 1983. 'The Rhetoric of Temporality.' In *Blindness and Insight: Essays in the Rhetoric of Contemporary Criticism*, 187–228. 2nd edition. Minneapolis: University of Minnesota Press.

———. 1984. 'Autobiography as De-Facement.' In *The Rhetoric of Romanticism*, 67–82. New York: Columbia University Press.

———. 1979. 'Excuses (*Confessions*).' In *Allegories of Reading: Figural Language in Rousseau, Nietzsche, Rilke and Proust*, 278–301. New Haven: Yale University Press.

Derrida, Jacques. 1982. 'White Mythology: Metaphor in the Text of Philosophy.' In *The Margins of Philosophy*, translated by Alan Bass. Chicago: The University of Chicago Press.

———. 2002. 'Typewriter Ribbon: Limited Ink (2).' In *Without Alibi*, edited and translated by Peggy Kamuf, 71–160. Stanford: Stanford University Press.

Freud, Sigmund. (1914) 1981. 'On Narcissism: An Introduction.' In *The Standard Edition of the Complete Psychological Works of Sigmund Freud Volume XIV*, translated by James Strachey, 73–104. Hogarth Press.

———. (1917) 1981. 'Mourning and Melancholia.' In *The Standard Edition of the Complete Psychological Works of Sigmund Freud Volume XIV*, translated by James Strachey, 243–258. Hogarth Press.

Galton, Francis. 1891. *Narrative of an Explorer in Tropical South Africa*. Ward, Lock and Co. Accessed 27 March 2022. https://galton.org/books/south-west-africa/

Gasché, Rodolphe. 2014. 'The Eve of Philosophy: On "Tropic" Movements and Syntactic Resistance in Derrida's *White Mythology*.' In *Focus: Philosophy as Literature*, edited by Günter Figal, 1–22. Mohr Siebeck.

Kristeva, Julia. 1989. *Black Sun: Depression and Melancholia*. New York: Columbia University Press.

Lacan, Jacques. 1992. *The Ethics of Psychoanalysis: Seminar VII*. Translated by Dennis Porter. New York: W.W. Norton & Company.

Lejeune, Philippe. 1989. *On Autobiography*. Translated by Katherine Leary. Minneapolis: University of Minnesota Press.

Kannemeyer, J.C. 2012. *J.M. Coetzee: A Life in Writing*. Translated by Michiel Heyns. Melbourne: Scribe.

Rousseau, Jean-Jacques. 1953. *The Confessions of Jean-Jacques Rousseau*. Translated by J.M. Cohen. New York: Penguin Books.

Warminski, Andrzej. 2009. 'Machinal Effects: Derrida with and without de Man.' *MLN* (124) 5: 1072–1090.

Notes

1 Meta-textual references to Coetzee's family name also feature prominently in both parts of Coetzee's first novel, *Dusklands* (1974), and more obliquely in *Diary of a Bad Year* (2007). If anything, this is an indication that the intertwining of autobiography and fiction has informed Coetzee's writing beyond his autobiographical works. However, *Boyhood* (1994) and, successively, *Youth* (2002) and *Summertime* (2009) are more serious attempts by Coetzee to write within the parameters of the genre of autobiography. Interestingly, the American editions of these texts categorises them under 'autobiography', while the British edition labels them as 'fiction'. These three novels were later published together as one edition titled *Scenes from Provincial Life: Boyhood, Youth, Summertime* (2012).

2 The fact that the narrative voice in Coetzee's *Boyhood* and *Youth* is not in the first-person singular, 'I', thereby linking the narrator with the principal character through the use of the first-person pronoun, would not be a cause for Lejeune to declassify them as autobiographical texts. Lejeune asserts that the third-person voice in autobiographical texts does not work as the 'non-person' third entity as it does in everyday speech. Instead, in autobiographies, Lejeune stipulates, the third-person voice constitutes a 'figure' for the first-person singular (1989, 33). For another example of an autobiography in the third-person voice that may have influenced Coetzee, see Henry Adam's *The Education of Henry Adams* ([1907] 1973). The third-person voice in Coetzee's autobiographical texts is perhaps not reducible to a 'figure' for the first person (as it is for Lejeune). However, I do not develop its larger implications in this chapter. Nonetheless, a study that would pursue this link would have to take into account the rift between the principal character in the third person and the narrative voice as a formal textual manifestation of shame.

3 I am somewhat selectively quoting from Paul de Man's 'Autobiography as De-Facement', first published in *MLN* in 1979 and later republished in *The Rhetoric of Romanticism* (1984) in this section. All pagination is from the later print. De Man's larger concern in this essay is to assess the stature of autobiography among other 'literary genres'. In this assessment, he finds autobiography to be incompatible 'with the monumental dignity

of aesthetic values' due to, among other reasons, its reliance on potential verifiability of events in a 'less ambivalent way than fiction' (De Man 1984, 68). I engage with de Man's reading of Rousseau's *Confessions* in *Allegories of Reading* in greater detail in the next section.

4 Although, almost everything Coetzee writes responds in one way or another to the problematics of identity and race, a quick summary of the most relevant texts would include 'Apartheid Thinking', *Giving Offense* (1996, 163–185; other essays in this collection are also relevant); *Life & Times of Michael K* (1984); *In the Heart of the Country* (1977); *Age of Iron* (1990); *Disgrace* (1999) and *Dusklands* (1974). This is by no means a comprehensive list. Lectures, essays and interviews published in *Doubling the Point* (1992) are just as relevant.

5 I am borrowing the concept of the 'lost object' from two distinct sources: Walter Benjamin's *Origin of the German Trauerspiel* ([1925] 2019, 144, 179, 188, 258) and Jacques Lacan's *The Ethics of Psychoanalysis* (1992, 52, 05, 294). For a more theoretical treatment of this underexplored passage between Benjamin and Lacan, see Julia Kristeva, 'Beauty: The Depressive's Other Realm' (1989, 95–103). Sigmund Freud's 'Mourning and Melancholia' ([1917] 1981) and 'On Narcissism' ([1914] 1981) are also central to the growth of this concept in 20th-century thought.

6 I borrow the phrase 'painful knowledge' from Paul de Man's 'The Rhetoric of Temporality,' *Blindness and Insight* (1983, 207).

7 This chapter is a reprint of an earlier publication of the same essay under the title 'The Purloined Ribbon' in *Glyph I* (1977). All pagination refers to the print in *Allegories*.

8 We may also consider Maurice Blanchot's brilliant analysis of the same problematic in 'Gazes from Beyond the Grave', *The Work of Fire* (1995). He writes,

> There is a sin in confession that no confession can atone for, since it is committed by being avowed and is aggravated as soon as it is absolved: the offense here is linked to justification, innocence. Yet wanting this innocence is necessary, we cannot do without it, so that everything is an offense, both the avowal and refusal of avowal. Such is pretty much the category of the demonic of which Kierkegaard spoke. (247–248)

9 I am drawing on the use of the term 'extra-metaphor' in Jacques Derrida's 'White Mythology: Metaphor in the Text of Philosophy,' *Margins of Philosophy* (1982, 219–220). He writes, 'This extra metaphor, remaining outside the field that it allows to be circumscribed, extracts or abstracts itself from the field, thus subtracting itself as a metaphor less' (220). My reading of this essay is indebted to Rodolphe Gasché (2014).

10 Reprinted as 'Typewriter Ribbon: Limited Link (2)' in Derrida (2002, 71–160). The title of the conference organised at UC Davis in 1998 where this lecture was first delivered is 'Culture and Materiality: A Post-Millenarian Conference—à propos of Paul de Man's *Aesthetic Ideology*—To Consider

Trajectories for "Materialist" Thought in the Afterlife of Theory, Cultural Studies, and Marxist Critique.' For further discussion on this conference and Derrida's reading of de Man, see Andrzej Warminski (2009).

11 For further reading on shame as the 'inadequacy of form', see Timothy Bewes (2011, 9–48).

12 For a comparative analysis between Coetzee's autobiographies and Kannemeyer's biography, see Elleke Boehmer's essay 'Reading between Life and Work: Reflections on "J.M. Coetzee"' (2016). For a more critical analysis of Coetzee's life and context, see David Attwell's *J.M. Coetzee and the Life of Writing: Face-to-Face with Time* (2015).

11

THE MÖBIUS STRIP OF LITERATURE AND CRITICISM: GABRIEL JOSIPOVICI'S *MOO PAK*[1]

Anirudh Karnick

I

From the very beginning, that is, from the publication of his first novel, *The Inventory* (1968), and his first book of criticism, *The World and the Book* (1971), Gabriel Josipovici has written both fiction and criticism. Throughout, he has said that he is a novelist first, by need, and a critic second, by inclination (Josipovici 2006, 308–310; Best 2015). He has continued to write both fiction and criticism in near equal measure, however, and in my experience, readers have read his critical work more than his fiction.

The subjects of Josipovici's criticism range from the Bible, *Piers Plowman* and Dante's *Commedia* to Rabelais and Cervantes and 20th-century writers such as Proust, Eliot, Aharon Appelfeld and Muriel Spark, but he returns over and over to Modernism: that is, the question of what it is to make art in a disenchanted world or, as Robert Pippin puts it, 'art produced under the pressure of art having become a problem for itself, in a period when the point and significance of art could no longer be taken for granted' (2013, 1).

Modernism is an elastic term. It has been discussed thematically (urban alienation, the wars) or technically (experiments in typography, poetic diction and so on) It has been understood as a chronological span, roughly from the late 19th century to the Second World War in Western Europe. (A geographically more inclusive conception of Modernism would naturally require some modification of its chronology as well as certain characteristics we associate with the term.) What Josipovici

1 Thanks to Tanya Desai, Labanya Unni and Vikrant Dadawala for their reading of and comments on the essay and to Prasanta Chakravarty for his editorial comments and support.

means by it is both more capacious and more restricted. I will return to this. For now, here is one of Josipovici's descriptions of Modernism:

> The temptation is strong to date Modernism in that hundred-year period [between 1850 and 1950]. This is certainly when it flourished and when its manifestations were so prevalent that no-one could ignore it. The danger in seeing it like that, though, is that Modernism is thereby turned into a style, like Mannerism or Impressionism, and into a period of art history, like the Augustan or the Victorian age, and therefore as something that can be clearly defined and is safely behind us. I, on the other hand, want to argue that Modernism needs to be understood in a completely different way, as the coming into awareness by art of its precarious status and responsibilities, and therefore as something that will, from now on, always be with us. Seen in this way, Modernism, I would suggest, becomes a response by artists to that 'disenchantment of the world' to which cultural historians have long been drawing our attention. (Josipovici 2010, 11)

II

Both more capacious and stricter. The novels of Rabelais and Cervantes and Sterne's *Tristram Shandy* are as much a part of Josipovici's writing on the challenge of making art in modernity as Proust and Kafka. On the other hand, writers such as Pound and Apollinaire and much avant-garde and experimental literature leave him cold. What is the difference, for Josipovici, between Eliot and Pound or Proust and Joyce? Pound and Joyce believe in the value of the new; they are 'more innocently artifactual' than Eliot or Proust (Kelly 1989). Eliot or Proust continue to write even as they doubt the value of the enterprise, and this doubt is formative of their poetry and fiction (Kafka is an extreme case of this). For Josipovici, academic understandings of Modernism do not adequately register the relationship of modernists to writing—their strong sense of a calling to write, which they felt had no basis, and their sense of producing something new, an alienation from past literature, even literature per se. This sense was emblematised by comments such as Woolf's: 'I have an idea that I will invent a new name for my books to supplant 'novel'. A new ___ by Virginia Woolf. But what?' (Woolf 1925) Also, Beckett's meditation: 'When one listens to oneself, it's not literature that one hears' (Fort 2014, 5).

For Josipovici, nothing is given to the modern artist. In the past, art had a function—whether produced in courtly or religious settings. It does not any longer, but the artist's need to make remains. The loss of the social apparatus that justified art and of the conventions that directed its making is experienced, at first, as liberatory. In the past, artists were trained in specific conventions and worked and innovated within that ambit. For modern artists, however, conventions come to seem to be no longer a 'part of the natural scheme of things, but *impositions*, which no-one, having seen the truth, could ever submit to again' (Josipovici 1999, 147).

This devaluation of genre and genre conventions brings two urgent questions in its wake: How do we make art? And why make art at all? Many writers in the past two centuries have simply ignored these questions, doubting little the value of expressing oneself or telling stories or representing reality or—here, Josipovici parts company with many partisans of Modernism—making it new. Josipovici is interested in and nourished by the minority of artists who are exercised by these questions—artists in whose works these questions are present, not absent; and constitutive, rather than a mandatory off-ticking of the box, 'Metafiction'.

III

Unlike much criticism, which begins from the finished work of literature as if it had always already existed, he wishes to write with an implicit awareness of the work's coming-into-being. He is as interested in incomplete works—whether abandoned (Kafka's novels) or suppressed (Proust's *Jean Santeuil*)—as in completed ones, interested, that is, in the process, the possibility of failure and the provisionality of a particular success. I attribute this to his being both a critic and a writer. Josipovici is at pains in his criticism to not take the finished work for granted. However, his critical writing cannot but help represent the fraught process of writing, to some extent and despite itself, as the explication and appreciation of an already achieved success.

The introduction to *The Mirror of Criticism*, Josipovici's selected reviews from 1977 to 1982, begins: 'Why is the profoundest criticism to be found in the letters and incidental remarks of artists?' (Josipovici 1983, 1) Might this, Josipovici asks, be because these need not be substantiated and because the writer 'feels no inhibition about showing doubt ... changing his mind in mid-sentence and doing all those other natural things which the critical book or essay has somehow to pretend we are not subject to' (1). The transition from incidental remarks in letters and diaries to a review or a critical essay demands that the writer make an argument that is substantiated by evidence. So Josipovici continues, could one not counter that 'true criticism is precisely that which has ... thought through the implications of certain responses ... for that very reason, a deeper and richer thing than a passing comment in a letter or a journal' (1). Something is gained in substantiating one's remarks, no doubt, but more, Josipovici writes, is perhaps lost: 'What the letter conveys, and what the book or essay, however sensitively written, conceals, is the sense of an *encounter*' (1). Unlike the dispassionate voice we often find in literary criticism, a letter makes it clear that when we read, we are entangled with what we are reading. We don't stand above it.

Criticism may manifest anxiety, of course, but most attempts at experimental criticism come across as gimmicky. Its expression of uncertainty comes across as 'being yet another *device*' (Josipovici 1983, 8). Criticism 'by its very nature, however tactful or sensitive it may be, always presents us with the finished object, and it is helpless to show how it might very well not have been, or at what cost it has come to be what it is' (8).

IV

Josipovici is a practising novelist. How does he answer the two questions: How do we make art? And why make it at all?[1] Until *Contre-Jour: A Triptych after Pierre Bonnard* (1986), his eighth novel, Josipovici poses these questions in his criticism via other writers. The critic's relatively assured Self is separated from the writer's restive Self even if the latter's restiveness has a central place in the criticism. No doubt, the two questions are immanent in his fiction, but they are never posed in as many words. I suspect the tension of this separation comes to a head in the late 1980s. A second phase of Josipovici's career starts with *The Big Glass* (1991). From this point, the questions—Why write? Write how?—are constitutive of his fiction, stated more or less explicitly.

Some of these novels are structured in relation to artists who were exercised by these two questions—Marcel Duchamp in *The Big Glass* (1991), Arnold Schoenberg in *Everything Passes* (2006), the eccentric Sicilian composer Giacinto Scelsi in *Infinity: The Story of a Moment* (2012) and Josipovici himself in *Moo Pak* (1994). In none of these cases do the novels aim for biographical accuracy—the central character is never named Duchamp or Scelsi, and what we find written about him is an amalgam of actual biographical events or stated opinions, modifications of these actual events or opinions and much that is invented or drawn from elsewhere. In each of these instances, the form of the work is *periscopic*, W.G. Sebald's term for the narrative perspective in Thomas Bernhard's novels (Sebald quoted in Silverblatt 2007). That is, what we are reading is presented as the *transcription* of the speech of the chief character or protagonist by the narrator. So what we read is 'at one remove, at two removes, at two or three' (Silverblatt 2007).[2]

In *The Big Glass*, Harsnet is the (Duchamp-like) central character, now dead. We read his notes about art and life during the preparation of *The Big Glass* (an actual work by Duchamp, now in the Philadelphia Museum of Art), as his former fellow artist Goldberg, now a critic and teacher, types these notes together with his own notations and explanations in the margin. In *Infinity: The Story of a Moment*, we have the transcription of an extensive interview with Massimo, the former manservant of the (Scelsi-like) Sicilian nobleman and composer, Tancredo Pavone.[3] In *Moo Pak*, the narrator Damien Anderson recounts conversations between the (Josipovici-like) Jack Toledano and himself (Josipovici 1994).

V

Like several of Bernhard's novels, *Moo Pak* is a single paragraph (or unparagraphed). Within the logic of the novel, Damien Anderson is writing/transcribing what Jack Toledano said, and this writing/transcription is what we read. The novel begins: 'On Tuesday I received a note from Jack Toledano asking me to meet him today at the Star and Garter in Putney at the usual time, *wrote* Damien Anderson' (Josipovici 1994, 9; emphasis mine). It continues:

> I am used to these notes. Jack does not need to specify the time. If I cannot make it, he goes for a walk himself, but I always try to be there because there is nothing better than going for a walk with Jack Toledano. London is a walker's paradise, he says, but you have to know where to go.[4] (9)

Moo Pak is not well known. I cannot take it for granted that most readers of this chapter will have read the novel, nor even that a single reader who wishes to read it will be able to procure a copy of the English original—translations into other European languages are more easily available—without much difficulty (sans access to an excellent library). A detailed description of the novel is merited. The novel's periscopic narrative and its being a single paragraph (or unparagraphed) have been noted. What is *Moo Pak* about and what are other features of its organisation?

The novel is about two friends—Jack Toledano and Damien Anderson—walking and talking. Jack talks, Damien listens; what we read is Damien's recounting of what Jack said. The attributive 'wrote Damien Anderson' recurs throughout the novel, from page 1 to 151. Most of what we read is presented to us as what 'Jack said' (or as what 'he says'), but the narrator's presence, Damien's presence, is not 'perfunctory almost to the point of nonexistence' (Robertson 2021). As we saw in the opening of the book earlier, there are short passages written by Damien that are not presented to readers as transcriptions of what 'Jack said'. There are occasional descriptions (always brief) throughout of what Damien and Jack were doing—walking next to a lake, sitting and having a drink, standing in a queue—when Jack said a particular thing to Damien. (For example: 'Hopeless confusion, he said, hopeless confusion. We went into the café and joined the queue. There is a country somewhere, he said, somewhere between cynicism and idealism, waiting to be explored' [Josipovici 1994, 92].)

VI

The first reported/transcribed conversation is about the mechanics of writing and Toledano's preference for the typewriter.

> People are always trying to persuade me to give up my typewriter and adopt an Apple or a Mackintosh or a Toffee or something like that, he said as we walked over the Hampstead Heath last July.... You can play around with the sentences, they say, you can sit there and play with the words and the sentences. But I don't want to play with the words and sentences, he said, once I start playing with the words and sentences I will never be able to move forward at all and I will grow less and less sure which of the many possibilities is the one that will suit me best and then I will grow more and more unsure of what best means and of what I was trying to do in the first place ... that's why I gave up writing by hand and learned how to type. With a typewriter you have to go forward, you have to keep typing, and that was the saving of me. If I switched now to a word-processor, he said, I would be back where I started. (Josipovici 1994, 9–11)

In beginning with this conversation, we are immediately alerted to the physical process of writing and the choice involved (Which possibility works best? What does best mean?) in writing. Since the work does not stop with these remarks—this is an important effect of the lack of paragraph breaks—we do not experience it as making a tired point about writing being 'embodied' or a 'process' or as a disquisition on writerly choice. Instead, the conversation segues into Jack's dislike for adjectives:

> The search for the *mot juste*, he said, leads to overwriting and dullness and the dreadful proliferation of adjectives.... People who cannot write and cannot think and yet believe that they adore literature are in love with adjectives, he said, for them literature is synonymous with adjectives, they pass their life in a bubble bath of adjectives. (Josipovici 1994, 11)

Then back into what one uses to write: 'Pens are for Victorian novelists, he said, and word-processors are for playful post-modernists. But if I am anything, he said, it is a modernist' (14).

The proliferation of adjectives and adverbs helps the reader populate a scene in a novel with details. Shiny burnished knees, rather dry champagne, reclining limply—all of these try to specify to the reader how to visualise a scene and the actions being performed there.[5] The Australian writer Gerald Murnane calls this kind of writing 'film-script fiction' in which the narrator wants us 'to see in mind a certain scene with a character moving through it, rather as [one] might see the opening scenes of a film. [The narrator] prefers, for the time being, to show me details rather than to impart information' (Murnane 2016). *Moo Pak*, on the other, describes little; it is a cascade of information.

This information is of a particular sort. Throughout the novel, Jack returns to what aids his writing (sitting at a desk) and his thinking (a walk with a friend when he's hit a dead end) and to remarks, both offhand and detailed, on art in general, particular artists and the contemporary world. Some of these remarks ring truer today than when I first read the novel in 2010 (or than it must have when the novel was first published in 1994):

> The truth of the matter is, he said, that it can only be by the greatest good fortune that we can nowadays be surprised by the world around us, that we can chance on a part of it that is not already packaged and prepared for our gaze.... Everywhere today, he said, people travel to have confirmed for them what they already know and take photographs to remind themselves that they have really been there. (Josipovici 1994, 42)

All of this is relayed to us as part of a flow: 'winged words ... that fly out of the mouth of one speaker and land in the chest of the other, but words that are so light that they soon fly on again' (15).

VII

Living and making art in modernity is the thematic thread—or, more aptly, ramifying strand of yarn—that runs through the conversations transcribed in the book.[6] Not coincidentally, this has been the thread that runs through all of Josipovici's criticism. As I have written earlier in the chapter, Josipovici has come at modernity and modernism in a variety of ways in his criticism. He has marked various points as the 'coming into awareness by art of its precarious status and responsibilities' (Josipovici 2010, 11).[7]

His interest in marking the moment of the emergence of this new awareness may be the reason for his attraction to literary hinge figures, whether Rabelais or Cervantes or 18th-century figures in English literature. In *On Trust* (1999), he writes at length about Samuel Johnson. In *Moo Pak*, the figure on the cusp of Romanticism, the last non-Romantic, is Jonathan Swift, whom Toledano is constructing a work around (see the final third of the chapter).

Toledano, however, knows he is no Swift nor was meant to be; he belongs to the post-Romantic world. He tells Damien about an early letter of Kafka's to Brod 'in which this inability to adapt to an environment in which air and not water is the medium, is caught with frightening clarity' (Josipovici 1994, 51–52).

> Kafka writes that now it is summer and he is on vacation he feels full of energy but does not know what to do with his energy. His arms are too long, his legs are too far away from him. In a kind of despair he wanders through the streets and squares of Prague, swinging his arms, twisting his torso, raising his legs too high, trying in effect to find a set of gestures that will correspond to his feelings but no doubt looking like a madman to those who come across him. (52)

Making art in modernity is like desperately trying to adapt one's style of swimming to (the freedom of movement afforded by) air instead of (the familiar friction of) water. This chimes with Toledano's not wanting to play with words. Why not? There is too much freedom. You can do as you like— no strictures or rules. Freeing at first, this freedom soon sours. You can make gestures that correspond to your feelings, but if these are incomprehensible, they make you look like a madman to others. The incomprehensibility of one's private language, however, is not the only risk involved with such expression.

Two other interrelated risks are that our notion of *which* gestures symbolise our feelings is often abstract and unrealistic and, so, sentimental. Saying 'I'm sorry' or 'Oh no!' in response to another's person's loss may appear formulaic and inadequate. But an attempt to mime sadness or empathy or to express actually felt sadness or empathy through a gesture adequate to it is fraught. It can come across as mawkish or as play-acting. This, I wager, is why adjectives and adverbs in modern literature are anathema to Jack Toledano. Through their mere use, by writing 'radiant smile' or 'wept inconsolably', they try to covertly bludgeon the reader into feeling, into agreement. (Background music is frequently used in this way in cinema and television.)

What do I mean by abstract and unrealistic? This idea may be explained with reference to both *Kutiyattam*, the centuries-old dramatic form from Kerala, and an example from Proust dear to Josipovici, Giotto's frescoes *Charity* and *Envy*. In Kutiyattam, along with an unusually drawn-out representation of what is happening (a one-act play in Sanskrit may be enacted over several nights) by the actor's body and face, there are precise gestures of the hands and specific ways in which Sanskrit verses are chanted to communicate information and emotion. The emotion—erotic desire, sadness, fear and so on—is both communicated pithily through these precise gestures and verses and embodied by the actor's body and face as part of the slow narrative unfolding over half an hour. The gestures and verses act as labels.

This labeling is what bothers Paul de Man about Proust's use of Giotto's *Charity* in his novel.

> The facial expression of the 'heavy and mannish' matron painted by Giotto connotes nothing charitable ... a literal reading of Giotto's fresco would never have discovered what it meant.... We know the meaning of the allegory only because Giotto, substituting writing for representation, spelled it out on the upper frame of his painting. (de Man 1979, 76)

Josipovici's reading of Proust in *On Trust* (the chapter is titled 'Proust and the Face of True Goodness') is via a carefully argued refutation of de Man's reading (Josipovici 1999, chap. 6). The initial response of Marcel, the narrator of Proust's novel, is like de Man's. It is the response of someone 'brought up on Romantic and post-Romantic art and criticism' (196). But Marcel comes to understand over time:

> The reason why Charity does not look charitable or Envy envious is not that the painter or the tradition substitutes the idea for thing, but rather that they recognise that human beings are always more than their thoughts or their feelings, that they are embodied and active in the world. What Giotto's images do is to relate Charity and Envy to all the other images and activities we can imagine of Charity and Envy, and to guide us in the exploration by choice of attribute given to them ... we are shown Charity in action, not someone who has a charitable disposition. (182)

VIII

The modern suspicion of labels as inadequate and inauthentic is perfectly understandable. The attempt to be authentic and, particularly, to try to appear authentic and to find labels false but to have one's gestures correspond to one's feelings or the feelings one thinks one should be feeling: this is a recipe for the sentimentality and mawkishness in contemporary writing and contemporary culture that one finds Jack Toledano railing against.

This is why he finds Sartre's rejection of the Nobel Prize repulsively ostentatious (Josipovici 1994, 43); why he finds Naipaul's reading of tragic passages from *The Enigma of Arrival*, a book he has loved, on television distasteful: 'as though asking us both to sympathise with his plight and admire his writing ... [in a way that was] symptomatic of our modern culture' (47). Toledano does not associate sentimentalism with vague effusions about nature or beauty. He understands that in the 20th century, sentimentalism often takes another form:

> What I am trying to say, Jack said, is that the modern imperative to immerse yourself in the filth and despair of life ... the modern insistence that life is to be found there with ... the addicts and the bums, the terrorists and the mafiosi, and that to read Raymond Queneau under a tree in Kew Gardens on a summer afternoon is to cut yourself off from reality—this must not go unchallenged. It is nothing but Romantic claptrap and sentimental nonsense, he said, fuelled by guilt and nostalgia and by a terrible confusion at the heart of our culture. Why is Webern less real than rock? he said, and darted through the tombstones away from the main path. Why is *An Ordinary Evening in New Haven* less real than *The Naked Lunch*?... Why should suffering be real and well-being not?... Why should the fist in the face be real and not the wind in the hair? I have no answer to these questions, he said, and a part of me is romantic enough to have a sneaking sympathy for ... [these] views. (60–61)

Why do people see suffering as real and well-being as trivial? The reason is the kinds of choices that are usually presumed to be on offer: 'After all, if we have to choose between *Last Exit to Brooklyn* and *Harper's Bazaar* the choice is pretty obvious. If we have to choose between Dostoevsky and Galsworthy, he said, we won't have to pause very long' (Josipovici 1994, 61). But perhaps, he continues, 'The lines have not been drawn in the right places' (61). He asks: 'What about having to choose between *The Faerie Queene* and *Speke Parrot*? or between *Anna Karenina* and *Pierrot mon ami*? Should we not draw the line between the supple and the rigid, the humourous and the humourless, the humanly vulnerable and the smugly self-assured?' (61)

Throughout *Moo Pak*, we have the production of such concepts to divide, describe or appraise works of art (but also artists). Jean-Michel Rabaté praises *On Trust* for eschewing foreign lexicons and the accompanying theoretical armature and for producing concepts like *trust* and *suspicion* instead, 'that are used immediately, to be absorbed or resorbed once they have accomplished their task' (Rabaté 2016, 1164–1165). We encounter this production and resorption at a greater velocity and in a more off-hand way in *Moo Pak*, such as Jack's distinction between 'the wet and the dry'.

> Swift's life and his books, he said as we reached the river again, are a rebuke to the whole tradition of the novel, of the *bildungsroman* in particular. His books are as angry as the plays of John Osborne, he said, but anger is only a small part of it. They are dry, and that is what I love about them. All art can be divided into two, he said, the wet and the dry. Aristophanes is dry, Euripedes is wet. Homer is dry, Virgil is wet. Dante and Chaucer are dry but Petrarch and Wyatt are wet. Donne is dry but Milton is wet. Jane Austen is dry but George Eliot and Goethe are both wet. Sterne is a complicated case, he said, wetness miming dryness miming wetness, or perhaps dryness miming wetness miming dryness. Shakespeare, as usual, defies the categories, he said, the murder of Macduff's children is wet and so is much of *Cymbeline* and *The Tempest* and *Othello* and *Lear*. But he gets away with it, he said, because you can never tell if he is wet himself or only dramatising wetness. Ivy Compton-Burnett is dry, he said, and E.M. Forster is wet. Coleridge, strangely, is dry, and Wordsworth wet. By and large though the nineteenth century is wholly wet. In England at any rate. You can be sure that all the winners of prizes will be wet, for the judges are invariably wet. Nature is dry and man is wet he said as we rounded the lake and stopped to look at the ducks. (Josipovici 1994, 103–104)

What Toledano's remarks do here is offer us a way of dividing artworks and the world in a way I found both funny and true. These are snap judgements, but they do not seem to us as readers to be stand-alone remarks, as they would have seemed in an interview or if they were accompanying a list of top ten books. They occur a hundred pages into *Moo Pak*, after we have spent that much time (those many pages) in Toledano's company. Earlier in the book, he contrasts the 'unspeakably awful' question-answer sessions after lectures to a conversation between two friends who have 'unspoken assumptions in common ... whereas the lecturer and his interlocutors share no assumptions' (Josipovici 1994, 15). Appearing as it does two-thirds of the way into the novel, we are well acquainted with Toledano's assumptions and opinions as we read this passage; whether we agree or disagree with Toledano's specific pronouncements, we know what he means.

In *On Trust*, Josipovici qualifies an important sentence—'It may simply be a matter of temperament or circumstance, but I obscurely feel that Kierkegaard and Mann have a point which the post-Modernist is missing and that the solutions he offers are thin and unreal' (Josipovici 1999, 23)—with an endnote: 'This is not rhetorical. Duchamp and Kundera, for example, seem to me to have a genuinely cold and ironic temperament which I respect and even admire in certain instances, although I cannot identify with it' (277).

I invoke this qualifying endnote for two reasons. The first is to point out that even in his criticism, Josipovici is not shy of mentioning temperament as a factor. His argument in favour of modernist trust and against post-modernist suspicion does not lean heavily on temperament, but we are glancingly told of why he felt the need to make this argument. The second is to indicate the kinds of terminology that Josipovici has used in his critical work. Trust and suspicion. Warm temperaments and cold. Beckett's 'wild beast of earnestness' and Duchamp's irony (Beckett 2009, 189).

By the time we read the passage given earlier, we have a good sense of Jack's temperament. We may laugh along, disagree, modify certain of those judgements and offer a few of our own. I have found that I have returned to this contrast in thinking about works of art and in conversations with friends. I prefer the wet Wordsworth to the dry Coleridge (despite the clear preference for dryness in this passage, it should not be presumed that dry equals good and wet bad). *Seinfeld* is dry; *Friends* is wet. Kishore Kumar is dry, Guru Dutt wet. Bangla poetry is wet; classical Urdu poetry is dryness miming wetness, though its reception nowadays is frequently wet. Ghatak is mostly wet; Ray is drier. The Godard of the 1960s is dry and cold, the French cinema of the 1960s overeager to be dry. Kiarostami, on the other hand, is bone-dry but warm.

IX

The form of *Moo Pak* allows the novel/Josipovici to have Toledano articulate strong views without substantiating them. Since it is the transcription of a conversation and of more than one conversation, Jack Toledano corrects and contradicts himself.

As an example, let me take Jack's mentions of Milton in *Moo Pak*, both deprecatory and approbatory. Milton's first appearance in the book is when Jack is criticising the humourlessness of Protestant culture ('Goethe and Milton ... Kant and Hegel ... George Eliot and van Gogh'; Josipovici 1994, 19), the hypocrisy and fanaticism of Catholicism and the Puritan legacy that weighs heavy on England. But then, Jack continues: 'And yet ... without Catholicism would we have had Dante and Langland, Evelyn Waugh and Muriel Spark? Without Protestantism would we have had Milton and Wordsworth, Nietzsche and van Gogh?' (19) Later in the book, Milton appears as an example of English Puritanism (a variant of Protestantism that was committed to purifying the Church of England by eliminating every aspect of Catholicism from its religious practices).

> The trouble with ... the so-called intellectual English, is that they ... seem, he said ... to be incapable of relaxing enough to let any new thought or idea disturb their certainties.... It was all foretold, he said, in that masterpiece of prophecy, Milton's *Comus*. Comus, he said, the spirit of the forest of the forests of Wales over which the English, from their redout (sic) in Ludlow Castle, tried to exercise control, Comus is the spirit of ... the vernacular, of Shakespeare's fools and their quick repartee, of Skelton and Rabelais.... And look at what Milton does to him. He transforms him in his Puritan imagination into ... the figure of the Tempter ... just as [he] ... transforms the poetry of Chaucer and Shakespeare into his marble periods. (34)

Readers today, Toledano continues, read *Comus* against its grain—they sympathise with Comus, the repressed spirit of the forest. Ironically, in doing so, these very readers are the ones compulsively repeating the pattern Milton puts forward in his poem. They are on the side of Comus because they are on the side of all the right causes. 'Thinking themselves to be fighting Puritanism and repression in the name of freedom, they demonstrate in the way they do it that they too cannot tolerate what does not fit in with their increasingly rigid systems' (Josipovici 1994, 34–35) Milton, here, is himself an example of English uptightness as well as the artist who foretold its effects on the English national character.

Still later, Milton appears in the context of the relationship between artists and the media. This appearance is a part of one of Toledano's diatribes against the relationship of contemporary writers with publicity, who thoughtlessly undo what their work asserts ethically with their simultaneously self-regarding and self-pitying media appearances: 'media people ... are themselves so bitter and feel themselves to be such failures ... that what they enjoy above all else is the sight of writers denying by their public actions and behaviour what they seem to be asserting in their work' (Josipovici 1994, 45). The Milton of *Paradise Lost* appears here as a writer who, with the Shakespeare of *Measure for*

Measure and *Othello*, understood this dynamic. Satan/Angelo/Iago (the cynical journalist) cannot bear for Eve/Isabella/Othello (the serious writer) to be pure (or relatively unsullied). By showing them up, they justify their own cynicism.

And in the final third of the novel: 'When religion dies morality is waiting to step into its shoes, he said. You can see it happening with Luther and with Milton and with George Eliot' (Josipovici 1994, 113). Since Jack's views are bracketed, since we read them through the writing of Damien Anderson, the effect is unlike, say, Adorno's lecturing or writing. Adorno's views, learned and perceptive and sensitive as he is, often seem to come from on high. This seeming to come from on high is not only something Jack remarks on in *Moo Pak* (29) but also how the essayist Eliot Weinberger reacted to Josipovici's tone in his review of the latter's *What Ever Happened to Modernism?* (Weinberger 2011). The cascading form of *Moo Pak* means that Toledano's strong views can be expressed without constant qualifications or exculpatory irony since the specific remark or opinion is embedded in a continuity.

X

From *The Singer on the Shore*: 'I start then not with an idea but with a *need*. Not the idea of literature but the need to write' (Josipovici 2006, 310).

From *100 Days*: 'There is nothing shameful about criticism, *pace* Beckett. It is more natural, actually, than "creative writing", for every time one recommends a book or a film to a friend with a little more than: "You must read this, see that", one is doing criticism' (Josipovici 2021, 121)

At various points, Josipovici has indicated that he was a novelist by need and a critic by inclination and, further, that writing a novel was fraught for him in ways that writing criticism was not. I don't dispute this. Yet there is a difference between literary criticism today and the commentary of old. In the introduction to their translation of the modernist Persian poet Sohrab Sepehri, Pouneh Shabani-Jadidi and Prashant Keshavmurthy capture this well:

> [The] difficulty of premodern poetry lay in its assumption of a traditional code that the connoisseur reader was expected to discover, the difficulty of modern poetry was peculiar to each poet or poem and demanded a new kind of reader: the critic who would provisionally invent a code proper to its difficulty.... It fell to the ... modern genre of literary criticism to *invent* a code for such poetry where the premodern genre of commentary had *discovered* one. (2022, 1–2)

Literary criticism may not seem shameful or feel unnatural in the way that writing fiction or poetry does. To announce that one is writing poetry or a novel seems presumptuous in a way that writing a book or an essay or a dissertation on something does not. Is this merely institutional? If the world had as many MFA programmes as it has colleges and universities, would we feel more embarrassed writing fiction or poetry than doing research? I cannot say.

Even if criticism is more natural than writing fiction, however, just as genre conventions are not given to modern poets or novelists, they are not given to modern critics. How is the modern critic to interpret and appraise a work of art? How is a critic to know that their ascription of value is not utterly subjective? In what form are they to write? If Kafka is a well-known emblematic case of the fastidious writer, Adorno may be just such a case of a fastidious critic. Josipovici is aware of this, as we have seen from his introduction to a selection of his reviews (see Section III earlier).

Moo Pak is constructed and driven in part by Josipovici's treatment of Modernism in his criticism, right from *The World and the Book* (1971) to *What Ever Happened to Modernism?* (2010). For any reader who has read Josipovici's criticism, a good deal of what Jack 'says' in *Moo Pak* resembles what Josipovici has written. Only a scholarly critic like Josipovici could have plausibly written all that Jack Toledano says in the book. In this, *Moo Pak* is unlike books and films about purportedly brilliant or erudite thinkers and scientists in which we get no real sense of their brilliance or erudition; Jack is a character credibly drawn. But why write a book structured around a character like Jack Toledano (and other novels structured around other artists and critics—see Section IV earlier)?

Moo Pak allows Josipovici to write criticism differently: to practice a modernist criticism of sorts, to allow himself unsubstantiated or quite partially substantiated remarks, to use terms such as 'wet' and 'dry' and to write about the entwinement of life and art without the distance kept by an academic or a connoisseur aesthete. If Josipovici had done this in a critical essay, it may have seemed gimmicky or mawkish; it may have been frowned upon. He may have been too self-conscious to do it freely. *Moo Pak* allows him to embed criticism within a novel, like Proust in the *Recherche*, and to use his aptitude as a literary critic to drive the novel. As readers, we encounter this criticism during the time we devote to reading the novel, as we read of Jack Toledano putting his own book together (see Sections XI–XIV later). We are aware throughout, as a result, of how all the finished works discussed in *Moo Pak* cannot be taken for granted, 'how [they] might very well not have been' (Josipovici 1983, 8).

XI

As *Moo Pak* proceeds, we learn that Jack Toledano is writing a book—a book about Jonathan Swift, his love interests Stella and Vanessa 'and especially his time as a secretary to Sir William Temple, the 17th-century diplomat and writer, and his country house at Moor Park in Surrey, at its centre' (Josipovici 2021, 158). While Sir Temple's country house at Moor Park actually existed and Swift did work there as Temple's secretary, in Jack's book, as he tells Damien, it metamorphoses into a variety of institutions:

> In my book Moor Park is, at different times … the home of Sir William Temple and his widowed sister, Swift's inveterate enemy, Lady Giffard, a school, a lunatic asylum, a college of theology, a center for the decipherment of codes during the Second World War, a centre for the study of primates and again a school [in which non-native English speakers, asked to write the history of Moor Park itself, would misspell it as Moo Pak]. (Josipovici 1994, 123)

These are all fictional but are presented in *Moo Pak* as though they were factual (as I had mistakenly assumed they were when I first read the book).

Jack's book and Swift are merely mentioned in the first third of *Moo Pak*. The frequency of reference to the book he is writing grows slowly, until the final third is devoted primarily to Jack's descriptions of this book, its organisation, his struggle to write it and how it is, at long last, slowly coming together. This, Jack tells Damien, is to be his big book:

> Everything I have published till now ... has really been in the form of sketches ... but all human beings have one big work in them, think of Virgil or Rabelais ... of Wordsworth, of Proust ... there comes a point in life when one has to accept that and leave the sketches ... behind. (Josipovici 1994, 58)

He repeats this later, but he is less sure.

> There comes to every writer, he said, at some time in his life, the idea that he will write one work which will finally justify him, one work into which he can pour himself for as long as it takes, a decade perhaps, or two, or the rest of his life, as with Proust and Dante. But perhaps, he said, that is one of these pernicious legacies Proust and Joyce and Musil have left us. (89)

It is a pernicious legacy for two reasons: First, writers, thinking that they must write a magnum opus at some point, produce grandiose, unreadable work. (Jack jokes that the writers who beat their chest about the environment are the same ones who write the biggest books.) Second, the magnum opus sanctifies the otherwise uncertain, lonely and perhaps pointless task of making art. A masterpiece, the public perception goes, will make it all worth it, all the time one has given to making art. Yet, his suspicion of the mid- or late-career pull of the masterpiece notwithstanding, Jack, as he tells Damien, keeps at his big book.

XII

Josipovici, I have remarked earlier, is fascinated with hinge figures and works of art that appear to be on the cusp of a world view that we take for granted. In *Moo Pak*, this figure, the last non-Romantic, is Jonathan Swift. Toledano is interested in Swift because he is both like and unlike himself.[8] On the one hand: 'You never find in Swift what you find so often in Pope, he said, and what is perhaps the hallmark of the Romantic sensibility, the assertion that *words fail him*, that *his heart is too heavy* for him to speak' (Josipovici 1994, 49) On the other:

> his love of masks, his extraordinary way of piling irony on irony, testify to his feeling that beyond the language men ordinarily use there is another, lying in the interstices of that language so to speak, and which cannot be brought fully out into the open, only made manifest by indirection. (122)

He tells us what he is *not* after: 'there is no point in writing about Swift as if he was Keats, or someone like him, as 19th-century writers were fond of doing. The challenge ... is to find a way of bringing out the non-modern complexity of Swift' (Josipovici 1994, 112). He also tells us what he *is* after:

> What I have been trying to do in my book ... what my book is trying to be is a moor park or a park moor.... A work which holds together too easily is of no interest.... Ditto a work which falls apart at the slightest touch ... the works which please me best ... are those which exist in such a state of tension that at every second we expect them to fly apart but at every second we are amazed because they do not fly apart. (122, 137)

The more Toledano talks about his book, the more the reader (a reader who has read Josipovici's work) realises, as Monika Fludernik has remarked, that Toledano's 'aesthetics bear uncanny affinities to the poetics of Josipovici's own work' (Fludernik 2000, 87). The description of a figure by Jack—'a white figure thrashing about in a white room, a trussed up madman in an underground cell who is the spirit of all that is not and cannot be said in the book' (123)—bears striking similarities to Josipovici's own *Migrations* (1977) (besides resembling certain figures from Beckett's fiction). Jack tells Damien that 'the whole of what is happening ... may perhaps be happening in the mind' of this figure, who has perhaps 'interiorised the history of the house, the life of Swift, the training of the apes' (Josipovici 1994, 124).[9]

But, of course, it is not Jack's book but his account of this book that we read in *Moo Pak*. And so, we are witness to all the decisions, vacillation and hesitation involved in writing such a book: from the title—he vacillates between *Moor Park* and *Animal Languages*—to what he is trying to get at. Josipovici has always written that what a writer is trying to get at does not precede or exist independent outside of the work of fiction. Yet, without the tension of there being something one is trying to get at, the work goes slack. He is bored by the French *nouveau romancier*s, with Barthes, Ricardou et al., when they do away with the anxiety involved in writing and pooh-pooh as naive the urge to say something, to get something just right, and when they conceive of writing, instead, as (mere/sheer) play. In *Moo Pak* (and in *The Big Glass* before that), Josipovici has found a way to write about the fear of not getting it right and of gesturing at the eddies of thought and conversation that swirl around a work by having Jack tell Damien of his thoughts on art, on realism, on what making art in the present means and on his various plans for the book and what he is trying to get at through it.

XIII

As *Moo Pak* draws to its end, we hear that Toledano's book is also approaching its end. He tells Damien how he has organised it.

> I have used a variant of the Fibonacci series to control the number of parts in the book, he said, and the number of sections in each part, and I have used palindromes, broken here and there according to further rules, to determine the relative length of each section. The themes, of which there are six—Swift, ciphers, monkeys, gardens, madness and language—make their appearance in accordance with the principles of the sestina, upon which I have superimposed another sestina, made up of the six subsidiary themes of love, masks, folly, age, boundaries and food. (Josipovici 1994, 123)

At one point, Jack tells Damien that he has 'classical aspirations but a romantic temperament' (Josipovici 1994, 125). In reading his descriptions of how he has dealt with the 'engineering problems' (128) in the construction of the book, it is as if we encounter the 'classical' Jack, dispassionately talking about how his project is nearing successful completion at long last, after 'twenty years or more of thought, ten years of writing' (122). But what will he do when the work is finished? ('This book has been my lifeline', he tells Damien (128).) Might it be a failure? In the most detailed analogy in *Moo Pak* between a life and a work, particularly a magnum opus, Jack tells Damien:

> A book is like a life.... When we start becoming conscious of ourselves there are many directions in which most of us feel we can go and each of them seems equally valid.... By the middle of our lives ... we are only too conscious that we have taken ... any number of false turnings but we are too far forward to do anything but press on. But as we near the end of our lives ... we realise that every step must now be the right one because now there will certainly be no second chance.... It is the same with the novel ... and with this one in particular. I have been working at it too long to be able to start again and I have given up too much of my life to countenance the thought that it might be a failure. (145)

As *Moo Pak* draws to its end, there are a couple of hints that indicate that it is turning in on itself, like a Möbius strip. Jack tells Damien that he is thinking of using the chimp Bertrand signing 'Me cry there' to his caretaker (on looking at a photograph of a chimp resisting a bathtub scrub) as his epigraph. This is the epigraph to the book we are reading (Josipovici 1994, 138). Later, in a passage that is ostensibly Jack speaking to Damien but that is unusual in its lack of attributives like 'he said', we read:

> At his desk the author has watched his hand move over page after page, covering it in signs which he dreads to reread, and he has walked through the parks and heaths of London talking to himself as though to another until the last little section has fallen into place. (146)

But these are only hints, and *Moo Pak* does not emphasise them.

XIV

In their last meeting, Jack tells Damien that there is no book and never has been. Damien writes, 'Three weeks ago for the first time that I can remember he arrived late for our rendezvous' (Josipovici 1994, 147).

They go to the park, but Jack feels their choice of venue has been a mistake and suggests taking a taxi to Hampstead Heath. Then:

> In the taxi he told me there was no novel. I asked him what he meant and he said he had been talking and talking about it in the hope that it would materialise but that it hadn't and he had to face up to the fact that it never would. I was confused and asked him to explain. He said they were notes but no novel. He said that far from almost finishing it he had never really started it. (148)

He tells Damien that he knew 'it was all over with my writing' ten years back but kept trying to tell himself that it might be 'the temptation of the devil' (Josipovici 1994, 149). Damien asks him if it couldn't still be:

> Yes, he said laughing of course. But what can I do? he said, and looked at me helplessly. I have done what I could, he said. I have done what I thought right. I have lived according to my precepts. Of course I have done many foolish and reprehensible things. But at least where my writing is concerned I have always tried to be true to myself. When you are young, he said, you do not ask yourself too many questions. After the age of fifty, he said, you have got to ask yourself what you are doing with your life. I have gone on trying, he said, because there did not seem to be any alternative, or rather, because all the alternatives seemed worse than what I was doing. Perhaps he said, I should have been a doctor like my grandfather or a lawyer like my great-grandfather. (149)

He continues, 'And yet, he said, despite everything, and despite even the disaster of *Moo Pak*, I cannot quite accept that I was wrong to spend so long trying vainly to write it' (Josipovici 1994, 150) The title *Moo Pak* (instead of *Moor Park* or *Animal Languages*) is the third hint of the book turning in on itself. But they are only hints, and there are only three of them. If these hints indicate, within the logic of *Moo Pak*, that Jack invented Damien, there are others that indicate that what we are reading is Damien's transcription-cum-invention of what Jack said, as we had thought all along.

For instance, on announcing that there is no book, Jack says that, in any case, it wouldn't have made a difference to anyone whether he finished it or not. When Damien protests that it would have made a difference to him, he laughs, and says: 'It might have made a difference to you if I had never talked about it .... But not now. Now ... you only have to go away and write it yourself' (Josipovici 1994, 149). Where Jack's monologue ends and Jack and Damien part, we read:

> That was three weeks ago. On Tuesday I received a note from him asking me to meet him today at the Star and Garter in Putney. I waited for over an hour, wrote Damien Anderson, and then, when it was quite obvious he was not going to turn up, I went home. (150)

The book begins, of course, with: 'On Tuesday I received a note from Jack Toledano asking me to meet him today at the Star and Garter in Putney at the usual time, wrote Damien Anderson' (Josipovici 1994, 9) Are we to surmise then, within the logic of the book, that Damien has written what we are reading over the past three weeks? After all, Damien continues:

> I had known, I think, he wrote ... that this would happen and that then I would have to write down, however inadequately, my memories of my meetings with him and what he had said to me on our walks. I think I had even known for some time prior to that, he wrote, that he was not really writing his book and that it would be left to me to put down what little I could recall of all he had said about it. But it is not the book I have wanted to write about, he wrote, it is the man. (150–151)

It ends: 'My life would have been the poorer had I never known him and had we never walked and talked together for over ten years in the parks and heaths and along the waterways of London. Let that suffice' (151).

Did *Moo Pak* take three weeks to write or did it take ten years? Is Jack Toledano the author of *Moo Pak* and Damien Anderson his invention? Is Damien Anderson the author of *Moo Pak* and Jack Toledano *his* invention? Is Damien Anderson the author of what we are reading, transcribing (and presumably writing in his own words) what he remembers Jack as having said to him over the past ten years?

This last, of course, is what we have lived with over the course of the book, and a couple of ambiguous hints may modify but will not dislodge our sense of our experience of reading the book. If we elect to look back at our reading of *Moo Pak*, assuming that Jack spoke to Damien and that Damien wrote it down, doesn't our sense of Jack change significantly when we learn that he did not write, had never even begun to write, his magnum opus? Do his tirades and diatribes—both learned and cranky—not seem a little pathetic once we learn that, for all his talk of his working at his desk and his 'optimistic nervous system', for all the humour and wisdom of his disdain for contemporary writers, he hasn't written a thing in ten years? At the end of *Moo Pak*, monologic—but *periscopically* monologic—for roughly nine-tenths of its length, these possibilities flicker into being and remain flickering as the book ends quietly, with 'Let that suffice'.

References

Beckett, Samuel. (1956) 2009. *Three Novels: Molloy, Malone Dies, The Unnamable*. New York: Grove Press.

Best, Victoria. 2015. 'The Mind of the Modern: An Interview with Gabriel Josipovici'. *Numero Cinq* 6 (12). Accessed 25 April 2022. http://numerocinqmagazine.com/2015/12/01/the-mind-of-the-modern-an-interview-with-gabriel-josipovici-victoria-best/

De Man, Paul. 1979. *Allegories of Reading: Figural Language in Rousseau, Nietzsche, Rilke, and Proust*. London: Yale University Press.

Fludernik, Monika. 2000. *Echoes and Mirrorings: Gabriel Josipovici's Creative Oeuvre*. Frankfurt: Peter Lang.

Fort, Jeff. 2014. *Imperative to Write: Destitutions of the Sublime in Kafka*. New York: Fordham University Press.

Josipovici, Gabriel. 1971. *The World and the Book*. London: Macmillan.

———. 1977. *The Lessons of Modernism*. London: Macmillan.

———. 1983. *The Mirror of Criticism: Selected Reviews 1977-1982*. Sussex: Harvester Press.

———. 1991. *The Big Glass*. Manchester: Carcanet Press.

———. 1992. *Text and Voice: Essays 1981-1991*. Manchester: Carcanet Press.

———. 1994. *Moo Pak*. Manchester: Carcanet Press.

———. 1996. *Touch*. London: Yale University Press.

———. 1999. *On Trust: Art and the Temptations of Suspicion*. London: Yale University Press.

———. 2006. *The Singer on the Shore: Essays 1991-2004*. Manchester: Carcanet Press.

———. 2010. *What Ever Happened to Modernism?* London: Yale University Press.

———. 2012. *Infinity: The Story of a Moment*. Manchester: Carcanet Press.

———. 2016. *The Teller and the Tale: Essays on Literature and Culture*. Manchester: Carcanet Press.

———. 2021. *100 Days*. Manchester: Little Island Press.

Murnane, Gerald. 2016. 'In Praise of the Long Sentence'. *Meanjin Quarterly*. Accessed 18 April 2022. https://meanjin.com.au/essays/in-praise-of-the-long-sentence

Kelly, Robert. 1989. 'Robert Kelly Interviewed by Bradford Morrow'. Conjunctions. Accessed 1 May 2022. https://www.conjunctions.com/print/article/robert-kelly-c13

Pippin, Robert. 2013. *After the Beautiful: Hegel and the Philosophy of Pictorial Modernism*. Chicago: Chicago University Press.

Rabaté, Jean-Michel. 2016. 'A 30 Years' War?'. *Textual Practice 30@ 30: The Future of Literary Thinking* 30 (7): 1164–1165. Compiled and edited by Peter Boxall, et al.

Robertson, Douglas. 2021. 'On Translating Thomas Bernhard's The Cheap-Eaters'. Minor Literatures, 21 April 2021. Accessed 6 July 2022. https://minorliteratures.com/2021/04/21/on-translating-thomas-bernhards-the-cheap-eaters-douglas-robertson/

Shabani-Jadidi, Pouneh, and Prashant Keshavmurthy. 2022. Introduction to *The Eight Books: A Complete English Translation*, by Sohrab Sepehri. Leiden: Brill.

Silverblatt, Michael. 2007. 'A Poem of an Invisible Subject'. In *The Emergence of Memory: Conversations with W.G. Sebald*, edited by Lynne Sharon Schwartz. London: Seven Stories Press.

Subrahmanyam, Sanjay. 2022. 'On the Spot: Sanjay Subrahmanyam'. *History Today*. Accessed 8 July 2022. https://www.historytoday.com/archive/interview/spot-sanjay-subrahmanyam

Thuswaldner, Gregor. 2020. 'Thomas Bernhard's Influence on Gabriel Josipovici's Monologue Novels'. In *Thomas Bernhard's Afterlives*, edited by Olaf Berwald, Stephen D. Dowden and Gregor Thuswaldner. New York: Bloomsbury Academic.

Weinberger, Eliot. 2011. 'Who Made It New?' *The New York Review of Books*, 23 June 2011. Accessed 8 April 2022. https://www.nybooks.com/articles/2011/06/23/who-made-it-new

Woolf, Virginia. 1925. 'Saturday 27 June'. Woolf Online. Accessed 10 March 2023. https://bit.ly/3FgCx8p

Notes

1 Three-fourths of the way through writing this chapter, I came across Josipovici's Sterne lecture in 2011, '*Tristram Shandy*: Not Waving but Drowning', which frames it exactly in this way (Josipovici 2016, 28).

2 As Bernhard translator Douglas Robertson points out in his essay on Bernhard's *The Cheap-Eaters*:

> In [English] translation this periscopic (so W.G. Sebald termed it) quality of the narrative perspective becomes evident thanks to the frequent interjections of 'so said Koller,' but in the German it is evident from the very start and remorselessly driven home at every moment along the way thanks to certain telltale markings of certain inflections of the helping-verbs haben and sein. (Robertson 2021)

3 *Infinity* puts one in mind of not only Bernhard's periscopic narration but also Robert Pinget's *The Inquisitory*, a work treasured by Josipovici. See the entry 'Robert Pinget' in Josipovici's *100 Days* (2021, 206).

4 See Thuswaldner (2020) for a comparison of this sentence with the first sentence of Thomas Bernhard's *Extinction* (1986).

5 These are all examples from Iris Murdoch's *A Fairly Honourable Defeat* (1970) that Josipovici lists in the entry 'Adverbs and Adjectives' in his recently published alphabetical lockdown journal, *100 Days* (2021).

6 I owe this turn of phrase to Douglas Robertson (personal correspondence).

7 In *The World and the Book* (1971), Josipovici is concerned with the art o the Middle Ages and its connections with Modernism. He argues that th dissolution of the medieval Christian view of the book as correspondin to the world leads, via a series of changes, to a gradual loss of faith i literary conventions and, thence, to literature being seen as either th Romantic expression of the Self or the Realist representation of externa reality. *The Lessons of Modernism* (1977) has essays on key figures fron the 20th century and, though primarily interested in literature, is als interested in music. *Text and Voice* (1992) is a book of literary criticisn and *Touch* (1996) is a book about the titular subject. The former attack modern theory's overvaluation of the (silent) text, while the latter argue that we can feel at home in a world indifferent to us only if we value touc over sight. Both are interested in ways of writing and reading books tha are not divorced from the body. *On Trust* (1999) argues that Modernisn is constituted as much by trust, albeit a difficult trust, in the process o making art as by its suspicion of the Romantic belief in art. In *What Eve Happened to Modernism?* (2010), Josipovici argues against restrictin Modernism to its late 19th-century and early 20th-century efflorescenc in Europe, arguing that the Modernist questions about art go as far back a the 1500s and remain with us today.

8 As Sanjay Subrahmanyam answers when asked why he works on the earl modern world: 'It's distant, yet close enough; familiar, yet not overly sc (2022).

9 However, *Moo Pak* is less concentrated than Josipovici's *Migrations* and say, Beckett's *Company*. Jack's diatribes are interrupted by Damien' 'topographical guidelines outlining their walks through Londor (Fludernik 2000, 86).

INDEX

T

U

V

W

ABOUT THE AUTHORS

Vijay Tankha retired as the head of the Department of Philosophy, St Stephen's College, New Delhi, in June 2017, where he taught a variety of papers in Western and Indian philosophy over the last thirty years. As a Commonwealth scholar, he did his PhD at McGill University, Montreal, Canada, specialising in Plato. Since then, he has written, presented and published papers and articles on both Plato and the Pre-Socratics as well as on other philosophical and literary topics and lectured in academic institutions around the country. He has authored *Greek Philosophy Thales to Gorgias* (2006). An expanded edition (*Ancient Greek Philosophy Thales to Socrates*) was published in 2014. *Poetry and Politics in Ancient Greece* (Cama Institute, Mumbai) was published in 2019.

***

D. Venkat Rao teaches at the English and Foreign Languages University, Hyderabad.

***

Aishwary Kumar (PhD, Trinity College, University of Cambridge) is the chair of Shri Shantinath Endowed Chair in Ahimsa Studies, director of the Ahimsa Center and associate professor of history at California State Polytechnic University, Pomona, Los Angeles, where he also directs the Democracy Institute. A political theorist and historian of global ideas, Kumar's work traverses South Asian, European and American religious and constitutional thought and questions of political and moral philosophy. He is the author of *Radical Equality: Ambedkar, Gandhi, and the Risk of Democracy* (Stanford University Press, 2015; Navayana, 2019) and *The Sovereign Void: Ambedkar's Critique of Violence* (forthcoming).

***

Rimli Bhattacharya is trained in comparative literature. She is the author of *Binodini Dasi: 'My Story' & 'My Life as an Actress'* (1998), *Sur Pippa: 'Notes on Running Feet'* (2012/co-authored), *Public Women in British India: Icons on the Urban Stage* (Routledge, 2018), *The Dancing*

Poet: Rabindranath Tagore and Choreographies of Participation (Tulika Books, 2019) and *Children's Literature in India: Many Tongues, Many Realities* (forthcoming, Bloomsbury Publishing). Her translations from Bangla into English include short stories, autobiographies, critical essays and classic novels. Bibhutibhushan Bandyopadhya's last novel, *Icchamati*, is her latest translation, titled *Restless Waters of Ichhamati* (Rupa, 2018). She has collaborated with artists and filmmakers on several projects and is currently working on an audio-visual script on expressive forms in the Indian Ocean world.

***

N.A. Jacob teaches English at Ramjas College, University of Delhi, New Delhi. His doctoral thesis at Rutgers University was titled 'Looking through Words: Histories of the Visual Image in Nineteenth-Century Literature'. His interests include philosophy, literary theory, aesthetics and photography studies.

***

Rahul Govind teaches history at the University of Delhi, New Delhi, and has held fellowships at Columbia University (for doctoral studies), the Centre for the Study of Developing Societies, New Delhi; The Indian Institute of Advanced Study, Shimla, and the University of Cambridge. Apart from his book *Infinite Double* (2015), he has published several articles in academic journals on themes ranging from political economy and philosophy to imperialism and jurisprudence.

***

Parul Dave-Mukherji is a professor at the School of Arts and Aesthetics, Jawaharlal Nehru University, New Delhi, India. She holds a PhD from Oxford University. She has held fellowships from Clark Art Institute, Williamstown, Massachusetts; South Asia Institute, Heidelberg; and British Academy Award, London. Her published books include *InFlux: Contemporary Art in Asia* (co-edited, Sage, 2013); 'Whither Art History in a Globalizing World,' in *The Art Bulletin* (2014); *Arts and Aesthetics in a Globalizing World* (co-edited, Bloomsbury, 2014); *Ebrahim Alkazi: Directing Art—The Making of a Modern Indian Art World* (ed., Mapin, 2016); and *Rethinking Aesthetics in a Comparative Frame* (co-edited, IIAS, 2020).

***

Babu Thaliath is a professor of philosophy and German studies at Jawaharlal Nehru University in New Delhi since 2013. His research focuses on the early modern philosophy of science and the late medieval *philosophia naturalis*, historical transition from medieval aporetics to early modern axiomatics, structural intuition (Martin Kemp), theory of perception and aesthetics. He studied civil engineering and German philology in India and pursued his PhD in philosophy at the Albert Ludwigs University of Freiburg and the University of Basel between 1997 and 2003. Subsequently, he completed several post-doctoral research projects in early modern mechanical philosophy at the Humboldt University of Berlin and the University of Cambridge (2005–2013). He has been a visiting scholar at the Department of History and Philosophy of Science and St Edmund's College, University of Cambridge, fellow at the International Kolleg Morphomata, University of Cologne (2016), and senior fellow at the Zukunftskolleg, University of Konstanz (2021–2022). His postdoctoral publications include the monographs *Wissenschaft und Kontext in der frühen Neuzeit* (2016), *Die Verkörperung der Sinnlichkeit* (2017) and *Vom Aufspüren der Axiome: Die Epistemisch-Strukturelle Intuition und das moderne Wissenssystem* (2021). His forthcoming publication (monograph) is Die hinterlassenen Objekte: Das Bildmotiv in den Filmen Andrej Tarkowskis (2024).

***

Prasanta Chakravarty is an associate professor of English, University of Delhi, New Delhi, and editor of the web journal Humanities Underground. His most recent work is *The Creature: In Power and Pain* (Bloomsbury, 2022). His other works include *Like Parchment in the Fire: Literature and Radicalism in the English Civil War* (Routledge, 2006), a monograph on early modern radical heretic culture; *The Opulence of Existence: Essays on Aesthetics and Politics* (Three Essays Collective, 2016), a collection of essays on literary forms and our political predicament and *Time, Doubt and Wonder in the Humanities: Between the Tick and the Tock* (Bloomsbury, 2019). A major project on the nature of classical sceptical approach to literature is forthcoming (Attention and Drift: Cavell and Santayana in the Present, 2024). He has edited two critical anthologies: *Shrapnel Minima: Writings from Humanities Underground* (2014) and *Populism and Its Limits: After Articulation* (2020). He has also co-edited *Machiavelli Then and Now* (2021) with Sukanta Chaudhuri.

***

Rachit Anand holds a PhD in comparative literature from the State University of New York, Buffalo. His doctoral dissertation, titled 'The Shadow of a Word: Thinking Allegorically with J.M. Coetzee', is a theoretical examination of the concept of allegory in the works of the South African novelist J.M. Coetzee. His article on allegorical thought and the apartheid mind will soon appear in *Cultural Critique*. His recent work has also appeared in *The Comparatist* and *Margins: A Journal of Literature and Culture*. In addition, he is working on a book project on the significance of allegorical thinking in twentieth and twenty-first century global Anglophone literatures.

***

Anirudh Karnick is a doctoral candidate at the University of Pennsylvania, Philadelphia. He is writing a dissertation on the transformation of poetics in North India from the late nineteenth century on and translating Udayan Vajpeyi's book-length interviews with Shamsur Rahman Faruqi (*Upanyāskār kā Safarnāmā* [A Novelist's Odyssey]) and Krishna Baldev Vaid (*Pravās aur Pravās* [Exile and Exile]).

***